BUDDHA:
HIS LIFE, HIS DOCTRINE, HIS ORDER

BUDDHA:
HIS LIFE, HIS DOCTRINE, HIS ORDER

BY

DR. HERMANN OLDENBERG,

PROFESSOR AT THE UNIVERSITY OF BERLIN, EDITOR OF THE VINAYA PITAKAM AND THE DIPAVAMSA IN PALI

Translated from the German

BY

WILLIAM HOEY, M.A., D. LIT.,

MEMBER OF THE ROYAL ASIATIC SOCIETY, ASIATIC SOCIETY OF BENGAL, ETC. OF HER MAJESTY'S BENGAL CIVIL SERVICE.

GYAN

Published by

GYAN

Gyan Publishing House
5, Ansari Road
Daryaganj, New Delhi-110002
Phone: 011-47034999, 9811692060
E-mail: books@gyanbooks.com

Distribution Network
gyanbooks.com
India, USA, Canada, UK, Australia, France

ISBN : 978-81-212-2482-6 (HB)
First Published, 1882

2nd Impression 2021

Printed at: Gyan Press, Delhi.

Buddha:
His Life His Doctrine His Order
Author: Dr. Hermann Oldenberg

BUDDHA:

HIS LIFE, HIS DOCTRINE, HIS ORDER,

BY

DR. HERMANN OLDENBERG,

PROFESSOR AT THE UNIVERSITY OF BERLIN, EDITOR OF THE VINAYA PITAKAM AND THE DÎPAVAMSA IN PÂLI.

Translated from the German

BY

WILLIAM HOEY, M.A., D.LIT.,

MEMBER OF THE ROYAL ASIATIC SOCIETY, ASIATIC SOCIETY OF BENGAL, ETC. OF HER MAJESTY'S BENGAL CIVIL SERVICE.

WILLIAMS AND NORGATE,

14, HENRIETTA STREET, COVENT GARDEN, LONDON;

AND 20, SOUTH FREDERICK STREET, EDINBURGH.

1882.

BUDDHA:

HIS LIFE, HIS DOCTRINE, HIS ORDER.

TRANSLATOR'S PREFACE.

This book is a translation of a German work, *Buddha, Sein Leben, seine Lehre, seine Gemeinde*, by Professor Hermann Oldenberg, of Berlin, editor of the "Pâli Texts of the Vinaya Pitakam and the Dîpavamsa." The original has attracted the attention of European scholars, and the name of Dr. Oldenberg is a sufficient guarantee of the value of its contents. A review of the original doctrines of Buddhism, coming from the pen of the eminent German scholar, the coadjutor of Mr. Rhys Davids in the translation of the Pâli scriptures for Professor Max Müller's "Sacred Books of the East," and the editor of many Pâli texts, must be welcome as an addition to the aids which we possess to the study of Buddhism. Dr. Oldenberg has in the work now translated successfully demolished the sceptical theory of a solar Buddha, put forward by M. Senart. He has sifted the legendary elements of Buddhist tradition, and has given the reliable residuum of facts concerning Buddha's life: he has examined the original teaching of Buddha, shown that the cardinal tenets of the pessimism which he preached are "the truth of suffering and the truth of the deliverance from suffering:" he has expounded the ontology of Buddhism and placed the Nirvâna in a true light. To do this he has gone to the roots of Buddhism in pre-Buddhist Brahmanism: and he has given Orientalists the original authorities for his views of Buddhist dogmatics in Excursus at the end of his work.

To thoughtful men who evince an interest in the comparative

study of religious beliefs, Buddhism, as the highest effort of pure intellect to solve the problem of being, is attractive. It is not less so to the metaphysician and sociologist who study the philosophy of the modern German pessimistic school and observe its social tendencies. To them Dr. Oldenberg's work will be as valuable as it is to the Orientalist.

My aim in this translation has been to reproduce the thought of the original in clear English. If I have done this, I have succeeded. Dr. Oldenberg has kindly perused my manuscript before going to press: and in a few passages of the English I have made slight alterations, additions, or omissions, as compared with the German original, at his request.*

I have to thank Dr. Rost, the Librarian of the India Office, at whose suggestion I undertook this work, for his kindness and courtesy in facilitating some references which I found it necessary to make to the India Office Library.

W. HOEY.

BELFAST, *October* 21, 1882.

* At p. 241-2, Dr. Oldenberg refers to the impossibility of Buddhist terminology finding adequate expression in the German language. I may make a similar complaint of the English tongue, and point in proof to the same word which occasioned his remark: Sankhâra. This term is translated in the German by "Gestaltungen," which would be usually rendered in English by "shapes" or "forms:" but the "shape" or "form," and the "shaping" or "forming," are one to Buddhist thought: hence I have used for "sankhâra" an English word which may connote both result and process, and is at the same time etymologically similar to, though not quite parallel to, "sankhâra." The word chosen is "conformations." The selection of the term is arbitrary, as all such translations of philosophical technicalities must be until a consensus of scholars gives currency to a fixed term.

The conception intended to be conveyed by the term "sankhâra" has, as far as I know, no exact parallel in European philosophy. The nearest approach to it is in the *modi* of Spinoza. Buddhist Sankhâra are *modi* underlying which, be there substance or be there not, we do not know.

CONTENTS.

INTRODUCTION.

CHAPTER I.

CHAPTER II.

CHAPTER III.

PART I.

BUDDHA'S LIFE.

CHAPTER I.

CHAPTER II.

CHAPTER III.

CHAPTER IV.

CHAPTER V.

PART II.

THE DOCTRINES OF BUDDHISM.

CHAPTER I.

CHAPTER II.

CHAPTER III.

PART III.

THE ORDER OF BUDDHA'S DISCIPLES.

EXCURSUS.

FIRST EXCURSUS.

SECOND EXCURSUS.

THIRD EXCURSUS.

INTRODUCTION.

CHAPTER I.

INDIA AND BUDDHISM.

The history of the Buddhist faith begins with a band of mendicant monks who gathered round the person of Gotama, the Buddha, in the country bordering on the Ganges, about five hundred years before the commencement of the Christian era. What bound them together and gave a stamp to their simple and earnest world of thought, was the deeply felt and clearly and sternly expressed consciousness, that all earthly existence is full of sorrow, and that the only deliverance from sorrow is in renunciation of the world and eternal rest.

An itinerant teacher and his itinerant followers, not unlike those bands, who in later times bore through Galilee the tidings: "the kingdom of heaven is at hand," went through the realms of India with the burden of sorrow and death, and the announcement: "open ye your ears; the deliverance from death is found."

Vast gaps separate the historical circle, in the middle of which stands the form of Buddha, from the world on which we are wont next to fix our thoughts, when we speak of the history of the world.

Those upheavals of nature which partitioned off India from the cooler lands of the west and north by a gigantic wall of vast mountains, allotted at the same time to the people, who should first tread this highly favoured land, a *rôle* of detached isolation. The Indian nation, in a manner scarcely paralleled by any other nation in the civilized world, has developed its life out of itself and according to its own laws, far removed alike from the alien and the cognate peoples, who in the west, within the compass of closer mutual relations, have performed the parts to which history called them. India took no share in this work. For those circles of the Indian race, among whom Buddha preached his doctrine, the idea of non-Indian lands had hardly a more concrete signification than the conception of those other worlds, which, scattered through infinite space, combine with other suns, other moons and other hells, to form other universes.

The day was yet to come, when an overpowering hand broke down the partition between India and the west—the hand of Alexander. But this contact of India and Greece belongs to a much later period than that which formed Buddhism: between the death of Buddha and Alexander's Indian expedition there elapsed perhaps about one hundred and sixty years. Who can conceive what might have been, if, at an earlier epoch, when the national life of the Indians might have opened itself more freshly and genially to the influences of a foreign life, such events had overtaken it as this incursion of Macedonian weapons and Hellenic culture? For India Alexander came too late. When he appeared, the Indian people had long since come, in the depth of their loneliness, to stand alone among nations, ruled by forms of life and habits of thought, which differed wholly from the standards of the non-Indian world. Without a past living in their memory, without a present, which they might utilize in love and hate, without a future, for which men might hope and work, they dreamed morbid and proud dreams of that which is beyond all time, and of the peculiar government which is within these everlasting realms. On scarcely any of the creations of the exuberant culture of India, do we find the stamp of this Indian characteristic so sharply, and therefore, too, so enigmatically impressed, as on Buddhism.

But the more completely do all external bonds between these distant regions and the world with which we are acquainted, as far as they consist of the intercourse of nations and the interchange of their intellectual wealth, seem to us to be severed, so much the more clearly do we perceive another tie, which holds closely together internally what are outwardly far apart and apparently foreign: the bond of historical analogy between phenomena, which are called into being in different places by the working of the same law.

Invariably, wherever a nation has been in a position to develope its intellectual life in purity and tranquillity through a long period of time, there recurs that phenomenon, specially observable in the domain of spiritual life, which we may venture to describe as a shifting of the centre of gravity of all supreme human interests from without to within: an old faith, which promised to men somehow or other by an offensive and defensive alliance with the Godhead, power, prosperity, victory and subjection of their enemies, will, sometimes by imperceptible degrees, and sometimes by great catastrophes, be supplanted by a new phase of thought, whose watchwords are no longer welfare, victory, dominion, but rest, peace, happiness, deliverance. The blood of the sacrificial victim no longer brings reconciliation to the dismayed and erring heart of man: new ways are sought and found, to overcome the enemy within the heart, and to become whole, pure, and happy.

This altered condition of the inner life gives rise externally to a new form of spiritual fellowship. In the old order of things nature associated religious unity with the family, the clan, and the nation jointly, and inside these unity of faith and worship existed of itself. Whoever belongs to a people has thereby the right to, and is bound to have a share in, the worship of the popular gods. Near this people are other people with other gods; for each individual it is determined as a natural necessity by the circumstances of his birth, what gods shall be to him the true and for him the operative deities. A particular collective body, which may be denominated a church, there is not and there cannot be, for the circle of all worshippers of the popular gods is no narrower and no wider than the people themselves.

The circumstances under which the later forms of religious life come to the surface are different. They have not an antiquity co-eval with the people among whom they arise. When they come into existence they find a faith already rooted in the people and giving an imprint to popular institutions. They must begin to gather adherents to themselves from among the crowds of professors of another faith. It is no longer natural necessity, but the will of the individual, which determines whether he hopes to find his salvation on this side or on that. There arise the forms of the school, the society, and the holy order. From the narrow social circle of teacher and disciples there may eventually grow a church, which, exceeding the limits of the nation, the limits of all seats of culture, may extend to distances the most remote.

Were it allowable to borrow from one particular instance

of those cases which illustrate this, a designation for this revolution of universal occurrence, which transforms the religious life of nations internally as well as externally, we might describe it as the transition from the Old Testament dispensation to the New Testament dispensation. The honour of having given the most unique and most marked expression to this transition in forms unequalled in history, belongs to the Semitic race. Somewhere about five hundred years earlier than in Palestine, analogous occurrences took place among the Indo-Germanic nations in two places, widely separated in locality, but approximate in time, in Greece and in India.

In the former case we find the most eccentric among the Athenians, the defining explorer of the bases of human action, who, in the market and over the wine-cup, to Alkibiades as well as to Plato, demonstrates that virtue can be taught and learned,—in the latter case there steps out as the most prominent among the world's physicians, who then traversed India in monastic garb, the noble Gotama, who calls himself the Exalted, the holy, highly Illuminated One, who has come into the world to show to gods and men the path out of the sorrowful prison of being into the freedom of everlasting rest.

What can be more different than the relative proportions in which in these two spirits—and historical treatment will permit us to add as a third their great counterpart in his mysterious majestic form of suffering humanity—the elements of thought and feeling, of depth and clearness, were arranged and mixed? But even in the sharply-defined difference of that which was, and still is, Socratic, Buddhistic, and Christian vitality, historical necessity holds good. For it was a matter of historical necessity that, when the step was attained at which this spiritual reconstruction was required and called for, the

Greeks were bound to meet this demand with a new philosophy, the Jews with a new faith. The Indian mind was wanting in that simplicity, which can believe without knowing, as well as in that bold clearness, which seeks to know without believing, and therefore the Indian had to frame a doctrine, a religion and a philosophy combined, and therefore, perhaps, if it must be said, neither the one nor the other; Buddhism. Our sketch is intended to keep in view, at every step in detail, the parallelism of these phenomena. While it obtains from the similar historical pictures of the western world a light which enables it in many a dark place within its own province to descry outlines and forms, it hopes on its part in return to aid thereby in suggesting bases founded on facts, sifted and assured, for the discovery of those universally valid rules, which govern the changes in the religious thought of nations.

The course which our sketch will have to follow, is clearly indicated by the nature of the case. Obviously, our first task is to describe the historical national antecedents, the ground and base on which Buddhism rests, above all the religious life and philosophical speculation of pre-Buddhist India; for hundreds of years before Buddha's time movements were in progress in Indian thought, which prepared the way for Buddhism and which cannot be separated from a sketch of the latter. Then the review of Buddhism will naturally divide itself into three heads, corresponding to that Triad, under which even in the very oldest time the Buddhist society in their liturgical language, distributed the whole of those matters which they esteemed sacred, the trinity of Buddha, the Law, the Order. Buddha's own person stands necessarily in our sketch also, as it did in that ancient formula, in the foreground. We must acquaint ourselves with his life and his death, with his *début* as teacher of his people, with his band of disciples, who gathered round him, and with his intercourse with rich and poor, high and low. We shall then turn, in the second place, to the dogmatic thought of the oldest Buddhism, above all to that which stands evermore as a focus in this world of thought, to the doctrine of the sorrow of all that is earthly, the deliverance from this sorrow, the goal of all effort to escape, the Nirvâna. There then remains the characteristic feature of Buddhism, as well as of Christianity, that which externally binds together all who are united by a common faith, and a common effort for deliverance, in bonds of a common church fellowship. In that formula of the Buddhist trinity we find the order named after Buddha and the Law as the third member. We shall follow this course and, when we have spoken of Buddha and his Law, we shall keep in view, in the third place, the Order and their corporate life. We shall come to understand the organization which Buddhism has given to the narrower circle of believers, who have taken their vows as monks and nuns, as well as to the lay community, who accept the doctrine of Buddha. With this will end the investigation of the most ancient Buddhism; or, more accurately expressed, the sketch of Buddhism in that form, which is to us the oldest; and to this investigation only will our sketch be confined.

Western and Eastern India—The Brahman-castes.

The stage upon which antecedent history as well as the most ancient history of Buddhism was enacted, is the Gangetic valley, the most Indian of Indian lands. In the times of which we have to speak, the Gangetic valley, almost alone in the whole peninsula, comprised within itself all centres of Aryan state-government and culture. The great natural divisions of this territory, which coincide with stages in the distribution of the Indian family-stock, and with stages in the extension of old-Indian culture, correspond also to stages in the course of development which this religious movement has taken.

At the outset we are carried into the north-west half of the Gangetic valley, to those territories where the Gangetic tracts and the Indus tracts approach each other, and to those through which the two twin streams of the Ganges and Yamunâ flow as they converge to their conjunction. Here, and for a long period here alone, lay the true settlements of Brahmanical culture; here first, centuries before the time of Buddha, in the circles of Brahman thinkers, at the place of sacrifice and in the solitudes of forest life, those thoughts were thought and uttered, in which the transition from the old Vedic religion of nature to the doctrine of deliverance began and ultimately found development.

The culture fostered in the north-west, and with it these thoughts, following the course of the Ganges, flowed on to the south-east through those powerful veins in which from of old beat most strongly the life of India. Among new peoples they assumed new forms, and when Buddha himself at last appeared, the two greatest kingdoms in the south-eastern half of the Gangetic valley, the lands of Kosala (Oude) and Magadha (Bihar), became the chief scenes of his teaching and labours. Thus there lie broad strips of land between the tracts in which, long before Buddha, Buddhism began its preparatory course of development, and those in which Buddha himself gathered round him his first believers; and this change of scenery and actors has had, it could not have been otherwise, an appreciable effect in more than one respect on the course of the play.

We next take a glance at the tribes, which successively meet us, some as the originators and others as the promoters of this religious movement.

The Aryan population of India came into the peninsula, as is well known, from the north-west. This immigration lay already in the remote past at the time to which the oldest monuments which we have of religious poetry belong. The Indians had as completely lost the memory of this as the corresponding events had been forgotten by the Greeks and Italians. Fair Aryans pressed on and broke down the strongholds of the aboriginal inhabitants, the "black-skinned," the "lawless," and "godless." The enemy was driven back, annihilated, or subjugated. When the songs of the Veda were sung, Aryan clans, though perhaps only as adventurous, solitary pioneers, had already pressed on to where the Indus in the west, and possibly also to where the Ganges in the east, empty their mighty waters into the sea; inexhaustibly rich regions in which the flocks of the Aryans grazed and the Aryan deities were honoured with prayer and sacrifice.

Probably the first immigrants, and, therefore, the farthest forward to the east, whether confederate or disassociated we know not, are those tribes which meet us later on east of the junction of the Ganges and Yamunâ, settled on both banks of the Ganges, the Anga and Magadha, the Videha, the Kâçi and Kosala.

A second wave of the great tide of immigration brought with it new groups of Aryans, a number of tribes closely interconnected, who, surpassing their brothers intellectually, have produced the most ancient great monuments of the Indian mind which we possess, and which we call by the name of the Vedas. We find these tribes at the time of which the hymns of the Rig Veda give us a picture, near the entrances of the Indian peninsula, at the Indus and in the Panjáb; later on they are driven to the south-east and have founded on the upper stream of the Ganges and on the Yamunâ those kingdoms, which are called in "Manu's Institutes" the land of the "Brahmarshis," the home and the type of holy, upright living: "By a Brahman who has been born in this land," says the Law (of Manu), "shall all men on earth be instructed as to their conduct." The names of the Bharata tribe, Kuru, Pancâla, stand out among the peoples of this classic land of Vedic culture, which lies before our gaze in clear illumination as a land rich in advanced intellectual creation, while the destinies of the other tribes, who had immigrated at an earlier date, remained in darkness until the period when they came into contact with the culture of their brother tribes.*

In a Vedic work, the "Brahmana of the hundred paths," we have a remarkable legend, in which is clearly depicted the course which the extension of the cult and culture of the Veda took. The flaming god Agni Vaiçvânara, the sacrificial fire, wanders eastward from the river Sarasvatî, beyond the old sacred home-land of the Vedic Sacra. Rivers cross his path, but Agni burns on across all streams, and after him follow the prince Mâthava and the Brahman Gotama. Thus they came to the river Sadânîrâ, which flows down from the snowy mountains in the north: Agni does not cross it. "Brahmans crossed it not in former ages for Agni Vaiçvânara had not burned beyond it. But now many Brahmans dwelt beyond it to the east. This was formerly very bad land, inundated soil, for Agni Vaiçvânara had not made it habitable. But now it is very good land, for Brahmans have since made it enjoyable

* Further proofs in support of the view here taken of the separation of the western Vedic and the eastern non-Vedic tribes, are advanced at the close of this work in Excursus I.

through offerings;"—in India bad land is not converted into good, as in the rest of the world, by peasants who plough and dig, but by sacrificing Brahmans. Prince Mâthava takes up his abode to the east of the Sadânîrâ, in the bad land, which Agni had not essayed to enter. His descendants are the rulers of Videha. The opposition is clear in which these legends place the eastern tribes to the western, among whom Agni Vaiçvânara, the ideal champion of Vedic life, is from of old at home. Whoever pursues an inquiry into the beginning of the extension of Buddhism, must remember that the home of the oldest Buddhist communities lies in the tracts or near the limits of those tracts, into which Agni Vaiçvânara did not cross in his flaming course when he travelled to the east.

We are unable to fix any graduated series of dates, either by years or by centuries, indicating the progress of this victorious campaign, in which Aryans and Vedic culture overran the Gangetic valley. But, what is more important, we are able from the layers of Vedic literature which overlie each other, to gather some idea of how, under the influences of a new home, of Indian nature and Indian climate, a change came over the life of the people—first and foremost of the Vedic peoples, the tribes of the north-west—and how the popular mind received that morbid impression of sorrow and disease, which has survived all changes of fortune, and which will last as long as there is an Indian people.

In the sultry, moist, tropical lands of the Ganges, highly endowed by nature with rich gifts, the people who were in the prime of youthful vigour when they penetrated hither from the north, soon ceased to be young and strong. Men and peoples come rapidly to maturity in that land, like the plants of the tropical world, only just as rapidly to fall asleep both bodily and spiritually. The sea with its invigorating breeze, and the school of noble national energy, play no part in the life of the Indians. The Indian has above all, at an early stage, turned aside from that which chiefly preserves a people young and healthy, from the battle and struggle for home, country, and law. The thought of freedom with all the quickening, and, it is true, also with all the deadly powers which it brings in its train, has always been unknown and incomprehensible in India. The free will of man may not chafe against the system of Brahma, the natural law of caste, which has given the people into the power of the king and the king into the power of the priest. Well might it awaken the astonishment of the Greek to see in India the peasant calmly go forth between opposing armies to till his fields:* "He is sacred and inviolable for he is the common benefactor of friend and foe." But in what the Greeks mention as a beautiful and sensible feature in Indian national life, there lies something more than mere soft mildness. When Hannibal came, the Roman peasant ceased to sow his fields. The Indians are wholly strangers to the highest interests and ideals which are at the basis of all healthy national life. Will and action are overgrown by thought. But when once the internal balance is disarranged and the natural relationship between the spirit and the reality of the world is disturbed, thought has no longer the power to take a wholesome grasp of what is wholesome. Whatever is, appears to the Indian worthless compared to the marginal illuminations with which his fancy surrounds it, and the images of his fancy grow in tropical luxuriance, shapeless and distorted, and turn eventually with terrific power against their creator. To him the true world, hidden by the images of his own dreams, remains an unknown, which he is unable to trust

* This fact mentioned by Megasthenes is also confirmed by modern writers, cf. Irving, "Theory and Practice of Caste," p. 75.

and over which he has no control: life and happiness in this world break down under the burden of excessively crushing contemplation of the hereafter.

The visible manifestation of the world to come in the midst of the present world is the caste of the Brahmans, who have knowledge and power, who can open and shut to man the approach to the gods, and make friends or enemies for him above. Those powers, which were excluded from development in political life, could find in the case of the Brahmans alone a sphere for creation, but verily for what a creation! Instead of a Lykurgus or a Themistokles, whom fate peremptorily denied to the Indians, they have had all the more Ârunis and Yâjnavalkyas, who knew how to found with masterly hand the mysteries of fire-offering and soma-offering, and to give currency in not less masterly fashion to those claims which are advanced against the secular classes by the champions of the kingdom which is not of this world.

No one can understand the course which Indian thought has taken, without keeping in view the picture, with its lights and shadows, of this order of philosophers, as the Greeks named the Brahmanical caste. And above all it must be remembered that, at that time at least, which has shaped the determinative fundamental thoughts for the intellectual efforts of a subsequent age and for Buddhism also, this priestly class was something more than a vain and greedy priestcraft, that it was the necessary form in which the innermost essence, the evil genius, if we may so call it, of the Indian people has embodied itself.

The days of the Brahman passed in solemn routine. At every step those narrow, restraining limits held him in, which the holy dignity that he represented imposed on the inner and outer man. He passed his youth in hearing and learning the sacred word, for a true Brahman is he alone "who has heard." And if he acquired the reputation "of having heard," his adult life passed in teaching, in the village or out in the solitude of the forest in the consecrated circle, on which the sun shone in the east, where alone the most secret instruction could be imparted openly to the muffled scholar. Or he was be found at the place of sacrifice, performing for himself and for others the sacred office, which, with its countless observances, demanded the most painful minuteness and the most laborious proficiency, or he fulfilled the life-long duty of Brahma-offering, that is, the daily prayer from the sacred Veda. Well might riches flow into his hands by the remuneration for sacrifice, which kings and nobles gave to the Brahmans, but he passed as most worthy, who lived, not by offerings for others, but by the gleanings of the field, which he gathered, or by alms for which he had not asked, or such charity as he had begged as a favour. Still, living even as a beggar, he looked on himself as exalted above earthly potentates and subjects, made of other stuff than they. The Brahmans call themselves gods, and, in treaty with the gods of heaven, these gods of earth know themselves possessed of weapons of the gods, weapons of spiritual power, before which all earthly weapons snap powerless. "The Brahmans," says a Vedic song, "carry sharp arrows: they have darts; the aim, which they take, fails not. They attack their enemy in their holy ardour and their fury, they pierce him through from afar." The king, whom they anoint to rule over their people, is not their king; the priest, at the coronation, when he presents the ruler to his subjects, says: "This is your king, O people; the king over us Brahmans is Soma." They, the Brahmans, standing without the pale of the State, bind themselves together in a great confederacy, which extends as far as the ordinances of the Veda are current. The members of this confederacy are the only teachers of the rising youth. The young Indian of Aryan birth is as good as out-caste, if he be not brought at a proper age to a Brahman teacher, to receive from him the sacred cord, the mark of the spiritual twice-born, and to be inducted into the wisdom of the Vedas. "Into my control," then says the teacher, "I take thy heart, let thy thought follow my thought, with all thy soul rejoice in my word." And through the long years, which the pupil passes in the master's house, he is coerced by his fear and obedience to him. The house of the Brahman is, like the army in the modern State, the great school, which demands of every one a share of the best part of his life, to discharge him eventually with the indelibly implanted consciousness of subordination to the idea embodied, in the one case in the State, in the other case in the Brahman-class.

In the strength and the weakness of the forms of life of this class of thinkers lies also, as it were in a germ, the strength and weakness of their thought. They were, so to speak, banished into a self-made world, cut off from the refreshing atmosphere of real life, by nothing shaken in their unbounded belief in themselves and in their unique omnipotence, in comparison with which all that gave character to the life of others, must have appeared small and contemptible. And thus, therefore, in their thought also the utmost boldness of world-disclaiming abstraction shows itself, which soars beyond all that is visible into the regions of the spaceless and timeless, to caper in sickly company in baseless chimeras, without limit or aim, in fancies such as can be conceived only by a spirit which has lost all taste for the sober realities of fact. They have created a mode of thought in which the great and profound has joined partnership with childish absurdities so uniquely that the history of the attempts of humanity to comprehend self and the universe affords no parallel. To study this thought in its development is our next task.

CHAPTER II.

INDIAN PANTHEISM AND PESSIMISM BEFORE BUDDHA.

Symbolism of the Offering—The Absolute.

The rudiments of Indian speculation extend back to the lyric poetry of the Rig Veda. Here, in the oldest monument of Vedic poetry, among songs at sacrifice and prayers to Agni and Indra for protection, prosperity, and victory, we discover the first bold efforts of a reflecting mind, which turns its back on the spheres of motley worlds of gods and myths, and, in conscious reliance on its own power, approaches the enigmas of being and origination :—

"Nor Aught nor Naught existed, yon bright sky
Was not, nor heaven's broad roof outstretched above.
What covered all? What sheltered? What concealed?
Was it the water's fathomless abyss?

"There was not death—yet was there naught immortal,
There was no confine betwixt day and night;
The only One breathed breathless by itself,
Other than It there nothing since has been.

"Darkness there was, and all at first was veiled
In gloom profound—an ocean without light—
The germ that still lay covered in the husk
Burst forth, one nature, from the fervent heat.

"Who knows the secret? who proclaimed it here,
Whence, whence this manifold creation sprang?
The gods themselves came later into being—
Who knows from whence this great creation sprang?

"He from whom all this great creation came,
Whether His will created or was mute,
The Most High Seer that is in highest heaven,
He knows it—or perchance even He knows not."*

And in another song a poet speaks, who, estranged from the faith in the old deities, seeks after the one God, "who alone is Lord over all that moves:"

"He who gives breath, He who gives strength;
Whose command all the bright gods revere,
Whose shadow is immortality, whose shadow is death;—
Who is the God to whom we shall offer our sacrifice?

"He through whose greatness these snowy mountains are,
And the sea, they say, with the distant river (the Rasâ)—
He of whom these regions are the two arms;—
Who is the God to whom we shall offer our sacrifice?

"He through whom the sky is bright and the earth firm—
He through whom the heaven was 'stablished, nay the highest heaven—
He who measured out the space in the sky?—
Who is the God to whom we shall offer our sacrifice?

"He who by His might looked even over the waters
Which held power and generated the sacrificial fire,
He who alone is God above all gods;—
Who is the God to whom we shall offer our sacrifice?†"

Each strophe of the lyric ends in these words: "who is the God to whom we shall offer our sacrifice?" The gap is clearly perceptible which lies between inquiring hymns like this and the positive faith of an earlier age, which knew, but

* Rig Veda, x. 129. Translated by Max Müller.
† Ibid., x. 121. Translated by Max Müller.

inquired not regarding the gods to whom they should make sacrifice.

We can only touch with brief comment this first flash of conscious thought of the Indians regarding the fundamental questions of the universe and life. The development of speculation—or, rather, its self-development out of a world of phantasms—first assumes a connected progressive form at a time which is later—probably much later—than that to which these hymns, quoted from the Rig Veda, belong. It was that period of widely ramified and exuberant literary production which has given birth to the endless mass of sacrificial works and mystic collections of dogmas and discourses, written in prose, which are usually named Brâhmana, Aranyaka, and Upanishad. The age of these works, upon which alone we can rely for this portion of our sketch, we can determine only approximately and within uncertain limits. We shall scarcely be much in error, if we place their origin somewhere between the ninth and seventh centuries before the Christian era. The development of thought, which was progressing in this period, while resting apparently on the basis of the old faith in gods, had really undermined that faith, and, forcing its way through endless voids of fantastic chimeras, had at last created a new ground of religious thought, the belief in the undisturbed, unchangeable universal-Unity, which reposes behind the world of sorrow and impermanence, and to which the delivered, leaving this world, returns. On this very foundation, moreover, centuries after the Brahmanical thinkers had laid it, were the doctrine and the church built, which were named after the name of Buddha.

We now proceed to trace step by step the process of that self-destruction of the Vedic religious thought, which has produced Buddhism as its positive outcome.

At the time when this process begins, all spiritual exercises which are performed in India are concentrated round one focus, the sacrifice. The world, which surrounds the Brahmans, is the place of sacrifice; the matters, of which, above all others, he has knowledge, are those relating to sacrificial duties. He must understand the sacrifice with all its secrets, for understanding is all-subduing power. By this power the gods have chained the demons—"mighty," so runs the promise for those who have knowledge, "doth he himself become, and powerless becomes his enemy and controverter, who possesses such knowledge."

The elements, of which this knowledge of the meaning of the sacred sacrificial rites consists, are twofold; some spring from the spiritual bequests of the past, and others are a newly-acquired possession.

On the one side, the legacy inherited from the time of the simple belief in Agni and Indra and Varuna, and all the hosts of gods, before whom fathers and ancestors had bowed themselves in prayer and sacrifice. Every hand laid on the offering points to these. When the offerer seizes the sacred implement, he says, "I grasp thee at the call of god Savitar, with the arms of the Açvins, with Pûshan's hands." If the sacrificial object is to be consecrated with sprinkling of water, he says to the waters, "Indra hath chosen you as his associates at the conquest of Vritra; ye have chosen Indra as your associate at the conquest of Vritra." And from early morn until evening there resound at the place of sacrifice praises and songs to Ushas, the redness of dawn, the divine maiden, who, with her glistening steeds, approaches the dwellings of man, dispensing blessings; to Indra, who, fired by the soma-draught, breaks in wild battle the legions of demons with his thunderbolt; to Agni, the benign god, the heavenly guest, who beams in the habitations of men, and bears their sacrificial gifts to heaven.

But the world of the old gods, the living gods of flesh and blood, can no longer of itself alone satisfy the mind of the later age. Ever stronger becomes the tendency to name by their proper names the powers which govern the wide world and the life of man. There is space; the Indians named it "the regions of the world." There is time, with its creating and destroying power; the Indians named it "the year." There are the seasons, the moon, day and night, earth and air, the sun—"he who burns," and the wind—"he who blows." There are the breath-powers, which pass through the human body. There are thought and speech, "which are one with each other and yet separate." The movements and operations of these powers govern the course of the universe, and bring men weal and woe.

And now men look for an answer, in the new language of their own age, to the question which the sacrifice and the world of gods, to whom sacrifice is made, suggest to the thought. Then the atmosphere assumes a state in which mysteries and symbols increase. In all the surroundings of the Brahman at the altar of sacrifice, and above all in the sacred office which he there performs, the god Agni and the god Savitar will no longer be present alone, but there shall be there all the hidden powers which move to and fro in the universe, "for the universe," it is said, "is swayed by the movement of sacrifice." What meets the eye in the offering is not merely what it is or appears to be, but there is something further—that which it signifies. Speech and action have a double signification, the apparent and the hidden; and, if human knowledge follows the apparent, yet the gods love the hidden and abhor the apparent.

Numbers have mysterious power, words and syllables have mysterious power, rhythms have mysterious power. There is an imaginary play between imaginary forces which is subject to no law of perceptibility. Consecration (dîkshâ) escapes from the gods; they search for it through the months; they find it neither with summer nor with winter, but they find it with the months of the cool season (çiçira); therefore man must consecrate himself when the months of the cool season have come round. The metra fly up to heaven to bring the soma-draught; the voice speaks standing in the seasons.

The system of offering is a type of the year, or, briefly, the sacrifice is the year; the officiating priests are the seasons of the year; the objects offered up are the months. We should import something foreign into these plays of thought if we attempted to trace in them any sharply-defined line of demarcation between the being and the signifying, between the reality and its representative; the one overlaps the other. "Prajâpati (the Creator) created as his image that which is the offering. Therefore people say the offering is Prajâpati. For he created it as his image."

Morning after morning, and evening after evening, two offerings are placed in the sacred fire; the one is the past, the other the future; the one is to-day, the other the morrow. To-day is certain; therefore, the first of both offerings will be made with an utterance of sacrificial formula, for speech is certainty. The morrow is uncertain; therefore, the second offering will be made in silence, for silence, as the Indian says, is the uncertain.

In the confused cloud-world of these mysteries, there lurk, concealed from the eye of the ignorant, countless enemies of the destinies of the children of men; days and nights roll on, and bear away with them the blessings which the good deeds of men had won for them; above the realm of changing days and nights the sun, "who shines," is enthroned; and "he who burns is death. Since he is death, therefore the creatures who dwell below him die; those who live beyond him are the gods; therefore are the gods immortal. His rays are the traces, wherewith all these creatures are yoked to life. Whosesoever life he wishes, he draws to himself and he departs—he dies." But the wise man knows formulas and offerings, which exalt him above the region of rolling days and nights, and above the world, in which the sun, with his heat, has power over life and death. Day and night rob not him of the reward of his works; he sets his life free from death—"that is the deliverance from death, which is in the Agnihotra offering."

The world thus darkens down for the fancy of this race to a dismal arena for the movement of unlimited lifeless shapes. Symbols are heaped unceasingly on symbols; wherever thought turns, new gods and new miraculous powers confront it, each as formless as the rest. That God, it is true, who was before all gods and all existences, the creator of worlds, Prajâpati, who was alone in the beginning and desired "might I become a plurality, might I produce creatures," stands out above all; and in the hot work of toilsome creation he gave forth from himself the worlds, and gods and men, and space and time, and thought and speech. But even the thought of Prajâpati, the lord of beings, evoked no louder response from the breast of the believer; the image of the Creator floats hazily among others in the great, gray, shapeless mist, which surrounds the world of creatures.

Wherever we look in the vast mass of monuments, which the strange activity of that age has bequeathed to us, there is nowhere to be seen an operation of the inquiring mind, proceeding from the depths, nowhere that effort of bold thought, which plays for a heavy stake and wins. That imbecile wisdom which knows all things and declares all things, sits enthroned in self-content in the middle of its absurd images, and not even quakes before the spectral hosts which it has conjured up; wherefore should the wise tremble, who knows the word before which spirits and demons bow? One generation after another grows up under the ban of confused thoughts, and one after another unwearied adds its quota to the contributions of departed races, and then it also passes away.

Our eyes must accustom themselves, until they have learned to see in the dim light of this shadow-land, in which the fanciful images of those ages move, crowding formlessly together. But then even here there reveals itself a kind of natural law operating in the region of the spiritual. Let us first on our part trace what is preserved to us in the oldest monuments of those speculations, and then the work of later generations successively, and thus as we mount up layer by layer, the picture which we see changes, and the changes have connection and meaning.

The more important of these conceptions of the fancy gradually emerge from the confused mass, press into the foreground, trample down the weak, and step triumphantly into the centre of every circle. The powers and symbols, on whose working the Indian thinker fancies the system of the universe to rest, are what they are, not in and by themselves alone, but the farther thought goes, the more clearly do they appear to rest on great fundamental forces, from which their existence is principally derived, or in which they are again merged, when the goal of their being is reached. From the surface, where each phenomenon presents itself as something different from every other, the speculative imagination strives to pierce into the depths below, in which lies the unifying bond of all diversity. Man looks for the essence in things, and the essence of the essence,* for the reality, the truth of phenomena, and the truth of the true. This quest of the substance is necessarily a search for unity in all diversity. And thus thought lays hold separately upon one single group of phenomena, connected by a common feature, and regards them as united in a common root, and ere long thought passes all bounds and boldly declares, so and so is the universe. And then it lets go what it laid hold of; that one phenomenon which had just now been declared to be the universe is lost again in the floating crowd of all the powers, which hold sway in man and the world, in space and time, in word and speech.

In none of the Vedic texts can we trace the genesis of the

* Cf. "Chândogya Upanishad," i. 1, 2:—"The essence of all beings is the earth, the essence of the earth is water, the essence of water the plants, the essence of plants man, the essence of man speech, the essence of speech the Rig Veda, the essence of the Rig Veda the Sâma Veda, the essence of the Sâma Veda the Udgîtha (which is Om). That Udgîtha (Om) is the best of all essences, the highest, deserving the highest place, the eighth."

The conception which lies at the bottom of this eight-fold series of essence, essence of the essence, and so on, is (in the words of Max Müller) something like this:—"Earth is the support of all beings, water pervades the earth, plants arise from water, man lives by plants, speech is the best part of man, the Rig Veda the best part of speech, the Sâma Veda the best extract from the *Rik*, Udgîtha, or the syllable Om, the crown of the Sâma Veda."

Later on, where the idea of the Brahma will claim our attention, we shall have to speak of the symbolical relation or of the hidden intrinsic identity, which the Indian fancy detects between nature and the world of language, especially the sacred word. This passage has an important bearing on this, inasmuch as it shows how, in the mind of the Indian, the objects of nature point back through a series of middle terms, to the word of the Veda, and finally to the Om, the most suitable expression of the Brahma, as it were to the life-giving power in them.

conception of the unity in all that is, from the first dim indications of this thought until it attains a steady brilliancy, as clearly as in that work, which, next to the hymns of the Rig Veda, deserves to be regarded as the most significant in the whole range of Vedic literature, the "Brâhmana of the hundred paths."

The "Brâhmana of the hundred paths" shows us first and foremost how from these confused masses of ideas the notion of the "ego" presses to the front of all others, and will domineer over them, in the language of the Indians: the Âtman, the subject, in which the forces and functions of human life find root and footing. The breath-powers penetrate the human body and give it life; the Âtman is lord over all breath-powers; he is the central power, which works and creates in the basis of personal life, the "innominate breath-power," from which the other "nominate" breath-powers derive their being. "A decade of breaths truly," so says the Brâhmana, "dwells in man; the Âtman is the eleventh, on him are dependent the breath-powers." "From the Âtman come all these members (of the human body) into being," "of all that is, the Âtman is the first."

A central point is here found for the domain of human personality, with its limbs and its faculties, that power which is the intrinsic and essential, working in all forms of life. And what the Indian thinker has conceived in the particular "ego" extends in his idea, by inevitable necessity, to the universe at large beyond him; according to him microcosm and macrocosm continuously play corresponding parts, and here and yonder similar appearances point significantly to each other. As the human eye resembles the cosmic eye, the sun, and as the gods, resembling in the general system the human breath-powers, act as the breath-powers of the universe, so also the Âtman, the central substance of the "ego," steps forth on the domain of the bare human individual, and is taken as the creating power that moves the great body of the universe. He, the lord of the breath-powers, the firstling, from whom the limbs of the body were formed, is at the same time the lord of the gods, the creator of creatures, who has caused the worlds to proceed from his "ego;" the Âtman is Prajâpati. Yea, the very expression occurs, "the Âtman is the universe." At this stage this phrase is only one play of the fancy among a thousand others, not the thought grasped in its fulness, that the boundless universe and the restricted "ego," which contemplates it, are in truth one. A crowd of other figures pushes to the front and diverts the attention from the Âtman, who is the universe; but the expression once uttered, though it die away, works on in secret and awaits the time when he who once uttered it, will turn his thoughts back to it.

Meanwhile from another train of conceptions another power not less potent pushes itself forward, with a claim to be recognized as the great cosmic energy. The sacred word, the established guide in sacrifice, is preserved in its three forms of hymn, formula, and song,* making up the "threefold knowledge" of those who knew the Vedas. The spiritual fluid, which bears the sacred word and its supporters, the Brahmans, floating above the profane word and the profane world, is the Brahma:† it is the power which dwells in hymn, formula, and song, as the power of holiness; "the truth of the word is the Brahma."

* That is Ric (hymn of the Rig Veda), Yajus (sacrificial formula of the Yajur Veda), Sâman (songs contained in the Sâma Veda).—*Translator.*

† It will not be superfluous to bear in mind that the times, of which we are speaking, know nothing of the god Brahman. While "brahman," "brâhmana" occur frequently enough in the oldest texts in the signification of "Priest," the god Brahman appears first only in the very latest parts of the Veda.

The world of the word is to the Indian another microcosm. In the rhythm of the sacred song he hears the echoes of the rhythm of the universe resound.* Thus must that substance from which the sacred word derives its being, also be a power which operates at the basis. of all things. The fanciful subtleties, regarding the enigma of the Brahma reposing in the

* Of the countless passages which could be quoted in illustration of this, let us merely refer to one, to the working out by the theologians of the Sâma Veda of the idea of the symbolic relation of the Sâman-(song-) diction with its five parts ("Chândogya Upanishad," ii. 2, etc.). "Let a man meditate on the fivefold Sâman as the five worlds. The hinkâra is the earth, the prastâva the fire, the udgîtha the sky, the pratihâra the sun, the nidhana heaven.—Let a man meditate on the fivefold Sâman as rain. The hinkâra is wind (that brings the rain); the prastâva is 'the cloud is come;' the udgîtha is 'it rains;' the pratihâra, 'it flashes, it thunders;' the nidhana 'it stops.' There is rain for him and he brings rain for others, who, thus knowing, meditates on the fivefold Sâman as rain."

And then it goes on through a series of other comparisons; the Sâman with its five parts represents the waters, the seasons, the animals, and more of the like. Often these symbolizings rest upon nothing more than the most meaningless superficialities, as when the matter treated of is the three syllables of the word udgîtha (sacred song), "ut (ud) is breath, for by means of breath a man rises (ut-tishthati); gî is speech, for speeches are called girah; tha is food, for by means of food all subsist (sthita)." ["Chând. Up.," i. 3, 6. To this passage Max Müller furnishes from Irish sources interesting parallels in the fanciful conceits of the Christians of the Middle Ages.] However senseless such fancies may appear to us, they cannot be overlooked as precursors of the most important event in the religious development of India. In the symbolical interpretation or mystical identification, which the individual word or the individual sacred song furnishes, of the individual phenomenon in the life of nature or of the ego, the ultimate tendency of this development is being shaped: the identification of the central power in the whole range of the sacred word (Brahma), with the central power of the human person (Âtman), and with the life-centre of nature: the genesis of the idea of the universal One.

Vedic text, and the priestly pride of the human supporters of the Brahma, combine to elevate this entity to a dominant position in the Indian's world of thought. "He makes," it is said of the priest who completes a specific sacrificial operation, "the Brahma the head of this universe; therefore the Brahman is the head of this universe." There was an ancient Vedic ode which began: "On truth is the earth founded, on the sun is the heaven founded. By the right do the Adityas (the supreme gods, the sons of the Aditi, the infinite) consist." Now it is said "the Brahma is the word, the truth in the word is the Brahma." "The Brahma is the right." "By the Brahma are the heavens and the earth held together."

Here is an example furnished more illustrative than anything else of the peculiarities of Indian thought. This gradual, persistent pressure of an idea, which arises not from the contemplation of visible nature, but from the speculation about the sacredness of the holy Vedic text—the pressure of this idea and of this word until all the loftiest and deepest conceptions which the mind can grasp are associated with this word.

This stage is not attained at one bound. When it is said, "The Brahma is the noblest among the gods," it is also said in another place in proximity to this, "Indra and Agni are the noblest among the gods." Well, the power of sacred truth, which the Indian calls the Brahma, has stepped into a position among the most prominent forces of the universe; it is recognized as the power which holds the heavens and the earth together, but it is not yet the first and last—the one and all. The young upstart among the ideas is not yet sufficiently powerful to push the ancient creator and ruler of the worlds, Prajâpati, from his throne; but he is become the nearest to this throne. "The spirit, Prajâpati," thus says the Brâhmana of the hundred paths, "wished: May I become a plurality—

may I propagate myself." He exerted himself—he took on himself severe pangs. When he exerted himself, when he had endured severe pangs, he created the Brahma first, the threefold knowledge. That became a support for him; therefore people say, "The Brahma is the support of this universe." Therefore, he who has learned (the sacred word) has gained a support, for what is the Brahma is the support. "The Brahma," it is also said, "is the first-born in this universe." It is not yet the everlasting unborn, from which everything that is has been born, but it is the first-born among the children of Prajâpati, the father of worlds.

There is something of the calm uncontrollable necessity of a natural process in this emerging or growth of both these notions, the Âtman and the Brahma, each of which first gains the dominant position in its own circle, and is then carried forward by the progress of thought into the expanse of worlds; and there also plays an ever-widening part. Though the images which were originally associated with each, in the mind of the Indian, were so different, yet it could not but be that, in the course of such a development, the thought of the Âtman should assimilate itself continually more and more to that of the Brahma, and that of the Brahma to that of the Âtman. "The first-born in this universe is the Brahma," as has been said. And of the Âtman it is said in another place, "Of all that exists, the first existent is the Âtman." The Brahma is the face of the universe, and "the firstling of this universe" is the Âtman. The Brahma displays himself in hymn, formula, and song; "the nature of the Âtman consists," it is further said, "of hymn, formula, and song." The definite, obviously presented, and limited meaning, which simple consciousness had at one time attached to the idea of the Âtman, and to the idea of the Brahma, extends itself to unlimited ranges, and then the difference between the two ideas gradually vanishes. The imagination of the Indian, eager to grasp the unity underlying things, is wanting in the power to preserve the images of the different notions within their several limitations, and in their separation from each other.

And the remaining barriers are passed at last. What heretofore emerged momentarily, and was again lost in the current of an erratic imagination, is grasped anew by the mind, to be lost no more again: the conception of the great everlasting and eternal One, in which all diversity vanishes, from which are spirit and universe, and in which they live and move. It is called the Âtman, it is called the Brahma; Âtman and Brahma converge in the One, in which the yearning spirit, wearied of wandering in a world of gloomy, formless phantasms, finds its rest. "That which was," it is written, "that which will be, I praise, the great Bráhma, the One, the Imperishable, the wide Brahma, the One Imperishable." "To the Âtman let man bring his adoration, the spiritual, whose body is the breath, whose form the light, whose soul the æther, who assumes what forms he will, quick as a thought, full of right purpose, full of right performance, the source of every vapour, of every essence, who extends to all the regions of the world, who pervades this universe, silent and unmoved. Small as a grain of rice, or barley, or hirse, or a millet-seed, this spirit dwells in the ego; golden, like a light without smoke, is he; wider than the heavens, wider than the æther, wider than this earth, wider than all the range of being; he is the ego of the breath, he is my ego (Âtman); with this Âtman shall I, when I separate from this state, unite myself. Whosoever thinketh thus truly, there is no doubt. Thus said Çândilya."

A new centre of all thought is found, a new god, greater than all old gods, for he is the All; nearer to the quest of man's heart, for he is the particular ego. The name of the thinker who was the first to propound this new philosophy, we know not;* the circle of people in which it found response must have been at that time very narrow. But they were the most enlightened of the Indian people, and we see how for them all other thoughts fade, and all other quests are merged in the one quest, the quest of the Âtman, the foundation of things. The parting words of the wise man, who leaves his home and speaks for the last time with his wife, have reference to the Âtman. The debates of the Brahmans, who come together at the gorgeous sacrificial solemnities at the courts of kings, deal with the Âtman. Many a lively description has come down to us, showing how Brahmans eager for the fray, and Brahman females not less eager for the contest, have crossed lances in argument regarding the Âtman. The wise Gârgî says to Yâjnavalkya, "As an heroic youth from Kâçi or Videha bends his unbent bow, and takes two deadly arrows in his hand, I have armed myself against thee with two questions, which solve for me." And another of those opponents, whom the legend of the "Brâhmana of the hundred paths" represents as confronting Yâjnavalkya in this great tournament of debate, and as being conquered by him, says to him, "When anyone says 'that is an ox, that is a horse,' it is thereby pointed out.

* The names of the teachers in whose mouths our texts put the discourses regarding the Âtman cannot be regarded otherwise than with distrust. In the "Çatapatha Br." Yâjnavalkya appears as the one who has most successfully advocated the new doctrines at the court of the Videha king. But while the first books of the said text, which must have been compiled at a not inconsiderable length of time before the development of these speculations, frequently quote Yâjnavalkya as an authority, the *rôle* which he plays in the later books must be a fabrication. The traditions, which give Çândilya a similar place in the history of Indian thought, are hardly deserving of greater credence.

Point out to me the revealed, unveiled Brahma, the Âtman, which dwells in everything: the Âtman, which dwells in everything, what is that, O Yâjnavalkya?" Thus the combatants commence, and the princes listen to the debate, to see which has the deeper knowledge of the Brahma; and he who conquers in the fight gains the Brahmani cows, with horns hung with gold. And side by side with these highly-coloured court scenes, where renowned masters from all lands, who have knowledge of the Âtman, contend with each other for fame, patronage, and reward, the same text gives us another very different picture: "Knowing him, the Âtman, Brahmans relinquish the desire for posterity, the desire for possessions, the desire for worldly prosperity, and go forth as mendicants." This is the earliest trace of Indian monasticism; from those Brahmans who, knowing the Âtman, renounce all that is earthly, and become beggars, the historical development progresses in a regular line up to Buddha, who leaves kith and kin, and goods and chattels, to seek deliverance, wandering homeless in the yellow garb of a monk. The appearance of the doctrine of the eternal One and the origin of monastic life in India, are simultaneous; they are two issues of the same important occurrence.

The Absolute and the External World.

We must more closely examine the various meanings attached by the Indian mind to the idea of the Âtman, the Brahma, alone and in its connection with the material world, for it is in and by these thoughts that those tendencies, which have given to the Buddhist world its characteristic stamp, were, at first imperceptibly but subsequently more decidedly, developed.

The doctrines of the Brahmans regarding the Âtman do not form a system: their mind has, it is true, the courage and strength for a great venture; but how could it, in the excitement of this creation, preserve at the same time the cool equanimity, necessary for arranging and harmonizing its creation? While the mind is ever seeking new paths, ever making new comparisons, which shall explain the enigma of the Âtman; while, no matter whether man's inquiry be as to the remote past of the world's beginning, or as to the future of the human soul in a world to come, the first and last word is invariably the Âtman, who can be astonished if often, in the accumulated masses of these notions, the most irreconcilable differences remained in juxtaposition, probably without their inherent contradictions having been even noticed?

I shall now abstract from one of the most important monuments which have come down to us from those times, from the concluding sections of the "Brâhmana of the hundred paths," a passage which seems to be connected with the first rude efforts of speculation regarding the Âtman. If the being who created the worlds out of himself, here also bears that name, which later times have given him, Âtman, one may well be tempted to believe that the thoughts themselves with their antique and crude stamp belong to the preceding age.

"The Âtman," it says, "existed in the beginning, in a spirit form; he looked round him and saw nothing else but himself; he spoke the first word: 'I am;' hence comes the name 'I;' therefore even now also, whoever is addressed by another, says first: 'It is I,' and then he names the other name which he bears. . . . He was afraid; therefore whoever is alone is afraid. Then he thought: 'There is nothing else but I, of what then am I afraid?' So his fear vanished. Of what had he to be afraid? Man experiences fear of another. But he did not feel content; therefore whoever is alone does not feel content. He desired another. He combined in himself the natures of female and male which are locked in each other's embrace. He divided this nature of his into two parts: by this came husband and wife; therefore each of us alike, is a half, says Yâjnavalkya; therefore is this void (of a man's nature) filled up by the woman. He joined himself to her; thus were men born."

It is then further narrated, how the two halves of the creating Âtman, as sire and dam, assume all animal forms after the human, and produce the animal kingdom, and how then the Âtman produces from himself fire and moisture, or the divinities Agni and Soma. "This is Brahma's creation superior to himself. Inasmuch as he has created gods greater than he himself is, inasmuch as he, a mortal, has created immortals, therefore it is a creating of the superior to himself. Whosoever has this knowledge, finds his place in this, his superior creation."

As the foregoing text may apparently resemble those ancient cosmogonies which begin: "In the beginning was Prajâpati"—so, internally also, this *naïve* conception of the highest being—or of the original being, for it is not the highest yet—scarcely differs from that which a preceding age had conceived in Prajâpati, the creator and ruler of the world. The Âtman here resembles a powerful first man more than a god, not to say the one great *bëent*, in whom all other being lives and moves. This Âtman is afraid in his loneliness, like a man; he feels desire, like a man; he begets and brings forth like human beings. It is true, gods are among his creatures, but these creatures are higher than the creator; creating greater than himself, he, a mortal, produces from himself immortal deities.

Side by side with this cosmogony we place other fragments of the same text, which are of an age probably not much later than the passage quoted.

Yâjnavalkya, the renowned Brahman, is about to leave his home, to wander as a mendicant. He divides his property between his two wives. Then his wife Maitreyî says to him as he is departing, "If my property included the whole earth, would I therefore be immortal?" He replies, "Thy life would be like the life of the rich: but of immortality riches bring no hope." She says, "If I cannot be immortal, what use is all this to me? Tell me, exalted one, whatever thou knowest." And he addresses her regarding the Âtman.

"As when the drum is beaten, a man cannot prevent its sound going forth, but if he seize the drum or the drummer, the sound is stayed;—as when the lute is played, a man cannot prevent its sound going forth, but if he seize the lute or the lute-player, the sound is stayed;—as when the trumpet is blown, a man cannot prevent its sound going forth, but if he seize the trumpet or the trumpeter, the sound is stayed;—as from a fire, in which a man places damp wood, clouds of smoke issue here and there, so truly is the exhalation of this great being; he is Rig Veda, he is Yajur Veda, he is Sâma Veda, the Atharvan and Angiras songs, tale and legend, knowledge and sacred doctrine, verses, rules, he is the explanation and the second explanation; all this is his exhalation.—As a lump of salt, which is thrown into the water, dissolves and cannot be gathered up again, but wherever water is drawn, it is salty, so truly it is with this great being, the endless, the unlimited, the fulness of knowledge: from these (earthly) beings it came into view and with them it vanishes. There is no consciousness after death; hearken, thus I declare unto thee." Thus spoke Yâjnavalkya. Then Maitreyî said, "This speech of thine, exalted one, perplexes me; there is no consciousness after death." Then said Yâjnavalkya, "I tell thee nothing perplexing; it is quite comprehensible; where there is a duality of existences, one can see the other, one can smell the other, one can speak to the other, one can hear the other, one can think of the other, one can apprehend the other. But where for each everything has turned into his ego (the Âtman), by whom and whom shall he see, by whom and whom shall he smell, by whom and to whom shall he speak, by whom and whom shall he hear, think and apprehend? By whom shall he apprehend him through whom he apprehends this universe? Through whom shall he apprehend him, the apprehender?"

This is the farewell conversation of Yâjnavalkya with his wife. Between this and those cosmogonic speculations, which we have already described, there lies a development of thought, which is not much less than a revolution. There is the Âtman, who is afraid, who soliloquizes, who experiences desire, who can be compared with his creatures, as to whether he or they be the greater, and who must fall back behind the highest of his creatures. Here is the Âtman, who is free from all limits of personal, human-like existence. Can there, man now inquires, be perception, thought, consciousness, in the Universe-Being? No, for all perception rests upon a duality, on the opposition of subject and object. In the external world with its unlimited plurality there is everywhere a field for this opposition, but in the absolutely existent all plurality ceases, and with it necessarily all perception, and all consciousness, which have their origin in a plurality. The Âtman is not blind and deaf—he is on the contrary the one great seer and hearer, who does all the seeing and hearing in the external world—but in his own domain he sees not and hears not, for in the unity, which there prevails, the opposition of seeing and seen, of hearing and heard, is removed. Like the ultimate supreme One of the Neoplatonics, which cannot be regarded as intellect nor yet as intelligible, but transcends the reason (*ὑπερβεβηκὸς τὴν νοῦ φύσιν*), the Âtman also, as these farewell words of Yâjnavalkya represent him, transcends the personal, is the root of all personality, the comprehensive fulness of all those powers, in which personal life finds its termination: but these powers come into operation only in this phenomenal world, not in the domain of the everlasting One, the everlasting unchangeable itself.

The one *bëent* is neither great nor small, neither long nor short, neither hidden nor revealed, neither within nor without; the "No, No" is his name, inasmuch as he cannot be comprehended by any epithets, and yet his representative is the syllable of affirmation, Om;* he is the *ens realissimum.*

There yet remained for Indian speculation the task of finding its way back from this ultimate ground of all being to the empirical state of being, to define the relation which subsists between the Âtman and the external world. Is the external world something separate, side by side with the Âtman; such that, apart from that which the Âtman is or works in it, something else, howsoever it have to be apprehended, may yet be left, which is not Âtman? or is the world of plurality absolved without residuum in the Âtman?

It was necessary to approach this question in some form, more or less definite, as soon as men came to speak at all of the Âtman and the material world; but the question is hinted at by the Indian thinkers of these ancient times, rather than put directly or point blank. In their estimation, this alone is

* In Sanscrit the same expression (ekam aksharam) has the same double meaning, "the one imperishable," namely, the Âtman; and "the one syllable," namely, the Om.

of all things most important, that the Âtman may be recognized as the sole source of life in all that lives, and as the thread in which all plurality finds its unity; but where the attempt is made to show how the problem of the co-existence of that plurality and this unity, or of their existence in each other, finds a solution, they speak in the vague language of similes and symbols, rather than in expressions which admit of their signification being sharply defined.

The Âtman, they say, pervades things, as the salt, which has dissolved in water, pervades the water; from the Âtman things spring, as the sparks fly out from the fire, as threads from the spider, as the sound comes from the flute or the drum. "As all the spokes are united together in the nave and the felly of a wheel, so in this Âtman are united all breath-powers, all worlds, all gods, all beings, all these ego-ities."

There is great danger, in interpreting such similes, of not keeping within the faint line which separates that which it was intended they should convey and that which lies in them beyond this, accidentally and unintentionally; yet he who would avoid this danger altogether must simply forbear to lift the veil which lies over the Indian world of thought, shrouded in types and symbols. And we, for our part, think we can detect behind these similitudes, by which men strove to bring the living power of the Âtman in the universe near to his understanding, a conviction, though at the same time but a half-conscious conviction, of the existence of an element in things separate from the Âtman. The Âtman, says the Indian, pervades the universe, as the salt the water in which it has dissolved; but we may easily go on to add, as a complement to this, although no drop of the salt water is without salt, the water continues, notwithstanding, to be something separately constituted from the salt. The spokes of the wheel are all fitted into the nave and the felly, and fastened in, and still the spoke is something which the nave and the felly are not. And thus we may infer, the Âtman is to the Indian certainly the sole actuality, light-diffusing, the only significant reality in things; but there is a remainder left in things, which he is not. "He who dwells in the earth," it is said of the Âtman, "being within the earth, whom the earth knows not, whose body is the earth, who operates within the earth, that is the Âtman, the in-dwelling ruler, the immortal. He who dwells in the water, who dwells in the fire, who dwells in the æther, who dwells in the wind, who dwells in the sun, moon, and stars, who dwells in space, who dwells in lightning and thunder, who dwells in all worlds, who is illatent in all Vedas, all offerings, all beings, whom all beings know not, whose body all beings are, who operates within all beings, that is the Âtman, the in-dwelling ruler, the immortal." And in another part of the same dialogue, from which these propositions have been excerpted: "by the command of this unchangeable being heaven and earth stand fast; by the command of this unchangeable being sun and moon stand fast, days and nights, half months and months, seasons and years stand fast; by the command of this unchangeable being some rivers flow from the snowy mountains to the east, and others to the west and other points of the heavens; by the command of this unchangeable being men commend the giver, the gods the offerer, and the libation made with the spoon is the proper part belonging to the Manes."

Though thus varied is the garb in which thought wraps itself in all these expressions, yet it is always the same, viz., that the Âtman, as the sole directing power, is in all that lives and moves, but that the world of creatures operated on stands side by side with the directing power, pervaded by his energy, and yet separate from him.

Though here and there, by all means, the language seems more free, and expressions are found which convey a hint that the Âtman is everything which lives and moves, yet, I take it, the contradiction lies more in the words employed than in the thought. Is it not allowable, for the bold language in which these hazardous ventures of young thought clothe themselves, to say that the Âtman is the universe, even where the thought, if it were accurately expressed, is only this, that in the universe the Âtman is the only valuable, the source of all life and all light?

Since, then, there remains in things a residue which is not Âtman, we ask: in what light was this residue viewed? whence comes it? what significance has it? Naturally comes the expectation that it was conceived to be matter, or dark chaos, which, formless in itself, receives its form from the Âtman, the source of forms and light. Our texts have preserved for us but few hints on this subject. The knowledge of the Âtman itself, which was inseparably associated with the ideas of the deliverance of the spirit from the domain of sorrow-fraught impermanence, had such unlimited value for the Indian, that the other side of the problem receded in speculative importance before it into the background. But where utterances bearing on these questions are found, they do actually point to the notion of a chaos, a world of potentialities, from which the operation of the Âtman produces realities. The *bĕent*, that was in the beginning alone, Uddâlaka thus instructs his son,* thought: may I become a plurality. It sent forth fire from itself: the fire sent forth water from itself: the water produced food. "Then thought this being: let me now enter these three beings with this living self and let me then

* "Chândogya Upan.," vi. 2, etc. Similar but much more involved is "Çat. Br.," xi. 2, 3.

reveal names and forms." And it enters with its breath of life into the fire, into the water, and into the food, mixes the elements of the one with those of the other, and thus the real world is prepared from the three original existents by the demiurgic operation of the Âtman.

It is clear that those three oldest existents, those original creations of the Âtman, in which he then reveals name and form by his breath of life, are treated before this act of revealing as a chaotic something, which is there, but is not as yet anything precisely determinate, older than the world of things we see, and not eternal like the Âtman, but the Âtman's first creation. But these attempts to demonstrate what in things is matter, bear very perceptibly the marks of immaturity. One would expect to find in the chaos, before the breath of life of the demiurgus produces in it "name and form," a nameless and formless, an absolute, indeterminate something, and yet it is in the very beginning organic, of the threefold nature, of fire, water, and food, and thus it has thereby originally in itself an element of distinctness and nomination. And similarily, on the other hand, is the Âtman, the creator and vivifier of the chaotic, less firmly maintained in that paramount position resulting from the abstraction which we found attained in the farewell discourse of Yâjnavalkya. It is not the simple One, from whose nature, for his unity's sake, all reflection and projection must be excluded, as involving the duality of subject and object; he thinks, and this, indeed, is his thought: may I become a plurality. Those thinkers who have pursued the idea of the unity in the nature of the Âtman to its ultimate consequence, would scarcely have ventured to attempt, in the way entered upon here, a solution of the problem of matter and its evolution from the Âtman; it is surely no mere accident that those passages in our texts also, which accentuate those consequences with the most marked emphasis, are silent on these problems: men may have felt that thought had here reached a chasm, over which to throw a bridge was not in their power.

PESSIMISM, METEMPSYCHOSIS, DELIVERANCE.

This is the place in which to speak of the inferences which the speculation of the Indians drew from the doctrine of the universal One side by side with and in the world of plurality, bearing on the estimate of the value of the world, life and death, and the ethical questions so closely connected therewith.

We stand here at the birthplace of Indian pessimism.

When thought, liberal to itself, had laden the idea of the Âtman with all attributes of every perfection, of absolute unity, of unlimited fulness, the world of plurality, measured by the standard of the everlasting One, must have necessarily appeared a state of disruption, restriction and pain. The unconstrained feeling of being at home in this world is destroyed at one stroke, as soon as thought has weighed it against its ideal of the supreme One, and found it wanting, and thus the glorification of the Âtman becomes involuntarily an ever increasingly bitter criticism of this world. If the Âtman be commended "who is far above hunger and thirst, above sorrow and confusion, above old age and death," who is there who does not detect in such words a reflection, though it be not openly expressed, on the world of the creature, in which hunger and thirst, sorrow and confusion are at home, and in which men grow old and die? "The unseen seer," thus Yâjnavalkya speaks to Uddâlaka, "the unheard hearer, the unthought thinker, the unknown knower; there is no other seer, no other hearer, no other thinker, no other knower. That is thy Âtman, the mover within, the immortal; whatever is besides him, is full of sorrow."—And it is said on another occasion: "as the sun, the eye of the universe, remains far off and unaffected by all sickness that meets the (human) eye, so also the One, the Âtman, who dwells in all creatures, dwells afar and untouched by the sorrows of the world." Here occurs for the first time the expression "Sorrow of the world." That the One, the happy Âtman, has chosen to manifest himself in the world of plurality, of becoming and decease, was a misfortune: this is not openly stated, for men are shy of a thought, which would trace to the happy One Being the roots of the sorrow of earth or even any fault, but they cannot have been very far from this thought when they proposed to man as the highest aim of his effort, the undoing in his case of this manifestation, and the finding for himself a return from the plurality to the One.

The place which Indian speculation allots to man, in and between the two worlds of the happy Âtman and the sorrowful state of the present life, is intimately connected with the conceptions of metempsychosis, the first traces of which appear in the Vedic texts not long before the doctrine of the everlasting One comes to the surface.

The thought that new wanderings, new repetitions of death and re-birth await the soul after death, are wholly foreign to the ancient times in which the hymns of the Rig Veda are sung. Men can talk of the habitations of the happy, where in Yama's kingdom those who have trodden the dark way of death enjoy everlasting pleasures—

> "Where joy and pleasure and gladness
> And rapture dwell, where the wish
> Of the wisher finds fulfilment"——

and men speak also of the deep places of darkness, and of the horrors which await the evil-doer in the world to come. But men have no other thought but the one, that on the entry into the world of the blessed, or into the world of everlasting darkness, destiny is for ever fixed.

We have shown how the age which followed the period of the Rig Veda created a new scheme of the universe. On all sides men descried gloomy formless powers, either openly displayed or veiled in mysterious symbols, contending with each other, and, like harassing enemies, preparing *contretemps* for human destiny. The tyranny of death also is enhanced in the estimation of the dismal mystic of this age; the power of death over men is not spent with the one blow which he inflicts. It soon comes to be averred that his power over him, who is not wise enough to save himself by the use of the right words and the right offerings, extends even into the world beyond, and death cuts short his life yonder again and again; we soon meet the conception of a multiplicity of death-powers, of whom some pursue men in the worlds on this side, and others in the worlds beyond. "Whoever passes into that world without having made himself free from death, will become in that world again and again the prey of death, in the same way that death shows no respect in this world and kills him when he wills." And in another place, "Through all worlds truly death's powers have dominion; if he offered to these no libations, death would pursue him from world to world—if he offers libations to the powers of death, he repels death through world after world."*

* We must refrain from asking the question, whether the influences of the belief of non-Aryan peoples in India have had any share in the origin of this idea of new existences and recurrences of the fate of death. This idea is quite capable of explanation, if we regard it as the outcome of the progressive course which the thought or imagination of the Brahmans has taken, entirely independent of the co-operation of extraneous impulses, the existence of which is as incapable of proof as of disproof.

In the texts of the times, in which these plays of a cheerless fancy first appear, there is little said of the idea of re-birth, or, as it first meets us in characteristic form, of that of re-dying. And yet the influence, which these ideas must have had on the aspirations of religious life, cannot have been small. The spirit can bear the thought of a decision of its destiny once for all, determined for all eternity; but the endless migration from world to world, from existence to existence, the endlessness of the struggle against the pallid power of that ever-recurring destruction—a thought like this might well fill the heart even of the brave with a shudder at the resultlessness of all this unending course of things. When other associations directed the thought to the opposition of a happy world of unity, of rest, to a second world of plurality, of change, the appalling prospect of re-birth—that is, of re-death—will have had no small share in causing men to paint the domain of plurality in those dark colours, as unhappy and desolated by sorrow.

But a thought such as that of more and still more deaths, which await the mortal in future forms of being, cannot be entertained without evoking its complement—or, we should rather say, perhaps, its neutralizer—the thought of the deliverance from death: without this the end would be despair. From the beginning, therefore, the idea of metempsychosis was not so conceived, as though there were in it an unavoidable fatality, to which every human life is subject without hope of escape. At the same time, with the belief in the transmigration of the soul, and as its necessary complement, the conception is formed that from the limitless change of birth and death a way out stands open; the thought and the word "deliverance" are now ready to step into the foreground of religious life.

The phases, both of style and matter, through which

Brahmanical thought passes at this time, in rapid succession, are reflected successively in the way in which the thought of deliverance is embodied.

So long as the way out of that confused maze of grotesque and formless symbolical conceptions to the idea of the Âtman, the universal One, had not been found, the notions of deliverance also bear the same stamp of an arbitrary fantastic externality, which is characteristic of the spiritual creations of that age. The offering, the great fundamental power, and the fundamental symbol of all being and of all procession of being, is also the power by which man bursts the bands of death; and next to the offering itself, the sacred knowledge of the sacrificial rites has the power to set free. Above all, the daily offering to the two luminaries of the day and the night: the morning offering to the sun, and the evening offering to Agni, the sun of the night, both accompanied by a silently-performed offering to Prajâpati, the lord of the created. In the sun dwells death; the sun's rays are the cords by which death has power to draw man's life-breath to himself. "If in the evening, after sunset, he makes the two offerings, he takes his stand with the two fore-quarters (of his being) in that death's power (*i.e.*, in the sun); if in the morning, before sunrise, he makes the two offerings, he takes his stand with the two hind-quarters (of his being) in that death's power. When he rises, then, he bears him with him as he rises; thus he delivers himself from that death. This is the deliverance from death which is inherent in the Agnihotra offering. He delivers himself from the recurrence of death who thus understands this deliverance from death in the Agnihotra." And in another place, "Those who have this knowledge, and perform this offering, will after death be born again; they will be born again to die no more. But those who have not this knowledge, or do not perform this offering, will after death be born again, and will become the prey of death anew, over and over again for ever."

These are the earliest appearances of the belief in the transmigration of souls and the deliverance from death, dressed in fanciful miraculous shapes. When these thoughts came to the front, events were in process which were to give a new aspect to the Brahmanical world of ideas; at that very time speculation directed itself to detect in the Âtman, or the Brahma, the everlasting, imperishable Being, the source of every state of existence, the unity resting at the back of all plurality. As soon as this step was taken, a ground was gained on which those thoughts of death and deliverance could be planted out, and from which they could derive new intrinsic value. The different elements of speculation of themselves here fitted together into a whole which left no joinings to be seen. On the one side a dualism—the everlasting Brahma, the ground of all being, the true nature also of the human spirit (Brahma =Âtman), and opposed to him the world of becoming and of decease, of sorrow and of death. On the other side a similar opposition—the undelivered soul, which death holds in his bonds, and ever anew hurries from one state of being into another, and the delivered soul, which has overcome death, and attained the goal of wayfarers. The result of the union of the two trains of thought could only be this: the wandering of the soul through the domains of death is the fruit of its non-union with the Brahma: the deliverance is the attained unity of the soul with its true mode of being, the Brahma. Unity there is not, as long as the human soul conducts itself in thought and will as a citizen of the world of plurality; so long does it remain subject to the law which operates in this world, the law of origination and decease, of birth and death.

But where the look and longing fixed on plurality have been vanquished, the soul, freed from the dominion of death, returns to the home of all life, to the Brahma. "As a weaver," says the Brâhmana of the hundred paths, "takes away a piece of a many-coloured cloth and weaves another, new, more beautiful pattern, so also the spirit (in death) shuffles off this body, and allows consciousness to be extinguished, and takes upon itself another, new form, of Manes or Gandharvas, of Brahma's or Prajâpati's nature, of divine or human or other manner of being. . . . . As he acted and as he walked, so he becomes: he who does good becomes a good being, he who does bad a bad; he becomes pure by pure action, evil by evil action. . . . . So with him who is in the net of desire. But he who desires not? He who is without desire, who is free from desire, who desires the Âtman only, who has attained his desire, from his body the breath-powers do not escape (into another body), but here draw themselves together; he is the Brahma, and he goes to the Brahma. The following couplet speaks of this:—

> 'When he has set himself free from every desire of his heart,
> The mortal enters immortal into the Brahma here below.'"

Desire (kâma) and action (karman) are here named as the powers which hold the spirit bound within the limits of impermanence. Both are essentially the same. "Man's nature," it is said in the same treatise from which we have taken the passage quoted, "depends on desire. As his desire, so is his aspiration; as his aspiration, so is the course of action (karman) which he pursues; whatever be the course of action he pursues, he passes to a corresponding state of being."

The form in which the idea of a moral retribution here appears, and in which, through long ages, it has constituted a fundamental principle of religious thought, with Buddhists as well as with Brahmans, is the doctrine of the *karman* (action) as the power which pre-determines the course of the migration of the soul from one state of being to another. Our sources of information show us that this new doctrine did not at first meet with general acceptance among the circles of philosophizing Brahmans; whoever knows it, has the feeling of possessing in it a mysterious secret, of which one should speak only covertly and in private. So in the great debate, of which the Brâhmana of the hundred paths gives an account, among the opponents who seek to trip up the wise Yâjnavalkya with their questions, Jâratkârava Artabhâga comes forward. He puts a question: "Yâjnavalkya, when man dies, his voice goes into the fire, his breath into the wind, his eye to the sun, his thought to the moon, his ear to the quarters of heaven, his body to earth, his personality to the æther, his hairs to the plants, the hair of his head to the trees; his blood and his semen find a place in the waters. But where, then, remains the man himself?" "Give me thy hand, my friend," is the answer. "Artabhâga! we two alone must be privy to this; not a word on that subject where people are listening." "And they two went out and conversed together. What they then said, they said regarding action (karman); and what they then propounded, they propounded regarding action: by pure action man becomes pure (fortunate), by evil action evil (unfortunate)."

But no action can lead into the world of deliverance and happiness. Even good action is something which remains confined to the sphere of the impermanent; it receives its reward, but the reward of the impermanent can only be an impermanent one. The everlasting Âtman is highly exalted alike above reward and effort, above holiness and unholiness. "He, the immortal, is beyond both, beyond good and evil;

what is done and what is left undone, cause him no pain; his domain is affected by no action." Thus, action and the being delivered are two things, quite separate from each other; the dualism of impermanence and permanence, which influences all thought in this age, here imposes from the first on the idea of deliverance, and on the ethical postulates which flow from it, this negative character: morality is not a form of active participation in the world, but a complete severance of self from the world.

The felicity of the perfection which has divested itself of all action and dealing, good and evil, has its prefiguration and illustration in the state of the deepest sleep, when the world, which surrounds the mind in its waking hours, has vanished from its view, and not even a dream is seen; when it sleeps "like a child, or like a great sage, when he, wrapt in sleep, feels no desire and sees no vision, that is the condition in which he desires only the Âtman, when he has attained his desire, when he is without desire."

The succeeding age turned, with a special predilection, to the description of conditions of the deepest self-contained abstraction, in which perception and feeling, space and all objectivity, vanished from the mind, and it hangs, as it were, in the middle, between the transient world and the Nirvâna. Disquisitions on these ecstasies of contemplation are among the pet themes of the discourses which the Buddhist Church have put in their master's mouth. We shall not be wrong if we here recognize the preliminary traces of these ideas. When man seeks for an earthly prefiguration of the return to the universal One, he must, before he lights upon those sickly conditions of semi- or complete unconsciousness, picture to himself the rest of deep, dreamless sleep as the most natural and readiest image.

Up to this point we have found the opposition of the delivered and undelivered associated with the opposition of desire and non-desire. The same thought is often expressed, with a slight alteration of such a turn that, instead of desire, knowledge and absence of knowledge are set up as the determinators of the ultimate destiny of the soul: the knowledge, on the one hand, of the unity, to which the individual ego and all beings draw together in Brahma; and, on the other hand, the being absorbed in the contemplation of the finite as a plurality. "Where all beings have become one's self, for the *knowing* how can there be delusion—how can there be pain for him who has his eye on the unity?" "He who has discovered and *understood* (pratibuddha) the Âtman dwelling in the darkness of this corporeity, he is all-creating, for he is the creator of the universe: his is the world, he is himself the world. They who know the breath of the breath, and the eye of the eye, the ear of the ear, the food of food, the thought of thought, they have comprehended the Brahma, the ancient, the supreme, attainable by thought alone; there is not in it any diversity. He attains the death of death who here detects any diversity; thought alone can behold it, this Imperishable, Everlasting."

If then deliverance be based at one time on the conquest of all desire, and at another on the knowledge of the Brahma, both may be regarded merely as the expression of one and the same thought. "If a man knows the Âtman:* 'that am I myself'—wishing what, for the sake of what desire, should he cling to the bodily state?" The main thing is knowledge; if it be obtained, all desire vanishes of itself. In other words, the deepest root of the clinging to the impermanent, is the absence of knowledge.

* These words also mean: "If a man knows himself."

Here we stand wholly in those very ranges of thought with which Buddha's teaching dealt. The question, which has suggested the Buddhist views on deliverance, is here already put exactly in the same form as afterwards, and the same twofold answer is given to this question. What keeps the soul bound in the cycle of birth, death, and re-birth? Buddhism answers: desire and ignorance. Of the two, the greater evil is ignorance, the first link in the long chain of causes and effects, in which the sorrow-working destiny of the world is fulfilled. Is knowledge attained, then is all suffering at an end. Under the tree of knowledge, Buddha, when he has obtained the knowledge that gives deliverance, utters these words:

> "When the conditions (of existence) reveal themselves
> To the ardent, contemplating Brahman,
> To earth he casts the tempter's hosts,
> Like the sun, diffusing light through the air."

Here Brahmanical speculation anticipates Buddhism in diction as well as in thought. Language even now begins to make use of those phrases, which have received at a later time from the lips of Buddha's followers, their established currency as an expression of the tenets of the Buddhist faith. When he who has come to know the Âtman, is mentioned in the "Brâhmana of the hundred paths," as delivered, the word then used for "knowing" is that word (pratibuddha) which also signifies "awaking," the word which the Buddhists are accustomed to use, when they describe how Buddha has in a solemn hour under the Açvattha tree gained the knowledge of the delivering truth, or is awake to the delivering truth: the same word from which also the name "Buddha," *i.e.*, "the knowing," "the awake," is derived.

Of all the texts in which the Brahmanical speculations as to the delivering power of knowledge are contained, perhaps not even one was known except by hearsay to the founder of the Buddhist community of believers. But, for all that, it is certain that Buddhism has acquired as an inheritance from Brahmanism, not merely a series of its most important dogmas, but, what is not less significant to the historian, the bent of its religious thought and feeling, which is more easily comprehended than expressed in words.

If in Buddhism the proud attempt be made to conceive a deliverance in which man himself delivers himself, to create a faith without a god, it is Brahmanical speculation which has prepared the way for this thought. It has thrust back the idea of a god step by step; the forms of the old gods have faded away, and besides the Brahma, which is enthroned in its everlasting quietude, highly exalted above the destinies of the human world, there is left remaining, as the sole really active person in the great work of deliverance, man himself, who possesses inherent in himself the power to turn aside from this world, this hopeless state of sorrow.

Every people makes for itself gods after its own ideal, and is not less made what it actually is by the reflex influence of what its gods are. A people with a history make themselves gods who shall show their power in their history, who shall fight their battles with them, and join in the administration of their state. The god of Israel is the Holy One, before whose flaming majesty the heart of man bows in adoration and supplication, and to whom it draws near in prayer as to a father with the confidence of a child; whose wrath causes men to disappear, whose tender mercy worketh good to children, and children's children even unto the thousandth generation. And the god of the Brahmanical thought? The Great One, before whom all human movement is stilled, where all colours pale and all sounds expire. No song of praise, and no petition, no hope, no fear, no love. The gaze of man is unmoved, is turned upon himself and looks into the depths of his own being, expecting his ego to disclose itself to him as the everlasting One, and the thinker, for whom the veil has risen, discovers as an enigma of deep meaning, the mystery of the Unseen Seer, the Unheard Hearer, to find out whom Brahmans leave goods and chattels, wife and child, and move as mendicants, homeless through the world.

The Tempter. Brahman.

Tradition enables us to gain but a very imperfect idea of how the remaining notions, images, expressions, which passed to Buddhism as an inheritance from Brahmanical speculation, ranged themselves one after another round the central point of the religious thought, with which our sketch has been dealing. If we except the oldest, fundamental texts of the doctrine of the Âtman, from which we have drawn material for our sketch up to the present, we are driven to conjectures of the most uncertain kind, when we ask what works may be received as pre-Buddhist and what not. Internal evidence, on which alone we are thrown in this case, is sufficient in very few instances to render it possible to form even a probable estimate, as to whether what is connected in these texts in thought or form of expression with the Buddhist, belongs to the stages preparatory to the Buddhist phase of thought, or has on its part been influenced by that phase. I might claim a pre-Buddhist origin for the Kâthaka Upanishad, a poem which in the rude grandeur of its composition reflects all the earnestness and all the singularity of that age of self-study. If I am correct in my surmise as to the time of the production of this Upanishad, it contains an important contribution to the history of thought preparatory to Buddhist thought: namely, we here find the Satan of the Buddhist world, Mâra, the Tempter, the demon death-foe of the deliverer, in the form of Mrityu, the God of Death. The identity of the conception is most unmistakably apparent notwithstanding the difference of the clothing, and indeed the Brahmanical poem has preserved that image, which it has in common with the Buddhist legends, in a form assuredly far more original.

"Uçant, son of Vâjaçravas," the Upanishad begins, "gave away all that he had.* He had one son, named Naciketas. In this youth faith was awakened, when the offerings† were being carried away. He then reflected:

> "Water-drinking, grass-eating, milked-out (creatures) whose strength is exhausted—
> Cheerless are the worlds called, to which he tends, who offers such gifts."‡

He said to his father: "Father, to whom wilt thou give me?" And a second and a third time (he asked this). Then his father said: "I give thee to Death."

THE SON.

> "Many come after me: many have before me trodden the path of death.
> The Prince of Death, the god Yama, what need can he have of me?"

THE FATHER.

> "Look forward, look backward; a like fatality rules here and yonder.
> The destiny of man resembles the grain, which ripens, falls, and again returns."

The poem passes over what now happens: Naciketas

* He divided these out to the priests as sacrificial remuneration.

† All his father's gifts, especially cows.

‡ The rewards for earthly gifts, such as those cows, are vain.

descends to the kingdom of Death. Yama, the God of Death, does not see him: so he remains three days unhonoured in the realms of the departed.

THE SERVANTS OF THE GOD OF DEATH.

A flaming fire is the Brahman who approaches the house as a guest. Yama presents water to the guest, thus the heat of the fire is allayed.

"Hope and wish, friendship and every joy,
The fruit of his actions, children and fruitfulness of the flock,
These the Brahman takes away from the foolish man
In whose house he tarries unfed."

YAMA (THE GOD OF DEATH).

"Unfed within my house three nights,
Brâhmana, a worthy guest, hast thou tarried.
Honour to thee, let prosperity attend me;
Three wishes shall be granted thee; choose!"

Naciketas chooses as the first wish, that his father may receive him without ill will on his return from the realms of the dead; as the second, that the God of Death may teach him the hidden knowledge of the sacrificial fire, by the help of which man wins the heavenly world. Death imparts to him the mystic knowledge of this fire and guarantees that it shall be called among men after his name the Naciketas-fire. Naciketas has now to express his third wish.

NACIKETAS.

"Inquiry is made regarding the fate of the dead:
'They are,' says one; 'they are not,' says another.
This I wish to know, resolve this (doubt) for me.
This is the third wish, which I choose."

THE GOD OF DEATH.

"The gods themselves sought after this long since;
Hard to fathom, dark is this secret.
Choose some other boon, Naciketas,
On this insist not; release me from my promise."

NACIKETAS.

"From the gods themselves is this hidden, thou sayest;
Hard to fathom hast thou, O Death, declared it.
There is no other who can reveal this to me as thou canst,
There is no other wish which I can choose instead of this."

THE GOD OF DEATH.

"Fulness of years, and children's children,
Choose gold, herds, elephants, horses,
Choose widely-extended rule upon the earth,
Have thy life long as thou desirest.
If this appear to thee acceptable instead of that other wish,
Then choose wealth, choose long life;
Rule broad realms, Naciketas;
I give thee the fulness of all pleasures.
What mortal men obtain but with difficulty,
Choose every pleasure on which thy heart is set.
Maidens here, with harps, with carriages,
Fairer than men may hope to gain,
These give I thee, that they may do thee service;
Ask not of death, Naciketas."

NACIKETAS.

"The lapse of days causes, O Lord of Death,
The power of the organs of life to fail in the children of men;
The whole life swiftly passes away;
Song and dance, chariot and horse, thine are they.
Riches cannot give contentment to man;
What is wealth to us when we have beheld thee?
We shall live as long as thou biddest us;
Still this wish alone is that which I choose.
Tell us of the far-reaching future of the world to come,
Whereon, O Death, man meditates in doubt.
The wish, which penetrates into hidden depths,
That alone it is which Naciketas chooses."

The reluctance of the God of Death is overcome, and he grants to the importunate inquirer his request. The two paths of knowledge and ignorance diverge widely from each other.

Naciketas has chosen knowledge; the fulness of pleasures has not led him astray. They who walk in the path of ignorance, endlessly wander about through the world beyond, like the blind led by the blind. The wise man who knows the One, the Everlasting, the ancient God, who dwells in the depths, has no part in joy and sorrow, becomes free from right and wrong, free from the present, and free from hereafter. That is Yama's answer to Naciketas's inquiry.

A strange picture coming from this great period of old Indian thought and poetry: the Brahman who descends to Hades, and, unmoved by all promises of transient pleasures, wrings from the God of Death the secret of that which lies beyond death.

We now turn from this Vedic poem to Buddhist legend.

Through many a long age, he who is destined to the Buddhahood pursues his quest of the knowledge which is to deliver him from death and re-birth. His enemy is Mâra, the Evil One. As the god Mrityu promises Naciketas dominion over extended realms, if he will forego the knowledge of the hereafter, so Mâra offers Buddha the sovereignty of the whole earth, if he will renounce his career of Buddha; as Mrityu offers Naciketas nymphs of more than earthly beauty, so Buddha is tempted by Mâra's daughters, named Desire, Unrest, and Pleasure. Naciketas and Buddha alike withstand all temptations, and obtain the knowledge which delivers them from the hand of death. The name Mâra* is no other than

* Both words signify "death," and are derived from the same root, *mar*, "to die." The mode of expression in many places of the Dhammapada makes the identity of Mâra and Mrityu (Pâli *maccu*) clearly evident. Compare ver. 34, "Mâradheyyam pahâtave," with ver. 86, "maccudheyyam suduttaraṁ; v. 46: chetyâna Mârassa papupphakâni adassanam maccurâjassa gacche." Cf. also ver. 57 with 170. See also "Mahâvagga," I, ii. 2.

Mrityu; the God of Death is at the same time the "Prince of this world," the lord of all worldly enjoyment, the foe of knowledge; for pleasure is in Brahmanical, as it is in Buddhist speculation, the chain which binds to the bondage of death, and knowledge is the power which breaks that chain. This aspect of the God of Death, as the tempter to pride and worldly pleasures, steps in the Buddhist legend in the shape of Mâra so prominently into the foreground that the original character of that god thereby almost disappears; the older poem of the Kâthaka-Upanishad preserves clearly the original nature of Mrityu, but it shows us at the same time in it the point from which the conception of the Prince of Death could be transformed into that of the Tempter.

Together with Mâra, we find in the Buddhist texts very frequently mentioned another spiritual being, the conception of whom had likewise been first formed in the later Vedic age, Brahman. The god Brahman's figure is an outcome of that idea of the Brahma, the development of which has occupied our attention in a previous passage. It is exceedingly characteristic of the influence which the most abstract speculation of the schools exercised in India over the notions of the people generally, that the Brahma, the colourless, formless absolutum, has become an important element in the popular faith; of course, not without the thought in its original purity having been modified or, more accurately speaking, lost sight of. The thing in the abstract would have been rather too unconcrete a god even for the Indians. So the neuter personified itself, and became masculine; the Brahma turned into the god Brahman, the "progenitor of all worlds," the first-born among beings.

We cannot here attempt to give a more detailed picture of this peculiar invasion of the popular consciousness by the speculative idea; our sources of information completely forbid it. This much only we know with certainty, that the process of which we speak had not only completed itself in the age of earlier Buddhism, but that a considerable period must have elapsed since its completion. Scarcely any divine being is so familiar to the imagination of the Buddhists as Brahmâ Sahampati; at all important moments in the life of Buddha and his followers, he is wont to leave his Brahma-heaven and to appear on earth as the profoundly humble servant of holy men. And from this one principal Brahman the Buddhist imagination has created whole classes of Brahma-gods, who have their place in different Brahma-heavens:—one more finger-post in addition to many others, indicating the impossibility of those Vedic texts, in which the origin of the doctrine of the universal One is exhibited, coming at all near the Buddhist period, in which the god Brahman has already developed himself from the Brahma, and the whole system of the Brahma-divinities from the god Brahman.

CHAPTER III.

Asceticism—Monastic Orders.

We now proceed to describe the forms of religious, monastic life which have sprung up in close connection with the already discussed speculations regarding the universal One and deliverance. As in those philosophical ideas the way was prepared for the dogmatics of Buddhism, so in those beginnings of monastic life the foundation of the outward forms of the Buddhist Church was laid.

The two lines of development, that of the inner side and that of the outer side of religious life, run—how could it be otherwise?—in close harmony.

Those speculations which represented the phenomenal world to be unstable and worthless as compared with the world's base, the Âtman, had at one blow deprived of their value all those aims of life which appear important to the natural consciousness of ordinary men. Sacrifice and external observance are unable to raise the spirit to the Âtman, to disclose to the individual ego his identity with the universal ego. Man must separate himself from all that is earthly, must fly from love and hate, from hope and fear; man must live as though he lived not. The Brahmans, it is said, "the intelligent and wise desire not posterity: what are descendants to us, whose home is the Âtman? They relinquish the desire for children, the struggle for wealth, the pursuit of worldly weal, and go forth as mendicants."

Many content themselves with a less strict renunciation; they go forth, it is true, from their houses, and give up their property and all the comforts and enjoyments of their customary mode of living, but they do not wander about homeless; they build themselves half-covered huts in the forest and live there, alone or with their women, on the roots and berries of the forest; their sacred fire also accompanies them, and they continue as before to perform at least a part of the duties of the sacrificial cult.

It is probable that there were from the beginning persons, chiefly Brahmans, who as beggars or forest hermits sought their deliverance in retirement from worldly concerns. But an exclusive right of Brahmans only to those spiritual treasures, to obtain which men parted with all earthly treasure, was not asserted in early times; we have no trace that before Buddha's time, or in Buddha's own time, the Brahman caste had come forward with claims of such a kind, or that there was need of any struggle whatever to win for prince and peasant, as well as Brahman, the right to leave wife and child, goods and chattels, in order to seek, as mendicant monks, in poverty and purity of life, the deliverance of their souls. Side by side with the Brahmans, who appear in the old philosophical dialogues speaking of the mysteries of the Âtman, we find in more than one place princes, and even wise women are not wanting in these circles; why should men desire to forbid those, whose discourses on deliverance they listened to and applauded, an entry on that life of holy renunciation, which leads man to this deliverance?

A point which seems highly characteristic of the religious

tone of this Vedic monasticism, is the strongly maintained esoteric character of the faith. There was a consciousness of possessing a knowledge which could and must belong to but a few, to chosen persons, a sort of select doctrine, which was not intended to penetrate the national life. The father might impart the secret to his son, and the teacher to his pupil, but, in the circle of the believers in the Âtman, there was wholly wanting that warm-hearted enthusiasm which holds that it then, and then only, properly enjoys the possession of its own goods, when it has summoned all the world to participate in their possession.

Our sources of information are quite too incomplete for us to be able, while resting on the sure ground of transmitted facts, to trace even the most prominent only of the landmarks in the further development of Indian monasticism. Conjectural constructions must here come to our aid, which, even where they show with tolerable certainty something like what must have taken place, yet utterly fail us if we seek for those touches, which could impart to the picture of this evolution an appearance of life.

Two events, which stand apparently in close connection with each other, must have played a prominent part in the development of this monasticism from its beginning up to the stage in which Buddha found it: the cohesion of monks and ascetics into organized fraternities, and therewith the emancipation of numbers, or even of a majority and the paramount, among these fraternities, from the authority of the Vedas.

It appears that these two important occurrences, were materially influenced by a change of geographical scene. We spoke in the beginning of this sketch of the difference of culture in the western and eastern parts of the Gangetic tract: the holy land of the Veda, the home of Vedic poetry and Vedic speculation lies in the west: the east has acquired the Veda and the Brahmanical system from the intellectually more advanced west, but this foreign element was not wholly assimilated, converted into flesh and blood. A different air blows in the east; like the language which gives a preference to the weak *l* above the rough *r* of the west, the whole being is more relaxed; the Brahman is here less, the king and the people more. The movement, which had its origin in the west, here loses much of the fantastically abstruse which was in it, probably also something of the bold vastness and clear sequence of ideas, and thereby gains in popularity; questions, which it was chiefly the schools and the intellectual aristocracy of the nation had touched in the west, change in the east into vital questions for the people. Here men trouble themselves but little about the mystic universal One of Brahmanical speculation;* so much the more decidedly into the foreground come the ideas of the sorrow of every state of being, of moral retribution, of purification of the soul, of deliverance.

It cannot be ascertained whether any political convulsions or social revolutions were also in play at that time, to direct people's minds with particular earnestness and energy to thoughts and questions such as these. Christianity founded its kingdom in times of the keenest suffering, amid the death struggles of a collapsing world. India lived in more settled peace; if the government of its small states was the evil despotism of the Oriental, men knew of no other government

* It is significant that, although the speculations of the Upanishads regarding the Âtman and the Brahma must, in Buddha's time, have been long since propounded, and must have become part of the standing property of the students of the Vedas, the Buddhist texts never enter into them, not even polemically. The Brahma, as the universal One, is not alluded to by the Buddhists, either as an element of an alien or of their own creed, though they very frequently mention the god Brahma.

and made no complaint; was the gulf between poverty and wealth, between knight and yeoman, a wide one—and it has always been so in that land by natural necessity—still it was by no means the poor and oppressed alone, or even chiefly, who sought in monastic robes freedom from the burdens of the world.

Voices are raised full of bitter lamentations over the degeneracy of the age, the insatiable greed of men, which knows no limit, until death comes and makes rich and poor alike: "I behold the rich in this world," says a Buddhist Sutra;* "of the goods which they have acquired, in their folly they give nothing to others; they eagerly heap riches together and farther and still farther they go in their pursuit of enjoyment. The king, although he may have conquered the kingdoms of the earth, although he may be ruler of all land this side the sea, up to the ocean's shore, would, still insatiate, covet that which is beyond the sea. The king and many other men, with desires unsatisfied, fall a prey to death; . . . . neither relatives nor friends, nor acquaintances, save the dying man; the heirs take his property; but he receives the reward of his deeds; no treasures accompany him who dies, nor wife nor child, nor property nor kingdom." And in another Sutra it is said:† "the princes, who rule kingdoms, rich in treasures and wealth, turn their greed against one another, pandering insatiably to their desires. If these act thus restlessly, swimming in the stream of impermanence, carried along by greed and carnal desire, who then can walk on the earth in peace?"

But from passages like these, current as they are among the

* Ratthapâla-Suttanta in the "Majjhima-Nikâya," fol. nṛi' of the Turnour MS.

† "Saṃyuttaka-Nikâya," vol. i, fol. ku' of the Phayre MS.

moral preceptors of all ages and all lands, we cannot infer that at that time there was an atmosphere prevalent something like that prevailing at Rome in the sultry period of the early days of the empire. No such period was necessary for the Indian to strike him with sudden terror at the picture of life which surrounded him, to bring to his notice the traces of death in that picture. From the unprofitableness of a state of being to which they had not learned to give stability by labours and struggles for ends worthy of labour and struggle, men fly to seek peace for the soul in a renunciation of the world. The rich and the noble still more than the poor and humble; the young, wearied of life before life had well begun, rather than the old, who have nothing more to hope from life; women and maidens, abandon their homes and don the garb of monks and nuns. Everywhere we meet pictures of those struggles, which every day must have brought in that period, between those who make this resolution, and the parents, the wife, the children, who detain those eager for renunciation; acts of invincible determination are narrated of those who, in spite of all opposition, have managed to burst the bonds which bound them to a home-life.

Soon teachers appeared in more than one place who professed to have discovered independently of Vedic tradition a new, and the only true path of deliverance, and such teachers failed not to attract scholars, who attached themselves to them in their wanderings through the land. Under the protection of the most absolute liberty of conscience which has ever existed, sects were added to sects, the Nigganṭha "those freed from fetters,"* the Acelaka "the naked," and by whatever

* This sect, founded by one of the older contemporaries of Buddha, has maintained its ground to this day under the name of Jaina, especially in the south and west of the Indian peninsula. The view of it, which we

other name those communities of monks and nuns named themselves, into whose midst the young brotherhood of Buddha entered. The name which people gave to these persons of self-constituted religious standing in contradistinction to the Brahmans, whose dignity rested on their birth, was "Samana," *i.e.,* Ascetic; thus Buddha was called the Samana Gotama; people called his disciples "the Samanas who follow the son of the Sakya house." It is probable also that already one and another among the older Samana-sects had gone so far as to attribute to the teacher round whom they gathered, dogmatic attributes in a way similar to that in which the Buddhists acted at a later time with reference to the founder of their Church; the man of the Sakya race is not the only, and probably not even the first, who has been honoured in India as "the enlightened one" (Buddha) or as "the conqueror" (Jina); he was only one among the numerous saviours of the world and teachers of gods and men who then travelled through the country, preaching in monastic garb.

The paths of deliverance, by which those masters led their believers in quest of salvation, were legion; for us, who possess on this subject only the hardly impartial reports of the Buddhists and Jainas, their serious thought is, it must be allowed, covered deeply over with dull or abstruse conceits. There were Ascetics who lived in self-mortification, denied themselves nourishment for long periods, did not wash themselves, did not sit down, rested on beds of thorns; there were adherents of the faith in the purifying efficacy of water, who were intent on purging by continued ablutions all guilt which clung to them; others aimed at conditions of spiritual

get from its otherwise comparatively modern sacred literature, corresponds in many essential points with Buddhism. One point of difference lay in the great importance which the Niggantha attached to penances.

abstraction, and sought, while separating themselves from all perception of external realities, to imbue themselves with the feeling of the "eternity of space," or of the "eternity of reason," or of "not-anything-whatever-ness," and whatever else these conditions were called. It may easily be imagined that, among this multiplicity of holy men, the whimsical were not unrepresented: we are told of a "hen-saint," whose vow consisted in picking up his food from the ground like a hen and, as far as possible, in all matters acting like a hen; another saint of a similar type lived as a "cow-saint," and thus the Buddhist accounts give a by no means short list of different kinds of holy men in those days, few among whom seem to have always been lucky enough to preserve their holiness from the fate of ridicule and from dangers more serious than ridicule.

SOPHISTIC.

Certain phenomena which developed themselves in the busy bustle of these ascetic and philosophizing circles, may be described as a species of Indian sophistic; wherever a Socrates appears, sophists cannot fail to follow. The conditions under which this sophistic arose are in fact quite similar to those which gave birth to their Greek counterpart. In the footsteps of those men, such as the Eleatics and the enigmatic Ephesian, who opened up the highways of thought with their simple and large ideas, there followed Gorgiases and Protogorases, and a whole host of ingenious, specious, somewhat frivolous virtuosi, dealers in dialetic and rhetoric. In exactly the same way in India there came after the earnest thinkers of the masculine, classical period of Brahmanical speculation, a younger generation of dialecticians, professed controversialists with an overweening materialist or sceptical air, who were not deficient in either the readiness or the ability to show up all sides of the ideas of their great predecessors, to modify them, and to turn them into their opposites. System after system was constructed, it seems, with tolerably light building material. We know little more than a series of war-cries: discussions were raised about eternity or transitoriness of the world and the ego, or a reconciliation of these opposites, eternity in the one direction or transitoriness in the other, or about infiniteness and finiteness of the world, or about the assertion of infiniteness and finiteness at the same time, or about the negation of infiniteness as well as finiteness. Then spring up the beginnings of a logical scepticism, the two doctrines, of which the fundamental propositions run, "everything appears to me true," and "everything appears to me untrue," and here obviously the dialectician, who declares everything to be untrue, is met forthwith by the question whether he looks upon this theory of his own also, that everything is untrue, as likewise untrue. Men wrangle over the existence of a world beyond, over the continuance after death, over the freedom of the human will, over the existence of moral retribution. To Makkhali Gosâla, whom Buddha is represented as having declared to be the worst of all erroneous teachers,* is ascribed the negation of free will: "there is no power (of action), there is no ability; man has no strength, man has no control: all beings, everything that breathes, everything that is,

* "As, O ye disciples, of all woven garments which there are, a garment of hair is deemed the worst—a garment of hair, my disciples, is in cold weather cold, in heat hot, of a dirty colour, has a bad smell, is rough to the touch—so, my disciples, of all doctrines of other ascetics and Brahmans the doctrine of Makkhali is deemed the worst."—*Anguttara Nikâya.*

everything that has life is powerless, without power or ability to control (its own actions); it is hurried on to its goal by fate, decree, nature;"—every being passes through a fixed series of re-births, at the end of which the fool as well as the wise "puts a period to pain." And the existence of a moral government is also denied; Pûrana Kassapa teaches: "If a man makes a raid on the south bank of the Ganges, kills and lets kill, lays waste and lets lay waste, burns and lets burn, he imputes no guilt to himself; there is no punishment of guilt. If a man crosses to the north bank of the Ganges, distributes and causes to be distributed charity, offers and causes to be offered sacrifices, he does not thereby perform a good work; there is no reward for good works." And another expression of similar doctrines: "the wise and the fool, when the body is dissolved, are subject to destruction and to annihilation; they are not beyond death." In disputations before adherents, opponents, and great masses of people, these professional wranglers and "hair-splitters"—this word was even then in use in India—made propaganda for their theories; like their Greek counterparts, though a good deal coarser, they caused swaggering reports of their dialectic invincibility to go before them. Saccaka says: "I know no Samana, and no Brahman, no teacher, no master, no head of a school, even though he calls himself the holy supreme Buddha, who, if he face me in debate, would not totter, tremble, quake, and from whom the sweat would not exude. And if I attacked a lifeless pillar with my language, it would totter, tremble, quake; how much more a human being!" Possibly, the Buddhists, on whose reports we are here dependent, may in their animosity against this class of dialecticians have drawn them in darker colours than was fair; the picture of such a sophistic is certainly not all a fabrication.

At this time of deep and many-sided intellectual movements, which had extended from the circles of Brahmanical thinkers far into the people at large, when amateur studies of the dialectic routine had already grown up out of the arduous struggles of the past age over its simple profound thoughts, when dialectic scepticism began to attack moral ideas—at this time, when a painful longing for deliverance from the burden of being was met by the first signs of moral decay, Ġotama Buddha appears upon the scene.

PART I.

BUDDHA'S LIFE.

CHAPTER I.

The Character of Tradition—Legend and Myth.

There is no lack of current legendary narratives which the Buddhists relate concerning the founder of their faith. Can we learn anything of the life of Buddha from them? Some have gone farther, and have asked: has Buddha ever lived? Or at least, as Buddhism must have had a founder: has that Buddha ever lived whom those narratives seem to present to us, though in a superhuman form and in miraculous surroundings?*

That ingenious student of Indian antiquity who has occupied himself most closely with this question, *Emile Senart*,† answers it with an absolute no. A Buddha may have lived somewhere at some period, but that Buddha, of whom Buddhist tradition speaks, has never lived. This Buddha is not a man: his birth, the struggles he undergoes, and his death, are not those of a man.

And what is this Buddha? From the earliest age the

* In the second Excursus at the end of this work the chief authoritative sources relative to Buddha's life are collected from the sacred Pâli texts and discussed.

† Senart, "Essai sur la légende du Buddha," Paris, 1875.

allegorical poetry of the Indians, like that of the Greeks and the Germans, treats of the destinies of the sun-hero: of his birth from the morning-cloud, which, as soon as it has given him being, must itself vanish before the rays of its illuminating child; of his battle with and victory over the dark demon of the thunder-cloud; how he then marches triumphantly across the firmament, until at last the day declines and the light-hero succumbs to darkness.

Senart seeks to trace step by step in the history of Buddha's life, the history of the life of the sun-hero: like the sun from the clouds of night, he issues from the dark womb of Mâyâ; a flash of light pierces through all the world when he is born; Mâyâ dies like the morning-cloud which vanishes before the sun's rays. Like the sun-hero conquering the thunder-demon, Buddha vanquishes Mâra, the Tempter, in dire combat, under the sacred tree; the tree is the dark cloud-tree in heaven, round which the battle of thunderstorm rages. When the victory is won, Buddha proceeds to preach his evangelium to all worlds, "to set in motion the wheel of the Law;" this is the sun-god who sends his illuminating wheel revolving across the firmament. At last the life of Buddha draws to a close; he witnesses the terrible destruction of his whole house, the Sakya race, which is annihilated by enemies, as at sunset the powers of light die away in the blood-red tints of the evening clouds. His own end has now arrived: the flames of the funeral pile, on which Buddha's corpse is burnt, are extinguished by streams of water, which come pouring down from heaven, just as the sun-hero dies in the sea of fire kindled by his own rays, and the last flames of his divine obsequies die out on the horizon in the moisture of the evening mist.*

* Cf. Senart's work already referred to, especially the *resumé*, p. 504, seq.

In Senart's opinion, Buddha, the real Buddha, did exist, it is true: his reality, he admits, is a logical necessity, inasmuch as we see the reality of the Church founded by him; but beyond this bare reality there is nothing substantial. The fancy of his followers attached to his person the great allegorical ballad of the life of the sun-god in human guise, the life of the man Buddha had been forgotten.

One cannot read the ingenious efforts of Senart without admiring the energy with which the French scholar constrains the Veda as well as the Indian epic, the literature of the Greeks as well as that of northern races—no small constraint was here necessary—to bear witness for his solar Buddha. But one is astonished that this so extensive reading has not availed itself, when dealing with the legends of Buddha, of one field, which would have presented not less important sources of information than the Homeric hymns and the Edda: the oldest available literature of Buddhism itself, the oldest declarations of the body of Buddha's disciples regarding the personality of their master. Senart bases his criticism almost wholly on the legendary biography, the "Lalita-Vistara," current among the northern Buddhists in Tibet, China and Naipal. But would it be allowable for any one, who undertook to write a criticism on the life of Christ, to set aside the New Testament, and follow solely the apocryphal gospels or any legendary works whatsoever of the Middle Ages? Or does the law of criticism, which requires us to trace back tradition to its oldest form, before forming an opinion on it, not deserve to be as closely observed in the case of Buddhism as in that of Christianity?

The most ancient traditions of Buddhism are those preserved in Ceylon and studied by the monks of that island up to the present day.

While in India itself the Buddhist texts experienced new

fortunes from century to century, and while the ceremonies of the original Church were vanishing continually more and more behind the poetry and fiction of later generations, the Church of Ceylon remained true to the simple, homely, "Word of the Ancients" (Theravâda). The dialect itself in which it was recorded contributed to preserve it from corruptions, the language of the southern Indian territories, whose Churches and missions had naturally taken the largest share, if not the initiative, in the conversion of Ceylon.* This language of the texts ("Pâli"), imported from the south of India, is regarded in Ceylon as sacred: and it is there supposed that Buddha himself, and all Buddhas of preceding ages, had spoken it. Though the legends and speculations of later periods might find their way into the religious literature produced in the island and written in the popular tongue of Ceylon, the sacred Pâli texts remained unaffected by them.

It is to the Pâli traditions we must go in preference to all other sources, if we desire to know whether any information is obtainable regarding Buddha and his life.

There we see first and foremost that from the very beginning, as far back as we can go to the time of the earliest utterances of Buddhist religious consciousness, there is a firm conviction that the source of saving knowledge and holy life is the word of a teacher and founder of the Church, whom they designate the Exalted One (Bhagavâ), or the Knowing, the Enlightened One (Buddha). Whoever proposes to enter the

* According to the Church history of the island which has attained a fixed canonical status in Ceylon, and which first meets us in texts of the fourth and fifth century after Christ, but which must be based on considerably older memoranda, Mahinda, the son of the great Indian king Asoka (circ. 260 B.C.), was the converter of Ceylon. The tradition is in some essential parts obviously a concoction; how much or how little truth it contains, cannot for the present be determined with certainty.

spiritual brotherhood, repeats this formula three times: "I take my refuge with Buddha; I take my refuge in the Doctrine: I take my refuge in the Order." At the fortnightly confession, the liturgy of which is among the oldest of all the monuments of Buddhist Church life, the monk, who leads in the confession, charges the brethren who are present, not to conceal by silence any sins which they have committed, for silence is lying, "And intentional lying, O brethren, brings destruction; thus hath the Exalted One said." And the same liturgy of confession describes monks, who embrace heresies, by putting in their mouths these words: "Thus I understand the doctrine which the Exalted One hath preached," etc. Throughout it is not an impersonal revelation, nor is it the individual's own thought, but it is the person, the word of the Master, the Exalted One, the Buddha, which is regarded as the source of the truth and holy life.

And this master is not regarded as a wise man of the dim past, but people think of him as of a man, who has lived in a not very remote past. A century is said to have passed from his death to the council of the seven hundred fathers at Vesâlî (about 380 B.C.), and it may be taken as a fact that the great bulk of the holy texts, in which from beginning to end his person and his doctrine are the central points, in which his life and his death are spoken of, had been already compiled before this council of the Church assembled: the oldest components of these texts, such as the liturgy of the confession to which we have referred, belong in all probability much rather to the beginning than to the end of this first century after Buddha's death. The period, therefore, which separates the deponent witnesses from the events to which they undertake to depose, is short enough: it is not much longer, probably not at all longer, than the period which elapsed between the death of

Jesus and the compilation of our gospels. Is it credible that during the lapse of such a time in the Church of Buddha, all genuine memory of his life could be extruded by ballads of the sun-god, transferred to his personality?—crushed out in a brotherhood of ascetics, in whose circle of ideas, according to the evidence of the literature which they have bequeathed to us, everything else possessed a higher value than these very ballads of nature?

Let us now examine more closely how far the collective picture of the age of which the sacred texts speak, bears on the question of Buddha's personality. The Pâli books give us an exceedingly concrete picture of the movements of the religious world of India at the period in which Buddha, if he really lived, must have played a part in it; we possess the most minute details of all the holy men who, sometimes standing alone and sometimes surrounded by communities of adherents, with and without organization, some in more profound and some in more shallow terms, preached to the people salvation and deliverance. There are mentioned, among others, as contemporaries of Buddha, six great teachers, to the Buddhists naturally false teachers, the heads of six sects holding other faiths; and we find one of them, Nâtaputta, according to Bühler's and Jacobi's learned researches, mentioned in the texts of the Jaina sects, still numerously represented in India at the present day, as the founder of their faith and the saviour of these sects, with whom he occupies a place analogous to that which is given to Buddha in the Buddhist texts. As regards this Nâtaputta, we are, therefore, in such a position that we possess two groups of accounts—those of his own followers, to whom he is the holy, the enlightened one, the victor (Jina), the Buddha—the texts of the Jainas also use this last expression—and the statements of the Buddhists, who stigmatize him as an ascetic leader, teaching an erroneous doctrine—as a pretender, claiming the dignity which properly belongs to Buddha. The Buddhists, as well as the Jainas, casually mention the place where Nâtaputta died; both name the same place, the town of Pâvâ—a small but by no means insignificant contribution to the value of these traditions. The harmony of the testimony regarding a collateral fact of this description makes us conscious that we are here treading on the sure ground of historical reality.

It is evident that Buddha was a head of a monastic order of the very same type as that to which Nâtaputta belonged; that he journeyed from town to town in the garb and with all the external circumstance of an ascetic, taught, and gathered round himself a band of disciples, to whom he gave their simple ordinances, such as the Brahmans and the other monastic brotherhoods possessed.

I hold that, even under the most unfavourable circumstances, we can lay claim to the possession of this much at least of reliable information, as reliable as any knowledge of such things can ever be.

But does all that we can gather end here? Are there not, in the masses of fable which tradition places at our disposal, some further, more specific traces of historical truth to be found, which contribute to give life to that first outline?

In order to be able to answer this question, we shall next describe the aspect of the tradition as regards its details.

Here it must be premised as a cardinal statement: a biography of Buddha has not come down to us from ancient times, from the age of the Pâli texts, and, we can safely say, no such biography was in existence then.* This is, moreover,

* This assertion is supported as well by what the Pâli texts contain, as by what they do not contain. They do not contain either a biography

very easily understood. The idea of biography was foreign to the mind of that age. To take the life of a man as a whole, its development from beginning to end, as a unified subject for literary treatment, this thought, though it appears to us natural and obvious, had not occurred to any one yet in that age.

To this was added that in those times the interest in the life of the master receded entirely behind the interest attached to his teaching. It was exactly the same in the circles of the early Christian Church and in the circles of the Socratic

of Buddha, or even the slightest trace of such a thing having been in existence before, and this alone is conclusive. The loss of texts, which were once possessed, and *à fortiori* the loss of all memory of them, is wholly unmentioned in the literary history of the Tipitaka. On the contrary, the texts contain here and there unconnected fragments of the history of Buddha's life, in a form which our Excursus II. will exemplify, and which cannot be construed as if the complete life of Buddha had at that time already found a connected literary exposition. Senart (p. 7, 8) has not overlooked the fact that in the sacred literature of the southern Buddhists there is no work like the "Lalita Vistara" in the north, in which there is a connected narrative of Buddha's life up to the beginning of his career as a teacher. But the explanation which the French scholar gives of this fact will scarcely gain acceptance with many. The legend of Buddha, with its popular character, he says, "a dû demeurer particulièrement vivace parmi les populations dont elle était réellement l'œuvre, et qui, dès le début, avaient activement collaboré à l'établissement et aux progrès de la secte nouvelle. À Ceylan au contraire, où le buddhisme, s'introduisit surtout par une propagande théologique et sacerdotale, des récits de ce genre n'avaient ni pour les prédicateurs ni pour leurs néophytes un intérêt si sensible ni si vivant." It will not be easy to prove this alleged difference between the dogmatic tendency of the Ceylonese, and the leanings of the northern Church to popular legend. In fact, the greater antiquity of the Pâli version of the sacred texts, compared with the northern editions, infected throughout by later literary currents, is the sole and completely satisfactory means of explaining the fact in question.

schools. Long before people began to commit to writing the life of Jesus in the manner of our gospels, there was current in the young communities a collection of discourses and sayings of Jesus (λόγια κυριακά); to this collection was appended just so much precise narrative matter as was necessary to call to mind the occasion when, and the external surroundings amid which, the several discourses were delivered. This collection of the sayings of Jesus laid no claim to any historical arrangement or sequence whatever, or to any chronological accuracy. Similarly the Memorabilia Socratica of Xenophon. The method and manner of Socratic action are here illustrated by a rich profusion of the individual utterances of Socrates. But neither Xenophon nor any other of the old Socratics has given us the life of Socrates. What should induce them to do so? The form of Socrates was memorable to the Socratics for the words of wisdom which came from the lips of that great, eccentric man, not for the poor external fortunes of his life.

The development of the traditions of Buddha corresponds as closely as possible to these parallel illustrations. His disciples had begun at an early date to fix those discourses which the great teacher had preached, or at any rate, discourses after the method and manner in which he had delivered them, and to deliver these to the Church. They did not omit to note where and to whom he had uttered or was supposed to have uttered each word; this was necessary in order to fix in concrete the situation, and thereby to place the authenticity of the respective words of Buddha beyond all doubt. But, *when* Buddha said so and so, they did not ask. The narratives begin: At one time—or: at this time the exalted Buddha was tarrying at such and such a place; as far as dates go, this is worthless. People in India have never had any organ for the when of things: and in the life of an ascetic, such as Buddha was especially, year after year rolled by so very uniformly that it must have appeared to them superfluous to ask: When did this or that happen? When was this or that word uttered?—provided any one had ever thought at all of the possibility of such a question arising.*

Special events in the course of his wandering life, meetings with this and that other teacher, with this and that worldly potentate, were associated with the memory of one or other authentic or invented discourse; the first stages of his public career, the conversion of his first disciples, and then again the end, his farewell address to his followers, and his death, stand out, as may be readily understood, most prominent of all in the foreground of these memories. Thus there were biographical fragments, but a biography was compiled from them for the first time at a much later period.

Comparatively few are the memoranda preserved in the older authorities regarding the early life of Buddha, the years preceding the beginning of his professional career, or, to put it as the Indians are wont to do, the period prior to the attainment of the Buddhahood, when he had not yet acquired, but was still seeking, that saving knowledge, which constituted him the teacher of the worlds of gods and men. That we hear less of these days than of others, is explicable. The interest of the Church was fixed not so much on his worldly character

* At a later time, indeed, this question was actually put, and then obviously there was no embarrassment felt for a moment in answering it. Then were drawn up those great lists of what Buddha had said and done in the sixth, seventh, eighth, etc., year of his Buddhahood (*e.g., vide* Bigandet, "Life of Gaudama," p. 160, etc.). The utter worthlessness of these later-produced lists is obvious, when we bear in mind the absolute silence of the sacred texts as to matters of chronology.

as the child and heir of the Sakya house, as on the person of the "exalted, sacred, universal Buddha." People desired to know what he had uttered from that time forward, when he had become the Buddha; behind that vanished the interest in everything else, even the interest in this struggle for the Buddhahood.* It is later centuries which have built up a history of Buddha with wonders piled on wonders on a scale quite different from older times, and which first devoted themselves with special zeal to surrounding the form of the blessed child with the extravagant creations of a boundless imagination.

Let us now examine the tradition, meaning, of course, the older tradition continued in the sacred Pâli texts, to define accurately of what kind are the fabulous elements contained in them.

It is obvious that the appearance of the deliverer of the world on earth, must have presented itself to the believer's mind as an event of incomparable importance; to the Indian, who was and is accustomed, in the most trivial incidents of his own daily life, to pay attention to concomitant omens, it would have been the most impossible contingency if the conception of the exalted, holy, universal Buddha had not

* Moreover, there is in the external form of the Sûtra, and Vinaya texts a point which essentially contributes to explain this receding of narratives of Buddha's youth. Inasmuch as these texts, with inconsiderable exceptions, do not contain arbitrary communications, couched in a freely chosen form, but always an instructive speech of Buddha or an ordinance prescribed by Buddha for his disciples, it was only occurrences in his career as Buddha which could be chosen for the introductory narratives on the occasions which called for these utterances of Buddha; his youth could only be touched on in occasional allusions or by putting in his own mouth communications regarding that period of his life.

been already announced by the mightiest wonders and signs, and if the whole universe had not joined in its celebration. An inconceivably bright flash of light pierces through the universe; the worlds quake; the four divinities, who have in their protection the four quarters of the heavens, combine to keep guard over the pregnant mother. The birth is attended by wonders in no less a degree. The Brahmans possessed lists of bodily signs which import good and bad fortunes to men; the infant Buddha must obviously bear on his person all auspicious marks in the highest perfection, in the same perfection as a world-ruling monarch; the soothsayers declare: "if he choose a worldly life, he will become a ruler of the world; if he renounce the world, he will become the Buddha."

We need not cite any more fabulous embellishments of this description: their character cannot be mistaken. As it seemed to the Christian Church an obvious necessity, that all power and excellence, which the prophets of the Old Testament possessed, must have dwelt with enhanced glory in the person of Jesus, it was in the same way natural that the Buddhists should attribute to the founder of their Church all wonders and perfections, which, in the Indian mind, were attributed to the most powerful heroes and sages. Among the foundations, on which Indian intuitions rest, regarding that which pertains to an all-powerful hero and conqueror of the world, the ancient nature-myth, the original signification of which had long since ceased to be understood, is obviously not wanting; and thus it is not a matter of surprise, if one and another of the traits which were mentioned in the circles of monks and lay-disciples as indicating the nobility of Buddha, comes at last through many media to be connected with that which many centuries before, among the herdsmen and peasants of the Vedic age, and much earlier still among the common forefathers of the Indian, Grecian, and German stocks, popular fancy had associated in song with the sun-hero, the beaming type of all earthly heroism. This is the element of propriety which cannot be denied to Senart's theory of the solar Buddha.

As regards another group of legendary touches, it may well be in part doubted whether we have not in them historical memories. The elements of the tradition regarding Buddha hitherto mentioned flowed from the universal belief in Buddha's all-overpowering might and nobility, but the much more important and more prominent characteristics, of which we shall now have to treat, have their origin partly in the special theological predicates which Buddhist speculation affirmed of the holy, knowing, Delivered One, and partly in the external events which regularly occurred in the life of the Indian ascetic, and which consequently, according to an inference so naturally drawn by legend, cannot have been wanting in the life of Buddha, the ideal ascetic.

What makes a Buddha a Buddha is, as his name indicates, his knowledge. He does not possess this knowledge, like a Christ, by virtue of a metaphysical superiority of his nature, surpassing everything earthly, but he has gained it, or, more strictly speaking, won it by a struggle. The Buddha is at the same time the Jina, *i.e.*, the conqueror. The history of the struggle for the Buddhahood must therefore precede the history of the Buddha.

Battle involves an enemy, a victor the vanquished. The Prince of Life must be opposed by the Prince of Death. We have seen how the Indian mind had settled for itself the identity of the kingdom of death, and the kingdom of this world. We call to mind the *rôle* of the Death-god in the Vedic poem of Naciketas, to whom he promises long life and fulfilment of all desire, in order that he might abandon the pursuit of knowledge. So also there comes to the ascetic seeking Buddhahood, as his opponent, Mâra, Death, the lord of all worldly desire, which indeed is nothing else than veiled death. Mâra follows his enemy step by step, and watches for a moment of weakness to overpower his soul. No such moment comes. Amid many failures and desperate fights within, Buddha remains throughout unshaken.

When he is on the point of reaching the saving knowledge, the purchase of all his efforts, Mâra approaches him to divert him by tempting words from the path of salvation. In vain. Buddha attains the knowledge "that bringeth salvation" and the supreme peace.

We choose the narrative of this last struggle and victory, to illustrate by it the difference between Senart's and our conception of the nature of these legends.

How does the primitive Church narrate the history of the attainment of the knowledge which "maketh free?" What are the real facts of the occurrence as accepted by them? This, and only this, that Buddha, passing through a series of stages of esctasy, sitting under a tree through the three watches of a certain night, obtains the threefold sacred knowledge, that his soul becomes free from all sinful taint, and he becomes partaker of deliverance with a knowledge of his deliverance.* These purely theological elements far transcend in importance, in the opinion of the primitive Church, the struggle with Mâra; wherever in the sacred Pâli texts the attainment of Buddhahood is described, there is not a word spoken of Mâra.

Some few passages in the texts† narrate distinct encounters

* *Vide* references to the sacred texts in Excursus II.

† The texts compiled in a verse form are here especially referred to, in which the legendary element as compared with the purely dogmatic always

of Buddha with Mâra: sometimes they are referred to a time not long before and sometimes to a time not long after the attainment of Buddhahood. Mâra endeavours by seductive speeches to turn him from the path of holiness; mention is also made of temptresses, who, when the tempter has given up all for lost, renew the fight; the daughters of Mâra, named Desire, Unrest, and Pleasure. Buddha remains unmoved in his peaceful quietude.

These are the unadorned representations of the primitive Church. The simple thoughts, from which these have been constructed, are, it seems, so very evident, that it would be no easy task even for the keen intellect of Senart, to show that this is the old myth of the victory of the sun-hero over the cloud-demons. Senart does not even attempt this, but he leaves this cast of the legends wholly untouched.

He bases his criticism instead on that romance of wonders into which the grotesque tastes of later ages have transformed this primitive story.* Buddha sits down under the tree of knowledge with the firm resolve not to rise until he has attained the knowledge which "maketh free." Then Mâra advances with his forces; hosts of demons assail him (Buddha) with fiery darts, amid the whirl of hurricanes, darkness, and the downpour of floods of water, to drive him from the tree; Buddha maintains his position unmoved; at last the demons fly.

Whoever wishes to give a complete picture of Senart's mythological fancies, must reproduce the history of this struggle of Buddha and the demons in much greater detail

comes more into the foreground, than in the prose Sûtras. *Vide* references in Excursus II.

* The chief sources of this later form of the legend, wholly foreign to the sacred Pâli texts, are the commentary of the "Jâtaka" (i, p. 69, seq.) and the "Lalita Vistara" (cap. 19, seq.).

than I can make up my mind to do for this wild and coarse tableau of miracles and sensations, wholly foreign to ancient Buddhism. I shall confine myself to the discussion of a few characteristic points.

The tree under which Buddha sits. Mâra is determined to drive him from it, *i.e.*, naturally, he will defeat his resolve not to rise until he has attained deliverance. The demon says: "this place does not belong to you, it belongs to me."

Thus, Senart concludes, the true object of the fight is the tree. The tree belongs to Mâra: Buddha has taken possession of it. Contesting with him the possession of the tree and contesting with him the possession of deliverance are the same. How does the tree come to have this importance? What is the tie which connects the possession of the knowledge that brings deliverance, to which Buddha's efforts are directed, with the possession of the tree?

The Veda mentions the heavenly tree which the lightning strikes down; the mythology of the Fins speaks of the heavenly oak which the sun-dwarf uproots. Yama, the Vedic god of death, sits drinking with bands of the blessed under a leafy tree, just as in the northern Saga Hel's place is at the root of the ash Yggdrasill.

The tree is the cloud-tree: in the clouds the heavenly fluid is stored, and it is guarded by the dark demons; in the hymns of the Veda the powers of light and the powers of darkness fight their great battle for the clouds and the ambrosia which they contain: this is the identical battle of Buddha with the hosts of Mâra. In the cloud-battle the ambrosia (amṛita), which is in the clouds, is won; the enlightenment and deliverance, which Buddha wins, are also called an ambrosia (amṛita); the kingdom of knowledge is the land of immortality (padam amṛitam).

This is Senart's explanation.

Would this acute scholar have ventured it, had he had before him the old account of the occurrence under the tree which is composed solely of dogmatic elements such as the description of the four ecstasies and the threefold knowledge attained by Buddha? If he had been aware that Buddha and Mâra in the older texts do not fight under the tree, still less for the tree? That the only reference we hear of, made to the tree of knowledge, the supposed cloud-tree and ambrosia-tree, is this, that Buddha sat at its foot, when he fell into those trains of thought, which led him to the highest knowledge?* Where else sat in India in Buddha's time, where else even down to our days do ascetics, who have no sheltering roof, and all vagrant folk, sit, but at the foot of a tree?† We are not comparative mythologists and we cannot forget that, besides these cloud-trees which are shattered by lightning or uprooted by

* It is exceedingly characteristic of the method of Senart's criticism, that he quotes a text of the stamp of the "Saddharmapuṇḍa Rîka" (p. 247, note 1), to show the inseparability of the notions, Buddha and a tree of knowledge; he should have quoted the sacred Pâli texts to show the complete non-essentiality of the tree.

† Buddha tarries seven days at the foot of the banyan tree Ajapâla ("Mahâvagga," i, 2 and 5), and for the same length of time at the foot of the Mucalinda tree (i, 3) and of the Râjâyatana tree (i, 4). On the way from Benares to Uruvelâ he leaves the street to sit down at the foot of a tree in a grove. Similarly the monk Kassapa ("Cullavagga," xi, 1, 1). Ânanda, urged by Buddha to leave him alone for awhile, "set himself down at the foot of a tree not far off" ("Mahâ Parinibbâna S.," p. 24). In a description of the ascetic exerting himself, it is said (in the "Cûlahatthipadopamasutta"): "He dwells in a lonely spot, in a grove, at the foot of a tree, on a mountain, in a cave, in a mountain grotto, in a burial-place, in the wilderness, under an open sky, on a heap of straw." (Cf. also "Cullavagga," vi, 1, 1.) The number of these instances of the tarrying of ascetics under trees may be multiplied *ad libitum*, if there be any necessity.

the sun-dwarf, there grow other trees also on the earth, and we go so far as to surmise, that the trees, at the foot of which Gotama Buddha was wont to sit and meditate, belonged to this latter, much less deep-meaning but more widely extended, class of trees.

Nor are we more successful in the effort to persuade ourselves of the mythical character of the remaining elements of the narrative,* than we have been in the case of the Tree of Knowledge. The demons, who make an assault on Buddha, fling mountains of fire, trees with their roots, glowing masses of iron, and "as if these so evident and obvious symbols did not suffice, rain, darkness and lightning complete the picture, and figure

* But not so regarding the mythological significance of the person of Mâra himself as a thunder-demon. It is entirely misleading to call up, in order to explain so simple and transparent a conception as that of Mâra, the whole host of Vedic mythology and symbolical conceptions from the first-born Kâma (Love) to the airy Agni and the demon Namuci. The original and prevailing idea which finds expression in the personification of Mâra, is that of death; the name indicates this clearly enough ("Mâra, in loc. Antaka;" cf. antea, p. 58, note). But that the prince of death is at the same time the ruler of the kingdom of earthly pleasure, the tempter to this pleasure, and is thus connected with Kâma, is adequately accounted for in the course of development, which pre-Buddhist as well as Buddhist speculation has taken (*vide* antea, p. 58). Least of all can it cause astonishment, when Buddhist poetry occasionally gives to Mâra, the evil enemy, the name of Namuci, a demon, who is named in the Veda as an enemy of Indra (the "Çatapatha Br," xii, 7, 3, 4, also observes in a discussion on Rig V. viii, 14, 13: pâpmâ vai Namuciḥ). The nature of the case forbids us seeking to draw mythological inferences from such uses of names as do not flow from the nature of the being of whom they are used, but are purely secondary. If we speak of the Titanic nature of a Faust, who would venture to build thereon mythological theories as to the origin of the Faust legend? The identity of the Buddhist Mâra with the Mairya (epithet of Ahriman, who tempts Zoroaster) of the Avesta is considerately waived by Senart (p. 244, note) and after his example by Darmesteter ("Ormazd et Ahriman," p. 202).

as the most characteristic touches of the whole scene."* It does seem to us as if nothing can be less characteristic than these very touches; nothing presents itself to the fancy as more natural or necessary for the assaults of bands of demons than the accessories of lightning, thunder and darkness.† Or are those spirits also, by whom Caliban is tormented on the magic island, thunder-demons?

The vanquished Mâra is compared to a trunk without hands and feet,‡ and precisely in the same way the cloud-demon Vritra, whom Indra crushes with his thunderbolt, is styled in the Veda "footless and handless." But what is thus said of Mâra is nothing more than one in a hundred similes used regarding him, and therefore means very little; and, furthermore, can one not lose hands and feet in any other battles beside the battle of the thunder-storm?

But enough of these vagaries of the sunshine theory. We may say in a word: the components which go to make up the history of the attainment of the Buddhahood, and, we may add, countless similar narratives in the legends of Buddha, are not to be explained by reference to the mythology of the Veda, and still less to that of the Edda, but by the dogmatics of the Buddhist doctrine of deliverance and the external conditions and habits of Buddhist monastic life.

One class of doubts, however, and this is evident, cannot be fully resolved by this method of explanation. In each individual instance in which we have succeeded in showing that

* Senart, p. 200.

† It is, perhaps, possible that one or other of these touches may have first received its concrete form in the fables of the battle of the clouds, and may thenceforward have kept its place before the fancy; but that would do very little for Senart's theory.

‡ Senart, p. 202.

occurrences narrated of Buddha are frequent, or even constant, events in the life of Indian ascetics generally, one may proceed to reason further in two different ways. Either, here we have before us credible memoranda, for we see that things were wont to take this course; or, here we have not credible memoranda before us, for, inasmuch as this course is the regular course which things took in the period succeeding Buddha's death, the legends of Buddha's life must have been concocted so as to suit this precise course of events and no other.

To decide with certainty which of the two lines of reasoning is proper to pursue in each case is absolutely impossible. He who has arrived at this stage of the investigation must unreservedly acknowledge the limits which are here placed to inquiry, or, at all events, he must acquiesce in making up his mind as to the greater or less degree of probability in the one or the other of the two alternatives, and, in doing so, it will be impossible, of course, quite to exclude the momentum of subjective feeling from the momenta determining this decision.

If we now abstract from the traditions those of the categories indicated, which are wholly unhistorical, or are at least suspected to be of unhistorical character, we then have left as the very pith of these stories regarding Buddha a thread of facts, which we may claim to be a perfectly reliable, though, it may be, a very meagre, historical acquisition.

We know about Buddha's native country and about the family from which he came. We know about his parents, the early death of his mother, and about her sister, who brought up the boy. We know a number of other facts which extend over the several parts of his life. It would indeed be quite inconceivable, even in India, if the Church which called itself by the name of the son of the Sakya house had, within a century after his death, ceased to preserve, even though veiled in legend, a correct memory of the most important names of the persons round Buddha, and of certain leading public events in his life. Who would admit it possible for the memory of Joseph and Mary, of Peter and John, of Judas and Pilate, of Nazareth and Golgotha, to be forgotten or supplanted by inventions in the early Christian Churches of the first century? Here, if anywhere, it is fair to accept simple facts as such.

Or are we in error, and is that criticism in the right which even here discovers gross deception? Must not even the name of Buddha's native town, Kapilavatthu, excite suspicion? The abode of the Kapila, the mythical primitive philosopher Kapila, the founder of the Sânkhya school?* Why should we not seek, aye, and find, arcana of mythology, allegory and literary history in such a name? Especially when of opinion, as Senart is,† that the very existence itself of such a town is not guaranteed to us on any satisfactory evidence whatever.

Is the evidence really unreliable? The Chinese pilgrims, who travelled in India in the fifth and seventh centuries after Christ, saw the ruins of the town.‡ But, interposes Senart, no

* The alleged derivation of Buddhism from the Sânkhya philosophy plays an important part in many sketches of this as well as of other philosophies. I know nothing better to say on this subject than what Max Müller has already said ("Chips from a German Workshop," i, 226): "We have looked in vain for any definite similarities between the system of Kapila, as known to us in the Sânkhyasûtras, and the Abhidarma, or the metaphysics of the Buddhists."

† P. 512, Cf. p. 380, sec., and also Weber, "Indische Literatur Geschichte" (2 Auflage), p. 303. Senart finds, as was to be expected, in Kapilavatthu, "la ville, la fortresse de l'atmosphère."

‡ It is much to be regretted that General Cunningham, when he travelled the districts concerned for his archæological researches, allowed himself to be so far led astray by his geographical theories, which are on this point decidedly erroneous, as to look for the ruins of Kapilavatthu

one can tell by looking at the ruins whether the town to which they belong, was called Kapilavatthu. Unfortunately, most assuredly no one can tell by a look, although there is always some weight to be attached to the local traditions connected with the place, and in this case also to the monuments still extant in the time of those Chinese pilgrims. The strongest confirmation, however, of what the Chinese pilgrims state, lies in the fact that, on the one hand, the occasional direct statements and indirect hints of the sacred Pâli works regarding the site of the town, and, on the other hand, the route of the pilgrims who looked for it, if both be traced on the map of India, coincide exactly: in addition to this, at the very place where, according to this evidence, Buddha's home must have been, there is a small stream which, even in the present day, bears the same name (Rohinî) as was borne by a stream in the territory of the Sakyas often mentioned in the Buddhist traditions. I hold, stronger indications it is impossible to expect of an early demolished town in a country in which systematic excavations have not yet been made.*

Buddha's mother Mâyâ (*i.e.*, "miraculous power") has also become a mark for criticism because of her significant name. To Senart, Mâyâ, who dies a few days after the birth of her

in a wrong place; a fresh search in the regions clearly indicated by the texts would be most desirable.

* When Senart feels the want of a positive authority for the existence of Kapilavatthu, he has in his mind the silence of the Brahmanical literature, especially the great epic poems. Whoever considers at once what the epics, which were composed in the more westerly parts of India and the subject-matter of which lies chiefly in the more westerly lands, do yield for the geography of the east of the peninsula, and what they do not yield, will find their silence very explicable in the matter of this certainly not very important, and moreover very early destroyed, town of Kapilavatthu.

son, is the morning vapour, which vanishes before the rays of the sun. Weber,* who thought at an earlier period that he had discovered in Mâyâ's name a reference to the cosmic power of Mâyâ in the Sânkhya philosophy, has himself revoked this opinion elsewhere at a later period, remembering that the notion of the Mâyâ belongs, not to the Sânkhya school, but to the Vedanta system; it may be added, that every philosophico-mystical idea of the Mâyâ is wholly foreign to the ancient Buddhist texts throughout, and consequently the name of Buddha's mother cannot have been invented out of deference to any such idea.†

We must admit that we place greater reliance on tradition. We believe that the town of Kapilavatthu had once an existence, that Buddha passed his youth there, and that the sacred texts name his mother Mâyâ, not because of any mythical or allegorical secrets, but because she was so called.

Having unfolded our estimate of the value of the tradition, we now proceed to sketch the history of Buddha's life.

* "Literaturgeschichte," l.c. Cf. Köppen, "Die Religion des Buddha," i, 76.

† Even Mâyâ's sister, Mahâprajâpatî, does not escape the fate, that curious secrets have been supposed to be veiled in her significantly sounding name. (Senart, p. 339, note 1.) Senart translates Prajâpatî "creatrix," not without himself seeing that this is contrary to grammatical rule. Did the variante Prajâvatî (in the "Lal. Vist.") rightly noticed by him, not remind the distinguished Pâli scholar, that the word does not mean "creatrix" at all, but stands for Prajâvatî, "prolific in descendants?" In Pâli pajâpatî (=prajâvatî) is a very common appellation for "wife." See Childers, sub. verb. and "Mahâvagga," i, 14, 1, 2; x, 2, 3, 8. The meaning of the proper name is therefore quite of a harmless nature.

CHAPTER II.

Buddha's Youth.

The noble boy Siddhattha was born in the country and the tribe of the Sakyas ("The Powerful") somewhere about the middle of the sixth century before Christ. Better known than this name which he seems to have borne in the family circle, are other appellations. As a preaching monk wandering through India he was to his contemporaries "The ascetic Gotama"—this surname the Sakyas had, in accordance with the custom of Indian noble families, borrowed from one of the ancient Vedic bard-families; to us no name for this renowned of all Indians is so familiar as that with which the disciples who accepted his faith have expressed his authoritative position as the overthrower of error, as the discerner of the truth which gives deliverance, the name Buddha, *i.e.*, "the enlightened," "the knower."

We can point out the native land of Buddha on the map of India with tolerable accuracy.

Between the Nepalese lower range of the Himalaya and the middle part of the course of the Rapti,* which runs through the north-eastern part of the province of Oudh, there stretches a strip of level, fruitful land,† some thirty English miles broad,

* This river often appears in the Buddhist literature as Aciravatî.

† The Chinese pilgrim Hiouen Thsang (about 650 A.C.) says of Buddha's native state (St. Julien's Translation, ii, 130): "La terre est grasse et fertile; les semailles et les récoltes ont lieu à des époques régulières; les saisons ne se dérangent jamais; les moeurs des habitants sont douces et faciles."

well-watered by the numerous streams that issue from the Himalayas. Here lay the not very extensive territory over which the Sakyas claimed supremacy and dominion. On the east the Rohinî separated their lands from their neighbours; to this day this stream has preserved the name which it bore more than two thousand years ago.* On the west and south the rule of the Sakyas extended quite up, or nearly so, to the Rapti.†

Scarcely anywhere does the appearance of a country depend so completely on the activity or sloth of its inhabitants, as in these parts of India adjoining the Himalayas. The mountains send forth year by year inexhaustible volumes of water: whether for the benefit or for the destruction of the country depends solely on man's activity. Tracts of land which in times of unrest and thriftlessness are a swampy wilderness, the homes of pestilential vapours, may by a few years of regular and steady industry pass into a state of high and prosperous culture, and, if the causes of decline set in anew, return still more quickly to the state of a wilderness.

In the time of Sakya sovereignty this land must have been highly cultivated, a condition which it again attained under the government of the great emperor Akbar, and which, after long periods of protracted disquiet and sore decay, it is just now beginning once more to approach under the beneficent

* The Rohinî falls into the Rapti near Goruckpore, some hundred English miles north of Benares.

† The territory of the Sakyas included, as far as it appears, according to the present divisions of the land, approximately the following circles (pergunnahs) belonging to the Goruckpore district: Binayakpore, Bansee, and the western half of pergunnah Haveli. For an exact estimate of the extent of this territory the data at hand are obviously insufficient; I might quite roughly estimate it at nine-tenths the area of Yorkshire.

hand of the British administration, which is intent on supplying the land with the necessary working power.*

Between tall forests of sál trees yellow rice-fields spread out in uniform richness. The rice plant, which the Buddhist texts here mention, constitutes to-day, as in ancient times, the chief crop of this country, where the water of the rainy season and of inundations remains long standing on the rich soil of the low lying flats, and renders in great measure superfluous that excessively troublesome artificial irrigation which is elsewhere necessary for rice.† Between the rice-fields we may here and there place villages in the days of the Sakyas such as exist to-day, hidden among the rich, dark-green foliage of mangos and tamarinds, which surround the village site. In the background of the picture, over the black masses of the mountains of Nepal, rise the towering snow-capt summits of the Himalayas.

The kingdom of the Sakyas was one of those small aristocratic governments, a number of which had maintained themselves on the outskirts of the greater Indian monarchies. We shall not be far astray if we picture to ourselves the Sakyas as the forerunners in some fashion of such Rajput families as have in later times, by the aid of armed bands, held their ground against neighbouring rajas.‡ Of these greater

* Cf. the descriptions of Buchanan, who travelled in the country about 1810 (Montgomery Martin, ii, 292, 402, etc.), with A. Swinton's "Manual of Statistics of the district of Goruckpore" (Allahabad, 1861), and the new official "Statistical description and historical account of the Gorakhpore district" (Allahabad, 1880), pp. 287-330.

† *Inter alia*, the importance of rice cultivation to the Sakyas is evident from the name of Buddha's father, "pure rice," probably also from the otherwise seemingly fictitious names of his four brothers: clear-rice, strong-rice, white-rice, and immeasurable-rice.

‡ An instructive picture of these occurrences is given by Sir W. H. Sleeman, in his "Journey through the Kingdom of Oude," for inst. vol. i, p. 240.

monarchies there stood in closest proximity to the Sakyas, the powerful kingdom of Kosala (corresponding pretty nearly with the Oudh of to-day), adjoining it on the south and west. The Sakyas looked on themselves as Kosalas, and the kings of Kosala claimed certain rights over them, though probably merely honorary rights; later on they are said to have brought the Sakya-land wholly within their power, and to have exterminated the ruling family.*

But though the Sakyas occupied but an insignificant position in respect of military and political power among their neighbours, the haughty spirit which prevailed in their ancient family was characteristic of the Sakya line. Brahmans who had entered the council chamber of the Sakyas could testify to the little notice which these worldly nobles, who derived their nobility from the king Okkâka (Ikshvâku), renowned in song, were inclined to take of the claims of spiritual dignataries.

Of the wealth also of the Sakyas† our authorities speak frequently. They talk of them as "a family blessed with prosperity and great opulence," and mention the gold which they possess, and which the land they rule produces. The chief source of their wealth was undoubtedly rice cultivation;

* The Kosala king to whom this act is ascribed, is Vidûdabha, the son of Buddha's contemporary and patron, Pasenadi. Though later legends represent the Sakyas as having been destroyed during Buddha's life-time, this is not, as far as I know, supported by any proof contained in the sacred Pâli texts. Moreover the history of Buddha's relics ("Mahâparin," S. p. 68) clearly states that the Sakya dynasty survived Buddha.

† Indeed, it must not be forgotten that the value of these statements is not quite indisputable; inasmuch as the object was to represent Buddha's separation from his kin, as being, from a worldly point of view, a very great sacrifice, the wealth which he renounced must have been painted in the strongest colours possible. This is to be noticed also in the biography of Mahavîra, Buddha's contemporary, the founder of the Jaina sect.

and the advantageous position of their territory, commercially, which had been formed, as it were, for a medium of communication between the mountain range and the Gangetic plains, cannot have been unavailed of.

A widespread tradition represents Buddha as having been a king's son. At the head of this aristocratic community there must certainly have been some one leading man, appointed, we know not by what rules, with the title of king, which can scarcely in this case have indicated more than the position of *primus inter pares*. But the idea that Buddha's father, Suddhodana, enjoyed this royal dignity is quite foreign to the oldest forms in which the traditions regarding the family are presented to us: rather, we have nothing more or less to contemplate in Suddhodana than one of the great and wealthy landowners of the Sakya race, whom later legends first transformed into the "great king Suddhodana."

The mother of the child, Mâyâ, also a member of the Sakya stock, died soon—seven days, it is said—after the birth of the boy. Her sister, Mahâpajâpatî, another wife of Suddhodana, filled for him the place of mother.

Traditional story represents with apparent truth that the young noble passed his youth in the capital of the Sakya realm, in Kapilavatthu ("red place," or red earth).* This town, wholly unknown† to Brahmanical literature, cannot have been of much importance, although in an old Buddhist dialogue it is

* Montg. Martin, i, 293, says of Goruckpore district: "No soil of a red colour was observed on the surface, although earths of this kind may be procured by digging." This is quite sufficient, if we consider the changes caused in the earth's surface by inundations in the course of more than two thousand years, to explain the name Kapilavatthu. Swinton (p. 33) mentions "red spots resembling carbonate of iron," in the sandy beds under the surface of the yellow earth.

† Antea, note p. 93.

spoken of as a densely populated place, in the narrow streets of which were thronging elephants, carts, horses, and men.

We know scarcely anything of Buddha's childhood. We hear of a step-brother and of a step-sister renowned for her beauty, children of Mahâpajâpatî. What was the difference of age between them and their brother, is not known.

In the training of nobles in those lands which were but slightly attached to Brahmanism, more attention was paid to martial exercises than to knowledge of the Veda. Buddhists have not attributed Vedic scholarship to their master. Many a day may have been passed by the boy out of doors on his father's estate, indulging in meditations, as an old text describes him to us, in a field under the cool shade of a fragrant jambu tree (rose-apple).

Among the opulent and gentle youth of that age, it was indispensable to the comfort of a style of life in keeping with their dignity, to have three palaces, which were constructed to be occupied by turns corresponding to the changes of winter, summer, and rains. Tradition states that the coming Buddha passed his early years in three such palaces, a life the background of which was the same scenery, the wonderful splendour of which then surrounded, and, still unchanged, now surrounds, the habitations of Indian nobles; shady gardens with lotus-pools on which the gently waving, gay-coloured lotus-flowers gleam like floating flower beds, and in the evening diffuse their fragrance afar, and outside the town the pleasure grounds to which the walks or elephant-rides lead, where rest and solitude await the comer, far from the bustle of the town, beneath the shade of tall and thick foliaged mango, pipal and sál-trees.

We are told that the coming Buddha was married—but whether to one or several wives is not known—and that he had a son, Râhula, who afterwards became a member of his religious order. These statements we can the less regard as concoctions, the more casually and incidentally they meet us in the older traditions, the person of Râhula or of his mother* being there employed neither for didactic purposes nor to introduce pathetic situations. If one takes into account the part which the obligation of austere chastity plays in the ethical views and the monastic rules of the Buddhists, he will understand that had we before us here not facts but gratuitous inventions, the tendency of the fabricators of the history must have been rather to throw a veil over a real existing marriage of Buddha than to invent one which had no existence.

These scanty traces exhaust all that is handed down to us, credible concerning Buddha's early life. We must forbear asking the question, from what quarter and in what form the germs of those thoughts entered his soul which drove him to change home for exile and the plenty of his palaces for the poverty of a mendicant.

We can very readily understand how, in the oppressive monotony of idle ease and satiated enjoyment, there may have come directly over an earnest and vigorous nature a mood of restlessness, the thirst for a career and a struggle for the highest aims, and the despair at the same time to find anything to assuage that thirst in the empty world of transitory pleasure. Who knows anything of the form which these thoughts may have assumed in the mind of the youth, and how far the impulse which pervaded that age, and led men and women to leave home for an ascetic life, acting from without upon these inner pre-dispositions, may have influenced him also?

* Her name appears to have been unknown to the ancient Church. Copious inventions of later times first filled up these gaps in various ways. Cf. Davids' and my notes to our English translation of the "Mahâvagga," i, 54.

We have in one of the holy texts a description which shows in bare simplicity, how the early disciples represented to themselves the awakening of the fundamental ideas of their faith in the mind of their master.

Buddha is speaking to his disciples of his youth, and after he has spoken of the abundance which surrounded him in his palaces, he goes on to say:

"With such wealth was I endowed, my disciples, and in such great magnificence did I live. Then these thoughts arose within me. 'A weak-minded, everyday man, although he is himself liable to decay and is not free from the power of old age, feels horror, revulsion and disgust, if he sees another person in old age: the horror which he then feels recoils on himself. I also am subject to decay and am not free from the power of old age. Should I also, who am subject to decay and am not free from the power of old age, feel horror, revulsion, and disgust, if I see another in old age? This would not be becoming to me.' While I thus reflected, my disciples, in my own mind, all that buoyancy of youth, which dwells in the young, sank within me. A weak-minded everyday man, though he be himself liable to sickness, and is not free from the power of disease," and so on—then the same train of thought, which has been stated regarding old age and youth, follows in reference to disease and health, and then in regard to death and life. "While I, my disciples," thus ends this passage, "thus reflected in my mind, all that spirit of life which dwells in life, sank within me."

A later age desired to see illustrated in concrete occurrences, how for the first time and with impressive power the thoughts of old age, disease, and death crept over the young man, healthy and in the freshness of life, and how he was directed by some significant example to that path which leads away beyond the power of all suffering. Thus was invented, or rather transferred to the youth of Gotama, a legend which was narrated of one of the legendary Buddhas of bygone ages—the familiar history of the four drives of the youth to the garden outside the town, during which the pictures of the impermanence of everything earthly presented themselves to him one after the other, in the form of a helpless old man, a sick person, and a dead body; and at last a religious mendicant with shaven head and wearing yellow garments meets him, a picture of peace and of deliverance from all pain of impermanence. In that way later tradition concocted this narrative preparatory to the flight of Gotama from his home. Of all this the early ages knew nothing.

When Gotama left home to lead a religious life, he was, according to good tradition, twenty-nine years old.

He must have been no mean poet in whose hand the history of this flight grew into that poem, rich in the splendour of Indian colouring, as we read it in the later books of legends.

The king's son returns from that drive during which, by the appearance of a religious mendicant, thoughts of a life of peaceful renunciation had come home to him. When he mounts his chariot, the birth of a son is announced to him. He says: "Râhula* is born to me, a fetter has been forged for me"—a fetter which tries to bind him to the home-life from which he is struggling to part. A princess, who is standing on the balcony of the palace, beholds him as he approaches the city on his chariot, diffusing a beaming radiance. She breaks out at the sight of him into these words: "Happy the repose of the mother, happy the repose of the father, happy the repose of the wife, whose he is, such a husband!" The young

* In the name Râhula there seems to be an allusion to Râhu, the sun and moon subduing (darkening) demon.

man hears her words and thinks to himself: "well might she say that a blessed repose enters the heart of a mother, when she beholds such a son, and blessed repose enters the heart of a father and the heart of a wife. But whence comes the repose which brings happiness to the heart?" And he gives the answer himself: "when the fire of lust is extinguished, when the fire of hatred and infatuation is extinguished, when ambition, error, and all sins and sorrows are extinguished, then the heart finds happy repose."

In his palace the prince was surrounded by beautiful, gaily-attired handmaids, who sought to dissipate his thoughts with music and dance: but he neither looks upon nor listens to them, and soon falls into sleep. He wakes up at night and sees by the light of the lamps those dancing-girls wrapt in slumber, some talking in their sleep, some with running mouths, and of others again the clothes have become disarranged and exposed repulsive deformities of the body. At this sight it was to him as if he were in a burial-place full of disfigured corpses, as if the house around him were in flames. "Alas! danger surrounds me," he cried, "alas! distress surrounds me! Now is the time come for me to go on the great pilgrimage." Before hastening away, he thinks of his new-born son: "I will see my child." He goes to his wife's chamber, where she is sleeping on a flower-strewn couch, with her hand spread over the child's head. Then the thought occurs to him: "If I move her hand from his head to clasp my child, she will awake. When I shall have become Buddha, I shall return and see my son." His trusty steed Kanthaka is waiting outside, and thus the prince flies, seen by no human eye, away from wife and child and from his kingdon, out into the night, to find rest for his soul and for the world and the gods, and behind him follows Mâra, the tempter, shadow-like, and watches till perchance a moment may come, when a thought of lust or unrighteousness, entering the struggling soul, will give him power over the hated enemy.

That is poetry; now listen to the bare prose, in which an older age speaks of the flight, or rather of the departure of Gotama, from his home:

"The ascetic Gotama has gone from home into homelessness, while still young, young in years, in the bloom of youthful strength, in the first freshness of life. The ascetic Gotama, although his parents did not wish it, although they shed tears and wept, has had his hair and beard shaved, has put on yellow garments, and has gone from his home into homelessness."

Or, as it is put in another place: "Distressing is life at home, a state of impurity: freedom is in leaving home: while he reflected thus, he left his home."

It is necessary, in the face of the highly coloured poetical form into which later ages have thrown the history of Buddha's departure from Kapilavatthu, to remember these unadorned fragments of the little which older generations knew or desired to know of these things.

After the early life passed at home comes the period of homelessness, of wandering ascetic life. Only in his case who has severed the ties of home and family, can the effort to attain eternal blessings lead to success; such was the conception of that age.

Seven years of inquiry are stated to have passed from the day when Gotama left his native town, till the consciousness of realization was imparted to him, till he felt himself to be the Buddha, the deliverer, and the preacher of deliverance to the worlds of gods and men.

He trusted himself during this period of seven years at first to the guidance of two successive spiritual teachers, to find what the language of that time termed "the highest state of sublime repose," the "unoriginated, the Nirvâna, the eternal state." The path, in which these teachers directed him, must have been grounded on the production of pathological conditions of self-concentration, such as have in later Buddhism played a not unimportant part: conditions in which, by a long-continued observance of certain bodily discipline, the spirit seeks to divest itself of all concrete subject-matter, of every entity, of every conception, and, as is added, even of conceptionlessness.

Then he left these teachers unsatisfied, and travelled through the land of Magadha until he came to the town of Uruvelâ.* An old narrative puts these words into his mouth when he speaks of this wandering: "Then, O disciples, I thought within myself: truly this is a charming spot of earth, a beautiful forest: clear flows the river, with pleasant bathing-places, and fair lie the villages round about, to which one can go: here are good quarters for one of high resolve, who is in search of salvation."

Then in the woods of Uruvelâ Gotama is said to have lived many years in the severest discipline. It is described how he sat there, his tongue pressed against his palate, resolutely "checking, repressing, chastening" his aspirations, waiting the moment, when the supernatural illumination should come upon him. It comes not. He struggles for a still more perfect performance by imposing the greatest strains on his physical frame: he holds his breath: he denies himself nourishment. Five other ascetics are living in his neighbourhood: in astonishment at the resolution with which he pursues his mortifications, they wait to see will he be made partaker of

* Buddha Gayâ, south of Patna. The oft-mentioned river Neranjarâ is there called Phalgu now. Cf. Cunningham, "Ancient Geography of India," p. 457.

the longed-for enlightenment, in order that they may tread as his disciples the path of deliverance indicated by him. His body becomes attenuated by self-inflicted pain, but he finds himself no nearer the goal. He sees that self-mortifications cannot lead to enlightenment: so he takes nourishment again freely to regain his former strength. Then his five companions abandon him: he seems to them to have deserted his own cause, and there appears to be nothing more to hope for or of him. So Gotama remains alone.

One night, the old traditions narrate, the decisive turning point came, the moment wherein was vouchsafed to the seeker the certainty of discovery. Sitting under the tree, since then named the Tree of Knowledge, he went through successively purer and purer stages of abstraction of consciousness, until the sense of omniscient illumination came over him: in all-piercing intuition he pressed on to apprehend the wanderings of spirits in the mazes of transmigration, and to attain the knowledge of the sources whence flows the suffering of the world, and of the path which leads to the extinction of this suffering.

"When I apprehended this," he is reported to have said of this moment, "and when I beheld this, my soul was released from the evil of desire, released from the evil of earthly existence, released from the evil of error, released from the evil of ignorance. In the released awoke the knowledge of release: extinct is re-birth, finished the sacred course, duty done, no more shall I return to this world; this I knew."

This moment the Buddhist regard as the great turning-point in his life and in the life of the worlds of gods and men: the ascetic Gotama had become the Buddha, the awakened, the enlightened. That night which Buddha passed under the tree of knowledge,* on the banks of the river Neranjarâ, is the sacred night of the Buddhist world.

Thus the holy text narrates the history of the inner struggles of Gotama and his untiring pursuit of knowledge and peace. Is there any historical fact in this narrative?

We are here face to face with a question, on which the analysis of the historical critic is unable to return a clear and bold verdict, a decisive Yes or No.

The character of the sources does not of itself determine whether we here have historical fact or legend before us. In the authorities unquestionable truth is mixed up with just as unquestionable romance: the history of the attainment of Buddhahood does not bear any direct traces of being either the one or the other.

So much is clear that, granted even that Buddha had not experienced, and had not even professed to have experienced, something analogous to this, still the existence of this narrative among the groups of his disciples can be readily understood. If he was the Buddha, if he possessed sacred knowledge, he must at some place and at some definite moment have become the Buddha, have attained that sacred knowledge, and before this moment there must have been—legend-weaving fancy could scarcely have overlooked this conclusion—a period in which the consciousness that he was still far from his goal, dominated strongly and painfully. What can this period of

* Cunningham ("Archæol. Reports," i, 5) says of the pipal tree (Ficus religiosa) at Buddha Gayâ, which is looked upon as being this tree: "The celebrated Bodhi tree still exists, but is very much decayed; one large stem, with three branches to the westward, is still green, but the other branches are barkless and rotten. The tree must have been renewed frequently, as the present pipal is standing on a terrace at least thirty feet above the level of the surrounding country."

bootless search have been like? At every step the disciples of Buddha had to contend against the tendencies of ascetics who expected to attain quietude through fasting and severe bodily discipline. It is not surprising that this opposition in which they felt themselves to be to these tendencies should have influenced the belief of the early Church regarding Buddha's own previous history: he, too, must, before he became partaker of the imperishable treasure of true deliverance, have sought for salvation in the mazes of bodily discipline; he must have surpassed all that Brahmans and devotees had accomplished before him in the way of self-mortification, and he must have realized for himself the fruitlessness of such a course, until he at last, turning from the false to the true path, became the Buddha.

It is, therefore, evident that the narrative concerned *may* be a myth: the conditions, which suffice to make the concoction of such a myth comprehensible, certainly exist. And this possibility of a purely mythical conception gains further support by the undoubted mythical character of the occurrences yet to be discussed, which followed on the attainment of Buddhahood.

But showing that a thing *may* be a myth is not equivalent to showing that it *is* a myth, and I am inclined to think that that which can be urged in favour of an opposite conception is by no means without weight.

The coming of such a sudden turning-point in Buddha's inner life corresponds much too closely with what in all times similar natures have actually experienced under similar conditions, for us not to be inclined to believe in such an occurrence. In the most widely different periods of history the notion of a revolution or change of the whole man perfecting itself in one moment meets us in many forms:

a day and hour it must be possible to determine, in which the unsaved and unenlightened becomes a saved and enlightened man: and if men hope and look for such a sudden, and probably also violent, breaking through of the soul to the light, they realize it in fact. Within the Christian Church we have the Methodists especially, but not they alone, who bear testimony to this. Furthermore, phenomena of this kind are not confined by any means to persons of a vulgar type, living in a dull religious atmosphere. On the contrary, natures which are endowed with the keenest spiritual sensibility, with the most versatile power of imagination, are especially susceptible of such experiences. A flash of thought, a sudden excitement of warm emotion or vivid imagination, or a moment of tranquil breathing-time following on times of internal strife, is metamorphosed for them into that opening of the heart, or that call by divine omnipotence, for which they were consciously or unconsciously waiting, and which is sufficient to give a new turn to their whole life.

In the age of which the sacred writings of the Buddhists give us a picture, and, we may add with probability, in Buddha's own time, the belief in a sudden illumination of the soul, in the fact of an internal emancipation perfecting itself in one moment, was universally prevalent: people looked for the "deliverance from death," and told one another with beaming countenance that the deliverance from death had been found: people asked how long it was till one striving for salvation is able to attain his goal, and gave one another to understand, with and without figure or parable, that of course the day and hour, in which the fruit of immortality will be given to man, are not in his power, but still the Master promised to his follower that, if he trod the right path, "after a short time that for which noble youths leave their homes to lead a pilgrim life, the highest achievement of religious effort, would be vouchsafed to him, that he would yet in this life apprehend the truth itself, and see it face to face." This visionary grasp of truth some pursued by mortification, others by abstraction of the mind, pushed to the utmost limit and accompanied by long-protracted retention of the body in fixed postures, all waiting the moment in which the attainment of their aim would be clearly realized by them with absolute certainty. When any one came to regard his natural state as impermanent and dark, that to which he aspired, and which he, therefore, expected finally to actually realize, could not but appear to him to be a condition of purer internal illumination and self-knowledge, and with this condition of pure internal illumination was combined the consciousness of his own power to look, by visionary intuition, through the whole concatenation of the universe.

We can scarcely doubt that such a mode of viewing things prevailed among religious inquirers at Buddha's time. Whoever left his home and became a mendicant did so looking for the coveted fruit of enlightenment. May we not also surmise that similar expectations filled the heart of the Sakya youth, when he left his native town? That he then experienced within himself those struggles, those combats between hope and doubt, of which the history of those who have paved new paths for religious feeling and thought have so much to say? That after periods of intense mental, and why not also bodily, anguish there arose in him at a particular moment the feeling of clearer rest and internal certainty, and he laid hold on this as the longed-for illumination, as a token of deliverance come? That he thenceforward felt himself to be the Buddha, the one called by a universal law to be a follower of the Buddhas of bygone ages, and determined to bring to others the blessing which had been imparted to him?

If the process was anything like this, it cannot but have followed that Buddha at a later time communicated to the disciples, to whom he pointed out the path to holiness, these inner experiences also, through which he was conscious of having himself attained his goal: and though the memory of these communications may have received in the Church in the course of time a stamp of scholastic dogmatism, yet their original character must always have shone through. In this sense it is quite possible that this narrative may cover actual fact.

The historical inquirer cannot create certainties where there are only potentialities. Let each individual come to a conclusion, or refrain from coming to a conclusion, as he thinks porper; let me be allowed, for my part, to declare my belief that, in the narrative of how the Sakya youth became the Buddha, there is really an element of historical memory.

CHAPTER III.

Beginning of the Teacher's Career.

With this decisive turning-point begins in our authorities a long-connected narrative.* This gives us a picture of how the early Church represented to itself Buddha's first public appearance, the winning of the first converts, and the triumph over the first opponents. They were still far from thinking of an attempt to delineate a continuous sketch of Buddha's life, but these first days of his public life, as well as his last days, were invested with an especial interest, and therefore this part of his life has already in very ancient times—for the narrative bears unmistakably the stamp of high antiquity—assumed the form of a fixed tradition. Who has not experienced in his own case that in long, monotonous periods of time, in which reminiscences float promiscuously and blur one another, the early beginnings, the days of freshness and self-adjustment, usually preserve themselves clear in the memory?

We cannot read the beginning of the narrative referred to without calling to mind the story in our gospels. There Jesus, before He begins openly to teach, spends forty days fasting in the wilderness, "and was tempted of Satan; and He was with

* "Mahâvagga," i, 1-24 (pp. 1-44 of my Edition).

the wild beasts; and the angels ministered unto Him." So Buddha also, before he sets out to propagate his doctrine, remains four times seven days* fasting in the neighbourhood of the tree of knowledge, "enjoying the happiness of deliverance." The idea which underlies this is readily understood: after a severe struggle the victory has been won: it is natural that the victor, before he betakes himself to new conflicts, should pause to enjoy what he had won, that the delivered, before he preaches deliverance to others, should himself taste its happiness.

Buddha spends the first seven days, wrapt in meditation, under the sacred tree itself. During the night following the seventh day, he causes his mind to pass through the concatenation of causes and effects, from which the pain of existence arises: "From ignorance come conformations;† from conformations comes consciousness"—and so on through

* The oldest form of the tradition in the "Mahâvagga." Later narratives give seven times seven days. The oldest tradition specifically states that Buddha at the end of the seventh day went from the tree of knowledge to the fig-tree Ajapâla ("tree of the goat-herds"); the later narrative here inserts three periods of seven days. The patristic commentator Buddhagosha is naturally anxious to explain away the difference between the two narratives. "It is as when one says: after he has eaten, he lays himself down to rest. Thereby it is not implied that he lies down without first washing his hands, rinsing out his mouth, having gone to his couch, having indulged in any conversation whatever—but it is only meant to convey: after dinner-time he lies down, he does not omit to lie down. So here also it is not meant: after he had risen from this meditation he immediately went forward, but it merely means: after he had risen, he went forward later on, he did not omit to go forward. But what did the Exalted One do immediately before he went forward? He tarried other three times seven days in the neighbourhood of the tree of knowledge," and so on.

† We shall have to return later on to these propositions, in the review of the Buddhist doctrine.

a long series of intervening links, until, "from desire comes clinging (to existence); from clinging (to existence) comes being: from being comes birth: from birth come old age and death, pain and mourning, suffering, sorrow, and despair." But if the first cause be removed, on which this chain of effects hangs, ignorance becomes extinct, and everything which arises from it collapses, and all suffering is overcome. "Realizing this the Exalted One at that time spoke these words:—

'When the conditions (of existence) reveal themselves
To the ardent, contemplating Brahman,
Then must every doubt give way,
When the origin of all becoming is revealed to him.'

"Three times, in the three watches of the night, he caused his mind to pass through all this series of causes and effects: at last he spoke thus:—

'When the conditions (of existence) reveal themselves
To the ardent, contemplating Brahman,
He casts to earth the tempter's hosts,
Like the sun, which sheds its light through space.'

"Then Buddha rose, when the seven days had passed, from the meditation in which he had been absorbed, left the spot under the tree of knowledge, and went to the fig-tree Ajapâla (tree of the goat-herds)."

Another and probably later cast of this tradition here inserts an account of a temptation: just as on Jesus also Satan made an attack, when He spent those forty days in the wilderness, trying, before He should enter on His career, to make Him unfaithful to His calling as the Saviour.*

* It seems scarcely necessary to observe that in both cases the same obvious motives have given rise to the corresponding narratives; the notion of an influence exerted by Buddhist tradition on Christian cannot

It would be going too far if we were to suppose that there is preserved to us in the Buddhist tradition the memory of single and specific visions of good and evil spirits, with which Buddha professed to have had intercourse: but it is beyond doubt that he himself and his disciples shared the beliefs of all the Indian world in such appearances, and that they were convinced that they had seen the like.

Mâra, the tempter, knows that fear or lust can have no further influence over Buddha: he had vanquished all earthly thoughts and emotions under the tree of knowledge. To undo this victory is impossible, but there is one thing still left which the tempter may effect: he may induce Buddha to turn his back at this stage on earthly life and to enter into Nirvâna. Then he alone would be delivered from Mâra's power: he would not have proclaimed the doctrine of deliverance to men.

"Then came"—thus Buddha afterwards relates the history of this temptation to his disciple Ânanda—"Mâra, the wicked one, unto me. Coming up to me, he placed himself at my side: standing at my side, Ânanda, Mâra, the wicked one, spake unto me, saying: 'Enter now into Nirvâna, Exalted One, enter Nirvâna, Perfect One: now is the time of Nirvâna arrived for the Exalted One.' As he thus spake, I replied, Ânanda, to Mâra, the wicked one, saying: 'I shall not enter Nirvâna, thou wicked one, until I shall have gained monks as my disciples, who are wise and instructed, intelligent hearers of the word, acquainted with the doctrine, experts in the Doctrine and the second Doctrine, versed in the ordinances, walking in the Law, to propagate, teach, promulgate, explain, formulate,

be entertained. The Buddhist history of the temptation is to be found in the "Mahâparinibbâna Sutta," p. 30, seq., and is inserted in the context of the whole continuous narrative in the "Lalita Vistara," p. 489.

analyze, what they have heard from their master, to annihilate and exterminate by their knowledge any heresy which arises, and preach the doctrine with wonder-working. I shall not enter Nirvâna, thou wicked one, until I shall have gained nuns as my disciples, who are both wise and instructed (and here, after the fashion of the Buddhist ecclesiastical style, what has been said of monks follows about nuns, lay brothers, and lay sisters). I shall not enter Nirvâna, thou wicked one, until the life of holiness which I point out, has been successful, grown in favour, and extended among all mankind, and is in vogue and thoroughly made known to all men.'"

We return to the older version of the narrative.*

Buddha still tarries thrice seven days in various places in the neighbourhood of the tree of knowledge "enjoying the happiness of deliverance." A sort of overture is here played to the great drama of which he is to be the hero: significant typical occurrences foreshadow the future. The meeting with a "Brahman of haughty air," causes us to think of a struggle with and conquest of Brahmanism. We hear nothing of the taunt with which that Brahman may have accosted Buddha: it

* In addition to the external ground of the history of this temptation being wanting in the "Mahâvagga," there is still another deeper consideration which determines me to believe that it was excluded from the older traditions. We shall afterwards come to the history of Buddha's internal struggle whether he should preach his doctrine and not rather enjoy the acquired deliverance himself alone: Brahma's appearance solved the doubt. This history conveys no other thought but the same which underlies the narrative of Mâra: Buddha's struggle with the possibility of permitting the sacred knowledge which he had won, to benefit himself only and not humanity at large. Had he repelled Mâra's tempting suggestion to do this, by saying that the time to enter Nirvâna would not come until he had gained disciples, male and female, and preached his doctrine to all the world, there would have been no opening left for the whole account of the dialogue with Brahma.

is only reported that he puts this question to him: "wherein, O Gotama, consists the nature of the Brahman, and what are the qualities which make a man a Brahman?" Buddha had, thinking of himself, spoken in that speech under the tree of knowledge of the Brahman, to whose ardent mind the procession of destiny reveals itself: a Brahman now disputes with him, the heir of worldly rank, the right to claim the title of a Brahman. Buddha tells him: he is a true Brahman who has put away all evil from himself, who knows nothing of contempt, nothing of impurity, a conqueror of self.

Human attacks have no power against Buddha: but the raging of the elements is also unable to disturb the abiding peaceful reposo which is his. Storms arise; for seven continuous days rain falls in torrents; cold, tempest, and darkness surround him. Mucalinda, the serpent-king, comes from his hidden realm, enfolds Buddha's body in a sevenfold covering with his serpent coils, and protects him from the storm. "And after seven days, when the serpent-king, Mucalinda, saw that the sky had become clear and cloudless, he loosed his coils from the body of the Exalted, concealed his serpent form, assumed the guise of a young man, and stepped before the Exalted One, worshipping him with folded hands. Seeing this, the Exalted One at this time spoke these words:

'Happy the solitude of the peaceful, who knows and beholds truth;
Happy is he who stands firmly unmoved, who holds himself in check at all times.
Happy he whose every sorrow, whose every wish is at an end.
The conquest of the stubbornness of the ego-ity is truly the supreme happiness.'"

A genuine Buddhist picture: the deliverer of the world, who, amid the raging of tempests, wrapped in a seven-fold casing by a serpent's body, enjoys the happiness of solitary repose.

Here follows the first meeting with men who honour him as Buddha. Two merchants come passing that way on a journey: a deity, who had been in earthly life related to the merchants, announces to them the nearness of Buddha, and prompts them to feed Buddha. The deities, who rule over the four quarters of the earth, present to him a bowl —for the perfect Buddhas accept no food except in a bowl— and he partakes of what the merchants give him, the first nourishment which he takes after long fasting.

"But the merchants, Tapussa and Bhallika, when they saw that the Exalted One, when his repast was over, had washed his bowl and his hands, bowed their heads to the feet of the Exalted One, and spake to the Exalted One, saying: 'we who are here, O sire, take refuge in the Exalted One and in his Doctrine: may the Exalted One accept us as his adherents* from this day forward throughout our life, we who have taken our refuge in him.' These were the first persons in the world who made their profession of the faith with the two words"— namely, the faith in the Buddha and his Doctrine, for as yet, the third member of the Buddhist triad, the Order, had not come into existence.

In this overture to the history of Buddha's labours we miss one element: a typical adumbration of the most prominent task of his life, the preaching of the doctrine of deliverance, and of the coming out of persons from among all classes to follow him in mendicant attire. Those two merchants take refuge in Buddha and the Doctrine, and nevertheless the Doctrine has not yet been preached to them. The narrative

* That is as lay-followers, not as monks.

which now follows has to do with the motive, in which all this seeming inconsistency finds its explanation. It is one thing to have realized for one's self the truth of deliverance, and another to proclaim it to the world. Buddha has accomplished the first: the resolution to do the second is not yet firmly fixed within him: apprehensions and doubt remain to be overcome before he adopts this resolve.*

I shall here let the text† speak for itself.

"Into the mind of the Exalted One, while he tarried, retired in solitude, came this thought: 'I have penetrated this deep truth, which is difficult to perceive, and difficult to understand, peace-giving, sublime, which transcends all thought, deeply-significant, which only the wise can grasp. Man moves in an earthly sphere, in an earthly sphere he has his place and finds his enjoyment. For man, who moves in an earthly sphere, and has his place and finds his enjoyment in an earthly sphere, it will be very difficult to grasp this matter, the law of causality, the chain of causes and effects: and this also will be very difficult for him to grasp, the extinction of all conformations, the withdrawal from all that is earthly, the extinction of desire, the cessation of longing, the end, the Nirvâna. Should I now preach the Doctrine and mankind not understand me, it would bring me nothing but fatigue, it would cause me nothing but trouble!' And there passed unceasingly through the mind of the Exalted One, this voice, which no one had ever before heard.

* In the language of Buddhist dogmatic, a Paccekabuddha (a Buddha for himself only) is not a Sammâsambuddha (universal Buddha and a teacher of the world). For Buddha's appearance as a Sammâsambuddha a special deliberation was necessary, which the legend gives in the narrative now following.

† "Mahâvagga," i, 5, 2, seq.

"'Why reveal to the world what I have won by a severe struggle?
The truth remains hidden from him whom desire and hate absorb.
It is difficult, mysterious, deep, hidden from the coarse mind;
He cannot apprehend it, whose mind earthly vocations surround with night.'

"When the Exalted One thought thus, his heart was inclined to abide in quietude and not to proclaim the Doctrine. Then Brahma Sahampati* with his thought perceived the thought of the Holy One and said thus to himself: 'Truly the world is lost, truly the world is undone, if the heart of the Perfect One, the holy, highest Buddha, be bent on abiding in quietude and not preaching the Doctrine.'

"Then Brahma Sahampati left the heaven of Brahma as quickly as a strong man stretches out his bent arm or bends his outstretched arm, and he appeared before the Exalted One. Then Brahma Sahampati made bare one of his shoulders from under his robe,† bowed his right knee to the earth, raised his folded hands to the Exalted One, and spake to the Exalted One thus: 'May it please, O sire, the Exalted One, to preach the Doctrine, may it please the Perfect One to preach the Doctrine. There are beings, who are pure from the dust of the earthly, but if they hear not the preaching of the Doctrine, they are lost: they will be believers of the Doctrine.' Thus spake Brahma Sahampati; when he had spoken thus, he went on to say:—

'In the land of Magadha there arose before
A doctrine of impure beings, sinful men.

* Sahampati is with the Buddhists the standing surname of the Supreme Brahma (cf. antea, p. 60); the word is not to be explained with certainty.

† A mark of respect.

Open thou, O Wise One, the door of eternity,
Let be heard what thou, O Sinless One, hast discovered.
Who stands above high on the mountain's rocky summit,
His eye looks afar over all people.
So mount thou also, O Wise One, up where on high
Far over the land stand out the battlements of truth,
And look down, Painless One, on mankind,
The suffering (creatures), whom birth and old age torture,
Rise, rise, thou valiant hero, rich in victories,
Go through the world, sinless preacher of the path,
Raise thy voice, O sire; many shall understand thy word.'"

(Buddha sets the solicitation of Brahma against the doubts and apprehensions, which made the preaching of the truth appear to him to be a fruitless undertaking. Brahma repeats his request three times: at last Buddha grants it:)

"As on a lotus stalk some water-roses, blue lotus flowers, white lotus flowers, generated in the water, growing up in the water, rise not out of the water, but bloom in the deep—other water roses, blue lotus flowers, white lotus flowers, generated in the water, growing up in the water, rise up to the surface of the water—and other water roses, blue lotus flowers, white lotus flowers, generated in the water, growing up in the water, rise up out of the water and the water damps not their blossoms: so likewise, when the Exalted One surveyed the universe with the glance of a Buddha, he saw beings whose souls were pure, and whose souls were not pure, from the dust of the earthly, with sharp faculties and with dull faculties, with noble natures and with ignoble natures, good hearers and wicked hearers, many who lived in fear of the world to come and of sin. When he saw this, he spake to Brahma Sahampati these words:—

'Let opened be to all the door of eternity;
He who hath ears, let him hear the word and believe.

I thought of affliction* for myself, therefore have I, O Brahma,
Not yet proclaimed the noble word to the world.'

"Then Brahma Sahampati perceived: The Exalted One has answered my prayer. He will preach the Doctrine. Then he bowed before the Exalted One, walked round him respectfully and vanished."

Thus has the legend conducted its hero to victory over the very last obstacle which stood between him and his calling as a deliverer, to victory over all doubt and dismay: the resolution to proclaim to the world the knowledge, in which he had himself found peace, now stands unshaken.

The Sermon at Benares.

Who should be the first to hear the new gospel? Legend makes Buddha think first of all of the two teachers, to whose guidance he had first confided himself as a disciple. If he were to preach his doctrine to them, they would understand him. A deity brings him the intelligence that they are both dead. Perhaps they were really so; in any case the meaning of this touch in the legend is clear. No one could have a higher claim than those two to be the first hearers of the gospel. It would have been ingratitude if Buddha had not made them before all others participators of his self-acquired treasure. But no one knew anything of his having done so: and others were known to be or said to be the first converts. These two were therefore represented as being no longer alive when Buddha began to preach his doctrine.

* Fruitless toil, if the doctrine found no hearers.

Could those, who had once been Buddha's teachers, not turn to him as his first disciples, yet the quondam partners of his quest and struggle, those five ascetics, could, who had long vied with him in penances, and had forsaken him when they saw that he gave up the pursuit of salvation by self-mortification (*vide* antea, p. 107). They are staying at Benares, and our narrative represents Buddha as now wandering thither. It is quite possible that tradition here rests on old and trustworthy memories.* Benares has at all times been

* It is a natural supposition that Buddha directed his first ministration to his quondam associates and admirers, in whom he could hope most surely to find willing hearers. Criticism has no means of determining absolutely, whether we are here to find in the internal probabilities of the case, a mark of genuineness, or of fiction. But, in my opinion, it is *à priori* probable that the recollection of where and to whom Buddha's first discourse, or at any rate his first successful discourse, was delivered, had not been lost. That some preceding unsuccessful attempts on Buddha's part to gain adherents, have been passed over in silence by tradition, is quite possible; but Mons. L. Feer's attempts ("Études Bouddhiques," i, p. 1-37) to point out traces of such events in the tradition, seem to me unsuccessful; the nature of these traditions does not admit of calculating from Buddha's proceedings any such pragmatic consecutive order of things, as this scholar has sought to make out therefrom, not without some violence towards the tradition in many places. If we follow the victorious march of Buddha, as we find it described in the "Mahâvagga," i, 1-24, on the map, there is not much to be said against the itinerarium: this to-and-fro movement is quite in accordance with the customs of these pious wanderers. When we call to mind the sharply defined analogy, which the imagination of the Buddhists traces between the victorious career of their master and the victorious progress of a world-subduing king, we can scarcely avoid opining that the former, if pure invention had here had full swing, would have been constructed according to the standing geographical scheme of the latter (*vide* "Lalita Vistara," p. 16, seq.). The direct contradiction in which the narrative of the "Mahâvagga" finds itself to this scheme, demonstrates essentially that it contains authentic matter.

regarded by the Buddhists as the town in which the gospel of deliverance was first heard and believed.

We reserve for a later passage the attempt to give a connected description of the manner in which Buddha preached his doctrine, what chords he was wont to strike in his hearers. In this place we merely give the old narrative. It shows us its hero now, at the beginning of his career, already wholly the same as it makes him appear to be throughout his long life. The monks, to whom we owe these notices, could not depict internal becoming, nor could they invent internal becoming, for they did not know what internal becoming is; and, even had they known it, how could they admit internal becoming in the case of the Perfect One, who had discovered for himself the path from the world of sorrowful becoming into the world of happy being?

The history of the first discourse of Buddha at Benares runs, in the solemn circumstantial narrative style which is peculiar to the sacred writings of the Buddhists, thus: *

"And the Exalted One, wandering from place to place, came to Benares, to the deer-park Isipatana, where the five ascetics dwelt. Then the five ascetics saw the Exalted One approaching from a distance: when they saw him, they said to one another: 'Friends, yonder comes the ascetic Gotama, who lives in self-indulgence, who has given up his quest, and returned to self-indulgence. We shall show him no respect, not rise up before him, not take his alms-bowl and his cloak from him: but we shall give him a seat, and he can sit down, if he likes.'

"But the nearer and nearer the Exalted One came to the five ascetics, the less could the five ascetics abide by their

* "Mahâvagga," i, 6-10, seq.

resolution: they went up to the Exalted One: one took from the Exalted One his alms-bowl and cloak: another brought him a seat, a third gave him water to wash his feet and a footstool. The Exalted One sat down on the seat which was set for him: when he had sat down, the Exalted One washed his feet.

"Now they addressed the Exalted One by his name and called him 'Friend.' When they addressed him thus, the Exalted One said to the five ascetics: 'Ye monks, address not the Perfect One* by his name and call him not "Friend." The Perfect One, O monks, is the holy, supreme Buddha. Open ye your ears, O monks; the deliverance from death is found: I teach you, I preach the Law. If ye walk according to my teaching, ye shall be partakers in a short time of that for which noble youths leave their homes and go into homelessness, the highest end of religious effort: ye shall even in this present life apprehend the truth itself and see face to face.'

"When he spake thus, the five ascetics said to the Exalted One: 'If thou hast not been able, friend Gotama, by that course, by those mortifications of the body, to attain superhuman perfection, the full supremacy of the knowledge and contemplation of sacred things, how wilt thou now, when thou livest in self-indulgence, when thou hast given up thy effort, and returned to self-indulgence, attain superhuman perfection, the full supremacy of the knowledge and contemplation of sacred things?'

"When they said this, the Exalted One spake to the five ascetics: 'O monks, the Perfect One liveth not in self-

* The word, which we translate "the Perfect One" (Tathâgata) is that which, most probably, Buddha was wont to use, when he was speaking of himself.

indulgence: he has not given up his effort and returned to self-indulgence. The Perfect One, O monks, is the holy, supreme Buddha. Open ye your ears, ye monks; the deliverance from death is found: I teach you, I preach the Law. If ye walk according to my teaching, ye shall be partakers in a short time of that for which noble youths leave their homes and go into homelessness, the highest end of religious effort: ye shall even in the present life apprehend the truth itself and see face to face.'"

(They repeat the same dialogue a second and a third time.)

"When they said this, the Exalted One spake to the five ascetics: 'Tell me, ye monks, have I ever before addressed you in these terms?'

"'Sire, thou has not.'

"'The Perfect One, O monks, is the holy, highest Buddha. Open ye your ears, ye monks, the deliverance from death is found,' etc.

"Then the five ascetics hearkened once more to the Exalted One. They opened their ears and directed their thoughts to knowledge.

"Then the Exalted One spake to the five ascetics, saying: 'There are two extremes, O monks, from which he who leads a religious life must abstain. What are those two extremes? One is a life of pleasure, devoted to desire and enjoyment: that is base, ignoble, unspiritual, unworthy, unreal. The other is a life of mortification: it is gloomy, unworthy, unreal. The Perfect One, O monks, is removed from both these extremes and has discovered the way which lies between them, the middle way which enlightens the eyes, enlightens the mind, which leads to rest, to knowledge, to enlightenment, to Nirvâna. And what, O monks, is this middle way, which the Perfect One has discovered, which enlightens the eye and enlightens the spirit, which leads to rest, to knowledge, to enlightenment, to Nirvâna? It is this sacred, eight-fold path, as it is called: Right Faith, Right Resolve, Right Speech, Right Action, Right Living, Right Effort, Right Thought, Right Self-concentration. This, O monks, is the middle way, which the Perfect One has discovered, which enlightens the eye and enlightens the spirit, which leads to rest, to knowledge, to enlightenment, to Nirvâna.

"'This, O monks, is the sacred truth of suffering: Birth is suffering, old age is suffering, sickness is suffering, death is suffering, to be united with the unloved is suffering, to be separated from the loved is suffering, not to obtain what one desires is suffering, in short the five-fold clinging (to the earthly*) is suffering.

"'This, O monks, is the sacred truth of the origin of suffering: it is the thirst (for being), which leads from birth to birth, together with lust and desire, which finds gratification here and there: the thirst for pleasures, the thirst for being, the thirst for power.

"'This, O monks, is the sacred truth of the extinction of suffering.: the extinction of this thirst by complete annihilation of desire, letting it go, expelling it, separating oneself from it, giving it no room.

"'This, O monks, is the sacred truth of the path which leads to the extinction of suffering: it is this sacred, eight-fold path, to wit: Right Faith, Right Resolve, Right Speech, Right Action, Right Living, Right Effort, Right Thought, Right Self-concentration.

* The clinging to the five elements, of which man's body-cum-spirit state of being consists: corporeal form, sensations, perceptions, conformations (or aspirations), and consciousness.

"'This is the sacred truth of suffering; thus my eye, O monks, was opened to these conceptions, which no one had comprehended before, and my judgment, cognition, intuition, and vision were opened. "It is necessary to understand this sacred truth of suffering."—"I have comprehended this sacred truth of suffering." Thus, O monks, my eye was opened to these conceptions, which no one had comprehended before, and my judgment, cognition, intuition, and vision were opened.'"

(Then follow similar passages regarding the other three truths.)

"'And as long, O monks, as I did not possess in perfect clearness this triple, twelve-part,* trustworthy knowledge and understanding of these four sacred truths, so long, O monks, I knew that I had not yet attained the supreme Buddhahood in this world, and the worlds of gods, of Mâra and of Brahma, among all beings, ascetics and Brahmans, gods and men. But since, O monks, I have come to possess in perfect clearness this triple, twelve-part, trustworthy knowledge and understanding of these four sacred truths, since then I know, O monks, that I have attained the supreme Buddhahood in this world, and in the worlds of gods, of Mâra and of Brahma; among all beings, ascetics and Brahmans, gods and men. And I have seen and know this: the deliverance of my soul is secured: this is my last birth: henceforth there is for me no new birth.'

"Thus spake the Exalted One: the five ascetics joyfully received the words of the Exalted One."

This is the sermon at Benares, which tradition gives as the

* Of each of the four truths Buddha possesses a tri-partite knowledge, *e.g.* of the first: "this is the sacred truth of suffering;" "one must understand this sacred truth of suffering;" "I have understood this sacred truth of suffering."

opening of the ministry of Buddha, by which he, as his disciples expressed themselves, "has set in motion the wheel of the law." One may entertain whatever opinion he pleases regarding the historical truth with which this sermon is reported—I am inclined, for my part, to entertain no very high opinion of it—but even the more freely concocted one may take this discourse to be, only the more highly must he rate its fundamental importance, for he is so much the more certain here to find, if not the words actually spoken on the occasion of a definite occurrence, at any rate the ideas which the ancient Church regarded, and certainly not improperly regarded, as the real lever in the preaching of their master. Clearly and sharply defined are the leading thoughts, which stand in the middle of the contracted solemn thought-world, in which the Buddhist Church lived: in the centre of all one sole idea, the idea of deliverance. Of deliverance, of that from which we are to be delivered, of the way in which we shall be delivered, of this and of nothing else does this sermon of Buddha's, and, we may add, do the sermons of Buddha as a rule, treat. God and the universe trouble not the Buddhist: he knows only one question: how shall I in this world of suffering be delivered from suffering? We shall have to return to the answer which the sermon at Benares gives to this question.

When Buddha finishes his discourse, there rises from earth through all the worlds of gods the cry, that at Benares the Holy One has set in motion the wheel of the law. The five ascetics, headed by Kondañña, who has hence obtained the name of Kondañña, the Knower, beg Buddha to initiate them as students of his doctrine, and he does so in these words: "Come near, O monks; well preached is the doctrine: walk in purity to make an end of all suffering." Thus is founded the Church of Buddha's followers: the five are its first, as yet its only, members. A fresh discourse of Buddha's, on the instability and impermanence of everything earthly, causes the souls of the five disciples to obtain the condition of sinless purity. "At this time," thus ends this narrative, "there were six holy persons in the world"—Buddha himself and these five disciples.

Further Conversions.

The number of believers soon increases. The next convert is Yasa, a scion of a wealthy house at Benares: his parents and his wife likewise hear Buddha's discourses and become adherents of the faith as a lay-brother and lay-sister. Numerous friends of Yasa, youths of the most prominent houses in Benares and the country roundabout, adopt the monastic life. The company of the faithful soon reaches sixty members. Buddha sends them forth to preach the law throughout the country. In nothing did the secret of the great power of rapid increase, which existed in the young Church, so much lie as in its itinerancy: here anon, there anon, appearing, vanishing, simultaneously at a thousand places. "O disciples," thus in our authorities run the words with which Buddha sends out his followers, "I am loosed from all bands, divine and human. Ye also, O disciples, are loosed from all bands, divine and human. Go ye out, O disciples, and travel from place to place for the welfare of many people, for the joy of many people, in pity for the world, for the blessing, welfare, and joy of gods and men. Go not in twos to one place. Preach, O disciples, the law, the beginning of which is noble, the middle of which is noble, and the end of which is noble, in spirit and in letter: preach the whole and full, pure path of holiness. There are beings, who are pure from the dust of the earthly, but if they hear not the gospel of the law, they perish: they shall understand the law. But I, O disciples, go to Uruvelâ, to the village of the general, to preach the law."

At Uruvelâ there reside Brahman hermits, a thousand in number, who keep alight the sacred fire of sacrifice according the rites of the Vedas, and perform their ablutions in the river Neranjarâ. Three brothers, Brahmans, of the Kassapa family, are the leaders of these ascetics. Buddha comes to one of them and overcomes with miraculous power the terrible serpent-king, who dwelt in Kassapa's sacrificial chamber. The Brahmans wonder-struck persuade him to spend the winter with them. He stops there, dwelling in the forest near Kassapa's hermitage, in which he takes his food every day. Miracle after miracle convinces the Brahmans of his greatness: gods come to listen to his discourses; they shine like flaming fire all night long. Kassapa, overcome with wonder, admits the superhuman greatness of his guest, but he cannot bring himself to submit to him. "Thus the Exalted One," as our old narrative states in this connection, "thought within himself: 'this simpleton will long continue thinking: "the great Sumana is very powerful and mighty, but he is not holy as I am." So then, I shall work on this hermit's heart.' Therefore the Exalted One spake to the hermit Kassapa of Uruvelâ: 'Thou art not holy, Kassapa, nor hast thou found the path of holiness: and thou knowest nothing of the way by which thou canst be holy and mayest reach the path of holiness.' Then the hermit Kassapa, of Uruvelâ, bowed his head to the feet of the Exalted One, and said to the Exalted One: 'Grant me, O sire, to receive the degrees of initiation, the lower and the higher.'"

All narratives of conversions in the Buddhist scriptures resemble this narrative more or less. Where any attempt at individuality is made, it turns out clumsy and poor. That earnest, deep feeling, and the impulse of strong emotion was not denied to these minds, is amply proved by the poetry of the Buddhists. But describe they could not, and what they were least capable of understanding was individual life.

Kassapa's two brothers and all the bands of hermits round them turn to Buddha and adopt monastic garb. Thus the number of believers is at one stroke raised to a thousand.

They now wander from Uruvelâ to Râjagaha, the near-lying capital of the Magadha kingdom. The halting-place is in a bambu-thicket outside the town. The young king Bimbisâra hears of Buddha's arrival, and goes out with a vast following* of citizens and Brahmans to make the acquaintance of the teacher who had acquired sudden fame. When the people saw Buddha and Kassapa together, doubts arose as to which of the two is master and which is the disciple. Kassapa rises from his seat, bows his head to Buddha's feet and says: "Sire, my master is the Exalted One: I am his pupil. Sire, my master is the Exalted One: I am his pupil." Buddha preaches before the king and his retinue: Bimbisâra, with a great number of his people, declares himself a lay convert of Buddha's Church. Thenceforth throughout his long life he became one of the truest friends and patrons of Buddha and his doctrine.

Tradition informs us that on that occasion at Râjagaha

* The text says that "twelve myriads of Brahmans and citizens of Magadha" surrounded the king. These extravagantly high figures differ far too widely from the statements regarding the number of disciples accompanying Buddha (a few hundreds, at most thousands), for us to be in a position to draw conclusions from them with any certainty whatever as to the excessive character of the latter, in themselves very credible, numbers.

Buddha also gained as disciples those two men, Sâriputta and Moggallâna, who came later on to be honoured as the first in rank after their master in the circles of the Church. These two young men, bound to each other by close ties of friendship, sons of a Brahman family, were at that time residing at Râjagaha as pupils of Sanjaya, one of the itinerant medicants and teachers so numerous in that age. In their common pursuit of spiritual possessions, they had, as is related, given each other this promise, that he who would first obtain the deliverance from death, should tell the other. One day Sâriputta saw one of Buddha's disciples, Assaji, walking the streets of Râjagaha to collect alms, peaceful and dignified, with downcast look. "When he saw him," our narrative* here informs us, "he thought: 'truly this is one of those monks who are already sanctified in this world, or have attained the path of purity. I shall go up to this monk and I shall ask him: "Friend, in whose name hast thou renounced the world? and who is thy master? and whose doctrine dost thou recognize?"' But then Sâriputta, the mendicant, reflected: 'Now is not the time to ask this monk. He is going from house to house and is collecting alms. I shall approach this monk, as one approaches a person from whom he desires something.' But when the venerable Assaji had collected alms at Râjagaha, he took the contributions he had received and turned back. Thereupon the mendicant, Sâriputta, approached the venerable Assaji: arrived near him, he saluted the venerable Assaji. After he had exchanged words of friendly salutation with him,

* The passage which I here translate is one of those which king Asoka, in the Bairât inscription (circ. 260 B.C.), commanded the monks and nuns, the lay-brothers and lay-sisters, intently to hear and learn. The text is there described as "the question of Upatissa," but Upatissa is a name of Sâriputta.

he placed himself near him. Standing near him, the mendicant, Sâriputta, addressed the venerable Assaji, saying: 'Thy visage, friend, is luminous, thy colour is pure and clear. In whose name, friend, hast thou renounced the world? and who is thy master? and whose doctrine dost thou recognize?' 'It is the great Samana, my friend, the Sakya's son, who comes from the Sakya's house and has renounced the world. In his name, the Exalted One's, I have renounced the world, and he, the Exalted One, is my master, and his law, the Exalted One's, I recognize.' 'And what, friend, does thy master say, and what does he teach?' 'Friend, I am but a novice; it is not long since I left the world; I have only recently conformed to this doctrine and this order. I cannot expound the doctrine to thee in its fulness, but I can tell thee its spirit briefly.' Then the mendicant, Sâriputta, said to the venerable Assaji: 'Be it so, friend. Tell me little or much, but tell me its spirit: I have a longing to know the spirit only: what great care canst thou have for the letter?' Then the venerable Assaji addressed to the mendicant, Sâriputta, this statement of the doctrine:

"'Existences which flow from a cause, their cause the Perfect One teaches, and how they end: this is the doctrine of the great Samana.'"*

* This sentence has become in later ages the briefly-expressed confession of faith of Buddhism; it is to be met inscribed on numerous monuments. Undoubtedly it refers to the doctrine of the concatenation of causes and effects, on which doctrine tradition, as we have seen (p. 114) represents Buddha's thoughts as being fixed, when he sits under the sacred tree of the Buddhahood. The painful destiny of the world works itself out in the chain of operations, which flow from ignorance; the doctrine of Buddha tells us what these existences are, dependent one on another, springing from ignorance, and how they come to an end, *i.e.*, how the suffering of the world is removed.

And when the mendicant Sâriputta heard this statement of the doctrine, he obtained the clear, undimmed vision of the truth, and he perceived: "Whatever is subject to the law of beginning, all that is also subject to the law of decay." (And he said to Assaji:) "If the doctrine be nothing else but this, thou hast at any rate attained the condition in which there is no suffering. That which hath not been seen by many myriads of bygone ages, hath in these days come near unto us."

Sâriputta now goes to his friend, Moggallâna. "Thy visage, friend," says Moggallâna, "is luminous, thy colour is pure and clear. Hast thou found the deliverance from death?" "Yes, friend, I have found the deliverance from death!" And he tells him of his meeting with Assaji, and on Moggallâna also "the clear, undimmed light of truth" dawns. Sanjaya, their instructor, in vain begs them to remain with him. They go with great crowds of ascetics into the wood where Buddha is resting: but a hot stream of blood bursts from Sanjaya's mouth. Buddha sees the two coming: he announces to those around him that those are now approaching who should be the foremost and noblest among his disciples. And the two of them receive the initiation from Buddha himself.

"At this time," continues our narrative, "many distinguished and noble youths of the Magadha territory joined themselves to Buddha, to lead a pure life. On this the populace became displeased, murmured, and were angry, saying: 'The ascetic Gotama is come to bring childlessness: the ascetic Gotama is come to bring widowhood: the ascetic Gotama is come to bring subversion of families. Already hath he turned the thousand hermits into his disciples, and he hath made the two hundred and fifty mendicant followers of Sanjaya his disciples, and now these many distinguished and noble youths of the Magadha kingdom are betaking themselves to the ascetic Gotama to lead a religious life.' And whenever the people saw any of the disciples they taunted them with these words:

> 'The great monk came in his travels to the capital of Magadha, seated on a hill.
> He has converted all Sanjaya's followers, whom will he draw after him to-day?'

"The disciples then learned how the populace was displeased, murmured, and was angry: and the disciples told the Exalted One. 'This excitement, O disciples,' said the Exalted One, 'will not last long. Seven days will it last: after seven days will it vanish. But ye, my disciples, if they taunt you with the saying:

> 'The great monk came in his travels to the capital of Magadha, seated on a hill.
> He has converted all Sanjaya's followers, whom will he draw after him to-day?'

answer them with these words:

> 'The heroes, the perfect ones, convert by their true discourse;
> Who will reproach the Enlightened One who converts by the power of truth?'"

Have we really here a pair of those rhymes before us, such as they were probably bandied at that time between the friends and foes of the young teacher among the gossiping populace of the streets of the capital?

CHAPTER IV.

BUDDHA'S WORK.

WITH the history of the conversion of those two most prominent of his disciples, and the account of the soon-allayed discontent of the people at Râjagaha, the connected narrative of Buddha's career breaks off, again to unite but once more, where the memory had to be fastened on the last wanderings of the aged teacher, on his parting utterances and his death. For the long period which lies between that beginning and the end, a period, as we are told, of more than four decades, there is in our tradition, at least in that which deserves this name, nothing in the way of a continuous description, but merely collections of countless real or feigned addresses, dialogues, and sayings of Buddha, to which is annexed a short note regarding the external circumstances of place and company, which led to these utterances.

To outward view it is a uniform life which lies before us in this uni-coloured tradition, and that wherein alone the true history of this life lay, the inner current of being with its ebb and flow, its coming and its going, is hidden from us. When and how the picture of the world and life comes to assume in Buddha's mind the form in which it presented itself to his followers, in what order above all his convictions regarding himself and his mission developed themselves within him, how far the prejudices of the Indian people and the criticism of the Indian schools eventually reacted on Buddha's thought and inclination,—even to ask these questions nobody who looks to our authorities will be bold enough. Of this we shall never learn anything: we cannot.

What we can do is, without attempting to draw any distinction of early and later periods, merely to unite the different features which tradition places at our disposal, so as to form a connected picture, a picture of Buddha's teaching and life, of his intercourse with high and low, of the circle of disciples gathered round him, and of the wider circles of partizans and antagonists.

Can we hope to attain historical truth in such a picture?

Yes and no.

No: for this picture shows us only the type of ancient Buddhist life, but not the individual characteristics which belonged to Buddha and him only, as peculiarly his own, in the sense that we have a picture of Socrates which truly resembles Socrates only and no one else, even no Socratic.

Still this, which on the one hand indicates a want in our knowledge, gives us on the other hand, however, a ground for trusting it.

India is altogether a land of types, not of individualities stamped with their own dies. Life begins and passes away there, as the plant blooms and withers, subject to the dull rule of the laws of Nature; and the laws of Nature can produce nothing but typical forms. Only where the breath of freedom floats are those proud forces of manhood unfettered, which enable man to become, and dare to become, something individual, like himself alone. Thus on all pictures in the Indian epics, despite their splendid colouring, there lies that strange torpor which makes men look like spectres, to which the draught of vivifying blood had been denied: and this effect is owing to this cause above all others, that the domain of this poetry does not extend to the point where the particularly characteristic life of the individual begins. This range was closed to Indian poetry because the Indian peoples themselves were denied the power to develope individualties. And in the same way in the history of Indian thought, there also the power at work is not the individual mind, but always merely the great Indian folk-mind, that which the Indians, if questioned regarding the origin of their sacred writings, denominate the sacred Vedic spirit. Through all there operates an unindividual universal, and the individual bears only those marks with which the universal mind has endowed him.

Are we not to believe that this same law has also governed the beginnings of Buddhist life? The great disciples, who clustered round the Master, Sâriputta and Moggallâna, Upâli, and Ânanda, completely resemble each other in the old narratives, and their picture is nothing else but the invariably uniform copy of Buddha himself, only on a reduced scale. The reality was hardly much otherwise: the individual was little more than a specimen, which the general spirit disclosed to view, and this general spirit again was, with reference to the forms in which it outwardly displayed itself, scarcely intrinsically different from the spirit of Buddha himself and the forms among which Buddha's life was passed.

Furthermore, the period between Buddha and the fixing of our traditions regarding him was in nothing so deficient as in minds capable of giving a new direction to the great movement, or of stamping it with the impress of their own life: the ancient Buddhist Church had not a Paul. But in this we have a guarantee that this movement, as it is sketched for us, is in its essence the same as Buddha and his first disciples made it. True, Buddha may have had many a noble mark of intellect and of creative power, which the puny natures, by which his picture has been preserved to us, have reduced to their own lower level, but a form like his can certainly not be fundamentally misconceived.

Thus, though only a few touches of the picture presented to us by tradition can be said to be absolutely reliable, in the sense of historically exact, still we shall have a right to look upon this picture itself in its entirety as reliable in a higher sense.

Buddha's Daily Life.

From year to year the change from a period of wandering to a period of rest and retirement repeated itself for Buddha and his disciples. In the month of June when, after the dry scorching heat of the Indian summer, clouds come up in towering masses, and the rolling thunders herald the approach of the rain-bearing monsoon, the Indian to-day, as in ages past, prepares himself and his house for the time during which all usual operations are interrupted by the rain: for whole weeks long in many places the pouring torrents confine the inhabitants to their huts, or at any rate to their villages, while communication with neighbours is cut off by rapid, swollen streams, and by inundations. "The birds," says an ancient Buddhist work, "build their nests on the tops of trees: and there they nestle and hide during the damp season." And thus also it was in those days an established practice with the members of monastic orders, undoubtedly not first in Buddha's time, but since ever there was a system of religious itinerancy in India, to suspend itinerant operations during the three rainy months and to spend this time in quiet retirement in the neighbourhood of towns and villages, where sure support was to be found through the charity of believers. To this custom they adhered all the more strongly because they could not, during the rainy season, which, after the scorching heat of summer, calls everywhere into being an infinite variety of vegetable and animal life, travel about, without infringing at every step the commandment which forbids the destruction of even the lowest form of life.

Buddha also every year for three months "kept vassa (rainy reason)," surrounded by groups of his disciples, who flocked together to pass the rainy reason near their teacher. Kings and wealthy men contended for the honour of entertaining him and his disciples, who were with him, as guests during this season in the hospices and gardens which they had provided for the community.

The rains being over, the itinerating began: Buddha went from town to town and village to village, always attended by a great concourse of disciples: the texts are wont to speak in one place of three hundred, and in another of five hundred, who followed their master.* In the main streets, through which the religious pilgrims like travelling merchants used to pass, the believers who dwelt near had taken ample care to provide shelter, to which Buddha and his disciples might resort: or, where monks who professed the doctrine dwelt, there was sure to be found lodging for the night in their abodes, and even if

* On the occasion of a prophecy of Buddha's regarding Metteyya, the next Buddha, who will in the far future appear upon the earth, it is said: "He will be the leader of a band of disciples, numbering hundreds of thousands, as I am now the leader of bands of disciples, numbering hundreds."—*Cakkavattisuttanta.*

no other cover was to be had, there was no want of mango or banyan trees, at the feet of which the band might halt for the night.

The territory through which these wandering excursions generally extended was the circuit of the "Eastern Land," *i.e.*, chiefly the old kingdoms of Kàsi-Kosala and Magadha, with the neighbouring free states, the territories known to-day as Oudh and Bihar. Contrasted with this were the kingdoms of "Western Hindostan," the ancient seat of Vedic culture and of the exclusive power of a Brahman order strongly opposed to the religious influences of the East, affected, it is true, if tradition rightly inform us, by the itinerant ministrations of Buddha, but still only seldom and superficially. The most important headquarters during these wanderings, at the same time the approximately extreme points, to the north-west and south-east, of the area, in which Buddha's pilgrim-life was passed, are the capital cities of the kings of Kosala and and Magadha, Sâvatthi (now Sahet Mahet on the Rapti) and Râjagaha (now Rajgir, south of Bihar).* In the immediate neighbourhood of these towns the community possessed numerous pleasant gardens, in which structures of various kinds were erected for the requirements of the members. "Not too far from, nor yet too near the town," thus runs the standard description of such a park given in the sacred texts, "well provided with entrances and exits, easily accessible to all people who inquire after it, with not too much of the bustle of life by day, quiet by night, far from commotion and the crowds of men, a place of retirement, a good spot for solitary meditation." Such a garden was the Veluvana ("Bambu-grove"), once a pleasure ground of king Bimbisâra

* The distance between these two capitals is about the same as between London and Edinburgh.

and presented by him to Buddha and the Church: another was the still more renowned Jetavana (at Sâvatthi), a gift made by Buddha's most liberal admirer, the great merchant Anâthapindika. Not alone the sacred texts, but equally also the monumental records, the reliefs of the great Stupa of Bharhut, recently explored, show how highly celebrated this gift of Anâthapindika's was from the earliest days in the Buddhist Church. It is narrated how Anâthapindika was in search of a spot which should be worthy to serve as a place of sojourn for Buddha and his disciples: the garden of the prince Jeta alone appeared to him to unite in itself all requirements, but the prince declined to sell it to him. After protracted negotiations Anâthapindika obtained the garden for as much gold as sufficed to cover the surface of the ground of the whole Jetavana. He gave it to Buddha, whose favourite place of sojourn it thenceforward was. Numberless passages of the sacred texts, in which the subject-matter consists of addresses and sayings of Buddha, begin: "At this time the holy Buddha was sojourning at Sâvatthi, in the Jetavana, the garden of Anâthapindika."

If it is possible to speak of a home in the homeless, wandering life of Buddha and his disciples, places like the Veluvana and Jetavana may of all others be so called, near the great centres of Indian life and yet untouched by the turmoil of the capitals, once the quiet resting places of rulers and nobles, before the yellow-robed mendicants appeared on the scene, and "the Church in the four quarters, present and absent," succeeded to the possession of the kingly inheritance. In these gardens were the residences of the brethren, houses, halls, cloisters, storerooms, surrounded by lotus-pools, fragrant mango trees, and slender fan-palms that lift their foliage high over all else, and by the deep green foliage of the Nyagrodha tree, whose roots dropping from the air to earth become new stems, and with their cool shady arcades and leafy walks seem to invite to peaceful meditation.*

These were the surroundings in which Buddha passed a great part of his life, probably the portions of it richest in effective work. Here masses of the population, lay as well as monastic, flocked together to see him and to hear him preach. Hither came pilgrim monks from far countries, who have heard the fame of Buddha's teaching and, when the rainy season is past, undertake a pilgrimage to see the master face to face. "It is customary," runs an oft-recurring passage in our texts, "for monks, when they have passed the rainy season, to set out to see the Exalted One. It is the custom of the exalted Buddha to welcome monks who come from afar." "Is it well with you, monks?" Buddha is accustomed to ask the arrivals. "Are you able to live? Have you passed the rains in peace and unity, and without discord, and have you experienced any want of support?"

We hear, for instance, of one of the faithful named Sona, in the land of Avanti (Malwa), far from the country in which Buddha lived, whom the fame of the new doctrine had reached, and there arose in him the desire to be received among its professors. Three long years he had to wait until he succeeded in bringing together in this distant land the ten monks, whose presence was indispensable to conferring the orders on a new member. Once, when he was in solitude, there occurred to him the thought: "I have, it is true,

* The Chinese pilgrim Fa Hian (in the beginning of the fifth century after Christ) writes regarding the Jetavana (according to Beal's translation, p. 75): "The clear water of the tanks, the luxuriant groves, and numberless flowers of variegated hues, combine to produce the picture of what is called the Vihâra of Chi-ûn (Jeta)."

heard of the Exalted One, he is so and so, but I have not seen him face to face. I will go to behold him, the exalted, holy, highest Buddha, if my teacher allows me to go." And his teacher, to whom he expressed his wish, answered him: "Good, Sona, good: go, Sona, to behold him, the exalted, holy, supreme Buddha. Thou shalt see him, Sona, the Exalted One, the bringer of joy, the dispenser of joy, whose organs of life are placid, whose spirit is at rest, the supreme self-subduer and peace-possessor, the hero who has conquered self and watches himself, who holds his desires in check." And Sona prepares for the journey to Sâvatthi, where Buddha is tarrying in the Jetavana, the garden of Anâthapindika.

Pilgrims of this class come together where Buddha is sojourning, and the meetings and greetings of the arriving groups with the clerical brothers who live on the spot, the interchange of news, the arrangement of lodging-places for the itinerant monks, then not unfrequently caused those noisy clamours so strange to western ears, which seem to be inseparable from such occasions in the East, and which are most earnestly deprecated more than once in the sacred texts.

The fame of Buddha's person also drew together from far and near crowds of such as stood without the narrower circles of the community. "To the ascetic Gotama," people remarked to one another, "folks are coming, passing through kingdoms and countries, to converse with him." Often, when he happened to halt near the residences of potentates, kings, princes, and dignitaries, came on waggons or on elephants, to put questions to him or to hear his doctrine. Such a scene is described to us in the opening of the "Sûtra on the fruit of asceticism," and reappears in pictorial representation among the reliefs at Bharhut. The Sûtra relates how king Ajâtasattu of Magadha in the "Lotus-night," that is in the full moon of October, the time when the lotus blooms, is sitting in the open-air, surrounded by his nobles on the flat roof of his palace. "Then," as it is recorded in that text, "the king of Magadha, Ajâtasattu, the son of the Videha princess, uttered this exclamation: 'fair in sooth is this moonlight night, lovely in sooth is this moonlight night, grand in sooth is this moonlight night, heart-enchanting in sooth is this moonlight night, happy omens in sooth giveth this moonlight night. What Samana or what Brahman shall I go to hear, that my soul may be cheered when I hear him?'" One counsellor names this and another that teacher: but Jîvaka, the king's physician, sits on in silence. "Then the king of Magadha, Ajâtasattu, the son of Vedehî, spake to Jîvaka Komârabhacca: 'Why art thou silent, friend Jîvaka?'—'Sire, in my mango grove he resteth, the exalted, holy, supreme Buddha, with a great band of disciples, with three hundred monks. Of him, the exalted Gotama, there spreadeth through the world lordly praise in these terms: He, the Exalted One, is the holy, supreme Buddha, the wise, the learned, the blessed, who knoweth the universe, the highest, who tameth man like an ox, the teacher of gods and men, the exalted Buddha. Sire, go to hear him, the Exalted One: perchance, if thou hearest him, the Exalted One, thy soul, O sire, may be refreshed'"—and the king orders elephants to be prepared for himself and the queens, and the royal procession moves with burning torches on that moonlight night through the gate of Râjagaha to Jîvaka's mango grove, where Buddha is said to have held with the king the famous discourse "On the fruits of asceticism," at the end of which the king joined the Church as a lay-member.

The pictures, which the sacred texts give us of meetings and scenes like these, are very numerous: no doubt, the concourse which moved round Buddha's person is faithfully reflected in them. If Buddha comes to the free towns, we hear of his meetings with the noble families who exercise rule there: at Kusinârâ the Mallas, the ruling family of that town, go out to meet him and issue an edict: "whosoever goeth not to meet the Exalted One is liable to a penalty of five hundred pieces." From the gayest of the Indian free towns, the dissolute and wealthy Vesâlî, the distinguished youths of the Licchavi house drive out to Buddha with their splendid teams, some in white garments with white trimmings, and others in yellow, black, or red. Buddha says to his disciples, when he sees the Licchavi youths coming in the distance: "who ever, my disciples, among you hath not seen the divine host of the thirty-three gods, let him gaze on the host of the Licchavis, let him behold the host of the Licchavis, let him view the host of the Licchavis." And besides the noble youth of Vesâlî, there comes driving with not less pomp, to see Buddha, another celebrity of the town, the courtesan Ambapâlî. She invites Buddha and his disciples to dine in her mango grove, and when they assemble there and dinner is over, she makes a gift of the grove to Buddha and the Church.

To complete the picture of the society which existed round Buddha, the class of dialecticians and theological disputants of all shades already flourishing prosperously in India at this period, must not be allowed to pass unnoticed: the distinguished Brahman, endowed by the king with the revenues of a village, who comes conducted by a great following, the young Brahmanical scholar, who is sent forth by his teacher, to bring him tidings of the much-spoken-of Gotama, and who is eager to win his spurs in a logical dispute with the renowned adversary, countless sophistic hair-splitters, persons of religious as well as worldly standing, who have heard that the Samana

Gotama is staying in the neighbourhood, and who prepare to lay traps for him with two-edged questions and to entangle him in contradiction, whatever be the answer he may give.

A frequent end of these dialogues is of course that the vanquished opponents or the partisans of Buddha invite him and his disciples to dine on the following day: "Sire, may it please the Exalted One and his disciples to dine with me to-morrow." And Buddha permits his consent to be inferred from his silence. On the following day about noon, when dinner is ready, the host sends word to Buddha: "Sire, it is time, the dinner is ready;" and Buddha takes his overcoat and alms-bowl and goes with his disciples into the town or village to the residence of his host. After dinner at which well-to-do hosts offer, except meat dishes, the best which the not-very-luxurious cooks of those days could provide, and at which the host himself and his family serve the guests, when the customary hand washing is over, the host takes his place with his family at Buddha's side, and Buddha addresses to them a word of spiritual admonition and instruction.

If the day be not filled by an invitation, Buddha, according to monastic usages, undertakes his circuit of the village or town in quest of alms. He, as well as his disciples, rises early, when the light of dawn appears in the sky, and spends the early moments in spiritual exercises or in converse with his disciples, and then he proceeds with his companions towards the town. In the days when his reputation stood at its highest point, and his name was named throughout India among the foremost names, one might day by day see that man before whom kings bowed themselves, walking about, alms-bowl in hand, through streets and alleys, from house to house, and without uttering any request, with downcast look, stand silently waiting until a morsel of food was thrown into his bowl.

When he had returned from his begging excursion and had eaten his repast, there followed, as the Indian climate demanded, a time, if not of sleep, at any rate of peaceful retirement. Resting in a quiet chamber, or better still in the cool shades of dense foliage, he passed the sultry, close hours of the afternoon in solitary contemplation, until the evening came on and drew him once more from holy silence to the bustling concourse of friend and foe.

Buddha's Disciples.

From the exterior aspect of that which we must be satisfied to accept as a picture of this life, our description now turns to the interior. We have yet to acquaint ourselves with the circle of those to whom Buddha's teaching was especially directed, the disciples who endeavoured by following him to find for their souls the path to rest.

To all appearance this circle of disciples was even in the earliest days by no means a free society, bound together by merely internal cords, something like the band of Jesus' disciples. We can scarcely doubt that it was from the beginning much more of a community of ascetics organized according to fixed rules, a formal monastic order with Buddha at its head. The forms and external technic of a religious life of this class had been already established in India long before the age of Buddha: a monastic order appeared then to the religious consciousness to be the reasonable, natural form, in which alone the life of those who are associated in a common struggle for release could find expression. As there was nothing in Buddha's attitude generally which could be regarded by his contemporaries as unusual, he had not to introduce anything fundamentally new; on the contrary, it would have been an innovation if he had undertaken to preach a way of salvation, which did not proceed on a basis of monastic observances.

The standing formula with which Buddha is supposed to have received the first believers into this circle has been preserved to us: "Come hither, O monk; well preached is the doctrine, walk in purity, to make an end of all suffering." We know not whether this tradition rests on any authentic memory, but the thought which here finds expression seems quite correct, that the circle of Buddha's disciples was from the very beginning a monastic brotherhood, into which the postulant had to be admitted by an appointed step, with the utterance of a prescribed formula.

The yellow garment of the monk and tonsure are the visible tokens of separation from the world and worldly life; the severance of the family bond, the renunciation of all property, rigorous chastity, are the self-evident obligations of the "ascetics who adhere to the son of the Sakya house" (Samanâ Sakyaputtiyâ), the oldest term with which the people designated the members of the young Church.

We know not how far the forms of that corporate life, of which we shall give a fuller description later on, severally extend back to Buddha's own time, of which we are now speaking. It is possible, those half-monthly confessional gatherings, to which so great significance is attached in the simple cult of ancient Buddhism, may have been observed by Buddha himself with the disciples who were with him. The tone which prevailed in the assembly of the believers was calm, composed, one might say, ceremonious. Were we permitted to judge by the impression conveyed to us by the sacred writings, we might opine that the sense of tranquil goodness and the quiet self-conscious joy, by which the associated life of these monks was pervaded, were not sufficient to compensate the lack of liveliness in expression and interchange of the experiences and emotions of each individual. Occasions of rapture were not unfrequent, and were desired as a high spiritual good: they consisted rather in quiet transport than in ecstatic excitement. Each aspired to them for himself alone; they knew nothing of that popular enthusiasm which seizes on whole assemblies, where one carries the others away and common emotion excites similar visions in the imagination of hundreds. To boast before the brothers of experiences of ecstasy was strictly forbidden.

The distinction of caste had no place in this band. Whosoever will be Buddha's disciple renounces his caste. In one of the speeches which the sacred writings put in Buddha's mouth, it is said on this subject: "As the great streams, O disciples, however many they be, the Gangâ, Yamunâ, Aciravatî, Sarabhû, Mahî, when they reach the great ocean, lose their old name and their old descent, and bear only one name, 'the great ocean,' so also, my disciples, these four castes, Nobles, Brahmans, Vaiçya and Çûdra, when they, in accordance with the law and doctrine which the Perfect One has preached, forsake their home and go into homelessness, lose their old name and old paternity, and bear only the one designation, 'Ascetics, who follow the son of the Sakya house.'" And in the discourse "On the fruit of asceticism," in which Buddha answers king Ajâtasattu's question regarding the reward of him who leaves his home and devotes himself to the religious life, Buddha speaks of this matter: if a slave or servant of the king puts on the yellow garment, and lives as a monk without reproach in thought, word and deed, "wouldest thou, then," asks Buddha of the king, "say: well, then, let this man still be my slave and servant, to stand in my presence, bow before me, take upon himself to perform my behests, live to minister to my enjoyments, speak deferentially, hang upon my word?." And the king answers, "No, sire; I should bow before him, stand before him, invite him to sit down, give him what he needed in the way of clothing, food, shelter, and of medicine, when he is ill, and I should assure him of protection, watch and ward, as is becoming."

Thus the religious garb of Buddha's disciples makes lords and commons, Brahmans and Çûdras equal. The gospel of deliverance is not confined to the high-born alone, but is given "to the welfare of many people, to the joy of many people, to the blessing, welfare and joy of gods and men."

We can quite understand how historical treatment in our times, which takes a delight in deepening its knowledge of religious movements by bringing into prominence or discovering their social bearings, has attributed to Buddha the *rôle* of a social reformer, who is conceived to have broken the chains of caste and won for the poor and humble their place in the spiritual kingdom which he founded. But any one who attempts to describe Buddha's labours must, out of love for truth, resolutely combat the notion that the fame of such an exploit, in whatever way he may depict it to himself, belongs to Buddha. If any one speaks of a democratic element in Buddhism, he must bear in mind that the conception of any reformation of national life, every notion in any way based on the foundation of an ideal earthly kingdom, of a religious Utopia, was quite foreign to this fraternity. There was nothing resembling a social upheaval in India. Buddha's spirit was a stranger to that enthusiasm, without which no one can pose as the champion of the oppressed against the oppressor. Let the state and society remain what they are; the religious man, who as a monk has renounced the world, has no part in its cares and occupations. Caste has no value for him, for everything earthly has ceased to affect his interests, but it never occurs to him to exercise his influence for its abolition or for the mitigation of the severity of its rules for those who have lagged behind in worldly surroundings.

While it is true that Buddhism does not reserve to Brahmans only the right of entry into a spiritual life, we must not fall into the error of supposing that Buddha was the first to stand up for this cause and do battle for it. Before his time, probably long before his time, there were religious orders, which received members of all castes, both males and females.* Side by side with the first exclusive religious order of ancient times, the Brahmans, there existed long ere this period, equal to the Brahmans in public estimation, the second religious order of the Samanâ, *i.e.*, ascetics, admission to whose ranks was open to every one who was resolved to renounce a worldly career, whether he was high born or low born. This fact is recognized in the Buddhist traditions as indisputable, as something of which there is no recollection that it had ever been otherwise. There is no need of overrating the value of these traditions, to find in them a guarantee that Buddha did not deem it necessary to undertake a struggle against the leaders of society and thought in behalf of the spiritual rights of the poor and humble: and least of all is it possible that in such a struggle lay the essential character of his life.

This by no means ends all that might be said against the historically untrue conception of Buddha as the victorious champion of the lower classes against a haughty aristocracy of birth and brain.

If one speaks of the equality of all within the pale of Buddha's

* *Vide* antea, p. 63.

confraternity, it is not altogether superfluous to contrast the theory, which was prevalent on this subject among Buddhists, with the actual facts.

It is the case, as we have seen, that the Buddhist theory acknowledged the equal right of all persons without distinction to be received into the order, and it could not but acknowledge it, or it would have given up the consequences of its own principles. And indeed it does not appear to have been likely to occur that postulants should be rejected contrary to the law, on the score of caste.* Nevertheless it seems as if the actual composition of the band, which surrounded Buddha's person, and the composition of the early Church especially, was by no means in due keeping with the theory of equality: if even Brahman exclusiveness was not maintained in its full extent, still a marked leaning to aristocracy seems to have lingered in ancient Buddhism as an inheritance from the past. The sacred writings, in what they openly record as well as in what they imply between the lines, give us sufficient means of drawing a conclusion as to these matters. In the first great address which tradition puts in Buddha's mouth, the sermon at Benares, there occurs an expression, which unwittingly characterizes, and withal criticizes, as briefly as it did sharply, the state of the early Church. Buddha speaks on that occasion of the highest consummation of religious aspirations, for the sake of which "the sons of noble families (kulaputtâ) leave their homes and go into homelessness." The disciples who gathered

* Otherwise we should expect to find in the Vinaya, the codex of ecclesiastical law, in which the section treating of the reception into the order is especially detailed, distinct regulations directed against this abuse. The Vinaya shows clearly that necessity existed much more to prevent improper concessions of admission (*i.e.*, in the case of persons by whose entry into the order the rights of the Third might have been infringed), than to guard against improper refusals of admission.

round the teacher coming from the noble house of the Sakyas, the descendant of king Ikshvâku, were themselves for the most part "sons of noble families." If we review the ranks of personages, whom we are accustomed to meet in the texts, we find it clearly indicated, that the real situation was by this phrase described conformably to fact; here are young Brahmans like Sâriputta, Moggallâna, Kaccâna, nobles like Ânanda, Râhula, Anuruddha, sons of the greatest merchants and highest municipal dignitaries, like Yasa, invariably men and youths of the most respectable classes of society, and with an education in keeping with their social status.* Besides there were the numerous ascetics of other sects, converts to the faith of Buddha, who undoubtedly occupied, by birth and breeding, the same social position.† I am not aware of any instance in which a

* Among the disciples who surrounded Buddha, the barber Upâli is picked out as being a man of low position. Not quite correctly: as barber of the Sakyas he was a courtier, and appears in the tradition as the personal friend of the Sakya youths. *Vide* "Cullavagga," vii, 1-4, and, as to the courtly standing of kings' barbers, cf. "Jâtaka," i, p. 342.

† It may be observed in this connection that, according to Buddhist dogmatic, a Buddha can be born only as a Brahman or as a noble: in this we have it clearly indicated, that the distinctions of caste have by no means vanished or become worthless to the Buddhist consciousness. There is still much else which points in this direction with characteristic significance. In the narrative of a respected young Brahman who appears in the cloister-garden and asks after Buddha, it is recorded: "Thus the disciples communed among themselves, saying: this youth Ambaṭṭha is respected and of high family, and he is the pupil of a respected Brahman, Pokkharasâti. Truly not undesired by the Exalted One is such an interview with such noble youths" (Ambuṭṭhasutta). And Buddha's beloved disciple, Ânanda, says to his master with reference to a man of the noble house of the Mallas, the rulers over Kusinârâ: "Sire, this Malla Roja, is a respected, well-known person. The good will of such a respected and well-known person towards this doctrine and ordinance is of the highest importance. So then, sire, may the Exalted One be

Caṇḍâla—the Pariah of that age—is mentioned in the sacred writings as a member of the order. For the lower order of the people, for those born to toil in manual labour, hardened by the struggle for existence, the announcement of the connection of misery with all forms of existence was not made,* nor was the dialectic of the law of the painful concatenation of

pleased to bring it about that the Malla Roja shall be won to this doctrine and ordinance." And Buddha willingly complies with this request of his disciple ("Mahâvagga," vi, 36). If the texts permit any person at random, not specified by name, to come to Buddha and to be taught by him, they describe such a person as a rule as "a certain Brahman" (especially numerous instances occur in the "Anguttara-Nikâya, Tika-Nipâta"). The text of the Jainas also furnish similar cases. In the simile of the lotus flower, which is to be delivered from the miry earth (in the Sûtrakṛidanga), the flower is not any man at large in need of deliverance, but "a king."

* By this it is not meant to imply that people of humble origin in no case appear in the old texts as members of the order. Interesting, but standing quite alone, is the narrative which is attributed to the Thera (Elder) Sunîta in the collection of "Sayings of the Elders" (Theragâthâ): "I have come of a humble family, I was poor and needy. The work which I performed was lowly, sweeping the withered flowers (out of temples and palaces). I was despised of men, looked down upon and lightly esteemed. With submissive mien I showed respect to many. Then I beheld the Buddha with his band of monks, as he passed, the great hero, into the most important town of Magadha. Then I cast away my burden and ran to bow myself in reverence before him. From pity for me he halted, that highest among men. Then I bowed myself at the Master's feet, stepped up to him and begged him, the highest among all beings, to accept me as a monk. Then said unto me the gracious Master, the compassionator of all worlds: 'Come hither, O monk;' that was the initiation which I received." (Sunîta further relates how he withdrew to the forest, and there wrapt in contemplation, longed for deliverance. The gods came to him and paid him reverence.) "Then the Master saw me, how the host of the gods surrounded me. A smile broke over his features, and he spake these words: "By holy zeal and chaste living, by restraint and self-repression, thereby a man becomes a Brahman: that is the highest Brahmanhood."

causes and effects calculated to satisfy "the poor in spirit." "To the wise belongeth this law," it is said, "not to the foolish." Very unlike the word of that Man, who suffered "little children to come unto him, for of such is the kingdom of God." For children and those who are like children, the arms of Buddha are not opened.

Of the several personages in the narrower circle of disciples we cannot expect to have a life-like individual portrait. Here, as everywhere else in the literature of ancient India, we always meet merely with types, not individualities. We have already touched on this peculiarity: each of the chief disciples resembles every other, so that one might be taken for the other, the same conglomerate of perfect purity, perfect internal peace, perfect devotion to Buddha. These are not real individuals but the incarnated *esprit de corps* of the pupils of Buddha.

The names and the more important surroundings in the life of the individual disciples are undoubtedly authentic. Tradition accords the foremost place among them to those two Brahmans, bound to each other from youth up in bonds of closest friendship, viz., Sâriputta and Moggallâna, who meet us among the converts gained by Buddha in the outset of his career (p. 134, seq.). Throughout his and their long life they followed him faithfully, and they died within a short interval of each other in extreme old age, not long before Buddha's death. It is Sâriputta whom Buddha is believed to have declared to be the most prominent among his followers: he is, it is said,* like the eldest son of a world-ruling monarch, who, following the king, helps him to put in motion the wheel of sovereignty, which he sets rolling over the earth.† Nearest

* "Anguttara Nikâya, Pañcaka-Nipâta."

† By this description of Sâriputta as "eldest son of the Church," it was not contemplated, however, that he might be called to be Buddha's

to these two Brahmans, among those who stand closest to Buddha, is his own cousin, Ânanda, who, when still a youth, adopted the garb of a monk in company with a whole group of young nobles of Sakya family;* his brother Devadatta, whom we shall discover to be the apostate and traitor in the band, was likewise among these Sakyas. The care of Buddha's person and the ordinary necessities of his daily life, were committed to Ânanda's hands: often, when Buddha had left all the other disciples behind, it is Ânanda alone who accompanies him, and the narrative of Buddha's last journeyings and of his farewell address gives, as we shall see, to Ânanda a *role*, which may well entitle him to be above all others known as the disciple "whom the Master loved." Another member of this select circle was Upâli, who had formerly served the noble Sakyas as a barber, and who entered Buddha's order at the same time with his masters. He is frequently mentioned in the sacred writings as the first propounder of the ecclesiastical law of the young Church; it is not improbable that he had a special share in the framing and the scholastic transmission of the old confessional liturgy, from which has sprung the whole ecclesiastical literature of Buddhism. Buddha's own son, Râhula, whom he had begotten before leaving his father's roof, also entered the order, and is not unfrequently mentioned with the great disciples already named; a prominent part, however, he does not seem to have played in this band.

successor, the head of the Church after the Master's death. The notion of any head of the Church but Buddha himself is, as we shall see, foreign to Buddhism, independently of the fact that tradition could not have chosen a person more ill-adapted to give expression to this idea, than a disciple, who died before Buddha.

* One of the few chronological statements contained in the sacred texts states that this happened twenty-five years before Buddha's death ("Theragâthâ," fol. gai of the Phayre MS.).

The Judas Iscariot among Buddha's disciples—except that his machinations were unsuccessful—is, as narrated, Buddha's own cousin, Devadatta.* Stimulated by ambition he seems to have aimed at stepping into the place of Buddha, who had already grown old, and at getting the management of the community into his own hands. When Buddha does not permit this, he attempts, in conjunction with Ajâtasattu, the son of king Bimbisâra, who is aiming at his father's throne, to put the Master out of the way. Their projects fail: miracles are related, by which the life of the Holy One is preserved: the defeated murderers are attacked by fear and trembling, when they come near Buddha; he speaks gently to them, and they are converted to the faith; the piece of rock which is intended to crush Buddha, is interrupted by two converging mountain peaks, so that it merely grazes Buddha's foot: the wild elephant, which is driven against Buddha in a narrow street, remains standing before him, paralyzed by the magic power of his "friendly thought," and then turns tamely back. At last Devadatta is said to have attempted to obtain the leadership of the Church in another way. He makes five propositions, of which we possess an account seemingly quite above suspicion.† On a number of points which affect monastic life, on which Buddha allowed a certain amount of freedom of action at the discretion of the individual member, Devadatta attempted to substitute a more rigorous ascetic praxis for these liberal

* The oldest form of the narratives regarding Devadatta is to be found in the seventh book of the "Cullavagga."

† "Cullavagga." It is possible, but naturally it cannot be demonstrated, that the history of these five propositions and the schism brought about by Devadatta are the only historical kernel of these narratives, and that the attempts at murder are an invention, which the orthodox Buddhist tried to tack on to the memory of the hated heretic.

regulations: for instance, he insisted that a monk should have his camping-place all his life long in the jungle, while Buddha permitted him to live in the neighbourhood of towns and villages, and was himself accustomed to live there; a monk was, furthermore, to live only on the contributions which he collected on his begging excursions, and was not to accept any invitations to dine with the pious laity; he was to dress himself only in clothes made up of gathered rags; and more of the like. Whoever acted otherwise, would be punished with expulsion from the community. Devadatta proposed these rules as the fundamental principles of a true and rigid spiritual life, in opposition to Buddha's arrangements as a lax concession to human frailties, and he tried to draw off to himself the monks around Buddha: if we may believe tradition, with a transient success, which then turned into total discomfiture. Devadatta is said to have come to a deplorable end.*

These are the most prominent figures in the band of Buddha's disciples; but disciples in deed and in truth those alone are who give up all that is earthly to, as the formula puts it, "walk in holiness, to put an end to all suffering:" monks and nuns, with the Indian designations, "bhikkhu" (beggar, *m.*) and "bhikkhunî" (beggar, *f.*). But, as in the history of Jesus, Lazarus and Nicodemus, Mary and Martha, stand side by side with Peter and John, so Buddhism also, side by side with the male and female mendicants recognize male and female votaries (upâsaka, *m.*; upâsika, *f.*) of Buddha and his law, believers, who honour Buddha as the holy preacher of deliverance and his

* According to the later wide-spread version of the narrative, the jaws of hell opened and swallowed him alive; the narrative of the "Cullavagga," as a matter of course, represents him going to hell, but says nothing of this departure to hell in living form.

word as the word of truth, but who remain in their worldly position, in wedlock, in the possession of their property, and make themselves useful to the Church, as far as they can, by gifts and charities of every kind. Yet the monks alone, not the lay-adherents, are exclusively members of the Church.*

The formation of this wider circle of worldly believers has been regarded as an inconsistent relaxation of original Buddhism, as a concession on the part of clear and rigorous thought to practicability and the weakness of human nature. It has also been supposed that in the oldest texts the distinction to be found is only between professed believers, *i.e.*, monks, and non-believers, *i.e.*, the laity, but not that of believing monks and believing laity. This is wholly erroneous. The oldest traditions which we possess speak of the laity, who

* A close examination of the relations between the monks proper and lay-associates must obviously be reserved for the sketch of "Church Life" (part iii). It will suffice in this place to point out that the idea of lay-members (upâsaka) in Buddhist Church-law cannot be taken in the same sense as a technical term as that of monks (bhikkhu): in the latter idea there is involved a definite *de jure* relationship, in the former the relationship is rather *de facto* than inherently *de jure*. For anyone to become a bhikkhu a special procedure is necessary on the part of the Church to complete the fact; the case of a person who desires to be considered an upâsaka expresses this, of course, and the texts have in this case also, as for everything that occurs with frequency, a definite formula ("I take, sire, my refuge with the Exalted One, and with the Doctrine, and with the Order of the disciples; may the Exalted One accept me as his votary [upâsaka] from this day forward through my life, me who have taken refuge with him"), but no special procedure follows, no recognition of the upâsaka as such on the part of the Church. Furthermore there were no ties which prohibited the Buddhist upâsaka from being at the same time the upâsaka of another Church (cf. "Cullav.," v, 20, 3), so that it appears in every way impossible to identify the position of the upâsaka with anything we understand to be among the components of a Church.

profess to be friends and votaries of Buddha and the order, and the nature of the case compels us to attach credit to those traditions. There must in fact, since ever there were mendicant monks in India, have also been pious laymen, who gave something to these religious beggars, and there must also soon have grown up, whether with or without recognized forms and names, it is quite immaterial, a certain relationship between definite monks or monastic orders and a definite laity, who felt themselves bound to each other, the one class to receive spiritual instruction, the other to obtain the little that they needed for their maintenance. And more than a connection of this class, the relation which subsisted between Buddha's order and the lay-believers has not been.

Princes and nobles, Brahmans and merchants, we find among those who "took their refuge in Buddha, the Law, and the Order," *i.e.*, who made their profession as lay-believers; the wealthy and the aristocrat, it seems, here also exceeded the poor; to reach the humble and wretched, the sorrowing, who endured yet another sorrow than the great universal sorrow of inpermanence, was not the province of Buddhism.

Prominent among the "adherents" stand the two royal friends of Buddha, Bimbisâra, the ruler of Magadha, and Pasenadi, the ruler of Kosala, both approximately of the same age as Buddha, and throughout their lives true protectors of his Church. Then comes Jîvaka, the renowned physician-in-ordinary to Bimbisâra,* who was appointed by the king to undertake medical attendance, not on him and his women only, but also on Buddha and Buddha's order; next, the merchant Anâthapindika, who had presented to the order the garden of Jetavana, Buddha's favourite place of resort. In all important

* The story of Jîvaka and the wonderful cures which he effects is related in the Eighth Book of the "Mahâvagga."

places which Buddha touched in the course of his wanderings, he found bands of such lay-believers, who went out to meet him, arranged for assemblies, in which Buddha spoke, who gave him and his companions their meals, who placed their residences and gardens at their disposal, or made them over to the order as Church property. If he went wandering about with hundreds of his disciples, pious votaries were sure to accompany him on his journey with carts and waggons, and they brought necessaries of life, salt, and oil with them, for each in his turn to prepare the wanderer a meal, and crowds of needy folk followed in their train to snatch the remains of these provisions.

Women.

Buddha and his disciples did not and could not fail to come into contact with women: every begging excursion,* every repast at the house of a lay-member, at which the female members of the household appeared with the master of the house and listened after the repast to spiritual instruction, necessarily involved such meetings. The seclusion of women from the outer world, which later custom has enjoined, was quite unheard of in ancient India; women took their share in the intellectual life of the people, and the most delicate and tenderest of the epic poems of the Indians show us how well they could understand and appreciate true womanhood.

But was it possible for a mind like Buddha, who in the severe determination of renunciation had torn himself away from all

* It was, as a rule, women who, in the houses of the laity, answered the monks who went on begging excursions, and handed them food into their bowls.—*Cullavagga*, viii, 5, 2.

that is attractive and lovely in this world, was he given the faculty to understand and to value woman's nature? And were those ideals, which evoked the exertions of Buddha's disciples, calculated in their impersonal transcendentalism, to kindle and satisfy women's hearts, to be even realized in their rigorous and stern consequences by womanly feeling?

Women are to the Buddhist of all the snares which the tempter has spread for men, the most dangerous; in women are embodied all the powers of infatuation, which bind the mind of the world. The ancient story books of the Buddhists are full of narratives and illustrations of the incorrigible artifice of women. "Unfathomably deep, like a fish's course in the water," the moral of one such history runs, "is the character of women, robbers with many artifices, with whom truth is hard to find, to whom a lie is like the truth and the truth like a lie."—"Master," Buddha is asked by Ânanda, "how shall we behave before women?"—"You should shun their gaze, Ânanda."—"But if we do see them, master, what then are we to do?"—"Not speak to them, Ânanda."—"But if we do speak to them, master, what then?"—"Then you must watch over yourselves, Ânanda."

We are told, and some trustworthy memory may possibly be at the bottom of this tradition, that for a long time only men were permitted to be received into Buddha's order, and that it was only with grave misgiving that Buddha yielded to the pressure of his foster-mother, Mahâpajâpatî, to receive women also as his disciples.* "As in a field of rice, Ânanda,

* "Cullavagga," x, 1. Agreeably to this, nuns do not appear as disciples in the narratives of Buddha's first experiences as a teacher.—The confessional formulary, "Pâtimokkha," notably one of the oldest literary monuments of Buddhism, mentions the nuns at every step, and king Asoka also remembers them in the Edict of Bairât.

which is in full vigour, the disease breaks out which is called mildew,—then the vigour of that field of rice continues no longer,—so also, Ânanda, if women be admitted in a doctrine and to an order to renounce the world and go into homelessness, holy living does not last long.—If, Ânanda, in the doctrine and the order, which the Perfect One has founded, it were not conceded to women to go out from their homes into homelessness, holy living would remain preserved, Ânanda, for a long time; the pure doctrine would abide for a thousand years. But now, Ânanda, that, in the doctrine and order, which the Perfect One has founded, women renounce the world and go into homelessness, under these circumstances, Ânanda, holy living will not be long preserved; only five hundred years, Ânanda, will the doctrine of the truth abide."

The narratives of the sacred writings, accordingly, unmistakably keep the female disciples, who have donned the garb of nuns, at a certain distance from the master, both in spiritual offices and in daily life. Buddhism has not had a Mary of Bethany. Buddha announces the rules, which he lays down for the order of nuns, to the monks and merely causes them to reach the nuns through them: and these regulations keep the nuns as regards the monks in perfectly submissive subjection: throughout they are treated merely as a tolerated, and reluctantly tolerated, element in the Church. Not one of the female disciples is near the master when he is dying, and it is made a matter of reproach to Ânanda, that he has granted access to Buddha's corpse to women, whose tears bedewed the corpse. "O Kriton, let some one lead this woman home," says Socrates, when Xanthippe appears in his prison to take a last farewell of him.

Thus, between the spirit, which animated Buddha and

Buddha's disciples, and that which woman's nature is and gives and seeks, there was a fundamental difference, which could not be reconciled. But instead we find the women of India all the more zealously engaged as fellow-labourers through charity, assistance, and service, in those practical spheres which the young Church opened up for religious usefulness. The stupendous munificence, which met the Buddhist order at every step, proceeded in great measure, perhaps in the greatest measure, from women.

In the sacred texts the type of a female votary of Buddha, as she ought to be, with her indefatigable zeal as a giver and as a helper, is the honourable matron Visâkhâ. She is a rich citizen commoner at Sâvatthi, the chief town of Kosala, the mother of many blooming children, the grandmother of countless grandchildren. Every one invites Visâkhâ to sacrificial ceremonies and banquets, and has the dishes offered to her first; a guest like her brings luck to the house. It is Visâkhâ, who is represented to have made the first liberal preparations on a large scale to provide for Buddha's disciples who came to Sâvatthi, the chief necessaries of life. I here insert the narrative in point;* it gives at once an intelligible picture of what people in the young brotherhood thought as to giving and receiving and as to which of the two is the more blessed: the only benefactor, who must be thanked, is not he who gives anything to Buddha and his order, but Buddha who accepts the gift and thereby puts the giver in the position to practice the virtue of charity and to become partaker of that reward, which is promised to this virtue.

Buddha is one day dining with his disciples at Visâkhâ's.

* "Mahâvagga," viii, 15.

After dinner Visâkhâ approaches him and says: "Eight requests, sire, I make of the Exalted One"—"The Perfect, Visâkhâ, are too exalted to be able to grant every wish."—"What is allowable, sire, and what is unblamable."—"Then speak, Visâkhâ."

"I desire as long as I live, sire, to give the brotherhood clothes for the rainy season, to give food to stranger monks who arrive here, to give food to monks who are passing through, to give food to sick brethren, to give food to the attendants on the sick, to give medicine to the sick, to distribute a daily dole of cooked rice, to give bathing dresses to the sisterhood of nuns."

"What object hast thou in view, Visâkhâ, that thou approachest the Perfect One with these eight wishes?"

(Visâkhâ now explains her several wishes. So she says:)

"A monk, O sire, who comes from foreign parts, does not know the streets and lanes and he goes about weary to collect alms. When he has partaken of the food which I shall provide for the monks who arrive, he may then, when he has inquired the ways and the streets, go out refreshed to collect alms. This end, O sire, I have in view: therefore I desire as long as I live to give food to monks when they arrive.—And again, sire, a monk who is travelling through will, if he has to seek for food for himself, fall behind his caravan, or will arrive late when he intends to rest, and he will walk on his journey wearily. If he has partaken of the food which I shall have provided for monks who are passing through, he will not fall behind his caravan, and he will arrive in proper time at the place where he intends to rest, and he will walk on his journey refreshed. This object I have in view, sire; therefore I desire, as long as I live, to give food to the monks who are passing through.—It has happened, sire, that nuns were bathing naked together in the river Aciravatî (Rapti) at the same bathing place with prostitutes. The prostitutes, sire, mocked the nuns, saying: 'Most respected ones, what do you need of your holy life, as long as you are young? Is it not proper to gratify desire? When you are old you may begin a holy life, so both will be yours, this life and that which is to come.' When the nuns, sire, were thus mocked by the prostitutes, they were put out of temper. Improper, sire, is nakedness for a woman, obscene and objectionable. This, sire, I consider; therefore I desire, as long as I live, to provide bathing-dresses for the sisterhood of nuns."

And Buddha says: "Good, Visâkhâ! thou doest well, that thou, seeking this reward, askest the Perfect One for these eight wishes. I grant thee these eight wishes, Visâkhâ."

Then the Holy One praised Visâkhâ, the mother of Migâra, in these words:

"Who gives food and drink with generous readiness,
The follower of the Holy One, rich in virtues,
Who, without grudging, gives gifts for the reward of heaven,
Who puts an end to pain, is ever intent on bringing joy,
Obtains the reward of a heavenly life.
She walks the shining, commendable path,
Free from pain, she joyfully reaps for a very long period
The reward of good deeds in the happy realm of heaven above."

Pictures like this of Visâkhâ, benefactresses of the Church, with their inexhaustible religious zeal, and their not less inexhaustible resources of money, are certainly, if anything ever was, drawn from the life of India in those days: they cannot be left out of sight, if we desire to get an idea of the actors who made the oldest Buddhist community what it was.

Buddha's Opponents.

Now that we have made the acquaintance of disciples and friends, our next inquiry is about the enemies and about the battles in which the new gospel had to prove its strength. If we might believe the Buddhist texts on this subject, Buddha's career was nothing but one great uninterrupted victorious march. Wherever he comes, the masses, it is told us time after time, flock to him. The other teachers are deserted; they are silent if he "raises his lion voice in the assemblies." Whoever hears his discourse, is converted.

This picture certainly does not wholly correspond with the truth, and we can, on some points at least, learn the actual facts tolerably well.

Above all it must be borne in mind that Buddha did not find himself like other reformers face to face with a great, united power, capable of resistance, and determined to resist, in which was embodied the old which he attacked and desired to replace by the new.

People are accustomed to speak of Buddhism as opposed to Brahmanism, somewhat in the way that it is allowable to speak of Lutheranism as an opponent of the papacy. But if they mean, as they might be inclined from this parallel to do, to picture to themselves a kind of Brahmanical Church, which is assailed by Buddha, which opposed its resistance to its operations like the resistance of the party in possession to an upstart, they are mistaken. Buddha did not find himself in the presence of a Brahmanical hierarchy, embracing the whole people, overshading the whole popular life. In the eastern districts religious movement, allowing itself free play, had ramified in many separate directions: sects upon sects exist side by side, at peace or at war as circumstances determined. The champions of the Veda, of Brahmanism, are really not more than one among many parties, and, indeed, to all appearance, by no means an especially powerful one. They wanted altogether compact organization; least of all did they, at any rate in the territories in which Buddha's work was prosecuted, represent a state-Church or had they power to enforce their commands by the assistance of worldly power. Their personal prestige was by no means undisputed there. From the great Brahman, who as an officer of high rank oppressed the people in the king's name and then deceived the king in turn, down to the small clerics, who, if invited to dine, made themselves disagreeably conspicuous by their behaviour at table, their personal appearance and manner of life provoked criticism, and men did not withhold that criticism. Long since a Samana (an ascetic) had come to be not a hair lighter in popular estimation than a Brahman. The Veda, the great patent of nobility of the Brahman class could not possibly give them a claim to power and popularity, such even as that the Pharisees had in the Mosaic law. Who among the people cared for the Veda, for the abstruse theories of sacrifice, the language of which no one understood, or for the ancient hymns, the language of which was still less understood, the hymns to forgotten deities, the heirlooms of grammarians and antiquaries? The propitiatory sacrifice with its plain external conception of guilt and purification, behind which the greedy exaction of a priestcraft lay concealed, must have kept alive in earnest and clear thinking natures, ill-will towards this priesthood.

Thus Brahmanism was not to Buddha an enemy whose conquest he would have been unable to effect. He may often have found the local influence of respected Brahmans an obstacle in his path,* but against this a hundred other

* The insignificant part which the western portions of Hindostan (the countries of the Kuru-Pancâlâ, and so forth) play in the narration of

Brahmans stood by him as his disciples or had declared for him as lay members.* Here no struggle on a large scale has taken place. The Brahmans had not the weapons of the world without at their disposal in such a warfare, and where the arbitrament was of intellectual weapons, they were sure to lose.

Buddha discredited the sacrificial system; he censured with bitter irony the knowledge of Vedic scribes as sheer folly, if not as shameless swindle; Brahmanical pride of caste was not more gently handled. He who repeats the lays and sayings of the poetic sages of antiquity and then fancies himself a sage, is like a plebeian or a slave, who should mount up to the place from which a king has addressed his retinue, and speak the same words and then fancy himself also a king.† The pupil believes what the teacher has believed, the teacher what he has received from the teachers before him. "Like a chain of blind men, I take it, is the discourse of the Brahmans: he who is in front sees nothing, he who is in the middle sees nothing, he who is behind sees nothing, what then? Is not, if this be so, the faith of the Brahmans vain?" ‡

The classical expression of the views of the old Buddhist

Buddha's wanderings arises not only from their remoteness, but also in a not less degrees from the more powerful position which the Brahmans occupied there, in the old home of the Vedic faith. When the law of Manu (9, 225) gives authority for expelling all heretical people from the state, there is in this a claim of Brahmanism which a code framed in the east could scarcely have dared to advance.

* It is worthy of observation that the usage of the Buddhist texts in no way connects with the word "Brahman" the notion of an enemy to the cause of Buddha, in the way that in the New Testament Pharisees and Scribes appear as the standing enemies of Jesus.

† Sic Ambaṭṭasutta (Dîgha-Nikâya).

‡ Cankîsuttanta (Majjhima N.).

Church, and, we may say, of Buddha, regarding the value of the Vedic sacrificial cult, is contained in a conversation of Buddha with a Brahman of position, who had asked Buddha about the essentials of a proper sacrifice.*

Buddha then narrates the story of a powerful and successful king of bygone days, who, after splendid victories and the conquest of the whole earth, formed the resolution of making a great offering to the gods. He summoned his family priest and asked his instructions, as to how he should set about his project. The priest admonishes him before offering a sacrifice, to establish first of all peace, prosperity, and security in his kingdom. Not until all injustices in the land are repaired, does he proceed to sacrifice. And at his sacrifice no life of sentient creature is taken; no cattle and sheep are killed; no trees are hewn down; no grass is cut. The servants of the king perform their work in connection with the sacrifice, not under pressure and in tears, in fear of the overseer's verge; each works willingly, as his own inclination prompts him. Libations of milk, oil, and honey are offered, and thus the king's sacrifice is performed. But there is, Buddha goes on to say, yet another offering, easier to perform than that, and yet higher and more blessed: where men make gifts to pious monks, where men build dwelling-places for Buddha and his order. And there is yet a higher offering: where a man with believing heart takes his refuge with Buddha, with the Doctrine, with the Order, when a man robs no being of its life, when a man puts far from him lying and deceit. And there is yet a higher offering: where a man separates as a monk from joy and sorrow and sinks himself in holy repose. But the highest offering, which a man can bring, and the highest blessing of

* Kûṭadantasutta of the Dîgha-Nikâya.

which he can be made participator, is, when he obtains deliverance and gains this knowledge: I shall not again return to this world. This is the highest perfection of all offering.

Thus speaks Buddha; the Brahman hears his discourse believingly, and says: "I take my refuge with Buddha, with the Doctrine and with the Order." He had himself intended to perform a great sacrifice, and had hundreds of animals ready for it. "I let them loose and set them free," he says, "let them enjoy green grass, let them drink cool water, let the cool wind fan them."

The expressions which we here find need no commentary to clearly elicit from them the attitude of the Buddhists towards the ancient cult. We do not hear how the Brahmans on their part fortified their position, what procedure they adopted against the new faith; but, if we possessed Brahmanical sketches of Buddha's appearance, our conviction would hardly be thereby destroyed, that from the very beginning the intrinsic superiority as well as the external advantage in this struggle was on the side of Buddha's disciples.

Buddha found in the rival ascetic leaders and their monastic orders more subtle and dangerous opponents than in the champions of the ancient faith. The spirit which animated many of these communities was allied to the spirit on which Buddha's own work was based. If we read the sacred books of the Jainas, it seems as if we heard Buddhists speaking.

We have no quite reliable opinion as to the terms upon which the monks of the rival communities mixed with each other. Openly expressed enmity appears to have not always prevailed; it was not unusual for members to visit each other in their hermitages, to exchange civilities, to speak to each other coolly and temperately on dogmatic subjects. That there was notwithstanding an incessant play of intrigue in progress will be obvious; where the object in view was to deprive each other of the protection of influential personages no trouble was spared. King Asoka found occasion in his edicts to point out to the spiritual brotherhoods, that he is only doing an injury to his own faith who thinks to set it in a clear light by abusing the adherents of another faith. But whether Buddha himself and the disciples immediately round him descended from the heights of holy meekness, on which the orthodox tradition enthrones them, to this religious scramble, is a point on which we are forbidden to hazard a conjecture.

What more than anything else distinguished Buddha from the most of his rivals was his dissentient attitude towards the self-mortifications, in which they saw the path to deliverance.* We saw how, according to tradition, Buddha himself in the period of search through which he passed when a young man, had endured self-mortifications in their most rigorous severity, and had found out their fruitlessness in his own case. What drives earthly thoughts out of the soul is not fasting and bodily agony, but self-culture, above all the struggle for knowledge, and for this struggle man derives the power only from an external life, which is far removed alike from luxury and from privation, and still more from self-inflicted pain. In

* I take the following passages from one of the sacred texts of the Nigganthа- or Jaina-sect, founded by Buddha's contemporary Nâtaputta: "By day motionless as a statue, the countenance turned to the sun, permitting himself to burn on a place exposed to the sun's rays, by night cowering, unclothed . . . by this conspicuous, great, intense, prominent, precious, efficacious, rich, promising, noble, exalted, high, supreme, conspicuous, very potent exercise of penance he appeared very debilitated . . . with penance richly covered, but impoverished in flesh and blood like a fire covered over with heaps of ashes, shining brilliantly through penance, through radiance, in nobleness of the radiance of penance, there he stands."

the sermon at Benares, in which tradition has undertaken to draw up something like a programme of Buddha's operations,* polemic directed against those errors of gloomy ascetics is not absent; the way which leads to deliverance keeps itself as far from all self-mortification as it steers clear on the other side of earthly pleasure; the one as well as the other is there termed unworthy and vain. The true spiritual life is once compared to a lute, the strings of which must not be too loose nor stretched too tensely, if it is to give a correct sound. The balance of the faculties, the internal harmony, is that which Buddha commands his followers to aim at securing.

So far as moral living can maintain a healthy development on the ground and within the limits to which Indian monasticism is once for all by its nature confined, so far we must claim for Buddha's work the merit of such inherent soundness. He has seen through the enveloping husks which conceal the kernel of the ethical more clearly than his contemporaries, and has bequeathed to the community of his followers this knowledge of the subject, the clear rejection of everything which is foreign thereto. It may be chance that has given his doctrine the victory over the doctrines of his rival contemporaries centuries after the deaths of all; but possibly the more the darkness which covers these centuries for us is dissipated, this game of chance may the more resemble the operation of a law of necessity.

Buddha's Method of Teaching.

Our task is now to give some idea of the form of Buddha's teaching;—we reserve the attempt to unfold its purport for the following Part. Buddha's whole work was carried on by

* See above p. 127.

oral communication; written he has not. Writing itself was in all probability not unknown in his day, but certainly book-writing was unheard of. Brief written communications, brief written notifications, appear to have been common in India even at that time: books were not written, but learned by rote and taught from memory. Those extensive treatises, such as were addressed by the apostles in the form of letters to the early Christian Churches, and which cast so rich a light on the history of those Churches and circles of thought, are wholly wanting in Buddhist literature.

Buddha spoke, not Sanscrit, but, like every one around him,* the popular idiom of eastern Hindostan. We can by inscriptions and the analogies of a closely allied, probably South Indian popular dialect, the Pâli, obtain an adequate picture of this dialect: a soft and agreeably-sounding language, which is distinguished from the Sanscrit by the same smoothing down of the conjoined consonants, the same tendency to vocalic terminations, which gives the Italian its character as opposed to the Latin language. People said *mutte* for *muktas* ("free"), *vijju* for *vidyut* ("the lightning"), as the Italian says *fatti* for *facti*, *ama* for *amat*. The syntax was simple and not very well suited to express fine and sharp shades of dialectic.

* The Brahmans also of this eastern land spoke undoubtedly in their daily intercourse the popular dialect; had the Sanscrit been here, as we find it later in the dramas, the language of the upper classes, some trace of this circumstance must have shown itself in the sacred Pâli texts. But, as far as I know, there is no reference to be found in them (except, perhaps, at "Cullavagga," v, 33) to the Sanscrit, which to all appearances was not, setting aside the Brahman schools, known in wider circles. And this is not at all difficult to account for, as the Sanscrit belongs originally to the western parts of Hindostan; its universal employment as the language of the educated classes through all India, it has, as also the inscriptions teach us, first acquired at a much later period.

In the early Church, moreover, no special importance was attached to the dialect in which the doctrine of deliverance had been first preached. Buddha's words are confined to no language. "I direct, O disciples," tradition* makes him say, "that each individual learn the words of Buddha in his own tongue."

Anyone who reads the lectures which the sacred texts put in Buddha's mouth, can scarcely refrain from asking whether the form, in which he himself taught his doctrine, can possibly have resembled these self-same panoramas of abstract and often abstruse structures with their endless repetitions piled high upon each other. Should we not like to see in the picture of those early times something else beside merely a living spirit operating with the fresh vigour of youth in the circle of master and pupils, and should we not for that reason be inclined to eliminate from this picture all that imparts to it an air of tension and fiction? And at the same time is it natural, when we endeavour to obtain a representation of Buddha's teaching and preaching, for us to resort to another source beside the tradition of the Buddhist Church, that is, when thought, consciously or unconsciously, recurs to the teaching of Jesus? Those homely sentences with their totally unstudied external setting and their deep internal wealth, seem to wear that very form, from which we may infer that it, or some similar form, may have accompanied the dissemination of the Buddhist doctrine, as long as the spirit of the early ages survived.

Reflections such as these are not easy to repress, but historical treatment, before committing itself to them, will do well not to leave untested the ground and foundation on which they rest.

It cannot be forgotten that the fundamental differences of

* "Cullavagga," v, 33, 1.

the thoughts and the dispositions with which the early Christian and early Buddhist communities dealt, were such that these differences must also find expression in the method of religious instruction.

Where the pure sentiment of the simple, believing heart is supreme, where there are children to whom the Father in heaven has given His kingdom to possess, there the brief and homely language, which comes from the depth of a pure heart, may touch the proper chords more effectually than the highly organized development of a system of ideas. But the mode of thinking of the world in which Buddha lived, moves in other paths: for it all weal and woe, depend on knowledge and ignorance; ignorance is the ultimate root of all evil, and the sole power, which can strike at the root of this evil, is knowledge. Deliverance is, therefore, above all, knowledge;* and the preaching of deliverance can be nothing less or more than the exposition of this knowledge, which means the unfolding of a series of abstract notions and abstract propositions.

* This mode of viewing things is not capable of a more significant and at the same time *naïve* expression than that which it has found in the narrative of the Singhalese Church records of the first conversation of Mahinda, the converter of Ceylon, with the king Devânampiya Tissa (circ. 250 B.C.). The Thera (elder) proceeds to a formal examination of the king in logic, "to find out: does the king possess a clear understanding?" There is a mango tree near. The Thera asks: "What is this tree called, O great king?" "It is called mango, sire." "Are there, O great king, beside this mango tree yet other mango trees or are there not?" "There are, sire, many other mango trees." "Are there, O great king, beside this mango tree and those mango trees still other trees?" "There are, sire; but they are not mango trees." "Are there beside those other mango trees and non-mango trees yet another tree?" "Yes, sire, this mango tree here." "Well done, great king, thou art clever." The Thera proceeds to apply another test which the

If, therefore, we do not wish, out of deference to a universal feeling of probability, which has based its standard on a ground other than Indian, to destroy the singularity and continuity of Indian developments, we must be on our guard against making a fanciful picture of Buddha, as if he were one of those aboriginal natures living only amid the concrete and tangible, to whom the spirit is everything, the letter nothing. His thought drew its nourishment from the long course of metaphysical speculation which preceded him; he shares the delight in the metaphysical which is inherent in the Indian blood, the taste for abstraction, classification, and construction, and viewing him from this aspect, we should compare him not so much to the founder of Christianity, as to its theological champions, something such as Origen was. Thus we cannot refuse credence to the tradition which, in however many forms it makes Buddha speak, yet represents the particular weight of his teaching as lying in great lectures, beside which dialogue and parable, fable and sententious sayings, appear to be something merely adventitious or marginal.

The Vedic literature gives us a picture of the forensic style of dogmatic teaching and debate, which had established itself long before Buddha's time in the Brahmanical schools and on the sacrificial ground. The word which is to convey holy things, needs a fitting garb: the setting of spiritual discourse bears a solemn, sacred character, the stateliness of which soon changes to ponderous gravity. The personal bearing of the

king stands as successfully. "Beside thy relatives and the non-relatives, is there any other man, O great king?" "Myself, sire." "Well done, great king, a man is neither relative nor non-relative to himself." "Thereupon the Elder said," the narrative proceeds, "that the king is clever and that he will be able to understand the doctrine, and he propounded to him the parable of the elephant's foot."—*Buddhaghosa, in the Vinaya Pitaka*, vol. iii, p. 324.

speaker also is not a matter of indifference: a strict ceremonial regulates his appearance and his movements. Thus men were wont to think in Brahman circles long before Buddha's time, thus they were wont to think in the Buddhist Church at the time in which our texts were compiled. Are we to suppose that Buddha and the circles around him, standing in the middle between this epoch and that, felt differently from both? However widely form, tone, and movement in the didactic lectures, which we find in the sacred texts, may differ from what appears to us the natural and necessary manner of living, spoken language, anyone who knows how to apply different standards to things differing in their conditions, will find it not impossible to believe that the solemnly earnest style of address of Buddha was much more nearly allied to the type of the addresses preserved to us by tradition, than to that which our feeling of the natural and the probable might be tempted to substitute for it.

The periods of these addresses in their motionless and rigid uniformity, on which no lights and shadows fall, are an accurate picture of the world as it presented itself to the eye of that monastic fraternity, the grim world of origination and decease, which goes on like clockwork in an ever uniform course, and behind which rests the still deep of the Nirvâna. In the words of this ministry, there is heard no sound of working within, no voice of yearning, nothing which—passing from person to person with the power which the utterance of a superior man possesses, and with all the relentlessness which is inseparable from that power—may fasten on the hearers. No impassioned entreating of men to come to the faith, no bitterness for the unbelieving who remains afar off. In these addresses, one word, one sentence, lies beside another in stony stillness, whether it expresses the most trivial thing or the most important. As worlds of gods and worlds of men are, for the Buddhist consciousness, ruled by everlasting necessity, so also are the worlds of ideas and of verities: for these, too, there is one, and only one, necessary form of knowledge and expression, and the thinker does not make this form but he adopts what is ready to hand—as Buddha speaks, so countless Buddhas in countless ages of the world have spoken and will speak. Therefore, everything which resembles a free or arbitrary dealing of the mind with the material, must be absent from the diction of this ministration of salvation; every idea, every thought, has the same right to be heard in full and uncurtailed at the place which belongs to it, and thus those endless repetitions accumulate which Buddha's disciples were never tired of listening to anew, and always honouring afresh as the necessary garb of holy thought, as something which should be so and not otherwise. One might often fancy that at Buddha's time the human mind had not yet discovered the magic word which joins together the lengths of disconnected co-ordinates into one compact whole, the insignificant but powerful word "and." Hear how one of the most renowned discourses expresses the thought that all man's senses and the world, which they apprehend, are attacked and wasted by the sorrow-bringing powers of the earthly and the impermanent as by a flaming fire.*

Then said the Exalted One to the disciples: "Everything, O disciples, is in flames. And what Everything, O disciples, is in flames? The eye, O disciples, is in flames, the visible is in flames, the knowledge of the visible is in flames, the contact with the visible is in flames, the feeling which arises from contact with the visible, be it pleasure, be it pain, be it neither pleasure nor pain, this also is in flames. By what

* "Mahâvagga," i, 21.

fire is it kindled? By the fire of desire, by the fire of hate, by the fire of fascination, it is kindled; by birth, old age, death, pain, lamentation, sorrow, grief, despair, it is kindled: thus I say. The ear is in flames, the audible is in flames, the knowledge of the audible is in flames, the contact with the audible is in flames, the feeling which arises from contact with the audible, be it pleasure, be it pain, be it neither pleasure nor pain, this also is in flames. By what fire is it kindled? By the fire of desire, by the fire of hate, by the fire of fascination, it is kindled; by birth, old age, death, pain, lamentation, sorrow, grief, despair, it is kindled: thus I say. The sense of smell is in flames—and then follows for the third time the same series of propositions;—the tongue is in flames; the body is in flames; the mind is in flames;—each time the same detail follows unabridged." Then the address goes on:—

"Knowing this, O disciples, a wise, noble hearer of the word becomes wearied of the eye, he becomes wearied of the visible, he becomes wearied of the knowledge of the visible, he becomes wearied of contact with the visible, he becomes wearied of the feeling which arises from contact with the visible, be it pleasure, be it pain, be it neither pleasure nor pain. He becomes wearied of the ear,—and then follows one after the other the whole series of ideas as above." The address concludes:—

"While he becomes wearied thereof, he becomes free from desire; free from desire he becomes delivered; in the delivered arises the knowledge: I am delivered; re-birth is at an end, perfected is holiness, duty done; there is no more returning to this world; he knows this."

The address on the flames of the conflagration of the senses purports to have been delivered by Buddha to the thousand hermits of Uruvelâ,* when they had already confessed the faith and received initiation, when in them, as the texts are wont to express it, "the pure and moteless eye of the truth was awakened: whatever is subject to the law of origination, every such thing is also subject to the law of decease." But if the object be to bring the doctrine of suffering and of deliverance near to a novice, who is still far from the revelation of Buddha, the variations of the sacred writings assume a somewhat different form. As a specimen of their type, place may here be given to the narrative of the village-fathers of the eighty thousand villages of the Magadha kingdom, who were assembled round the king of Magadha, and at the end of their deliberations were sent by him to Buddha.†

"But when the king of Magadha, Seniya Bimbisâra, had instructed the eighty thousand village elders in the laws of the visible world, he dismissed them and said: Friends, ye have now been instructed by me in the rules of the visible universe; go now and approach him, the Exalted One; he, the Exalted One, will instruct you in the things of the hereafter." Then the eighty thousand village elders went to the mountain Gijjhakûta (vulture peak). At that time the venerable Sâgata was on duty with the Exalted One. The eighty thousand village elders went on to where the venerable Sâgata was; when they had come up to him, they said to the venerable Sâgata: "Here come eighty thousand village elders, sire, to see the Exalted One. Come, sire, vouchsafe to us to see the Exalted One." "Tarry here a while, my friends, that I may announce you to the Exalted One." Then vanished the venerable Sâgata from the steps (at the entrance to the monastery) in the presence of the eighty thousand village elders, and before their eyes rose up in the presence of

* *Vide* antea, p. 132.

† "Mahâvagga," v, 1.

the Exalted One and spoke to the Exalted One: "The eighty thousand village elders are come hither, sire, to see the Exalted One. Sire, let the Exalted One be pleased to do what he now thinks right for the occasion." "Then place a seat for me, Sâgata, in the shadow of the monastery." "Yes, sire," replied the venerable Sâgata to the Exalted One, took a stool, vanished before the face of the Exalted One, came up again before the face of the eighty thousand village elders and before their eyes on the steps, and prepared a seat in the shadow of the monastery. Then the Exalted One went out of the monastery and took a seat on the stool which had been set for him in the shadow of the monastery. Then the eighty thousand village elders approached to where the Exalted One was; when they had come up to him they bowed themselves before the Exalted One and sat down near him. But the eighty thousand village elders directed their thoughts to the venerable Sâgata alone, and therefore not to the Exalted One. Then the Exalted One knew in his mind the thoughts of the eighty thousand village elders, and said to the venerable Sâgata: "Come, Sâgata, show yet greater marvels of superhuman ability." "Yes, sire," the venerable Sâgata answered the Exalted One, rose up into the air, and walked on high in the atmosphere, stood, descended, sat down, emitted smoke and flames, and vanished. When the venerable Sâgata had exhibited in various ways, on high in the atmosphere, such marvels of superhuman power, he bowed his head at the feet of the Exalted One, and said to the Exalted One: "My master, sire, is the Exalted One; I am his disciple; my master, sire, is the Exalted One; I am his disciple." Thereupon thought the eighty thousand village elders: "truly this is glorious, truly it is wonderful: if the disciple is so exceedingly mighty and exceedingly powerful, what will the Master be!" and they directed their thoughts to the Exalted One alone and not to the venerable Sâgata. Then the Exalted One knew in his mind the thoughts of the eighty thousand village elders, and preached to them the word according to the law, as it is: the discourse on giving, the discourse on uprightness, the discourse on the heavens, the corruption, vanity, impurity of desires, the glory of being free from desire. When now the Exalted One perceived that their thoughts were prepared, susceptible, free from obstructions, elevated, and directed towards him, he preached to them what is pre-eminently the teaching of the Buddhas, suffering, the origin of suffering, the removal of suffering, the way to the removal of suffering. As a clean garment, from which all impurity is removed, wholly absorbs within itself the dye, so opened in these eighty thousand village elders, as they sat there, the pure moteless eye of the truth: whatever is subject to the law of origination, all such is subject to the law of decease. And discerning the doctrine, having pierced through to the doctrine, knowing the doctrine, sinking themselves in the doctrine, overcoming doubt, free from vacillation, having penetrated to knowledge, needing nothing else in their faith in the Master's doctrine, they spoke to the Exalted One thus: "Excellent, sire, excellent, sire; as a man, O sire, straightens that which is bowed down, or uncovers the hidden, or shows the way to one who has gone astray, or shows a light in the darkness, so that he who has eyes may be able to see the forms of things, even so has the Exalted One proclaimed the doctrine in manifold discourses. We, O sire, take our refuge with the Exalted One, and with the Doctrine and with the Order of his disciples: may the Exalted One receive us as his lay disciples, for from this day henceforth we have taken our refuge with him as long as our life endures."

This narrative of the visit of the elders to Buddha may be

taken as a typical one, the features of which reappear in the sacred texts on all similar occasions. Buddha does not speak at starting of the things which constitute the scope and kernel of his teaching, but he begins by admonishing to the practice of virtues in worldly vocations, to generosity, to rectitude in every earthly occupation: he speaks of the heavens with their rewards which await him who has led a life of earnest purpose here below. And as soon as he knows that his hearers are fitted to receive something deeper, he proceeds to speak to them of that which, as the texts say, "is pre-eminently the revelation of the Buddhas," the doctrines of suffering and deliverance. These are always the same subjects of Buddha's preaching, and we over and over again meet the same expressions of joy and gratitude on the part of the converted, then finally the formula with which they take their refuge as lay brothers or lay sisters in the ancient trinity of the Buddhist Church, the Buddha, the Doctrine, and the Order. Here and there there is inserted a story of some wonder which rises in no way above the level of quaint and tedious miracle. All these narratives are absolutely wanting in individuality; we seek in vain to gather something therefrom as to how Buddha penetrated and operated on the private, personal life of the individual among his disciples. Whenever we open our gospels, we find portrayed the most delicate and deepest traces of the work of Jesus, which, providing, consoling, healing, and building up, passes from man to man: very different from the picture which the Buddhist Church has preserved to us of its master's work; the living human, the personal hides itself behind the system, the formula; no one to seek out and to console the suffering and the sorrowing; it is only the sorrow of the whole universe of which we again and again hear.

Here and there the outward garb of such narratives is somewhat altered; instead of a sermon we find a dialogue; Buddha questions or is questioned. In the task of producing a life-like picture of such conversations as took place in Buddha's time, or in their own circles, the compilers of our sacred texts, who had not many things to go upon, but had nothing less than a dramatic vein, have certainly in their mode of treatment failed most signally. Those who converse with Buddha are good for nothing else but simply to say "yes," and to be eventually converted, if they have not yet been converted.* But any one who does not suffer himself to be

* An amusing illustration of the manner in which the sacred texts deal with the claims of character of the speakers and the other requirements of description by dramatic dialogue, is to be found in the history of Buddha's conversation with Anâthapindika's daughter-in-law (in the "Anguttara-Nikâya," Sattakanipâta). Buddha comes in his begging excursion to the house of his wealthiest and most liberal admirer, the great wholesale merchant Anâthapindika. He hears loud conversation and wrangling, and asks: "Why are the people screaming and crying in thy house? One would think fishermen had been robbed of their fish." And Anâthapindika pours out his grief to Buddha: a daughter-in-law of a rich family has come into his house, who will not listen to her husband and her parents-in-law, and declines to show due reverence to Buddha. Buddha says to her: "Come, Sujâtâ." She answers: "Yes, sire," and comes to Buddha. He says to her: "There are seven kinds of wives which a man may have, Sujâtâ. What seven are they? One resembles a murderess, another a robber, another a mistress, another a mother, another a sister, another a friend, another a servant. These Sujâtâ, are the seven kinds of wives which a man may have. Which kind art thou?" And Sujâtâ has forgotten all obstinacy and pride, and says deferentially: "Sire, I do not understand the full meaning of that which the Exalted One has stated in brief; therefore, sire, may the Exalted One so expound to me his doctrine, that I may be able to understand the full meaning of that which the Exalted One has stated briefly." "Hearken, then, Sujâtâ, and take it well to heart: I shall state it to thee."—"Yes, sire," said Sujâtâ. And Buddha describes to her then the seven kinds of women, from the worst who goes after other men, despises her husband, and tries

deterred by this want of living concrete reality from following up the logical train of these conversations, will here find more than one trace, though dim and unskilful, of the same maieutic method of dialectic, which history has properly denominated Socratic, after the name of the man who has practised it incomparably more perfectly, among a more brilliantly-gifted people—the same sifting of spiritual truths by argument from analogies which daily life supplies, the same rudiments of the inductive method.

Thus is related to us the conversation of Buddha with Sona,* a young man, who had imposed on himself an excess of ascetic observances, and now, when he becomes aware of the fruitlessness of his practice, is on the point of turning to the opposite extreme, and reverting to a life of enjoyment. Buddha says to this disciple: "How is it, Sona, were you able to play the lute before you left home?"—"Yes, sire."—"What do you think then, Sona, if the strings of your lute are too tightly strung, will the lute give out the proper tone and be fit to play?"—"It will not, sire."—"And what do you think, Sona, if the strings of your lute be strung too slack; will the lute then give out the proper tone and be fit to play?"—"It will not, sire."—"But how, Sona, if the strings of your lute be not strung too tight or too slack, if they have the proper degree of tension, will the lute then give out the proper sound and be fit to play?"—"Yes, sire."—"In the same way, Sona, energy too much strained tends to excessive

to take his life, up to the best who, like a servant, is always submissive to her husband's will, and bears without a murmur all he says and does. "These, Sujâtâ, are the seven kinds of wives which a man may have. What kind among these art thou?"—"From this day forward, sire, may the Exalted One esteem me one who is to her husband a wife who resembles a servant."

* "Mahâvagga," v, 1-15, seq.

zeal, and energy too much relaxed tends to apathy. Therefore, Sona, cultivate in yourself the mean of energy, and press on to the mean in your mental powers, and place this before you as your aim."

Another conversation,* carried on between Buddha and a Brahman, deals with the relation between the four castes and the claim to service and obedience which the Brahmans advance against all other castes, and each higher among other castes advances against the lower castes. Buddha couches his criticism in the form of a dialogue, with question and answer. "If anyone were to ask a Kshatriya (noble) as follows: 'To whom wouldst thou render service: to him with whom, if thou doest him service, thou wilt fare worse for thy service, not better; or to him with whom, if thou doest him service, thou wilt fare better for thy service, not worse?' The Kshatriya would, if he answers properly, answer thus: 'Him with whom, if I did him service, I should fare worse for my service, not better, him would I not serve; but him with whom, if I did him service, I should fare better for my service, not worse, to him would I render service.'" And then the induction goes on in its stiff consecutive course: "If anyone were to ask a Brahman as follows—if anyone were to ask a Vaiçya as follows—if anyone were to ask a Çûdra as follows." The answer is naturally every time the same, and the exposition eventually yields this result: "Where by the service which anyone renders to another, his faith increases, his virtue increases, his understanding increases, his knowledge increases, there, I say, it is that he should render him service."

Here and there, as in our gospels, parables alternate with doctrine and admonition: "I shall show you a parable," Buddha says, "by a parable many a wise man perceives the meaning of

* Phasukâri Suttanta (Majjhima Nikâya).

what is being said." The operations of man as well as the life of nature are the fields of observation, with which these similes for spiritual life and effort, for deliverance, and the company of the delivered, deal. Buddha's preaching of deliverance is compared to the work of the physician, who draws the poisoned arrow from a wound, and overcomes the power of the poison with remedial herbs. The company of disciples, the gathering of noble spirits, in whom all worldly differences of high and low cease, resembles the sea with its wonders, in the depths of which lie pearls and crystals, in which gigantic creatures have free play, into which the rivers flow, and lose their names, and make up the ocean, so many of them there are. As the lotus flower raises its head out of the water, unaffected by the water, so the Buddhas born in the world, rise above the world, unaffected by the impurity of the world. As the peasant ploughs his fields and sows the seed and irrigates, but has not the power to say: the grain shall swell to-day, to morrow it shall germinate, next day it shall ripen, but must wait till the proper time comes and brings growth and ripeness of his corn, so also it is with the disciple who seeks deliverance: he must regulate his course according to strict discipline, practise religious meditation, study diligently the doctrine of salvation, but he has not the power to say: to-day or to-morrow shall my spirit be delivered from every impure habit, but he must wait until his time comes for deliverance to be vouchsafed to him. For the tempter who tries to shut up against man the path of salvation and to lure him to false paths, and the deliverer, who leads him back to the right path, this simile is employed:* "As when, O disciples, in the forest, on a mountain slope, there lies a great tract of low land and water, where a great herd of deer lives,

* Dvedhâvitakka Sutta (Majjh. N.).

and there comes a man, who devises hurt, distress and danger for the deer; who covers over and shuts up the path which is safe, good, and pleasant to take, and opens up a false path, a swampy path, a marshy track. Thenceforward, O disciples, the great herd of deer incurs hurt and danger and diminishes. But now, O disciples, if a man comes, who devises prosperity, welfare, and safety for this great herd of deer: who clears and opens up the path which is safe, good and pleasant to take, and does away with the false path, and abolishes the swampy path, the marshy track. Thenceforth, O disciples, will the great herd of deer thrive, grow, and increase. I have spoken to you, O disciples, in a parable, to make known my meaning. But the meaning is this. The great lowland and the water, O disciples, are pleasures. The great herds of deer, O disciples, are living men. The man, O disciples, who devises hurt, distress, and ruin, is Mâra, the Evil One. The false path, O disciples, is the eight-fold false path, to wit: false faith, false resolve, false speech, false action, false living, false effort, false thought, false self-concentration. The swampy way, O disciples, is pleasure and desire. The swampy track is ignorance. The man, O disciples, who devises prosperity, welfare, salvation, is the Perfect One, the holy, supreme Buddha. The safe, good way, O disciples, in which it is well to walk, is the holy eight-fold path, to wit: right faith, right resolve, right speech, right action, right living, right effort, right thought, right self-concentration. Thus, O disciples, has the safe, good path, in which it is well to walk, been opened up by me; the false path has been done away, the swampy path, the swampy track has been abolished. Everything, O disciples, that a master, who seeks the salvation of his disciples, who pities them, must do out of pity for them, that have I done for you."

Such similes run through the discourse on sorrow and

deliverance. Through the measured formality of the monastic church-diction, we constantly feel the breath of intelligent sympathy with life and nature, that genuine human desire to observe this motley world, and see whether it cannot by its figurative language throw some light on the spirit world and its secrets.

From similes to fable and romance is not a long way; the Buddhist mendicant monks were sufficiently Indian to have an abundant share of the old Indian delight in romance. Sometimes the sacred writings make Buddha tell his disciples a fable of animals, sometimes a history of strange occurrences, and all kinds of human actions, thoughtful or amusing: "There were once two wise brothers," or "there was once at Benares a king, called Brahmadatta," the history of the banished king Long-grief, and his sagacious son Long-life, or the fable, how the partridge, the ape, and the elephant have learned to live together in virtue and harmony; at the end of every history came, as is fitting, a moral.*

But the most beautiful embellishments of Buddha's preaching are those poetical sentences in which all the most delicate powers of light and warmth, which dwell within the Buddhist mind, are concentrated as it were in a focus. Here we need not by any means see merely a poetic embellishment which the Church has attributed to its master's teaching; sentences of this kind, short improvisations, to which the pliant nature of

* Some of these stories—hardly all—are so applied that their leading hero is identified with Buddha in one of his previous existences, and the other personages who appear with persons in Buddha's society or in the circles of his opponents. Later on new stories, but always with the same points, were invented by the hundred, or even old legendary matter has been wrought up *in majorem Buddhæ gloriam*; these make up a particular book of the sacred writings, the collection of the Jâtaka (stories of earlier births), cf., however, also my note to Suttavibhanga, Pâcittiya, 2, 1.

the Çloka-metre readily adapted itself, may very well have been actually a feature of Buddha's mode of speech, and of that specially-gifted among his disciples.* These apothegms are so unlike the dry numbness of the prose lectures, that we may be tempted to ask whether they were really the same spirits which have composed the one and the other. We feel how that prose confined and bound up those who spoke in it; but when the domain of prose ceases, where men are expressing not dry, subtle systems of ideas, but the simple emotions, the sorrows and hopes of their own hearts, life is roused and the blood of life, poetry. Thoughtful feeling, clad in the grand and rich attire of Indian metaphor, looks out upon us, and the Çlokas with their gently measured rhythms, so peculiarly combining uniformity and diversity, flow up and down like the surging billows of the sea, on which the clear sky is reflected amid variegated, fragrant lotus flowers. The soul of this poesy, too, is nothing else but what the soul of the Buddhist faith itself is, the one thought, which rings out in sublime monotony from all these apothegms: Unhappy, impermanence, happy he who has the eternal. From this thought there pervades the proverbial wisdom of the Buddhist, that tone of deep, happy repose, of which that proud sentence says that the gods themselves envy it, that repose which looks down upon the struggling world, stoops to the most distressed and quietly extends to him the picture of absolute peace. For the elucida-

* Tradition allots specially the task of improvisation (paṭibhâna) among Buddha's disciples to Vangîsa ("Dîp.," iv, 4), who is the hero of one particular section in the holy texts, the Vangîsathera-Saṃyutta. There it is often said: this and that thought "dawned on Vangîsa" (paṭibhâti), and then he utters a verse in which he gives expression to the collateral circumstances, praises Buddha, and so on. He then says of these verses, they are not prepared beforehand (pubbe parivitakkitâ) but "they suddenly dawned on me" (ṭhânaso maṃ paṭibhanti).

tion of Buddhism nothing better could happen than that, at the very outset of Buddhist studies, there should be presented to the student by an auspicious hand the Dhammapada,* that most beautiful and richest of collections of proverbs, to which anyone who is determined to come to know Buddhism must over and over again return, and to which we shall often have to allude in our sketch of the Buddhist teaching.

* Here a few sayings of the Dhammapada (60, 153 seq. 383, 82) may find a fitting place; I have avoided attempting to reproduce the metrical form:

"Long is the night to him who keeps watch, long is the road to the weary, long is the wandering path of re-births for the foolish, who know not the word of truth."

"A path of many re-births have I vainly traversed, seeking the builder of the house (of corporeity); full of suffering is birth (recurring) over and over again. Now have I seen thee, O builder of the house; thou shalt not again build the house. Thy rafters are all broken, the battlements of the house are demolished. The soul, having escaped changeability, has attained the end of desire."

"Stem the current with might, banish from thee all desire, O Brahman; if thou hast sighted the end of the changeable, thou art a knower of the uncreated, O Brahman."

"A rest like that of the deep sea, calm and clear, the wise find, who hear the truth."

CHAPTER V.

Buddha's Death.

Buddha is said to have reached the age of eighty years; forty-four years of this term belong to his public career, to what his followers term his Buddhahood. The year of his death is one of the most firmly fixed dates in ancient Indian history; calculations, by which the sum of possible error is confined within tolerably narrow limits, give as a result, that he died not long before or not long after 480 B.C.

Regarding the last months of his life and his last great journey from Râjagaha to Kusinârâ, the place of his death, we possess a detailed account in a Sûtra of the sacred Pâli Canon.* The external features of this narrative bear for the most part, though perhaps not in every particular,† the stamp of trustworthy tradition; in the utterances and addresses of Buddha, most of which convey a clear or covert intimation of his approaching end, fancy has undoubtedly allowed itself freer range. A portion at any rate of the narrative may here be

* The "Mahâparinibbâna Sutta," by which the northern Buddhist versions of this narrative are rendered superfluous.

† It especially excites distrust, to find that the occurrences at Pâṭaliputta and the meeting with Ambapâli ("Childers' Ed.," p. 10 seq.) are narrated at another place in quite a different connection ("Mahâvagga," vi, 28 seq.).

reproduced, partly in *resumé*, and partly in a verbal translation.

From Râjagaha, the chief town in the Magadha territory, Buddha goes northward. He crosses the Ganges at the place where the new capital, Pâtaliputta (Παλίβοθρα), is then being built, the chief city of India in the following centuries. Buddha foretells the coming greatness of this town. Then he journeys on to the opulent and brilliant free-town Vesâlî. Near Vesâlî, in the village of Beluva, he dismissed the disciples who were with him, to pass in solitary retirement the three months at the damp period of the year, the last rainy season of his life. At Beluva he was attacked by a severe illness; violent pains seized him, he was near dying. He then bethought him of his disciples. "It becomes me not to enter into Nirvâna, without having addressed those who cared for me, without speaking to the community of my followers. I shall conquer this illness by my power, and hold life fast within me." Then the Exalted One subdued the sickness by his power and held the life fast within him. And the illness of the Exalted One vanished. And the Exalted One recovered from his sickness and soon after, when he had recovered from his sickness, he went out of the house and sat down in the shade of the house, on the seat which was prepared for him. Thereupon the venerable Ânanda went to the Exalted One: when he was near him and had made his salutations to the Exalted One, he sat down beside him; sitting by his side, the worthy Ânanda spake to the Exalted One thus: "Sire, I see that the Exalted One is well; I see, sire, that the Exalted One is better. All nerve had left me, sire; I was faint; my senses failed me because of the sickness of the Exalted One. But still I had one consolation, sire: the Exalted One will not enter Nirvâna, until he has declared his purpose concerning the body of his followers." "What need hath the body of my followers of me now, Ânanda? I have declared the Doctrine, Ânanda, and I have made no distinction between within and without; the Perfect One has not, Ânanda, been a forgetful teacher of the Doctrine. He, Ânanda, who says: I will rule over the Church, or let the Church be subject to me, he, O Ânanda, might declare his will in the Church. The Perfect One, however, O Ânanda, does not say: I will rule over the Church, or let the Church be subject to me. What shall the Perfect One declare, Ânanda, to be his purpose regarding the Church? I am now frail, Ânanda, I am aged, I am an old man, who has finished his pilgrimage and reached old age; eighty years old am I. . . . . Be ye to yourselves, Ânanda, your own light, your own refuge; seek no other refuge. Let the truth be your light and your refuge, seek no other refuge . . . . . whosoever now, Ânanda, or after my departure shall be his own light, his own refuge, and shall seek no other refuge, whosoever taketh the truth as his light and his refuge and shall seek no other refuge, such will henceforth Ânanda, be my true disciples, who walk in the right path."

Buddha now goes on to Vesâlî and makes his usual begging excursion through the town. Here Mâra comes to him and calls on him to enter at once into Nirvâna. Buddha repels him, saying, "give thyself no trouble on that score, thou evil one. After a short time the Nirvâna of the Perfect One will be accomplished; three months hence will the Perfect One enter Nirvâna." And Buddha dismisses the volition which atttached life to himself: earthquakes and thunderings accompany his resolution to enter into Nirvâna.

In the evening Buddha sends for all the monks, who are tarrying in the neighbourhood of Vesâlî, and he seats himself in the midst of them and he addresses them:—

"Learn ye then fully, O my disciples, that knowledge which

I have attained and have declared unto you, and walk ye in it, practice and increase, in order that this path of holiness may last and long endure, for the blessing of many people, for the joy of many people, to the relief of the world, to the welfare, the blessing, the joy of gods and men. And what, O disciples, is the knowledge which I have attained and have declared unto you, which you are to learn fully, walk in it, practice and increase, in order that this path of holiness may last and long endure, for the blessing of many people, for the joy of many people, to the relief of the world, to the welfare, the blessing, the joy of gods and men? It is the four-fold vigilance, the four-fold right effort, the four-fold holy strength, the five organs, the five powers, the seven members of knowledge, the sacred eight-fold path. This, O disciples, is the knowledge which I have attained, and have declared unto you," etc.

And the Exalted One spake further to the monks: "Hearken, ye monks, I say unto you: all earthly things are transitory; strive on without ceasing. In a short time the Perfect One will attain Nirvâna; three months hence will the Perfect One enter Nirvâna."

Thus spake the Exalted One: when the Perfect One had thus said, the Master further spake as follows:—

"My existence is ripening to its close, the end of my life is near.
I go hence, ye remain behind; the place of refuge is ready for me.
Be watchful without intermission, walk evermore in holiness;
Aye resolute and aye prepared keep ye, O disciples, your minds.
He who evermore walks without stumbling, true to the word of truth,
Struggles into freedom from birth and death, presses through to the end of all suffering."

On the following day Buddha once more makes a begging excursion through Vesâlî, then looks back upon the town for the last time and sets out with a large concourse of disciples for Kusinârâ,* which he had chosen as the place for his entry into Nirvâna. On the way that sickness, which was to terminate his life, attacked him at Pâvâ. Our text, with a *naïveté* far removed from modern affectation, has in the course of the narrative of Buddha's last addresses, preserved to us the information that his illness was brought on by eating pork, which Cunda, the son of a goldsmith at Pâvâ, put before him.

Buddha journeys on, sick and weary, to Kusinârâ. A few verses, of which this journey is the subject, have come down to us :—

> "Travel-worn came Buddha to the river Kakutthâ,†
> Peaceful, pure, with clear waters,
> Down into the water went the Master, weary,
> The supreme Perfect One, without equal.
> When he had bathed, the Master drank of the river
> And went up out of it with the bands of his disciples,
> The holy Master, the preacher of the truth,
> The sage went on to the mango grove.
> Then spake he to Cunda, the monk : Fold me
> My robe in four folds, that I may lay me down.
> And Cunda did cheerfully as the Master bade him;
> He quickly spread out the robe folded in four folds.
> There the Master laid himself down, the weary one,
> And Cunda also sat down beside him."‡

* Now Kasia, east of Goruckpore, on the Chota Gandak. Cunningham, "Ancient Geography of India," 430.

† On the way between Pâvâ and Kusinârâ. According to Cunningham (l. c. 435) the Kakutthâ is the small stream Badhi or Barhi, which flows into the Chota Gandak, eight English miles below Kasia.

‡ These very old verses, which plainly and truly depict a plain situation, belong beyond all doubt to the most trustworthy reminiscences, which we have of Buddha's life. In the face of the wild phantasms of later works like the "Lalita Vistara," they should not be forgotten by those, who are in doubt as to whether the biography before them is that of a man or of a sun-hero.

At last Buddha arrives at Kusinârâ. There lay on the bank of the river Hiranyavatî (Chota Gandak) a grove of sâl trees. "Go, Ânanda," says Buddha, "and prepare a bed for me between two twin trees, with my head to the north. I am tired, Ânanda; I shall lie down."

It was not the season for sâl trees to bloom, but these two twin trees were covered with blossoms from crown to foot. Buddha laid himself down under the blooming trees, like a lion taking his rest, and blossoms fell down on him; a shower of flowers fell from heaven; and heavenly melodies sounded over head, in honour of the dying saint.

"Then spake the Exalted One to the venerable Ânanda: Although this is not the time for flowers, Ânanda, yet are these two twin trees completely decked with blossoms, and flowers are falling, showering, streaming down on the body of the Perfect One, . . . heavenly melodies are sounding in the air, in honour of the Perfect One. But to the Perfect One belongeth another honour, another glory, another reward, another homage, other reverence. Whosoever, Ânanda, male disciple or female follower, lay-brother, or lay-sister, lives in the truth in matters both great and small, and lives according to the ordinance and also walks in the truth in details, these bring to the Perfect One the highest honour, glory, praise, and credit. Therefore, Ânanda, must ye practise, thinking: Let us live in the truth in matters great and small, and let us live according to the ordinance and walk in the truth also in details."

But Ânanda went into the house and wept, saying: "I am not yet free from impurities, I have not yet reached the goal, and my master, who takes pity on me, will soon enter into Nirvâna." Then Buddha sent one of the disciples to him, saying: "Go, O disciple, and say to Ânanda in my name; the Master wishes to speak with thee, friend Ânanda." Thereupon

Ânanda went in to the Master, bowed himself before him, and sat down beside him. But Buddha said to him: "Not so, Ânanda, weep not, sorrow not. Have I not ere this said to thee, Ânanda, that from all that man loves and from all that man enjoys, from that must man part, must give it up, and tear himself from it. How can it be, Ânanda, that that which is born, grows, is made, which is subject to decay, should not pass away? That cannot be. But thou, Ânanda, hast long honoured the Perfect One, in love and kindness, with cheerfulness, loyally and unwearyingly, in thought, word and deed. Thou hast done well, Ânanda; only strive on, soon wilt thou be free from impurities."

When night came on, the Mallas, the nobles of Kusinârâ, went out in streams to the sâl grove with their wives and children, to pay their respects for the last time to the dying Master. Subhadda, a monk of another sect, who had desired to speak with Buddha, turned to him as the last of the converts who have seen the Master in the flesh.

Buddha, shortly before his departure, said to Ânanda: "It may be, Ânanda, that ye shall say: the Word has lost its master, we have no master more. Ye must not think thus, Ânanda. The law, Ânanda, and the ordinance, which I have taught and preached unto ye, these are your master when I am gone hence."

And to his disciples he said: "Hearken, O disciples, I charge ye: everything that cometh into being passeth away: strive without ceasing." These were his last words.

His spirit then rose from one state of ecstasy to another, up and down through all the stages of rapture, until he passed into Nirvâna. The earth quaked and thunders rolled. At the moment when Buddha entered Nirvâna, Brahma spake these words:—

"In the worlds beings all put off corporeity at some time,
Just as at this present time Buddha, the prince of victory, the supreme master of all worlds,
The mighty, Perfect One, hath entered into Nirvâna."

Towards sunrise the nobles of Kusinârâ have burned Buddha's body before the city gates with all the honours that are shown to the relics of universal monarchs.

PART II.

THE DOCTRINES OF BUDDHISM.

CHAPTER I.

The Tenet of Suffering.

"At one time," as we read,* "the Exalted One was staying at Kosambî in the Sinsapâ grove. And the Exalted One took a few Sinsapâ leaves in his hand and said to his disciples: "what think ye, my disciples, whether are more, these few Sinsapâ leaves, which I have gathered in my hand, or the other leaves yonder in the Sinsapâ grove?"

"The few leaves, sire, which the Exalted One holds in his hand are not many, but many more are those leaves yonder in the Sinsapâ grove."

"So also, my disciples, is that much more, which I have learned and have not told you, than that which I have told you. And, wherefore, my disciples, have I not told you that? Because, my disciples, it brings you no profit, it does not conduce to progress in holiness, because it does not lead to the turning from the earthly, to the subjection of all desire, to the cessation of the transitory, to peace, to knowledge, to illumination, to Nirvâna: therefore have I not declared it unto

* In the "Saṃyuttaka Nikâya," at the end of the work (vol. iii, fol. as of the Phayre MS.).

you. And what, O disciples, have I preached unto you? 'This is suffering'—thus, O disciples, have I proclaimed unto you. 'This is the origin of suffering'—thus have I proclaimed unto you. 'This is the cessation of suffering'—thus have I proclaimed unto you. 'This is the path to the cessation of suffering'—thus have I proclaimed unto you."

This passage states briefly and clearly what the doctrine of Buddhism is and what it is not. It does not purport to be a philosophy, which inquires into the ultimate grounds of things, unfolds to thought the breadths and depths of the universe. It addresses itself to man plunged in sorrow, and, while it teaches him to understand his sorrow, it shows him the way to exterminate it, root and all. This is the only problem with which Buddhist thought is concerned. "As the vast ocean, O disciples, is impregnated with one taste, the taste of salt, so also, my disciples, this Law and Doctrine is impregnated with but one taste, with the taste of deliverance."*

Yet this deliverance is not an inheritance for the poor in spirit but only for the wise. And therefore the Buddhist doctrine of deliverance is by no means content with merely those simple ethical reflections, which appeal more to the sensation of a pure heart than to the intellectual faculty of a trained mind. The main outlines of the doctrine might be grasped by every one endowed with a lively feeling among the members of the Church; the more detailed dialectical deductions, however, the proficiency in which was by no means regarded as an unnecessary accomplishment, can have been within the grasp of but comparatively few individuals, even among a people so exceptionally highly endowed with a capacity for dealing with abstract thought as the Indians, and among men who devoted their whole life exclusively to

* "Cullavagga," ix, 1, 4.

these very thoughts. In the circles of the ancient Church also they were fully conscious of this. "To men concerned with worldly pursuits, who have their occupation and find their pleasure in worldly pursuits, will this matter be difficult to comprehend, the law of causality, the chain of causes and effects;" thus Buddha is said to have remarked to himself, before he took upon himself to preach his doctrine (p. 120). And so we find, when we open the sacred writings of the Buddhists, side by side with those simple, beautiful apothegms, such as are contained in the Dhammapada, those most abstruse dogmatic expositions also, those circuitous, much-involved systems of ideas, comprehensive classifications, long lists of categories, which are held together by a causal nexus or some other logical tie. "If this be, that also is; if this arises, that also arises; if this be not, then that also is not; if this perishes, that also perishes:"* thus they were accustomed to reason in the period in which the sacred writings originated, and we have already (p. 182) seen that it is probable, that Buddha's own mode of thought and speech moved in these very paths of abstract discussion, of technical, often scholastic expression and of a, it may be, not very dexterous dialectic.

On the whole we shall be authorized to refer to Buddha himself† the most essential trains of thought which we find

* Cûlasakuludâyi Suttanta, in the Majjhima Nikâya.

† A distinction of earlier and later can as yet be drawn in but few cases, and only with tolerable accuracy, in the collection of Buddha's didactic discourses (the "Sutta-Piṭaka"). This affects the greater and lesser antiquity of dogmatic notions and doctrines as well as that of the texts. One of the oldest, if not the oldest, of these texts is the "Sutta-Nipâta," frequently quoted in other works. We find in it already all the more important dogmatic categories and tenets enumerated or alluded to. In fact when we think what the mental labours of Brahmanism and the

recorded in the sacred texts, and, in many places, it is probably not too much to believe that the very words, in which the ascetic of the Sakya house couched his gospel of deliverance, have come down to us as they fell from his lips. We find that throughout the vast complex of ancient Buddhist literature which has been collected, certain mottoes and formulas, the expression of Buddhist convictions upon some of the weightiest problems of religious thought, are expressed over and over again in a standard form adopted once for all. Why may not these be words which have received their currency from the founder of Buddhism, which had been spoken by him hundreds and thousands of times throughout his long life, devoted to teaching?

The meaning which he conveyed by such words we can often only approximately determine. Here, as in every case where the word has a preponderant importance over the thought, where it does not smoothly fit the thought, but compresses it within its own straight form, the inquirer who desires to reconstruct remote and foreign forms of thought, has not that surest key which consecutive progression, the inherent necessity of the thought, can give him. Those hundred-fold repetitions, those permutations and combinations of every kind, in which dogmatic technicalities meet us, but through which a living current of dialectic movement does not flow, hardly render the meaning of those expressions more comprehensible to us. Moreover, we find the same technical term

older sects have transmitted to Buddhism ready made, it does not seem improbable that the latter started at the very beginning with a very comprehensive and very definitely formulated dogmatic apparatus. It is not impossible, but not quite probable, that, if the Sutta texts be given to the public in their full extent, we may be able to go farther in the process of eliminating later elements than we can go at present.

used often in distinctly different meanings, or we find the same thought expressed in different settings, which can be only partially harmonized with each other. The most serious obstacle, however, which stands in the way of our comprehending Buddhist dogmatics is the silence with which everything is passed over which does not lead "to the separation from the earthly, to the subjection of all desire, to the cessation of the transitory, to quietude, knowledge, illumination, to Nirvâna." We remarked that an extensive stock of metaphysical, and especially psychological technicalities, was esteemed anything but superfluous for him who seeks after quietude and illumination; but advance in this direction was made only up to a certain point, and no farther. Speculations like those which were proposed can only be thoroughly comprehensible when they present themselves as a complete, self-contained circle. But here we have a fragment of a circle, to complete which, and to find the centre of which, is forbidden, for it would involve an inquiry after things which do not contribute to deliverance and happiness. When we try to resuscitate in our own way and in our own language the thoughts that are embedded in the Buddhist teaching, we can scarcely help forming the impression that it was not a mere idle statement which the sacred texts preserve to us, that the Perfect One knew much more which he thought inadvisable to say, than what he esteemed it profitable to his disciples to unfold. For that which is declared points for its explanation and completion to something else, which is passed over in silence—for it seemed not to serve for quietude, illumination, the Nirvâna—but of which we can scarcely help believing that it was really present in the minds of Buddha and those disciples, to whom we owe the compilation of the dogmatic texts.

The Four Sacred Truths. The First, and Buddhist Pessimism.

Ancient tradition, like Nature, provides us with a starting-point, equally commended to us by ancient tradition and by the natural condition of the question itself, from which we must begin our sketch of Buddhist teaching. At the basis of the whole body of Buddhist thought lies, like a permeating and leavening principle, the contemplation of the suffering of every form of life here on earth.* The four sacred truths of the Buddhists treat of suffering, of the origin of suffering, of the removal of suffering, and of the path to the removal of suffering: it is evermore the word and the idea of suffering which gives the key-note to Buddhist thought.

In these four truths we have the oldest authentic expression of this thought. We may describe this as the Buddhist creed. While most of the categories and propositions which we find imbedded in Buddhist teaching are treated, not as something peculiar to this faith, but as the obviously common property of all reflecting religious minds,† the four sacred truths always appear to us as something which the Buddhists hold beyond

* If Buddhism be treated strictly as philosophical doctrine, it must indeed be admitted that it looks upon the suffering of the universe not as an ultimate hypothesis, but as the product of deeper-lying factors. We might therefore be tempted in reviewing the system to begin preferably with the latter, with the fundamental metaphysical notions of Buddhism. It appears to me, however, more in keeping with the subject to follow the course laid down by our authorities themselves, and to state the result first, instead of the premises, the former being foremost and most important for the religious consciousness, though probably not so in strict dialectic.

† *E.g.*, the doctrine of metempsychosis, of ecstatic conditions, the idea of the saint (Arhat), etc.

all non-Buddhists,* as the kernel and the pole of the Dhamma (the Doctrine). Many were the steps of knowledge which Buddha had taken on his long and toilsome journey to the Buddhahood: yet evermore was there something wanting to his attainment of the knowledge that gives deliverance. On that night, under the Açvattha tree at Uruvelâ, the four truths at last dawn on him; they become the key-stone of his knowledge; now he is the Buddha. And when he goes to Benares to preach to the five monks what he has himself learned—"Open ye your ears, ye monks; the deliverance from death is found: I instruct you, I preach the Law"—again there are those very four sacred truths which constitute the gospel of the newly-discovered path of peace (p. 128 seq.). And throughout the long career of Buddha as a teacher, as it is depicted for us in the sacred texts, the discourse on the four truths is constantly coming to the front as that "which is the most prominent announcement of the Buddhas." The Buddhists describe ignorance as being the ultimate and most deeply-hidden root of all the suffering in the universe: if anyone inquires the ignorance of what is regarded as this fatal power, the uniform answer comes: the ignorance of the four sacred truths. And thus we find these propositions times without number in the canonical texts repeated, discussed, and their importance magnified in extravagant terms. It is difficult to avoid the presumption that the thoughts they convey and the wording in which they are expressed go back to Buddha himself, or at any rate to Buddha's first circle of followers.

* To give but one proof out of many: if sun and moon do not shine, it is said in the "Saṃyuttaka Nikâya" (vol. iii, fol. aṃ), darkness prevails in the world; day and night, months and years are not observable. So also darkness prevails in the world, if perfect, saintly Buddhas do not appear in it; then the four sacred truths are not preached, taught, proclaimed, revealed, etc.

We here repeat these propositions, as they have already met us in the sermon at Benares, in order to lay them as a foundation for our sketch of the Buddhist teaching.

"This, O monks, is the sacred truth of suffering: Birth is suffering, old age is suffering, sickness is suffering, death is suffering, to be united with the unloved is suffering, to be separated from the loved is suffering, not to obtain what one desires is suffering, in short the five-fold clinging (to the earthly*) is suffering.

"This, O monks, is the sacred truth of the origin of suffering: it is the thirst (for being) which leads from birth to birth, together with lust and desire, which finds gratification here and there: the thirst for pleasures, the thirst for being, the thirst for power.

"This, O monks, is the sacred truth of the extinction of suffering: the extinction of this thirst by complete annihilation of desire, letting it go, expelling it, separating oneself from it, giving it no room.

"This, O monks, is the sacred truth of the path which leads to the extinction of suffering: it is this sacred, eight-fold path, to wit: Right Faith, Right Resolve, Right Speech, Right Action, Right Living, Right Effort, Right Thought, Right Self-concentration."†

* The hankering after corporeal form, after sensations, perceptions, conformations, and after consciousness.—Köppen (i, 222, *n.* 1) finds quite groundlessly in these last words a "metaphysical postscript" to the original text of the four truths. Buddhism has at all times possessed as much of metaphysical terminology as is comprised in these words.

† "Köppen," i, 225, *n.* 2: "These eight divisions or branches also do not belong originally to the simple dogma." We cannot enter a strong enough protest against this setting aside of everything which militates against this gratuitous conceit of a peculiar simplicity of the earliest Buddhism. It cannot count up to eight without it being suspected of "metaphysical postscripts!"

The four truths give expression to Buddhist pessimism in its characteristic singularity.

They teach us first of all to direct attention to what this pessimism is not.

A widespread opinion finds the ultimate ground of this pessimism in the thought that, of all that is, the true existence is the Nothing.—The Nothing is alone certain. And if the world which surrounds us, or appears to surround us, is not wholly unreal, if it contains a certain, though ever so hollow a degree of existence, which cannot be ignored, this is a misfortune; and it is wrong, for right is only the Nothing. The wrong must be removed; we must remove it. Being, which originated in and from nothing, must again go to nothing, for it is essentially nothing.*

A strange error is this picture of what Buddhism is represented to have been. Whoever looks, not into the metaphysical speculations of later centuries, but into what the oldest traditions disclose to us of the teaching of Buddha, of the belief of that order of wandering mendicants, will not find therein one tenet of these all lucubrations regarding the Nothing. Neither openly expressed nor otherwise, neither in the foreground, nor in the farthest background of the religious thought, does the idea of the Nothing find a place. The tenets of the sacred truths show us clearly enough that, if this world has been weighed by the Buddhists and found wanting, the ground of this is not, that it, an illusory, specious something, is in reality a mere nothing, but the sole ground is that it consists of suffering and nothing but suffering.

All life is suffering: this is the inexhaustible theme, which,

* Adolf Wuttke has made by far the most clever and intelligent efforts to evolve Buddhism from these fundamental thoughts, *vide* "Geschichte des Heidenthums," ii, 520 seq., especially pp. 55, 535. Cf. also "Köppen," , 214 seq.

now in the strict forms of abstract philosophical discussion and now in the garment of poetical proverb, evermore comes ringing in our ears from Buddhist literature. We may take as the standard dialectic expression of this thought one of those discourses which Buddha, according to tradition, held at Benares soon after his first sermon, before those five earliest disciples, to whom he first proclaimed the four sacred truths.*

"And the Exalted One," so the tradition narrates, "spake to the five monks thus:

"The material form, O monks, is not the self. If material form were the self, O monks, this material form could not be subject to sickness, and a man should be able to say regarding his material form: my body shall be so and so; my body shall not be so and so. But inasmuch, O monks, as material form is not the self, therefore is material form subject to sickness, and a man cannot say as regards his material form: my body shall be so and so; my body shall not be so and so.

"The sensations, O monks, are not the self"—and then follows in detail regarding the sensations, the very same exposition which has been given regarding the body. Then comes the same detailed explanation regarding the remaining three component elements, the perceptions, the conformations, the consciousness, which in combination with the material form and the sensation constitute man's sentient state of being. Then Buddha goes on to say:

"How think ye then, O monks, is material form permanent or impermanent?"

"Impermanent, sire."

"But is that which is impermanent, sorrow or joy?"

"Sorrow, sire."

* This discourse is usually described as the "Sutta of the tokens of not-self" (of the non-ego). The text is to be found in the "Mahâvagga," i, 6, 38 seq.

"But if a man duly considers that which is impermanent, full of sorrow, subject to change, can he say: that is mine, that is I, that is myself?"

"Sire, he cannot."

Then follows the same exposition in similar terms regarding sensations, perceptions, conformations, and consciousness: after which the discourse proceeds:

"Therefore, O monks, whatever in the way of material form (sensations, perceptions, etc., respectively) has ever been, will be, or is, either in our cases, or in the outer world, or strong or weak, or low or high, or far or near, it is not self: this must he in truth perceive, who possesses real knowledge. Whosoever regards things in this light, O monks, being a wise and noble hearer of the word, turns himself from material form, turns himself from sensation and perception, from conformation and consciousness. When he turns therefrom, he becomes free from desire; by the cessation of desire he obtains deliverance; in the delivered there arises a consciousness of his deliverance: re-birth is extinct, holiness is completed, duty is accomplished; there is no more a return to this world, he knows."

The characteristic fundamental outlines of Brahmanical speculation turn up again in this discourse of Buddha's with dominant force. We have shown how that speculation works in the conception of a dualism. On one side the eternal immutable, which is endowed with the predicates of supreme freedom and happiness: that is the Brahma, and the Brahma is nothing else but man's own true self (Âtman). On the other side the world of origination and decease, birth, old age, death, in a word, of suffering. From this very dualism flow the ground-axioms, on which Buddha's discourse on the not-self proceeds: that proposition, which needed no proof for the

Buddhists, that refuge can only be had where origination and decease have no dominion, the identity of the ideas of change and sorrow, the conviction that the self of man (attâ = sansk. âtman) cannot belong to the world of evolution. The elements, in which the empirical state of man matures itself, are liable to continual change; the bodily as well as the spiritual life flows on, while one event is linked to another and closes up with another. Man stands helpless in the middle of this stream, the waves of which he cannot keep back or control. He cannot attain happiness or peace; how can happiness and peace be thought of, where there is no continuance, but only uncontrollable change holds sway? But if he cannot press this impermanence into his service, he can sever himself from it: where all contact with the earthly ceases, there are deliverance and freedom.*

At one point this discourse on the transitory nature of the earthly, shows a gap in its train of thought; to fill up which was, as we shall see later on, with a definite purpose omitted. One portion of the old Brahmanical dualism, the belief in an external world involving origination, decease and suffering, is adopted without reservation. What is the attitude of Buddha's doctrine with reference to the other side of this dualism? What does it teach regarding the eternal, the Âtman? It is said that whatever is subject to change and suffering cannot be the self. Is, then, the self something raised above this phenomenal world, separated from it, or has it no existence at all? Is deliverance a return of the self which is involved in change to itself, to its freedom? or is there nothing left, which

* "What is inconstant, is sorrow; what is sorrow, is not-self; what is not-self, that is not mine, that am not I, that is not myself." "Saṃyuttaka Nikâya," vol. ii, fol. ka, where the equivalence of the categories here indicated is carried out to a great length in repetitions of all kinds.

in the disappearance of the transitory, shows itself real and permanent? We note for the present that the sermon at Benares leaves these questions open. The answer to them, so far as Buddhism has given any answer at all to them, can claim our attention only in another connection.

We return to the Buddhist thoughts of the impermanence and sorrow of earthly things. The abstract and ideal development of these thoughts has been unfolded to us in the discourse quoted. But this is only a one-sided, imperfect expression. In a form, the most concrete, with the convincing and overwhelming force of a painful reality, there is ever present to the vision of the Buddhist, the picture of the universe and man enveloped in suffering. There are not shadows only, not clouds, which sorrow and death cast over human life, but sorrow and death pertain inseparably to every state of being. Through the delusion of happiness and youth the Buddhist looks on to the sorrow into which happiness and youth must soon turn. Behind the sorrowful present lies an immeasurable sorrowful past, and there extends equally immeasurably through the endless distance, which the belief in the transmigration of souls discloses to the awe-struck imagination, a future full of sorrows for him who does not succeed in attaining deliverance, "putting an end to sorrow."

"The pilgrimage (Saṃsâra) of beings, my disciples," Buddha says,* "has its beginning in eternity. No opening can be discovered, from which proceeding, creatures, mazed in ignorance, fettered by a thirst for being, stray and wander. What think ye, disciples, whether is more, the water which is in the four great oceans, or the tears which have flown from you and have been shed by you, while ye strayed and

* "Saṃyuttaka Nikâya," vol. i, fol. ṭho.

wandered on this long pilgrimage, and sorrowed and wept, because that was your portion which ye abhorred and that which ye loved was not your portion? A mother's death, a father's death, a brother's death, a sister's death, a son's death, a daughter's death, the loss of relations, the loss of property, all this have ye experienced through long ages. And while ye experienced this through long ages, more tears have flown from you and have been shed by you, while ye strayed and wandered on this long pilgrimage, and sorrowed and wept, because that was your portion which ye abhorred and that which ye loved was not your portion, than all the water which is in the four great oceans."

Birth, old age, death, are the leading forms in which the sorrow of earthly existence is depicted. "If these things were not in the world, my disciples, the Perfect One, the holy, supreme Buddha, would not appear in the world, the law and the Doctrine, which the Perfect One propounds, would not shine in the world. What three things are they? Birth and old age and death."* Impermanence holds sway with the pitiless, inexorable power of natural necessity. "There are five things which no Samana, and no Brahman, and no god, neither Mâra, nor Brahma, nor any being in the universe, can bring about. What five things are these? That what is subject to old age, should not grow old, that what is subject to sickness, should not be sick, that what is subject to death, should not die, that what is subject to decay, should not decay, that what is liable to pass away, should not pass away—this can no Samana bring about, nor any Brahman, nor any god, neither Mâra, nor Brahma, nor any being in the universe."†

* "Anguttara Nikâya," vol. iii, fol. thai.

† From the discourse with which the monk Nârada consoled the king Muṇḍa at Pâtaliputta on the death of the Queen Bhaddâ.—*Anguttara Nikâya*, vol. ii, fol. khai.

The actions of men who pursue earthly pleasures, are under the curse of impermanence, illusion, vanity. Paining, deceiving, sweeping, destroying, turning hoped-for enjoyments into sorrow and death, the inexorable necessity of progression holds dominion over all life and hopes. Whoever seeks to acquire worldly goods, the merchant, the farmer, the shepherd, the soldier, the civil servant of the crown, must expose himself to the inconveniences of heat and cold, the bite of serpents, to hunger and to thirst.* If he does not gain the object of his pursuit, he laments and grieves: in vain did I exert myself, in vain was all my labour. If he attains his object, he must guard his gains with anxiety and trouble, that kings or robbers may not wrest them from him, that fire may not burn them, that floods may not sweep them away, that they may not fall into the hands of hostile relations. To gain property and gratify desire, kings wage war, father or mother quarrels with son, brother with brother, warriors make their arrows fly, and their swords flash, and they brave death and mortal agonies. To gain pleasure, men break their word, commit robbery, murder, adultery: they endure excruciating tortures as human punishments, and when their bodies succumb in death, they go the way of evil-doers; in the kingdoms of hell they will be born again to new torments.

And these same powers of decadence and sorrow, to which human life is subject and which extend through all hells, have also power over heaven. The gods may have assured to them an incomparably longer and more happy state of being than earthly humanity: still even they are not immortal or free from sorrow. "The three and thirty gods, and the Yâma-gods, the happy deities, the gods who joy in creation, and the ruling gods, bound by the chain of desire, return within the

* I here paraphrase briefly a part of the "Mahâdukkhakkhandha Suttanta" (in the Majjhima Nikâya).

power of Mâra. The whole universe is consumed with flames, the whole universe is enveloped in smoke, the whole universe is on fire, the whole universe trembles."*

The proverbial wisdom of the "Dhammapada" gives the truest picture of all of Buddhist thought and feeling, how the disciples of Buddha saw in everything earthly the one thing, vanity and decay.

"How can ye be gay,"† it is said, "how can ye indulge desire? Evermore the flames burn. Darkness surrounds you: will ye not seek the light?"

"Man gathers flowers; his heart is set on pleasure. Death comes upon him, like the floods of water on a village, and sweeps him away."

"Man gathers flowers; his heart is set on pleasure. The Destroyer brings the man of insatiable desire within his clutch."

"Neither in the aërial region, nor in the depths of the sea, nor if thou piercest into the clefts of the mountains, wilt thou find any place on this earth where the hand of death will not reach thee."

"From merriment cometh sorrow: from merriment cometh fear. Whosoever is free from merriment, for him there is no sorrow: whence should come fear to him?"

"From love cometh sorrow: from love cometh fear: whosoever is free from love, for him there is no sorrow: whence should come fear to him?"

"Whoso looketh down upon the world, as though he gazed on a mere bubble or a dream, him the ruler Death beholdeth not."

"Whosoever hath traversed the evil, trackless path of the

* From the "Bhikkhunî Saṃyutta," vol. i, fol. ghai.

† "Dhammapada," v, 146, 47, 48, 128, 212, 213, 170, 414.

Sansâra, of error, who hath pushed on to the end, hath reached the shore, rich in meditation, free from desire, free from irresolution, who, freed from being, hath found rest, him I call a true Brahman."

Is it dialectic only with its comparison between the notions of becoming, decease, sorrow, which causes the world to appear to the Buddhist that immeasurable, painful waste?

It is true, indeed, that wherever the popular mind cannot obtain a sure anchorage for itself in the firm and clear realities of practical life, where it is under the overpowering influence of thought, of dreamy fancy without any counterpoise, there speculation, with its real or supposed logical conclusions, gains an incalculable influence as to which shall be the answer given by individuals as well as collective masses, to the question whether life is worth living. But it is not merely the speculation of the Indian which furnishes the answer. Speculation is bound up with his wishes and hopes; it shares with them the character of impatient impetuosity, untrained to deal with realities. Thought, which passes over everything, and arrives with one bound at the absolute, finds its counterpart in a craving whose impatience pushes from itself all goods, which are not the supreme, everlasting good. But what is the supreme good? As the glow of the Indian sun causes rest in cool shades to appear to the wearied body the good of goods, so also with the wearied soul, rest, eternal rest, is the only thing for which it craves. Of this life, which promises to the cheerful sturdiness of an industrious, struggling people, thousands of gifts and thousands of good things, the Indian merely scrapes the surface and turns away from it in weariness. The slave is tired of his servitude, the despot is still sooner and more completely wearied of his despotism, its unlimited enjoyment. The Buddhist propositions regarding the sorrow of all that is transitory are the sharp and trenchant expression, which these dispositions of the Indian people have framed for themselves, an expression, the commentary to which is written not alone in the sermon at Benares and in the apothegms of the "Dhammapada," but in indelible characters in the whole of the mournful history of this unhappy people.

In some of the sayings, which we have quoted from the "Dhammapada," the thought of the impermanence and unsubstantiality of the earthly world is blended with the praise of him who has succeeded in breaking the fetters which bind him to the prison-house. And this brings us to fill in a necessary part without which our sketch of the Buddhist pessimism would be very incomplete. Some writers have often represented the tone prevailing in it, as if it were peculiarly characterized by a feeling of melancholy which bewails in endless grief the unreality of being. In this they have altogether misunderstood Buddhism. The true Buddhist certainly sees in this world a state of continuous sorrow, but this sorrow only awakes in him a feeling of compassion for those who are yet in the world; for himself he feels no sorrow or compassion, for he knows he is near his goal which stands awaiting him, noble beyond all else. Is this goal annihilation? Perhaps it is. We cannot here answer this question yet. But be this as it may, the Buddhist is far from bewailing as a misfortune, or as an injury, to which he must submit with sad resignation as to an unalterable destiny, the constitution of things, which has provided just this goal and only this goal for man's existence. He seeks Nirvâna with the same joyous sense of victory in prospect, with which the Christian looks forward to his goal, everlasting life.

The following sayings also of the "Dhammapada" reflect this spirit*:—

* Verse 94, 197 seq. 373.

"He whose appetites are at rest, like steeds thoroughly broken in by the trainer, he who has put away pride, who is free from impurity, him thus perfect the gods themselves envy."

"In perfect joy we live, without enemy in this world of enmity; among men filled with enmity we dwell without enmity."

"In perfect joy we live, hale among the sick; among sick men we dwell without sickness."

"In perfect joy we live, without toil among toilers; among toiling men we dwell without toil."

"In perfect joy we live, to whom belongeth nothing. Our scrip is pleasantness, as of the effulgent gods."

"The monk who dwells in an empty abode, whose soul is full of peace, enjoys superhuman felicity, gazing solely on the truth."

It is not enough to say that the final goal to which the Buddhist strives to pass as an escape from the sorrow of the world, is Nirvâna. It is also necessary to any delineation of Buddhism to note as a fact assured beyond all doubt, that internal cheerfulness, infinitely surpassing all mere resignation, with which the Buddhist pursues this end.

CHAPTER II.

THE TENETS OF THE ORIGIN AND THE EXTINCTION OF SUFFERING.

THE FORMULA OF THE CAUSAL NEXUS.

IN order to understand the first of the four sacred truths, the tenet of suffering, we needed to acquaint ourselves only with the criticism which Buddha's discourses give of the events of daily life, the dispositions and inclinations which govern our actions, and the consequences which follow from them. The tenets of the origin of suffering and its extinction bring us out of the domain of the popular speculative view of life, into the realms of abstract notions of Buddhist dogmatic, and therewith into a region where the ground vanishes from beneath our feet at every step.

"This, O monks, is the sacred truth of the origin of suffering: it is the thirst (for being), which leads from birth to birth, together with lust and desire, which finds gratification here and there: the thirst for pleasures, the thirst for being, the thirst for power.

"This, O monks, is the sacred truth of the extinction of suffering: the extinction of this thirst by complete annihilation of desire, letting it go, expelling it, separating oneself from it, giving it no room."

The state of being, as it surrounds us in this world, with its restless oscillation between origination and decease, is our misfortune. The ground of our existing is our will. This is our besetting sin, that we will to be, that we will to be ourselves, that we fondly will our being to blend with other being and extend. The negation of the will to be, cuts off being, for us at least. Thus the two tenets of the origin of suffering and its cessation, comprise the sum of all human action and all human destiny.

But the sum must be resolved into the elements of which it is composed. The former tenet, as we have quoted it, speaks of the thirst for being, which leads from one birth to another. Whence this birth? It, the ground of our being, on what ground does it itself rest? And what law, what mechanism is there, what intermediate links are there, by which the repetition of our being, re-birth with its sorrows, is connected with it?

The very oldest traditions from which we draw our account of Buddhist speculations, show that these questions had been asked. People found the brief and concise setting of the sacred truths obviously inadequate and two formulas, or, more correctly speaking, a bipartite formula was drawn up, which was intended to supplement, or rather strengthen, the tenets regarding the origin of suffering and its cessation, the formula of the "*Causal Nexus of being*" (paṭiccasamuppâda).*

Tradition assigns to this formula the next place in sacredness to the four truths. The knowledge of the four verities is what makes Buddha Buddha; the formula of the causal nexus, which had occurred to him already before the attainment of

* This is frequently designated in later literature the formula of the twelve nidânas (Bases of Existence), an expression which, as far as I know, occurs neither in Buddha's discourses nor in the Vinaya texts.

Buddhahood had been vouchsafed to him, occupied his mind while he sits under the tree of knowledge, "enjoying the happiness of deliverance."* And when he combats the fear that his gospel will not be comprehended on earth, it is especially the law of the causal nexus of being, to which this fear attaches: "Men who move in a worldly sphere, who have their lot cast and find their enjoyments in a worldly sphere, will find this matter hard to grasp, the law of causality, the chain of causes and effects."†

Occasionally the sacred texts make the formula of the causal nexus actually an integral portion of the sacred truths themselves, by omitting the second and third truths and inserting in their stead this formula in its two branches.‡

The propositions of the causal nexus of being, in the form which is most commonly met with in the traditions, and which may be regarded as the most ancient form, with their double, their positive and negative, arrangement—"forwards and backwards," as the texts express themselves—are worded as follows:—

"From ignorance come conformations (sankhârâ); from conformations comes consciousness (viññâṇa); from consciousness come name and corporeal form; from name and corporeal form come the six fields;§ from the six fields comes

* "Mahâvagga," i, 1 (supra, pp. 116, 117). In the "Saṃyutta Nikâya" (Phayre MS., vol. i, fol. ja) Buddha says that, in his case as in the case of the prior Buddhas, the knowledge of this hitherto unheard-of wisdom dawned on him before the attainment of the Buddhahood (pubbeva me bhikkhave sambodhâ anabhisambuddhassa).

† *Vide* supra, p. 120.

‡ So in the "Anguttara Nikâya" (Tikanipâta, Phayre MS., vol. i, fol. ce').

§ The fields of the six senses and their objects. In addition to the five senses the Indians reckoned understanding (mano) the sixth.

contact (between the senses and their objects); from contact comes sensation; from sensation comes thirst (or desire); from thirst comes clinging (to existence: upâdâna); from clinging (to existence) comes being (bhava); from being comes birth; from birth come old age and death, pain and lamentation, suffering, anxiety and despair. This is the origin of the whole realm of suffering.

"But if ignorance be removed by the complete extinction of desire, this brings about the removal of conformations; by the removal of conformations, consciousness is removed; by the removal of consciousness, name and corporeal form are removed; by the removal of name and corporeal form, the six fields are removed; by the removal of the six fields, contact (between the senses and their objects) is removed; by the removal of contact, sensation is removed; by the removal of sensation, thirst is removed; by the removal of thirst, the clinging (to existence) is removed; by the removal of the clinging (to existence), being is removed; by the removal of being, birth is removed; by the removal of birth, old age and death, pain and lamentation, suffering, anxiety, and despair are removed. This is the removal of the whole realm of suffering."

The attempt is here made by the use of brief pithy phrases to trace back the suffering of all earthly existence to its most remote roots. The answer is as confused as the question was bold. It is utterly impossible for anyone who seeks to find out its meaning, to trace from beginning to end a connected meaning in this formula. Most of the links of the chain, taken separately, admit of a passable interpretation; many arrange themselves also in groups together, and their articulation may be said to be not incomprehensible; but between these groups there remain contradictions and impossibilities in the consecutive arrangement of priority and sequence, which an exact exegesis has not the power, and is not permitted to clear up. Even the ancient Buddhist theologians, who were by no means accustomed to construe too strictly in every case the requirement that "ein Begriff muss bei dem Worte sein,"* found here a stumbing-block; the variations, with which the formula of causality is found in the sacred writings, afford unmistakable evidence of this.

The Third Link in the Chain of Causality.

It seems advisable for the explanation of the formula of causality not to begin at the beginning. The first links of the series—the ultimate ground of earthly existence, ignorance, and the "conformations" which develop themselves from ignorance—are in their nature much more difficult of comprehension by concrete explanation than the following categories. We shall return later on to the attempt here made to denominate the cause of causes; at present we begin where consciousness appears in the chain of categories and with it we step upon the ground of conceivable reality. The sacred texts also apparently justify us in proceeding thus, as they themselves often begin the chain of causality with the category of consciousness, omitting the first members. "Ignorance" and "conformations" are evidently among the things, of which Buddhist dogmatists have, as far as possible, omitted to speak. "From consciousness"—runs the third proposition in the series—"come name and corporeal form."

* Göthe's "Faust," Dialogue of Mephistopheles and the Student. Anglicé: "A meaning must underlie words."—[*Translator.*]

One of the dialogues on this subject in the collection of the sacred texts, in which Buddha unfolds to his beloved disciple, Ânanda, the greater part of the formula of causality,* gives us a very concrete explanation of this proposition, which undoubtedly expounds the original meaning. "If consciousness, Ânanda, did not enter into the womb, would name and corporeal form† arise in the womb?"—"No, sire."—"And if consciousness, Ânanda, after it has entered into the womb, were again to leave its place, would name and corporeal form be born into this life?"—"No, sire."—"And if consciousness, Ânanda, were again lost to the boy or to the girl, while they were yet small, would name and corporeal form attain growth, increase, progress?"—"No, sire."

Thus the proposition, "From consciousness comes name and corporeal form," leads us to the moment of conception. We shall, when treating of the Buddhist notions of soul and metempsychosis, come to understand from another point of view still more completely the ideas which meet us here; here we must only state this much, that in death the other elements, which constitute the body-cum-spirit state of being of a man, are dissolved; the body, the sensations, the perceptions vanish, but not the consciousness (viññâṇa). Consciousness forms, so long as the existent is bound in metempsychosis, the connecting

* The Mahânidânasutta (Dîgha Nikâya).

† I reserve for the Excursus the more particular statements which the acred texts make regarding this double notion of "name and corporeal form," derived from older Brahmanical speculation. Originally in this expression undoubtedly the Name, in so far as it expresses what is only this person and no other, is regarded as a peculiar element annexed to the body, somehow connected with the body, and this interpretation has not wholly disappeared from the Buddhist texts. Meanwhile another view grew up, by which "name" was understood to include the more subtle immaterial functions connected with the body in contradistinction to the body formed of earth, water, fire, and air.

link which connects the old existences with the new; not till the bourne of deliverance, the nirvâna is reached, does the consciousness also of the dying perfect one vanish into nothing. As the human body is formed out of the material elements, so consciousness also is regarded as consisting of an analogous spiritual element. "There are six elements, my disciples," says Buddha, "the element of earth, the element of water, the element of fire, the element of air, the element of æther, the element of consciousness." The stuff of which consciousness is made is highly exalted above the other elements; it dwells, as it were, in its own world. "Consciousness," it is written, "the indemonstrable, the everlasting, the all-illuminating; it is where nor water nor earth, nor fire nor air, finds a place, in which greatness and smallness, weakness and strength, beauty and non-beauty, in which name and material form cease altogether."

That which in the dying man is constructed of this highest of earthly elements, the consciousness-element, becomes at the moment when the old being dies the germ of a new being; this germ of consciousness seeks and finds in the womb the material stuffs, from which it forms a new state of being coined in name and material form.

But as name and material form rest on consciousness, so also the latter rests on the former. Those passages in the texts, which do not carry back the line of causality to the ultimate end, to Ignorance, are wont to make it run in a circle with these two categories interchangeably dependent on one another We have already quoted from Buddha's and Ânanda's dialogue the passage bearing on the one side of this subject, on the allegation that name and material form rest on consciousness. On the other side, then, it is said in the same conversation: "If, Ânanda, consciousness were not to find name and materia form as its resting-place, would then birth, old age, and death, the origin and development of sorrow, reveal themselves in succession?"—"No, sire, they would not."—"Therefore, Ânanda, is this the cause, this the ground, this the origin, this the basis of consciousness: name and material form." And thus comprehensively are the bases on which all nameability and all existence of the existent, their birth, death, and re-birth, rest, described as "name and material form combined with consciousness."

We extract from other texts some more characteristic passages for the elucidation of this subject:—

"What must there be, in order that there may be name and material form? Whence come name and material form?—Consciousness must be in order that there may be name and material form; from consciousness come name and material form.—What must there be in order that there may be consciousness? Whence comes consciousness?—Name and material form must be, in order that there may be consciousness; from name and material form comes consciousness. Then, my disciples, the Bodhisatti Vipassi* thought: consciousness conversely depends on name and material form: the chain goes no farther."†

And in another place‡ the following simile is put into the mouth of Sâriputta, the greatest authority among Buddha's disciples: "My friend, as two bundles of sticks leaning against each other stand, so also, my friend, consciousness grows out of name and material form, and name and material

* Vipassi is one of the mythical Buddhas of the past, to whom are attributed these reflections on the chain of casuality, while he was still Bodhisatta (pursuing the path to the Buddhahood).

† Mahâpadhânasutta (Dîgha Nikâya), second Bhâṇavâra.

‡ "Saṃyatta N." vol. i, fol. ñâḥ˙.

form out of consciousness." It "grows out of" it—this is not intended to convey that consciousness is the element, out of which name and material form are made: it is merely tantamount to saying, that consciousness is the forming power, which originates from the material elements or being, which bears a name and is clothed with a body.

The Fourth to the Eleventh Link in the Chain of Causality.

When the spirit has found its body and the body found the spirit and united itself to it, this being compounded of spirit and body, provides itself with organs to put itself into communication with the external world. "From name and material form," runs the fourth term of the formula, "come the six fields"*—the "six fields of the subject" (ajjhattika âyatana), eye, ear, nose, tongue, body (as organ for sensations of touch), understanding,† and the six corresponding fields of the object world, corporeal forms as the object of the eye, and so on—sounds, odours, taste, tangibility, and last, as the object of the understanding, thoughts (or ideas, notions, "dhammâ"), which are represented evidently as something standing present before the thinking faculty in quite an objective

* The version contained in the "Mahânidânasutta" (Dialogue between Buddha and Ânanda) skips the categories of the "six fields," and goes on from "name and material form" straight to the next following category of contact. (*Vide* infra.)

† "Understanding" (mano) and "consciousness" (viññâṇa) are always quite distinct in the sacred texts, wherever they express themselves strictly. Turns such as these: "What people are accustomed to call thought (citta) or understanding (mano) or consciousness (viññâṇa)" occur, as far as I know, only in such a connection that they may be described as an intentional accommodation to customary modes of speech.

existence and realized by it, in the same way as visible bodies before the eyes.

The organs of the subject now step into communication with the objective world. "From the six fields comes contact. From contact comes sensation." We meet also with a certainly not very clearly expressed, and at the same time scarcely well-thought-out, attempt, to still further analyze these processes. Before the organ of sense grasps the object, an operation of the central organ, consciousness, on the organ of sense in requisition, gives it the command to join communication with the object, apparently in such a way that the former sets the latter in a certain manner to work. And when this communication follows, then by means of it, besides the two elements primarily concerned, the organ of sense and the object, the third element, consciousness, the author and supervisor of this communication, is at the same time in play. It is somewhat in this way, I believe, that we must understand the following proposition which recurs not unfrequently in the sacred texts: "From the eye and visible bodies comes consciousness, directed to the eye (cakkhuviññâṇa), the conjunction of the three, the contact." And similarly in that address of Buddha's already quoted (p. 185 seq.), the series of ideas and processes treated of in this connection, is expressed in the following fashion: "Eye—body—consciousness directed to the eye—contact of the eye (with the objects)—the sensation, which arises from the contact of the eye (with the objects), be it pleasure be it pain, be it neither pain nor pleasure."* Of course similar processes take place in the case of the other organs of sense to those which occur in the case of the eye.

* Pleasure, pain, and what is neither pleasure nor pain: a classification of sensations under three heads found frequently repeated in the sacred texts.

The formula goes on: "From sensation arises thirst." Here the point is reached, which the tenets of the origin and the extinction of suffering had made a starting-point, "the thirst which leads from re-birth to re-birth," not the ultimate but the most powerful cause of suffering. We be, because we thirst for being; we suffer, because we thirst for pleasure. "Whomsoever it holds in subjection, that thirst, that contemptible thing, which pours its venom through the world, his suffering grows as the grass grows. Whosoever holds it in subjection, that thirst, that contemptible thing, which it is difficult to escape in this world, suffering falls off from him as the water-drops from the lotus flowers."* "As, if the root be uninjured, even a hewn tree grows up anew mightily, so, if the excitement of thirst be not wholly dead, suffering ever and anon breaks out again." "The gift of the truth transcends all other gifts; the sweetness of the truth transcends all other sweetness; joy in the truth surpasses all other joy; the extermination of thirst, this subdues all suffering."

The idea of thirst, usually divided by scholastic teaching into six heads, according to whichever one or other of the six senses it is that has caused the sensation which generates the thirst, is usually met in close connection with the category, which follows next in the formula of causality, that of clinging, to wit, clinging to the external world, to existence.† "From

* "Dhammapada," v. 335 seq. The following quotations are taken from the same text, v. 338, 354.

† Scholastic terminology specially distinguishes four classes of clinging: clinging by desire, clinging by (mistaken) intentions, clinging by building on virtue and monastic observances (as though these were alone sufficient to obtain salvation), and clinging by thinking of the ego. We shall not be able to explain the last point, the attitude of Buddhist teaching as to the idea of the ego, until we reach a later stage.

thirst," says the formula, "comes clinging." The Pâli word for "clinging" (upâdâna) involves a metaphor which is highly descriptive of the idea which is here underlying. The flame which, as a scarcely material existence, freely urges its way on, spreading and rising, "clings" still to the fuel (upâdâna): it cannot be contemplated without fuel. Even if the flame be carried into the distance by the wind, there is still a fuel there to which it clings, the wind. The existence of every being is like the flame; like the flame, our being is to a certain extent a continuous process of burning. Deliverance is the extinction (nirvâna) of the flame; but the flame is not extinguished so long as it is supplied with fuel to which it "clings." And as the flame clinging to the wind presses on into far off distance, so also the flame of our existence is not laid on the spot, but presses on in transmigration to far off distances, from heaven to hell, from hells to heaven. What is it, to which the flame-resembling process of our being clings in the moment of such transmigration, like the flame to the wind? "Then, say I, (the being of the existent) has thirst as the substratum to which it clings; for this thirst, O Vaccha, is at that time (at the moment of transmigration) its (the being's) clinging."*

Even the slightest residue of clinging prevents deliverance. Whosoever separates from everything that is transitory, who-

* From a dialogue between Buddha and a monk of another persuasion named Vaccha ("Saṃyutta Nikâya," vol. ii, fol. tau). Here may be seen an illustration of the disconnectedness of the sacred texts already animadverted on, as regards the succession of the categories appearing in the formula of causality. We pointed out, that the proposition "from consciousness come name and material form" refers to the moment of conception, that is of transmigration of the soul. And here the categories of thirst and clinging, which appear much later in the formula, are carried back to the very same moment.

soever attains the most perfect quietude, but clings with his thought even to this very quietude and is glad of this quietude, he is still in bondage. The best, but still the minimum of clinging is the clinging to the condition of deepest self-suppression where consciousness and non-consciousness are alike overcome; complete deliverance has overcome even this last clinging.* "By the cessation of clinging his soul was delivered from all sinful existence"—this is the standing phrase with which the texts intimate that a disciple of Buddha has become a partaker of holiness, of deliverance.

Up to this point the connection of the causes and effects in our chain of categories was tolerably clear. The impression will have been formed that the being whose conception ("from consciousness come name and material form") was the starting-point of the series, has long since, in the later terms of the formula, entered on real life, struggles with the outer world, the clinging to its goods. In this light also the oft-mentioned dialogue between Buddha and Ânanda puts it; to the proposition; "from sensation comes thirst," it appends a picture of human toil and struggles for pleasure and gain: there are met the words seek, obtain, possession, guard, envy, quarrel, strife, backbiting, lying. It is therefore very surprising, when the formula of causality, which in its theory of the world seemed to have already arrived at the dealings of social life, at the struggle of egoism against egoism, suddenly turns back and causes that being whom we have already seen taking part in the transactions of the world to be born. The formula runs thus in its three last terms: "From clinging (to existence) comes becoming (bhava); from becoming comes birth; from birth come old age, and death, pain and lamentation, sorrow, anxiety and despair."

* "Anañjasappâya Suttanta" (Majjh. N.).

It seems to me evident that there is here a gap in the train of thought which our efforts of elucidation cannot, and are not even permitted to bridge over. What was more ready than to recognize in birth the sources from which come old age and death? "If three things were not in the world, my disciples, the Perfect One, the holy, supreme Buddha, would not appear in the world, the Law and the Doctrine, which the Perfect One propounds, would not shine in the world. What three things are they? Birth and old age and death."* Thus these so closely associated ideas were thrown together in the two last terms of the causal-chain, but it was omitted to weld these new groups of categories with those preceding, so as to form a harmonious whole. The idea of "becoming," which was thrust into the middle, inevitably creates by its very vagueness†—which you may regard as you like, as either of very little or of very great import—the impression as if it were intended for a shift or sleight to get over the break in continuity.

We close with some proverbs of the "Dhammapada,"‡ which translate these last terms of the formula of causality from the language of ideas into that of emotion and poetry.

"Behold this painted picture, the frail, scarred form of corporeity, wherein many an aspiration dwells, which has no happiness and no stability."

"To age comes as its lot this form, frail, a nest of diseases: the perishable body fails: life in it is death."

* *Vide* supra, p. 217.

† This is not removed by the explanation frequently occurring in the sacred texts, that there is a triple becoming: the becoming in desire, the becoming in form, the becoming in formlessness, according as a being is born again in the lower worlds ruled by desire, or in the higher states, the worlds of form and formlessness.

‡ Vers 147-149, 46.

"Those bleached bones, which are thrown out yonder like gourds in the autumn—when anyone sees them, how can he be happy?"

"Esteeming this body like a bubble, regarding it as a mirage, breaking the flower-shafts of the tempter, press on to the bourne where the monarch Death shall gaze no more on thee."

But death is not the end of the long chain of suffering: upon death follows re-birth, new sorrow, another death.

The First and Second Links of the Causal-chain.

From the end of the formula of causality we must turn back to its beginning, to speak of the two first members of the series.

"From ignorance (avijjâ)," the formula begins, "come conformations (sankhârâ).

"From conformations comes consciousness."

If ignorance be designated the ultimate source of suffering, the question must arise: Who is here the ignorant? What is that of which this ignorance is ignorant?

It is tempting, by the place assigned to the category of "ignorance," at the beginning of the whole line of causality, to allow one's self to be carried away by interpretations which see in this idèa, as it were, a cosmogonical power working at the primitive foundation of things. Or one might be tempted to read in it the history of a crime preceding all time, an unlucky act by which the non-*bëent* had doomed itself to be *bëent*, that is to suffer. The philosophy of later Brahmanical schools speaks in similar fashion of Mâyâ, that power of delusion, which causes the deceptive picture of the created world to appear to the One, the uncreated, as if it were *bëent*. "He, the knowing, gave himself up to confused fancies, and when he fell into the slumber prepared for him by Mâyâ, he beheld in amazement multiform dreams: I am, this is my father, this my mother, this my field, this my kingdom." Some have compared the ignorance of Buddhism with this Mâyâ of the Brahmanical theosophy; only with this note that, as Mâyâ is the deceptive reflection of the true everlasting *bëent*, so ignorance is the reflection of that which, as they thought, took the place of the everlasting *bëent* for the Buddhists, that this, the Nothing.

Interpretations of this kind, which find in the category of ignorance an expression for the deceptive Nothing appearing as a *bëent*, completely correspond in fact with the explicit utterances of later Buddhist texts. The construction alluded to is met with in the great standard text-book of mystic-nihilistic speculation, which was an authority among Buddhist theologians in the first century after Christ. In this most sacredly esteemed text, the "Perfection of Knowledge" (Prajnâpâramita), we read as follows:—*

Buddha said to Sâriputra: "Things, O Sâriputra, do not exist as ordinary and ignorant men, clinging closely to them, fancy, who are not instructed on the subject." Sâriputra said: "How then, sire, do they exist?" Buddha answered: "They exist, O Sâriputra, in so far that they do not exist in truth. And inasmuch as they do not exist, they are called Avidyâ, that is, the non-existent, or ignorance.† To this ordinary, ignorant men, who are not instructed on the matter, cling closely. They represent to themselves all things, of which in truth not one has any existence, as existent."

* The passage is quoted by Burnouf, "Introduction à l'histoire du Buddhisme indien," p. 473 seq. 478.

† This is the same term which occurs at the beginning of the formula of causality (avidyâ = Pâli, avijjâ).

Then Buddha asks the holy disciple Subhûti: "What thinkest thou now, Subhûti, is illusion one thing and material form another? Is illusion one thing and sensations another? perceptions another? conformations another? consciousness another?" Subhûti answered: "Nay, Master, nay; illusion is not one thing and material form another. Material form is itself the illusion and the illusion itself is material form, sensations, perceptions, conformations, and consciousness." And Buddha says: "It is in the nature of the illusion that that lies which makes beings what they are. It is, O Subhûti, as if a clever magician, or the pupil of a clever magician, caused a vast concourse of men to appear at a cross road, where four great thoroughfares meet, and, having caused them to appear, caused them again to vanish."

Thus the speculations contained in the treatise on the "Perfection of Knowledge," make ignorance the ultimate cause of the appearing of the world and at the same time the essential character of its state of being, which is in truth rather not-being: ignorance and not-being here coincide.

We have taken this glance at this later phase of the development of Buddhist thought merely with the intention of being put on our guard against assigning any of these ideas to ancient Buddhism and against framing any interpretation of the old texts, especially of the formula of causality, influenced by such a process. Inquirers, who had access to the propositions of the chain of causes and effects only in the garb of that later period, found themselves in fact in a not very different position from that in which a historian of Christianity would be placed, if he were directed to string together some account of the teaching of Jesus from the phantasms of the Gnostics.

The course, which we must follow, is clearly enough indicated: we have only to inquire from the oldest tradition of

Buddhist dogmatics, obtainable in the Pâli texts, what is that ignorance, the ultimate ground of all suffering.

Wherever in the sacred Pâli literature this question is mooted, as well in the addresses which Buddha himself and his chief disciples are said to have delivered, as in the systematizing compilations of a later generation of dogmatists, the answer is invariably the same. The ignorance is not declared to be anything in the way of a cosmic power, nor anything like a mysterious original sin, but it is within the range of earthly, tangible reality. The ignorance is the ignorance of the four sacred truths. Sâriputta says :* "Not to know suffering, friend, not to know the origin of suffering, not to know the extinction of suffering, not to know the path to the extinction of suffering: this, O friend, is called ignorance." "Not seeing the four sacred truths as they are, I have wandered on the long path from one birth to another. Now have I seen them: the current of being is stemmed. The root of suffering is destroyed: there is henceforward no re-birth."†

The method and procedure of old-Buddhist dogmatic is here clearly exemplified: when it tracks personality back on its way through the world of sorrow beyond that moment when consciousness clothes itself with "name and material form," that is, to the moment of conception, their thought is not on that account lost in the arcanum of pre-existence prior to all consciousness, but it makes this empirical existence take root in another equally empirical conceivable existence. That ignorance, which is stated to be the ultimate ground of your present state of being, involves that, at an earlier date, a being who then occupied your place, a being who has lived in not

* "Sammâdiṭṭhisuttanta" (Majjhima Nikâya). Similar passages occur frequently.

† "Mahâvagga," vi, 29.

less tangible reality than you now do, on earth or in a heaven or in a hell, has failed to possess a specific knowledge, definable in certain words, and bound for that reason in the bonds of transmigration, must have brought about your present state of being. We saw (p. 52) that old-Brahman speculation, in reply to the question, what is the power which holds the spirit bound in impermanence, what enemy must be overcome in order that deliverance may be obtained, has answered with the very same conception, that of ignorance. With the Brahmans this ignorance was the ignorance of the identity of the particular ego with that great ego, which is the source and the sum of all egoity. Buddhism has given up these thoughts and all metaphysical hypotheses which rendered them possible, but still the word proved itself more lasting than the thought: now, as before, the ultimate root of all suffering continues to be called "ignorance." And there it was natural, when inquiry was made as to the illatent import of this idea of "ignorance," it should be described as non-possession of that knowledge, the possession of which appeared to the Buddhist the highest aim of every struggle for deliverance, the knowledge of suffering, of the origin of suffering, of the extinction of suffering, and of the path to the extinction of suffering. The ultimate root of all suffering is the delusion which conceals from man the true being and the true value of the system of the universe. Being is suffering: but ignorance totally deceives us as to this suffering: it causes us to see instead of suffering a phantom of happiness and pleasure.

And the next consequence of this delusion? The formula of causality expresses it in its first proposition: "From ignorance come conformations (Sankhâra)."

Here the impossibility of Buddhist terminology finding adequate expression in our language makes itself keenly felt.

The word Sankhâra is derived from a verb which signifies to arrange, adorn, prepare. Sankhâra is both the preparation and that prepared; but these two coincide in Buddhist conceptions much more than in ours, for to the Buddhist mind —we shall have more to say on this point later on—the made has existence only and solely in the process of being made; whatever is, is not so much a something which is, as the process rather of a being, self-generating and self-again-consuming being. Now, nothing can be imagined at any time any how coming under observation in this world of becoming and decease, to which the idea of forming or of becoming formed does not attach, and thus we shall farther on meet with the word Sankhâra as one of the most general expressions for everything that is in it. In our formula, however, which has not to do with the universe, but with the origin and decease of personal life, the idea of Sankhâra suitable to the connection is a much narrower one: here a forming is meant which is consummated in the domain of the personal body-cum-spirit existence. We might translate Sankhâra directly by "actions," if we understand this word in the wide sense in which it includes also at the same time the internal "actions," the will and wish. The old scholastic teachers divide "conformations" or "actions" under two heads, always in three classes, either viewing them as corresponding to the three categories of thought, word, and deed, or proceeding on the basis of a moral principle of division, into conformations which have a pure end in view (good actions), those which have an impure end in view, and those which have a neutral end in view. "Pure" and "impure," in the language of Indian theology, are nothing more than moral merit, which will be rewarded hereafter, and guilt, which finds its punishment hereafter. Thus the category of "conformations" brings us to the doctrine of Kamma, *i.e.*, the law of moral retribution, which traces out for the wandering soul its path through the world of earthly being, through heaven and hell.

What we are, is the fruit of that which we have done. As an acquisition of pre-Buddhist speculation we have already come across the proposition: "whatsoever he does, to a corresponding state he attains;"* and Buddhism teaches: "My action is my possession, my action is my inheritance, my action is the womb which bears me. My action is the race to which I am akin, my action is my refuge."† What appears to man to be his body is in truth "the action of his past state, which then assuming a form, realized through his endeavour, has become endowed with a tangible existence."‡ The law of causality, substantially regarded by Buddhist speculation as a natural law, here assumes the form of a moral power influencing the universe. No man can escape the effect of his actions. "Not in the heavens," it is said in the Dhammapada,§ "not in the midst of the sea, not if thou hidest thyself away in the clefts of the mountains, wilt thou find a place on earth where thou canst escape the fruit of thy evil actions."|| "Him, who has been long

* *Vide* supra, p. 49.

† "Anguttara Nikâya," Pañcaka Nipâta.

‡ "Saṃyutta Nikâya," vol. i, fol. jhe'.

§ Verses 127, 219 seq.

|| He who obtains deliverance does not thereby escape punishment for the evil which he has not yet expiated. Yet this punishment assumes a form for the delivered, in which none of its terrors remain for them. The history of the robber Angulimâla gives an illustration. This man, who had on his conscience countless deeds of robbery and murder, is converted by Buddha and obtains sanctity. When he goes into the city of Sâvatthi to collect alms, he sustains injuries from the populace by stone-throwing and the hurling of other objects at him. Covered with blood, with broken alms-bowl and torn garments, he comes to Buddha. The latter says to him: "Seest thou not, O Brahman? The reward of evil actions,

travelling and who returns home in safety, the welcome of relatives, friends and acquaintances, awaits. So him, who has done good works, when he passes over from this world into the hereafter, his good works welcome, like relatives a home-returning friend." Through the five regions of transmigration, through divine and human existence, and through the realms of goblins, of animal-life and hells, the power of our actions leads us. The exaltation of heaven awaits the good. The warders of hell bring up the wicked before the throne of king Yama; who asks him, whether he, when he lived on earth, did not see the five messengers of the gods who are sent for the admonition of men, the five visions of human weakness and human suffering; the child, the old man, the sick man, the criminal suffering punishment, and the dead man. Of course he has seen them. "And hast thou, O man, when thou reachedst riper years and becamest old, not thought within thyself: 'I also am subject to birth, old age, and death; I am not exempt from the dominion of birth, old age, and death. Well, then! I will do good in thought, word and deed?'" But he answers: "I was unable to do it, sire; I neglected it, sire, in my frivolity." Then king Yama addresses him: "These thy evil deeds thy mother hath not done, nor thy father, nor thy brother, nor thy sister, nor thy friends and advisers, nor thy connections and blood-relations, nor ascetics, nor Brahmans, nor gods. It is thou alone that hast done these evil actions; thou alone shalt gather their fruit." And the warders of hell drag him to the places of torment. He is riveted to glowing iron, plunged in

for which thou shouldst otherwise have had to suffer for long years and many thousands of years in hell, that thou art now receiving already in this life." (Angalimâla Suttanta, Majjh. Nikâya. The extract given in Hardy's Manual, p. 260 seq., does not fully meet the theological points of the narrative.)

glowing seas of blood, or tortured on mountains of burning coals, and he dies not until the very last residue of his guilt has been expiated.*

It is quite in keeping with the spirit of the old dogmatic, when a later text† compares the cycle of ever-recurring existence, connected throughout by Kamma, by merit and demerit, to a wheel which recoils upon itself, or with the reciprocal generation of the tree from the seed, of the seed corn from the fruit of the tree, of the hen from the egg, and of the egg from the hen. Eye and ear, body and spirit, move into contact with the external world; thus arises sensation, desire, action (kamma); the fruit of the action is the new eye, and the new ear, the new body and the new spirit, which will go to make up the being in the coming existence.

It is this group of thoughts, associated with the idea of Kamma, which we must next take up in order to render intelligible the *rôle* which the category of the Sankhâras plays in the formula of causality. Yet the sacred texts point also to another more distinct interpretation of this category, which lies somewhat in another direction.

In one of the great collections of Buddha's addresses, we meet a sermon "on re-birth according to the Sankhâras."‡ Now this very "re-birth according to the Sankhâras" is that with which the formula of causality has to do at the place, where we are now arrived, for this formula speaks here precisely of the Sankhâras, in so far as they cause the consciousness of the dying being to become the germ of a new being ("from the Sankhâras comes consciousness. From consciousness come name and material form"). We are thus entitled to expect in the expositions of this Sûtra a com-

* Devadûta Sutta. † "Milinda Panha," seq., etc.

‡ Sankhâruppati Suttanta in the Majjhima Nikâya.

mentary upon this part of the formula of causality: and in fact we find it.

It runs as follows:—

"It happens, my disciples, that a monk, endowed with faith, endowed with righteousness, endowed with knowledge of the doctrine, with resignation, with wisdom, communes thus with himself: 'Now then, could I, when my body is dissolved in death, obtain re-birth in a powerful, princely family.' He thinks this thought, dwells on this thought, cherishes this thought. These Sankhâras and internal conditions (vihârâ), which he has thus cherished within him and fostered, lead to his re-birth in such an existence. This, disciples, is the avenue, this the path, which leads to re-birth in such an existence."

The train of thought is then similarly repeated in detail with reference to the several classes of men and gods. The believing and righteous monk, who has in his lifetime directed his thoughts and wishes to these forms of existence, will be re-born in them. So on up to the highest classes of gods, who are separated from Nirvâna by a diminishing residuum of the earthly, the "gods of the spheres, in which there is neither perception nor absence of perception." And finally, in the last place, the Sûtra speaks of the monk "who thus reflects: 'Now then, were I but able by the destruction of sinful existence, to discover and behold for myself the sinless state of deliverance in action and in knowledge even in this present life, and find in it my abode.' He will, by the destruction of sinful existence, discover and behold for himself the sinless state of deliverance in action and in knowledge even in this present life, and will find in it his abode. This monk, O disciples, will never be re-born."

We see what are here the Sankhâras, which have a decisive influence on the re-birth of man: the inner form of the spirit, which anon readily contents itself with the aspirations of the spheres of earthly greatness, raises itself anon with purer energy to the worlds of the gods, even to the highest altitudes, and soars in re-birth to existence actually in these altitudes. Still, however, sorrow pushes even into the most exalted regions. The wise man, therefore, aspires neither to human nor divine happiness; his self-forming directs itself only to the cessation of all conformations. The ignorant, on the contrary, led astray by lies, ignorance of the suffering of all states of being, becomes a settler in the world of impermanence. As the fuel will not permit the flame to be extinguished, so this inner forming of one's self, this hankering after an impermanent object, holds the dying being fast bound to existence. The spirit clothes itself with a new garment of name and material form, and in a new existence repeats the old cycle of birth and old age, of sorrow and death.

Being and Becoming.—Substance and Conformation.

We have attempted to explain the several elements of the line of causality: it remains for us, viewing it as a whole, to point out what view of the structure of being, if the expression be admissible, what answer to the question: what it amounts to, and what is implied by, anything being stated to be, is given in the formula itself and in the elsewhere-occurring utterances connected therewith in the Buddhist texts. First of all, however, we must here insert a proviso: we have only to deal with that which in this material transient realm of things, in which we live, constitutes being. The question whether there is for Buddhism, beyond this form of being, another realm of life, existing under peculiar laws, whether there is beyond the temporal an everlasting, cannot yet be grappled.

As a suitable starting-point for our inquiry there is a

discourse put into Buddha's mouth in sacred tradition, concerning the reflections by which a monk striving for deliverance is led to dissociation from joy and pain. It is therein recorded:—

"In this monk, O disciples, who thus guards himself and rules his consciousness, who is immovably intent thereon in holy effort and is steadfast in self-culture, there arises a sensation of pleasure. Then he knows as follows: 'In me has arisen this pleasurable sensation; this has arisen from a cause, not without a cause. Where lies this cause? It lies in this body of mine. But this body of mine is impermanent, has become (or, been formed), been produced by causes. A pleasurable sensation, the cause of which lies in the impermanent, originated, cause-produced body, how can it be permanent?' Thus, as well with regard to the body as to the pleasurable sensation, he commits himself to the contemplation of impermanence, transitoriness, evanition, renunciation, cessation, resignation. While he commits himself to the contemplation of impermanence, etc., as well with regard to the body as to the pleasurable sensation, he desists from all yearning propensity based on the body and on pleasurable sensation."

He who is not repelled by the tedious minuteness of this discursive style, will here find a view very important for the thought-fabric of Buddhism: the association of the impermanent and transitory with that which is produced by an operation of causality. Causality, or, to translate more accurately the Indian word (paṭiccasamuppâda), the origin (of one thing) in dependence (from another thing), represents a

* "Saṃyuttaka Nikâya," vol. ii, fol. jhu of the Phayre MS.

† Later on follows an exactly identical soliloquy regarding painful sensations, and sensations which are neither pleasurable nor painful.

relation existing between two members, of which the one, and because of it necessarily the other, is at no moment unaltered. There is no being subject to the law of causality, that does not resolve itself, when analyzed, into a process of self-changing, of becoming. In the continuous oscillation, ruled by the natural law of causality, between being and not-being, consists alone the reality of the things which make up the contents of this world. "This world, O Kaccâna," as we read,* "generally proceeds on a duality, on the 'it is' and the 'it is not.' But, O Kaccâna, whoever perceives in truth and wisdom how things originate in the world, in his eyes there is no 'it is not' in this world. Whoever, Kaccâna, perceives in truth and wisdom how things pass away in this world, in his eyes there is no 'it is' in this world. . . . Sorrow alone arises where anything arises; sorrow passes away where anything passes away. 'Everything is,' this is the one extreme, O Kaccâna. 'Everything is not,' this is the other extreme. The Perfect One, O Kaccâna, remaining far from both these extremes, proclaims the truth in the middle: 'From ignorance come conformations'"—and here follows the wording of the formula of causality. The world is the world's process, the formula of causality is the expression of this process of the world, or at least of that side of the process with which alone man, bound in sorrow and seeking deliverance, has anything to do. The conviction of an absolute law, which rules the world's process expressed in this formula, deserves to be set out in bold relief as one of the most essential elements of the body of Buddhist thought.†

* "Saṃyuttaka Nikâya," vol. i, fol. dhi.

† In another department, as may here be incidentally remarked, there is evinced this same thoroughly rationalistic mode of thought of Buddhism in its interesting attempts to explain on the principle of cause and consequence, the origin of the state and classes (Aggaññasutta, Dîgha Nikâya). Of a primeval difference of castes, rooted in mystic depths, as Brahmanism

Things or substances, in the sense of a something existing by itself, as we are accustomed to understand these words, cannot, according to all we have stated, be at all thought of by Buddhism. As the most general expression for those things, the mutual relation of which the formula of causality explains, the being of which, one might almost say, is their standing in that mutual relation, the language of the Buddhists has two terms: Dhamma* and Sankhâra: we may give an approximate rendering of them by "order" and "formation" (p. 247). Both designations are really synonymous; both include the idea that, not so much something ordered, a something formed, as rather a self-ordering, a self-forming, constitutes the subject-matter of the world; with both there is inseparably associated in the feeling of the Buddhist the thought that every order must give place to another order, and every formation to another formation. Bodily as well as spiritual evolutions, all sensations, all perceptions, all conditions, everything that is, *i.e.*, all that passes, is a Dhamma, a Sankhâra. While older speculation had confined all being to the Âtman, the great unchangeable "I," it was now laid down as a fundamental

regarded it, we do not now speak. In old times beings possessed the rice, on which they lived, in common. Later on they divided it among them. One being encroached on the share of another. The others at first punished the evil-doer on their own responsibility. Then they resolved: "We desire to appoint one being, who shall reprimand for us him who deserves reprimand, censure him who deserves censure, banish him who deserves banishment; therefore we desire to give him a share of our rice." Thus was the first king chosen on earth. The origin of the priestly class is described in similar fashion.

* The word Dhamma (Sansk. dharma, in the oldest form dharman), "order, law," usually signifies in Buddhist terminology "essence, idea," in so far as the essence of anything constitutes its own immanent law. Thus the word is also used as the most general designation of the doctrine or truth preached by Buddha.

proposition: all Dhammas are "not-I"* (an-attâ, Sansk. an-âtman);† they are all transitory. Time after time the words uttered by the god Indra when Buddha entered Nirvâna recur in the sacred texts: "Impermanent truly are the Sankhâras, liable to origination and decease; as they arose so they pass away; their disappearance is happiness."

Some have expressed the difference between the Brahman and the Buddhist conceptions of the existence of things, as if, of the component parts which together form the idea of becoming (being and not-being), the former had laid hold of the idea of being only, and the latter of non-being only. We prefer to avoid every expression which would make Buddhism regard non-being as the true substance of things, and to express ourselves thus. The speculation of the Brahmans apprehended being in all becoming, that of the Buddhists becoming in all apparent being. In the former case substance without causality, in the latter causality without substance.

Where the sources lie, from which this causality derives its sanction and its power, Buddhism does not ask. It is as little

* N.B.—It is not said, "there is no ego," but merely: "the Dhammas —*i.e.*, all things which go to make up the contents of this world—are non-ego."

† Verses 277-279 of the "Dhammapada" are very significant as the most general expression of these propositions. In them at the same time the synonymousness of Dhamma and Sankhâra is characteristically evidenced. In the two first of these three exactly similarly constructed verses mention is made of the Sankhâra; in the third verse, where a syllable must be curtailed for metrical reasons, Dhamma is used instead of Sankhâra:

"All Sankhâras are impermanent: when he perceives this in truth, he turns from sorrow; this is the path of purity.

"All Sankhâras are full of sorrow: when he perceives this in truth, he turns from sorrow; this is the path of purity.

"All Dhammas are non-ego: when he perceives this in truth, he turns from sorrow; this is the path of purity."

concerned whether the world was created by a god, or whether it was evolved by an absolute substance or by a creative natural *sub-stratum* out of its own interior. He accepts its presence and the working of the law of the world as facts. Should any one wish to express, though by no means in full accord with Buddhist habits of thought, what is the absolute within this domain of impermanence—we should, perhaps, rather say the most absolute—he might name as such the controlling law of the universe, that of causality. Where there is no being, but only becoming, it is not a substance, but only a law, which can be recognized as the first and the last.

A beginning of time from which the working of this law takes effect, and a limit of space, which encloses the world in which it operates, cannot be discovered. Is there in fact no such limit? "This has the Exalted One not revealed." "O disciples, think not such thoughts as the world thinks: 'The world is everlasting, or the world is not everlasting. The world is finite, or the world is not finite.' . . . If ye think, O disciples, thus think ye: 'This is suffering;' thus think ye: 'This is the origin of suffering;' thus think ye: 'This is the extinction of suffering;' thus think ye: 'This is the path to the extinction of suffering.'"*

THE SOUL.

It is only now, in this connection, that we are in a position to thoroughly understand a much-talked-of dogma of Buddhism: the negation of soul.

It is not incorrect to say that Buddhism disaffirms the existence of soul, but this cannot be understood in a sense

* "Saṃyutta N.," vol. iii, fol. kyâ.

which would in any way give this thought a materialistic stamp. It might be said with equal propriety that Buddhism denies the existence of the body. The body, as well as the soul, exists only as a complex of manifold inter-connected origination and decease; but neither body nor soul has existence as a self-contained substance, sustaining itself *per se*. Sensations, perceptions, and all those processes which make up the inner life, crowd upon one another in motley variety; in the centre of this changing plurality stands consciousness (viññâṇa), which, if the body be compared to a state, may be spoken of as the ruler of this state.* But consciousness is not essentially different from perceptions and sensations, the comings and goings of which it at the same time superintends and regulates: it is also a Sankhâra, and like all other Sankhâras it is changeable and without substance. We must here divest ourselves wholly of all customary modes of thinking. We are accustomed to realize our inner life as a comprehensible factor, only when we are allowed to refer its changing ingredients, every individual feeling, every distinct act of the will, to one and an ever identical ego, but this mode of thinking is fundamentally opposed to Buddhism. Here as everywhere it condemns that fixity which we are prone to give to the current of incidents that come and go by conceiving a substance, to or in which they might happen. A seeing, a hearing, a conceiving, above all a suffering, takes place: but

* "Saṃyutta Nikâya," vol. ii, fol. jo; "Milindapañha," p. 62.—Compare also the following passage, often repeated in the sacred texts (*e.g.* in the "Sâmaññaphala Sutta"): "This is my body, the material, framed out of the four elements, begotten by my father and mother . . . , but that is my consciousness, which clings firmly thereto, is joined to it. Like a precious stone, beautiful and valuable, octahedral, well polished, clear and pure, adorned with all perfection, to which a string is attached, blue or yellow, red or white, or a yellowish band," &c.

an existence, which may be regarded as the seer, the hearer, the sufferer, is not recognized in Buddhist teaching.

It may be allowable in this place to go beyond the range of the sacred texts, and here insert those very clear expressions which we find on this group of problems in a later and in many respects exceedingly remarkable dialogue, the "Questions of Milinda." In the centuries which followed Alexander's invasion of India, which was so highly important an event in Indian history—in those times, the traces of which meet our eyes in the Greek coins struck in India, and the half-Hellenic figures of ancient Buddhist reliefs—there cannot but have been in the Indus territory meetings of argumentative Greeks with Indian monks and dialecticians, and Buddhist literature has preserved one record of such encounters in that dialogue, which bears the name of the Yavana king Milinda, that is, the Ionian or Greek prince Menander (ca. 100 B.C.).

King Milinda* says to the great saint Nâgasena: "How art thou known, venerable sire; what is thy name, sire?"

The saint replies: "I am named Nâgasena, O great king; but Nâgasena, great king, is only a name, an appellation, a designation, an epithet, a mere word; here there is no subject."

Then said the king Milinda: "Well to be sure! let only the five hundred Yavanas and the eighty thousand monks hear it: this Nâgasena says: 'Here there is no subject.' Can anyone assent to this?"

And king Milinda went on to say to the venerable Nâgasena: "If, O venerable Nâgasena, there is no subject, who is it then that provides you with what you need, clothes and food, lodging and medicine for the sick? Who is it that enjoys all

* "Milindapañha," p. 25 seq. I take the liberty of omitting a few unnecessary repetitions in my translation.

these things? Who walks in virtues? Who expends labour upon himself? Who attains the path and the fruits of holiness? Who attains Nirvâna? Who kills? Who steals? Who walks in pleasures? Who deceives? Who drinks? Who commits the five deadly sins? Thus there is then no good and no evil; there is no doer and no originator of good and evil actions; good action and evil action bring no reward and bear no fruit. If anyone were to kill thee, venerable Nâgasena, even he would commit no murder.

"Sire, are the hairs Nâgasena?"

"No, great king."

"Are nails or teeth, skin or flesh or bone Nâgasena?"

"No, great king."

"Is the bodily form Nâgasena, O sire?"

"No, great king."

"Are the sensations Nâgasena?"

"No, great king."

"Are the perceptions, the conformations, the consciousness Nâgasena?"

"No, great king."

"Or, sire, the combination of corporeal form, sensations, perceptions, conformations, and consciousness, is this Nâgasena?"

"No, great king."

"Or, sire, apart from the corporeal form, and the sensations, the perceptions, conformations, and consciousness, is there a Nâgasena?"

"No, great king."

"Wherever I look then, sire, I nowhere find a Nâgasena. A mere word, sire, is Nâgasena. What is Nâgasena then? Thou speakest false then, sire, and thou liest; there is no Nâgasena."

Then spoke the venerable Nâgasena to king Milinda thus: "Thou art accustomed, great king, to all the comfort of a princely life, to the greatest comfort. If then, O great king, thou goest out on foot at midday on the hot earth, on the burning sand, and treadest on the sharp stones, gravel, and sand, thy feet are hurt; thy body is fatigued, thy mind upset; there arises a consciousness of a bodily condition associated with dislike. Hast thou come on foot or on a chariot?"

"I do not travel on foot, sire: I have come on a chariot."

"If thou hast come on a chariot, great king, then define the chariot. Is the pole the chariot, great king?"

And now the saint turns the same course of reasoning against the king which the king himself had used against him. Neither the pole, nor the wheels, nor the body, nor the yoke is the chariot. The chariot, moreover, is not the combination of all these component parts, or anything else beyond them. "Wherever I look then, O great king, I nowhere find the chariot. A mere word, O king, is the chariot. What then is the chariot? Thou speakest false then, O king, and thou liest; there is no chariot. Thou art, O great king, suzerain of all India. Of whom, therefore, hast thou any dread, that thou speakest untruth? Well to be sure! let the five hundred Yavanas and the eighty thousand monks hear it. This king Milinda has said: 'I have come here in a chariot.' Then I said, 'If thou hast come on a chariot, O great king, then explain the chariot?' And he could not point out the chariot. Can anyone assent to this?"

When he spoke thus, the five hundred Yavanas shouted approval of the venerable Nâgasena and said to king Milinda: "Now, O great king, speak, if thou canst."

But king Milinda said to the venerable Nâgasena:

"I do not speak untruly, venerable Nâgasena. In reference

to pole, axle, wheels, body and bar, the name, the appellation, the designation, the epithet, the word 'chariot' is used."

"Good indeed, great king, thou knowest the chariot. And in the same way, O king, in reference to my hair, my skin and bones, to corporeal form, sensations, perceptions, conformations, and consciousness, the word Nâgasena is used: but here subject, in the strict sense of the word, there is none. Thus also, great king, has the nun Vajirâ explained in the presence of the Exalted One (Buddha):

"'As in the case where the parts of a chariot come together the word 'chariot' is used, so also where the five groups* are, there is a person; that is the common notion.'"

"Well done, venerable Nâgasena! wonderful, Nâgasena! Many questionings indeed arose in my mind and thou hast resolved them. If Buddha were alive, he would applaud thee. Bravo! bravo! Nâgasena; many questionings arose in my mind and thou hast resolved them."

We have selected for quotation this passage of the "Questions of Milinda," because it controverts the idea of a soul-substance more fully and clearly than is done in the canonical texts. But the old texts themselves virtually rest on the same ground and the dialogue does not omit to authenticate it, by expressly quoting the canonical books. Although the "Milinda-pañha" was written apparently in the north-west of the Indian peninsula, and the sacred texts lie before us in the form in which they were preserved, and still are preserved, in the cloisters of Ceylon, nevertheless the words of the nun Vajirâ quoted in the dialogue are actually to be found in these texts.

* The five groups of the elements, which make up the being of any one that exists: material form, sensations, perceptions, conformations, consciousness.

I have succeeded in finding them there,* and the connection in which they occur is a guarantee that the conversation of the saint Nâgasena and the Greek king Menander truly reflects the old Church teaching on the subject. Mâra, the tempter, who seeks to confuse men by error and heresy, appears before a nun and says to her: "Thou art that by which personality is constituted, the creator of the person; the person that has an origin, that thou art; thou art the person that passes away." She answers: "What meanest thou, Mâra, that there is a person? False is thy teaching. This is only a heap of changeful conformations (Sankhâra); here there is not a person. As in the case where the parts of a chariot come together the word 'chariot' is used, so also where the five groups are, there is a person; that is the common notion. Pain alone it is that comes, pain that exists and that passes away; nothing else but pain arises, nothing else but pain vanishes again."

Thought has smitten down the stony, unvarying entity of Brahmanism; here it realizes in full consciousness the ultimate consequences of its act: if it is the absolutely restless movement of things which creates suffering, it cannot be said any more, "I suffer, thou sufferest;" there is left alone the certainty that there is suffering, or better still, that suffering keeps on coming and going. For the stream of Sankhâras appearing and again vanishing admits no "I" and no "thou," but only a phenomenon of the "I" and "thou," which the many in their hallucination address with an appellation of personality.†

* In the Bhikkhunî Saṃyutta, "Saṃy. Nik." vol. i, fol. ghai'-gho.

† The difficulty of bringing this doctrine of the non-existence of a subject in the complex of the body-cum-spirit attributes of man into harmony with the doctrine of moral retribution of our actions, has been keenly felt. "If material form be not the ego, if sensations, perceptions, formations, consciousness be not the ego, what ego is there to be affected

Imagination, which in the service of inquiring thought seeks for types and symbols of formless ideas in the form-world of nature, has at all times when its object was to represent a being, the characteristic of which is movement, chosen with decided preference two images: the flowing stream of water and the self-consuming flame. In the dark sayings of Buddha's great contemporary, Heraklitos, who in his theory of the being of beings more nearly approaches Buddha than does any other Greek thinker, both comparisons are constantly recurring in the foreground: "Everything flows on;" the universe is "an ever-living fire." The figurative language of Buddhism also employs both the stream and the flame as symbols of the restless movement involved in every state of being. But in this the Buddhist figure differs from that of the Ephesian, that Buddhism, ignoring every metaphysical interest which has not its root in an ethical interest, does not in its view of the water and the flame contemplate the mere movement, the bare becoming only, but above all the to-human-life-so-momentous and destructive power of this movement, this becoming. There are four great currents which break in with destructive force upon the human world: the stream of desire, the stream of being, the stream of error, the stream of ignorance. "The

by the work, which the non-ego now performs?" Thus a monk asks. Buddha answers the question: "With thy thoughts, which are under the dominion of desire, dost thou dream thou canst overhaul the teaching of the Master" ("Saṃyutta Nikâya," vol. i, fol. du). In fact Buddhism does not allow itself to be confused by metaphysical questions as to the identity of the subject, in its belief that the reward and punishment of our actions overtakes us. If in our present state of being this or that happens to us, it is a result of the fact, that we have done this or that in a previous existence: in this simple belief, universally comprehensible, this idea is firmly kept in view, heedless of theoretical difficulties, that he who performs an evil action, and he who suffers the punishment thereof, are one and the same person.

sea, the sea: thus, O disciples, saith a child of this world, who hath not received the Doctrine. But this, O disciples, is not that which is called the sea in the Doctrine of the Holy One; this is only a great mass of water, a great flood of water. The eye of man, O disciples, is the sea; things visible are the foam of this sea. He who hath overcome the foaming billows of visible things, of him, O disciples, it is said: That is a Brahman who hath in his inner man outridden the sea of the eye, with its waves and whirlpools, with its depths profound and its prodigies; he hath reached the shore; he stands on firm earth." (The same follows regarding the sea of hearing and the other senses.) "Thus spake the Exalted One; when the Perfect One had thus spoken, the Master went on to say:

"'If thou this sea with its abyss of waters,
Full of waves, full of deeps, full of monsters,
Hast crossed, wisdom and holiness are thy portion;
The land hast thou, the goal of the universe hast thou reached.'"*

But no other picture was so perfectly adapted for Buddhism to express the nature of being as the figure of flame, which, remaining in apparently restful invariability, is yet only a continuous self-production and self-consumption, and in which at the same time is embodied, with a still more impressive reality for the Indians than for us, the tormenting power of heat, the enemy of blissful coolness, the enemy of happiness and peace. "As, where there is heat, coolness is also found, so also where there is the threefold fire—the fire of love, hate and infatuation—the extinction of the fire (Nirvâna) must be sought."†—"Everything, O disciples, is in flames. And what Everything is in flames? The eye is in flames, and so on. By what fire is it kindled? By the fire of desire, by the fire of

* "Saṃyutta Nikâya," vol. ii, fol. chi.

† "Buddhavaṃsa."

hate, by the fire of fascination, it is kindled; by birth, old age, death, pain, lamentation, sorrow, grief, despair, it is kindled: thus I say."*—"The whole world is in flames; the whole world is wrapped in smoke, the whole world is wasted by fire; the whole world quakes."†

But to us in this connection more important than the employment of the metaphor of fire, from an ethical point of view, is its introduction to illustrate the metaphysical nature of being as of a continuous process. It is reserved to later texts to work up this metaphor to perfect clearness; but it already exists in the sacred writings, although we feel how thought has here to struggle with expression. Beings resemble a flame; their state of being, their becoming re-born is a flaming cleaving of self, a feeding of self upon the fuel which the world of impermanence supplies. As the flame, clinging to the wind, borne by the wind, inflames even distant things, so the flame-like existence of beings, presses on in the moment of re-birth into far distances; here the being puts off the old body, there it clothes itself with a new body. As the wind carries on the flame, so the thirst which clings to being carries on the soul from one existence to another.‡

In the previously quoted dialogue "The Questions of Milinda,"|| the conversation turns upon the problem of the identity or non-identity of the being in his several existences. The saint Nâgasena says: it is not the same being and yet they are not separate beings which relieve one another in the

* "Mahâvagga," i, 21, *vide* supra, p. 182, seq.

† "Saṃyutta Nikâya," vol. i, fol. ghai.

‡ Cf. the above (p. 234) quoted dialogue of Buddha and the monk Vaccha.

|| P. 40.

series of existences. "Give an illustration," says king Milinda. "If a man were to light a light, O great king, would it not burn on through the night?"—"Yes, sire, it would burn through the night."—"How then, O great king, is the flame in the first watch of the night identical with the flame in the midnight watch?"—"No, sire."—"And the flame in the midnight watch, is it identical with the flame in the last watch of the night?"—"No, sire."—"But how then, O great king, was the light in the first watch of the night another, in the midnight watch another, and in the last watch of the night another?"—"No, sire, it has burned all night long feeding on the same fuel."—"So also, O great king, the chain of elements of being (Dhamma) completes itself: the one comes, the other goes. Without beginning, without end, the circle completes itself: therefore it is neither the same being nor another being, which presents itself last to the consciousness."

Being is, we may say, the procession—regulated by the law of causality—of continuous being at every moment self-consuming and anew begetting. What we term a souled being, is one individual member in the line of this procession, one flame in this sea of flame. As in consuming the flame is always seeking fresh fuel for itself, so also this continuity of perception, sensation, action and suffering, which seems to the deluded gaze, deceived by the appearance of unbroken invariability, to be a being, a subject, maintains itself in the general influx and evanescence of ever fresh elements from the domain of the objective world.

The Saint—The Ego—The Nirvâna.

Sitting under the tree of knowledge Buddha says to himself: "Difficult will it be for men to grasp the law of causality, the chain of causes and effects. And this also will be very hard for them to grasp, the coming of all conformations to an end, the loosening from everything earthly, the extinction of desire, the cessation of longing, the end, the Nirvâna." These words divide the circle, which Buddhist thought describes, into its two natural halves. On the one side the earthly world, ruled by the law of causality. On the other side—is it the eternal? Is it the Nothing? We may doubt. We know this much only to begin with, that it is the domain over which the law of causality has no power.

Our sketch will follow this clearly indicated division.

From the flames of becoming, decease, and suffering, the believer, he who has knowledge, saves himself in the world of "extinction" (Nirvâna), in the cool quiet of everlasting peace. He overcomes ignorance and thereby sets himself free from the painful fruits which are bound up with it through the natural necessity of the law of causality. He knows the four sacred truths, and "while he thus knows and apprehends, his soul is freed from the calamity of desire, freed from the calamity of becoming, freed from the calamity of error, freed from the calamity of ignorance. In the delivered there arises the knowledge of his deliverance; ended is re-birth, fulfilled the law, duty done, there is no more any returning to this world: this he knows."

Buddha's disciple hopes to attain this happiness not merely in the hereafter. He who has conquered ignorance and got rid of desire enjoys the supreme reward already in this life.

His outer man may still be detained in the world of suffering; he knows that it is not he himself whom the coming and going of the Sankhâras affects. Buddhist proverbial philosophy attributes in innumerable passages the possession or Nirvâna to the saint, who still treads the earth:

"The disciple who has put off lust and desire, rich in wisdom, has here on earth attained the deliverance from death, the rest, the Nirvâna, the eternal state."

"He who has escaped from the trackless, hard mazes of the Sansâra, who has crossed over and reached the shore, self-absorbed, without stumbling and without doubt, who has delivered himself from the earthly, and attained Nirvâna, him I call a true Brahman."*

It is not an anticipation in parlance, but it is the absolutely exact expression of the dogmatic thought, when not merely the hereafter, which awaits the emancipated saint, but the perfection which he already attains in this life, is called the Nirvâna. What is to be extinguished has been extinguished, the fire of lust, hatred, bewilderment. In unsubstantial distance lie hope and fear; the will, the hugging of the hallucination of egoity is subdued, as a man throws aside the foolish wishes of childhood. What matters it whether the transitory state of being, the root of which is nipped, lay aside its indifferent phenomenal life instantaneously or in after ages?

If the saint will even now put an end to his state of

* "Suttasangaha," fol. cû; "Dhammapada," 414. The prose texts contain very numerous similar expressions. For instance, a Brahmanical ascetic addresses to Sâriputta this question: "Nirvâna, nirvâna, so they say, friend Sâriputta. But what is the Nirvâna, friend?" "The subjugation of desire, the subjugation of hatred, the subjugation of perplexity; this, O friend, is called Nirvâna." Thereon follows in the same way the question: "Holiness, holiness (arahatta), so they say," &c. The answer is word for word similar to the preceding ("Saṃy. Nik." ii, ñaṃ).

being he can do so, but the majority stand fast until nature has reached her goal: of such may those words be said which are put in the mouth of the most prominent of Buddha's disciples: "I long not for death, I long not for life; I wait till mine hour come, like a servant who awaiteth his reward. I long not for death, I long not for life; I wait till mine hour come, alert and with watchful mind."*

If we are to indicate the precise point at which the goal is reached for the Buddhist, we must not look to the entry of the dying Perfect One into the range of the everlasting—be this either everlasting being or everlasting nothing—but to that moment of his earthly life, when he has attained the status of sinlessness and painlessness; this is the true Nirvâna. If the Buddhist faith really make the saint's state of being disembody itself into nothingness—we shall come directly to the question whether it does so—still entry into nothingness for nothingness' sake is not at all the object of aspiration which has been set before the Buddhist. The goal to which he pressed was, we must constantly repeat this, solely deliverance from the sorrowful world of origination and decease. Religious aspiration did not purposely and expressly demand that this deliverance should transport to nothingness, but when this was taught at all expression was merely given thereby to the indifferent, accidental consequences of metaphysical reflections, which prevent the assumption of an everlasting, immutable, happy existence. In the religious life, in the tone which prevailed in the ancient Buddhist order, the thought of annihilation has had no influence. "As the great sea, O disciples, is permeated by but one taste, the taste of salt, so also, O disciples, this Doctrine and this Law are pervaded by but one taste, the taste of deliverance."

* "Milindapañha," p. 45, cf. Therag. fol. ko.

Our speculations must not seek to discover what is the essence of a faith; we must permit the adherents of each faith themselves to determine this, and it is for historical inquiry to point out how they have defined it. If any one describes Buddhism as a religion of annihilation, and attempts to develope it therefrom as from its specific germ, he has, in fact, succeeded in wholly missing the main drift of Buddha and the ancient order of his disciples.

Has the saint attained the goal of his earthly life, then is true of him what an old text says of Buddha:* "The body of the Perfect One, O disciples, subsists, cut off from the stream of becoming. As long as his body subsists, so long will gods and men see him; if his body be dissolved, his life run out, gods and men shall no more behold him." While in the case of beings who are committed to the path of metempsychosis, consciousness (viññâṇa), escaping from the dying, becomes the germ of a new state of being, the consciousness of the dying saint is extinguished without residuum. "Dissolved is the body," says Buddha, when one of the disciples has entered into Nirvâna, "extinct is perception; the sensations have all vanished away. The conformations have found their repose: the consciousness has sunk to its rest."†

When the venerable Godhika has brought about his own death by opening a vein, the disciples see a dark cloud of smoke moving to and fro on all sides round his corpse. They ask Buddha what the smoke means. "That is Mâra, the wicked one, O disciples," says Buddha: "he is looking for the noble Godhika's consciousness: 'where has the noble Godhika's consciousness found its place?' But the noble

* "Brahmajâlasutta" (at the end).

† "Udâna" (Phayre MS.), fol. ñu.

Godhika has entered into Nirvâna; his consciousness nowhere remains."*

Does this end of the earthly existence imply at the same time the total cessation of being? Is it the Nothing which receives the dying Perfect One into its dominion?

Step by step we have prepared the ground so as now to be able to face this question.

Some have thought to find the answer to this question contained in the word Nirvâna itself, *i.e.*, "Extinction." It seemed the most obvious construction that extinction is an extinction of being in the Nothing. But doubts were soon expressed as to the propriety of so summary a disposal of this question. It was quite allowable to speak of an extinction in the case—and the term was most incontrovertibly used by the Indians in the case—where being was not annihilated, but where it, freed from the glowing heat of suffering, had found the path to the cool repose of painless happiness.† Max Müller has above all others maintained with warm eloquence the notion of Nirvâna as the completion but not as an extinction of being.‡ His position is, that although later Buddhist metaphysicians have

* "Saṃyutta Nikâya," vol. i, fol. ghi'. The story is also narrated in the commentary to the "Dhammapada," p. 255.

† How universally in the language of that age the word Nirvâna denoted the *summum bonum*, without any reference to the close of existence, is clearly shown by the following passage, in which the view considering earthly enjoyments as the highest good is spoken of: "There are, O disciples, many Samanas and Brahmans, who thus teach and thus believe: If the ego moves, gifted and endowed with the pleasure of all the five senses, then has this ego, tarrying in the visible world, attained the highest Nirvâna."—*Brahmajâlasutta.*

‡ Introduction to Rogers, "Buddhaghosha's Parables," p. xxxix, seq.

undoubtedly regarded the Nothing as the supreme object of all effort, yet the original teaching of Buddha and the ancient order of his disciples was different: for them the Nirvâna was nothing more than the entry of the spirit upon its rest, an eternal beatitude, which is as highly exalted above the joys, as it is above the sorrow of the transitory world. Would not, asks Max Müller, a religion, which lands us at last in the Nothing, cease to be a religion? It would no longer be what every religion ought to be and purports to be, a bridge from the temporal to the eternal, but it would be a delusive gangway, which suddenly breaks off and shoots a man, just when he fancies he has reached the goal of the eternal, into the abyss of annihilation.

We cannot follow the famous inquirer, when he attempts to trace the limits between the possible and the impossible in the developement of religion. In the sultry, dreamy stillness of India, thoughts spring and grow, every surmise and every sensation grows, otherwise than in the cool air of the west. Perhaps what is here beyond comprehension may there be comprehensible, and if we reach a point which is to us a limit of the comprehensible, we shall permit much to pass and stand as incomprehensible, and await the future, which may bring us nearer the solution of the enigma.

Max Müller's researches, which could under the then circumstances of the case be based on only a portion of the authentic texts bearing on this branch of the subject, did not fail to attract the attention of native literati in Ceylon, the country which has preserved to the present day Buddhist temperament and knowledge in its purest form. And by the joint labours of eminent Singhalese students of Buddhist literature, such as the late James d'Alwis, and European inquirers, among whom we may mention especially Childers, Rhys Davids, and

Trenckner, literary materials for the elucidation of the dogma of Nirvâna have been amply unearthed and ably treated. I have endeavoured to complete the collections, for which we have to thank these learned scholars, in that I have submitted all the testimony of the sacred Pali canon, that contained in the discourses of Buddha as well as that in the writings upon the rights of the Order, to a detailed examination, so that I believe I am in a position to hope that no essential expression of the ancient dogmatics and doctrinal poets has been omitted.* Before I undertook this task, it was my conviction that there is in the ancient Buddhist literature no passage which directly decides the alternative whether the Nirvâna is eternal felicity or annihilation. So much the greater therefore was my surprise, when in the course of these researches I lit not upon one passage, but upon very numerous passages, which speak as expressly as possible upon the point, regarding which the controversy is waged, and determine it with a clearness which leaves nothing to be desired. And it was no less a cause of astonishment to me when I found that in that alternative, which appeared to have been laid down with all possible cogency, viz., that the Nirvâna must have been understood in the ancient Order to be either the Nothing or a supreme felicity, there was finally neither on the one side nor on the other perfect accuracy.

We shall now endeavour to state the question as it must have presented itself to Buddhist dogmatic on its own premises, and then the answer which the question has received.

A doctrine which contemplates a future of eternal perfection behind transitory being, cannot possibly admit of the kingdom

* In Excursus iii, further quotations are given from the materials here mentioned, and the dogmatic terminology is discussed in detail at greater length than appeared expedient in this place.

of the eternal first beginning only at the point where the world of the transient ends, cannot conjure it up immediately, as it were out of the Nothing. In the kingdom of the transient itself there must be contained, veiled perhaps like a latent germ, but still present, an element which bears in itself the pledge of everlasting being stretching out beyond origination and decease. It is possible that, where the claims of strict dialectic sequence are opposed by motives of another kind, thought pauses before accepting this so obvious conclusion; but it is important before we examine these deviations from the logical consequence, which we may possibly expect to find, to obtain a view of the form in which the logical consequence must have presented itself to Buddhist thought.

The finite world appears in the dogmatic of Buddhism to rest wholly upon itself. Whatever we see, whatever we hear, our senses as well as the objects which are presented to them, everything is drawn within the cycle of origination and decease; everything is only a Dhamma, a Sankhâra, and all Dhammas, all Sankhâras are transitory. Whence this cycle? No matter whence; it is there from a past beyond ken. The existence of the conditional is accepted as a given fact; thought shrinks from going back to the unconditional.

This is specially evident in the question as to the soul, the personality. "This is only a heap of Sankhâras; here there is not a person" (p. 258).

We see: the finite world bears in itself no traces which point to its connection with a world of the eternal. How could it possibly be otherwise? Where the opposition of the transient and eternal is carried to the point which Indian thought has here reached, there can in fact be no union conceived between the two extremes. Had the eternal any share whatsoever in the occurrences of the world of the changeable, a shadow of the changeable would fall on its own unchangeability. The conditional can only be thought of as conditioned through another conditional. If we follow the dialectic consequence solely, it is impossible on the basis of this theory of life to conceive how, where a series of conditions has run out, annihilating itself, anything else is to be recognized as remaining but a vacuum.

This is the consequence. Does Buddhism actually admit this?

We must here insert a few remarks upon the standard technical terms, which our texts are wont to use in dealing with these questions.

The word which we have translated "Person" (Satta) in the passages quoted, is not the precise technical term which the Brahmanical speculation, discussed by us at an earlier stage, had coined as the most exact and special expression for the eternal in man: Âtman, "the self," "the ego." The Buddhist texts deal with the Âtman (in Pâli: Attâ) also. If the demands of dialectic alone be regarded, it cannot be understood how the question regarding the "ego" was to be answered otherwise than the question as to the "person"—it seems clear enough that both words are only different names for the same idea, and that he who denies the existence of the "person," cannot maintain the existence of the "ego" or even admit it possible.

Beside the expression Âtman (attâ) we place another, of which the same may be said, the name Tathâgata, "the Perfect One." Buddha is in the habit of calling himself Tathâgata in his Buddhahood (p. 126). If a question be raised as to the essentiality and everlasting continuance of the Tathâgata, this is altogether parallel to the question regarding the essentiality and continuance of the ego; if there be an ego, the sacred perfect personality of the Tathâgata must undoubtedly be the ego, which deserves this name in the highest sense, which bears in itself the greatest claim to everlasting being. But as we might expect, with the lot of the "person" (satta) the lot of the Tathâgata, as well as that of the ego (attâ), is cast.

Let us see whether the expressions of the Buddhist texts are in accordance with this view.

"Then the wandering monk* Vacchagotta went to where the Exalted One was staying. When he had come near him, he saluted him. When, saluting him, he had interchanged friendly words with him, he sat down beside him. Sitting beside him the wandering monk Vacchagotta spake to the Exalted One, saying: "How does the matter stand, venerable Gotama, is there the ego (attâ)?"

When he said this, the Exalted One was silent.

"How then, venerable Gotama, is there not the ego?"

And still the Exalted One maintained silence. Then the wandering monk Vacchagotta rose from his seat and went away.

But the venerable Ânanda, when the wandering monk Vacchagotta had gone to a distance, soon said to the Exalted One: "wherefore, sire, has the Exalted One not given an answer to the questions put by the wandering monk Vacchagotta?"

"If I, Ânanda, when the wandering monk Vacchagotta asked me: 'Is there the ego?' had answered: 'the ego is,' then that, Ânanda, would have confirmed the doctrine of the Samanas and Brahmanas who believe in permanence.† If I, Ânanda, when the wandering monk Vacchagotta asked me:

* A monk of a non-Buddhist sect. The dialogue here translated is to be found in the "Saṃyuttaka Nikâya," vol. ii, fol. tan.

† "A few Samanas and Brahmanas, who believe in permanence, teach that the ego and the world are permanent."—*Brahmajâlasutta.*

'is there not the ego?' had answered: 'the ego is not,' then that, Ânanda, would have confirmed the doctrine of the Samanas and Brahmanas, who believe in annihilation.* If I, Ânanda, when the wandering monk Vacchagotta asked me: 'is there the ego?' had answered: 'the ego is,' would that have served my end, Ânanda, by producing in him the knowledge: all existences (dhamma) are non-ego?"

"That it would not, sire."

"But if I, Ânanda, when the wandering monk Vacchagotta asked me: 'Is there not the ego?' had answered: 'The ego is not,' then that, Ânanda, would only have caused the wandering monk Vacchagotta to be thrown from one bewilderment into another: 'My ego, did it not exist before? but now it exists no longer!'"

We see: the person who has framed this dialogue, has in his thought very nearly approached the consequence, which leads to the negation of the ego. It may almost be said, that, though probably he did not wish to express this consequence with overt consciousness, yet he has in fact expressed it. If Buddha avoids the negation of the existence of the ego, he does so in order not to shock a weak-minded hearer. Through the shirking of the question as to the existence or non-existence of the ego, is heard the answer, to which the premises of the Buddhist teaching tended: The ego is not. Or, what is equivalent: The Nirvâna is annihilation.

But we can well understand why these thinkers, who

* "A few Samanas and Brahmans, who believe in annihilation, teach that the person (satta) is, and that it undergoes annihilation, destruction, and removal" (ibidem).—It is meant, that the ego, even without being purified from sins, undergoes no transmigration, but becomes extinct in death.

were in a position to realize this ultimate consequence and to bear it, abandoned the erection of it as an official dogma of the Buddhist order. There were enough, and more than enough, of hopes and wishes, from which he who desired to follow the Sakya's son, had to sever his heart. Why present to the weak the keen edge of the truth: the victor's prize of the delivered is the Nothing? True, it is not permissible to put falsehood in the place of truth, but it is allowable to draw a well-meant veil over the picture of the truth, the sight of which threatens the destruction of the unprepared. What harm did it do? That which was alone of intrinsic worth and essential to excite the struggle for deliverance was maintained in unimpaired force, the certainty that deliverance is to be found only where joys and sorrows of this world have ceased. Was the emancipation of him, who knew how to free himself from everything transitory, not perfect enough? Would it become more perfect, if he were driven to acknowledge that beside the transitory there is only the Nothing?

Therefore the official teaching of the Church represented that on the question, whether the ego is, whether the perfected saint lives after death or not, the exalted Buddha has taught nothing.*

From the texts, in which this shirking of the question is inculcated, the following epitomized dialogue may be given.†

The venerable Mâlukya comes to the Master and expresses his astonishment that the Master's discourse leaves a series of

* The first scholar, who has given the correct interpretation of a text having an important bearing on this connection and has directed attention to this disallowing of the question as to continuance in the hereafter, is, as far as I know, V. Trenckner ("Milinda P." 424). I am glad to find my independently formed conclusion confirmed by the opinion of this able Danish scholar.

† "Cûla-Mâlukya-Ovâda" (Majjhima Nikâya).

the very most important and deepest questions unanswered. Is the world eternal or is it limited by bounds of time? Does the perfect Buddha (Tathâgata) live on beyond death? Does the Perfect One not live on beyond death? It pleases me not, says that monk, that all this should remain unanswered, and I do not think it right; therefore I am come to the Master to interrogate him about these doubts. May it please Buddha to answer them if he can. "But when anyone does not understand a matter and does not know it, then a straightforward man says: I do not understand that, I do not know that."

We see: the question of the Nirvâna is brought before Buddha by that monk as directly and definitely as could ever be possible. And what answers Buddha? He says in his Socratic fashion, not without a touch of irony:—

"What have I said to thee before now, Mâlukyaputta? Have I said: Come, Mâlukyaputta, and be my disciple; I shall teach thee, whether the world is everlasting or not everlasting, whether the world is finite or infinite, whether the vital faculty is identical with the body or separate from it, whether the Perfect One lives on after death or does not live on, or whether the Perfect One lives on and at the same time does not live on after death, or whether he neither lives on nor does not live on?"

"That thou hast not said, sire."

Or hast thou, Buddha goes on, said to me: I shall be thy disciple, declare unto me, whether the world is everlasting or not everlasting, and so on?

This also must Mâlukya answer in the negative.

If a man, Buddha proceeds, were struck by a poisoned arrow, and his friends and relatives called in a skilful physician: what if the wounded man said: "I shall not allow my wound to be treated until I know who the man is by whom I have been wounded, whether he is a noble, a Brahman, a Vaiçya, or Çûdra"—or if he said: "I shall not allow my wound to be treated, until I know what they call the man who has wounded me, and of what family he is, whether he is tall, or small, or of middle stature, and how his weapon was made, with which he has struck me." What would the end of the case be? The man would die of his wound.

Why has Buddha not taught his disciples, whether the world is finite or infinite, whether the saint lives on beyond death or not? Because the knowledge of these things does not conduce to progress in holiness, because it does not contribute to peace and enlightenment. What contributes to peace and enlightenment, Buddha has taught his own: the truth of suffering, the truth of the origin of suffering, the truth of the cessation of suffering, the truth of the path to the cessation of suffering.* "Therefore, Mâlukyaputta, whatsoever has not been revealed by me, let that remain unrevealed, and what has been revealed, let it be revealed."

Our researches must accept this clear and decisive solution of the question, recurring often in the sacred texts, as it is given; it needs no interpretation, and admits of no strained construction. Orthodox teaching in the ancient order of Buddhists inculcated expressly on its converts to forego the knowledge of the being or non-being of the perfected saint.

But, besides the question as to what was recognized as the orthodox dogma, there is yet another which we have to take up. Who would believe that he has fathomed the faith and

* The wording of the passage of which an epitome is here given is identical with that given before at p. 204.

hope of the devout heart, when he knows the dogma, which the Church prescribed and to which the believer subscribed? Was the waiving of the question which the religious consciousness cannot cease altogether to put to itself over and over again, sufficient to eliminate from the spirits of Buddha's disciples the craving for a Yes or No? Certainly the Yes or the No might not be declared as doctrine; this would be heretical disobedience of Buddha's injunction. But it might make itself perceptible like a vibration, like a gentle flutter of light or shadow, something felt rather than definable; it might, even where the honest purpose to faithfully enunciate the dogma existed, betray itself between the lines, in an incautious expression, in a word too many or too few. In the dialogue between Buddha and Ânanda (p. 272, seq.), a trace seemed to show itself of how some resolute spirits in the order were not far from perceiving that the conclusion of the doctrine involves the negation of the ego, the negation of an eternal future. But this very circumstance, that the official dogmatic abstained from answering these questions, was sure to lead to greater liberty and variety in the solutions which individual thought worked out, than could be the case with regard to problems, for which a recognized orthodox solution had been furnished. Could not that negative answer, which we have come to recognize as the true answer of close dialectic, be met by an affirmative also? Might not hearts, that quailed before the Nothing, that could not relinquish the hope of everlasting weal, gather from Buddha's silence above all this one response, that it was not forbidden to them to hope?

It appears to me that among the many utterances on these questions, which are bound up together in the great complex of the sacred writings, traces of such agitations, as I have here described, are unmistakably enough to be seen.

King Pasenadi of Kosala, we are told,* on one occasion on a journey between his two chief towns, Sâketa and Sâvatthi, fell in with the nun Khemâ, a female disciple of Buddha, renowned for her wisdom. The king paid his respects to her, and inquired of her concerning the sacred doctrine.

"Venerable lady," asked the king, "does the Perfect One (Tathâgata) exist after death?"

"The Exalted One, O great king, has not declared: the Perfect One exists after death."

"Then does the Perfect One not exist after death, venerable lady?"

"This also, O great king, the Exalted One has not declared: the Perfect One does not exist after death."

"Thus, venerable lady, the Perfect One does exist after death, and at the same time does not exist after death?—thus, venerable lady, the Perfect One neither exists after death, nor does he not exist?"

The answer is still the same: the Perfect One has not revealed it. We see how great pains are taken, with that somewhat clumsy subtlety which is characteristic of thought at every step in this stage of development, not merely to exhaust the two alternatives immediately confronting each other, but in the most careful manner to close up all joinings and loopholes, by which the true facts of the case might escape being caught in the logical net. But it is in vain; the Exalted One has not revealed this.

The king is astonished. "What is the reason, venerable

* "Saṃyutta Nikâya," vol. ii, fol. ṇo, seq.

lady, what is the ground, on which the Exalted One has not revealed this?"

"Permit me," answers the nun, "now to ask thee a question, O great king, and do thou answer me as the case seems to thee to stand. How thinkest thou, O great king, hast thou an accountant, or a mint-master, or a treasurer, who could count the sands of the Ganges, who could say: there are there so many grains of sand, or so many hundreds, or thousands, or hundreds of thousands of grains of sand?"

"No, venerable lady, I have not."

"Or hast thou an accountant, a mint-master or a treasurer, who could measure the water in the great ocean, who could say: there are therein so many measures of water, or so many hundreds or thousands, or hundreds of thousands of measures of water?"

"No, venerable lady, I have not."

"And why not? The great ocean is deep, immeasurable, unfathomable. So also, O great king, if the existence of the Perfect One be measured by the predicates of corporeal form:* these predicates of the corporeal form are abolished in the Perfect One, their root is severed, they are hewn away like a palm-tree, and laid aside, so that they cannot germinate again in the future. Released, O great king, is the Perfect One from this, that his being should be gauged by the measure of the corporeal world: he is deep, immeasurable, unfathomable as the great ocean. 'The Perfect One exists after death,' this is not apposite; 'the Perfect One does not exist after death,' this also is not apposite; 'the Perfect One at once exists and does not exists after death,' this also is not

* Afterwards, what is here said of corporeal form, will be repeated in detail regarding the four other groups of elements, of which earthly being is constituted (sensations, perceptions, conformations, consciousness).

apposite; 'the Perfect One neither does nor does not exist after death,' this also is not apposite."

"But Pasenadi, the king of Kosala, received the nun Khemâ's discourse with satisfaction and approbation, rose from his seat, bowed reverently before Khemâ the nun, turned and went away."*

We shall scarcely be astray in supposing that we discover in this dialogue a marked departure from the sharply defined line to which the course of thought confines itself in the previously quoted conversation between Buddha and Mâlukya (p. 274, seq.). True, the question as to the eternal duration of the Perfect One is as little answered here as there, but why can it not be answered? The Perfect One's existence is unfathomably deep, like the ocean: it is of a depth which terrestrial human thought with the appliances at its command, cannot exhaust. The man who applies to the strictly unconditional predicates such as being and non-being, which are used properly enough of the finite, the conditional, resembles a person who attempts to count the sands of the Ganges or the drops of the ocean.

When such a reason is assigned for the waiving of the question as to whether the Perfect One lives for ever, is not this very giving of a reason itself an answer? And is not this answer a Yes? No being in the ordinary sense, but still assuredly not a non-being: a sublime positive, of which thought has no idea, for which language has no expression, which beams out to meet the cravings of the thirsty for immortality in that same splendour, of which the apostle says: "Eye

* The texts relates then how the king at a later opportunity addressed the same questions to Buddha and obtained from him word for word the same answers which he had received on this occasion from the nun Khemâ.

hath not seen, nor ear heard, neither have entered into the heart of man, the things which God hath prepared for them that love Him."

We here proceed to insert another passage,* which adopts a position on this question similar to that last quoted.

"At this time a monk named Yamaka had adopted the following heretical notion: 'I understand the doctrine taught by the Exalted One to be this, that a monk who is free from sin, when his body dissolves, is subject to annihilation, that he passes away, that he does not exist beyond death.'"

Whoever names the absolute Nothing as the goal, in which, according to the Buddhist creed, the life of the Perfect One ends, may learn from the opening words of this passage, that the monk Yamaka advocated this very interpretation and that he had thereby been guilty of heresy.

The venerable Sâriputta undertakes to instruct him.

"How thinkest thou, friend Yamaka, is the Perfect One (Tathâgata) identical with the corporeal form (*i.e.*, does Buddha's body represent his true ego)? Dost thou hold this?"

"I do not, my friend."

"Is the Perfect One identical with the sensations? the perceptions? the conformations, the consciousness? Dost thou hold this?"

"I do not, my friend."

"How thinkest thou, friend Yamaka, is the Perfect One comprised in the corporeal form (. . the sensations, and so on)? Dost thou hold this?"

"I do not, my friend."

"Is the Perfect One separate from the corporeal form? Dost thou hold this?

* "Samyutta Nikâya," vol. i, fol. de, seq.

"I do not, my friend."

"How thinkest thou, friend Yamaka, are the corporeal form, sensations, perceptions, conformations, and consciousness (in their aggregate) the Perfect One? Dost thou hold this?

"I do not, my friend."

"How thinkest thou, friend Yamaka, is the Perfect One separate from corporeal form, sensations, perceptions, conformations, and consciousness? Dost thou hold this?

"I do not, my friend."

"Thus then, friend Yamaka, even here in this world the Perfect One is not to be apprehended by thee in truth. Hast thou therefore a right to speak, saying, 'I understand the doctrine taught by the Exalted One to be this, that a monk who is free from sin, when his body dissolves, is subject to annihilation, that he passes away, that he does not exist beyond death'?"

"Such, indeed, was hitherto, friend Sâriputta, the heretical view which I ignorantly entertained. But now when I hear the venerable Sâriputta expound the doctrine, the heretical view has lost its hold of me, and I have learned the doctrine."

Thus are all attempts to define dialectically the ego of the Perfect One, repelled. The idea is certainly not that some other attempt might prove successful, but is kept in concealment by Sâriputta; no more does the unavailingness of all these attempts to find a solution imply that the Perfect One does not exist at all. Thought, Sâriputta means to say, has here reached an unfathomably deep mystery, on the solution of which it must not insist. The monk, who seeks the happiness of his soul, has something else to pursue.

One who clearly and indefinitely renounced an everlasting future would speak in another strain; behind the veil of the mystery there flies the longing for escape from opposing reason, which declines to admit the conceivableness of everlasting existence, the hope for an existence, which is beyond reason and conception.

The terms, which can be applied to such an existence, are obviously exclusively negative. "There is, O disciples, a state, where there is neither earth nor water, neither light nor air, neither infinity of space, nor infinity of reason, nor absolute void, nor the co-extinction of perception and non-perception, neither this world nor that world, both sun and moon. That, O disciples, I term neither coming nor going nor standing, neither death nor birth. It is without basis, without procession, without cessation: that is the end of sorrow."* "There is, O disciples, an unborn, unoriginated, uncreated, unformed. Were there not, O disciples, this unborn, unoriginated, uncreated, unformed, there would be no possible exit from the world of the born, originated, created, formed."†

These words seem to sound as if we heard Brahmanical philosophers talking of the Brahma, the unborn, intransient which is neither great nor small, the name of which is "No, No," for no word can exhaust its being. Yet these expressions, when viewed in the connection of Buddhist thought, convey something wholly different. To the Brahman the uncreated is so veritable a reality, that the reality of the created pales before it; the created derives its being and life solely from the uncreated. For the Buddhist the words "there is an uncreated" merely signify that the created can free himself from the curse of being created‡—there is a path

* "Udâna," fol. ghau.

† "Udâna," fol. ghau'.

‡ In the "Dhammapada" it is said (v. 383): "If thou hast learned the destruction of the Sankhâra, thou knowest the uncreated." Max Müller (Introduction, l.c., p. xliv) adds to these words the remark: "This surely shows that even for Buddha a something existed which is not made, and

from the world of the created out into dark endlessness. Does the path lead into a new existence? Does it lead into the Nothing? The Buddhist creed rests in delicate equipoise between the two. The longing of the heart that craves the eternal has not nothing, and yet the thought has not a something, which it might firmly grasp. Farther off the idea of the endless, the eternal could not withdraw itself from belief than it has done here, where, like a gentle flutter on the point of merging in the Nothing, it threatens to evade the gaze.

I close with a few sentences from the collections of aphorisms of ancient Buddhist literature. These aphorisms may add nothing new to what has been said, but they will show more clearly than all abstract treatment, what melodies were awakened in the circle of that ancient monastic order, when the chord of the Nirvâna was touched.

"Plunged into meditation, the immovable ones who valiantly

which, therefore, is imperishable and eternal." It appears to me, that we can find in the expression another meaning, and if we consider it in connection with the Buddhist theory of the world, we must find another meaning: Let thine own aim be, to discover the cessation of impermanence. If thou knowest that, thou hast the highest knowledge. Let others pursue the uncreated by their erroneous paths, which will never carry them beyond the realm of the created. As for thee let the attainment of the uncreated consist in this, that thou reachest the cessation of the created. In the "Alagaddûpama Sutta" (Majjh. N.) we read: "The belief which says: 'This is the world, this is the self (attâ), this shall I dying become, firm, durable, everlasting, unchangeable; so shall I be yonder in eternity'—is not that, O disciples, merely sheer folly?"—"How can it be, sire, aught else but sheer folly?"—"How think ye then, O disciples, is corporeal form everlasting or impermanent?"—and then there follow the familiar doctrines of the impermanence of the five complexes (*vide* supra, p. 218), a significant commentary to the allegation, that the Buddhist asking after the eternal is the same as asking after the cessation of the impermanent.

struggle evermore, the wise, grasp the Nirvâna, the gain which no other gain surpasses."

"Hunger is the most grievous illness; the Sankhâra are the most grievous sorrow; recognizing this of a truth man attains the Nirvâna, the supreme happiness."

"The wise, who cause no suffering to any being, who keep their body in check, they walk to the everlasting state: he who has reached that, knows no sorrow."

"He who is permeated by goodness, the monk who adheres to Buddha's teaching, let him turn to the land of peace, where transientness finds an end, to happiness."*

* "Dhammapada," 23, 203, 225, 368.

CHAPTER III.

THE TENET OF THE PATH TO THE EXTINCTION OF SUFFERING.

Duties to others.

Following the course which the rule of faith (*i.e.* the four sacred truths) marks out for us, we have delineated, as corresponding with the second and third of these tenets, what may be described as the metaphysic of Buddhism: the picture of the world bound in the chain of causality, of the sorrow-fraught present, and the picture of the hereafter, in which origination and decease have come to a pause, the flame of sorrow has been extinguished. The fourth tenet of the sacred truths teaches us to know the path which leads out of that world into the domain of deliverance; the group of thoughts which it covers, may be termed the ethic of Buddhism.*

* If the sketch of Buddhism be divided according to the two categories on which the division of the sacred texts proceeds, Dhamma and Vinaya, *i.e.*, Doctrine and Ordinance, ethic must be referred, according to the Buddhist view, to the head of "Doctrine," for not only does that briefest expression of the Doctrine, the sacred truths, include within itself ethic in the last of the four tenets, but the matters falling under the scope of ethic have throughout found their place in the "Basket of the Doctrine," *i.e.*, in the complex of the sacred texts dealing with Dhamma. "Ordinance," as opposed to "Doctrine," is not to be understood in an ethical, but in a legal sense; it is ordinances to govern the associated life of the monastic order.

"This, O monks," so runs this tenet, "is the sacred truth of the path to the extinction of suffering: it is this sacred, eightfold path, to wit: Right Faith, Right Resolve, Right Speech, Right Action, Right Living, Right Effort, Right Thought, Right Self-concentration."

The ideas here placed before us gather significance and colour from the many discourses of Buddha, in which the path of salvation leading to deliverance is described. That scholastic apparatus, from which Indian thought can never shake itself wholly free, is employed in no sparing manner. Everything has its established, ever recurring expression. Virtues and vices have their number: there is a fourfold onward effort; there are five powers and five organs of moral life. Heretics and unbelievers also know the five impediments and the seven elements of illumination, but Buddha's disciples alone know, how that cinq becomes a dix, and this seven a fourteen.*

More valuable than this scholastic, as an aid to understanding how the moral presented itself to the Buddhist view, are the beautiful utterances of the poetical collections, as well as fables and parables, above all the ideal form of Buddha himself as the religious fancy of his disciples has sketched him. Not only in his final stage of earthly existence, but in hundreds of preceding existences has he unintermittingly arrived at all those perfections which were bringing him nearer and nearer to the supreme Buddhahood, and has in numberless displays of invincible strength of will and devoted self-sacrifice created an example for his believers. The components, which go to make up this ethical ideal, obviously disclose at every step the monastic character of Buddhist morality. The true holy life, is the life of the monk; the worldly life is an imperfect, necessarily unsatisfying life, the preliminary step of the weak.

* "Saṃyutta Nikâya," vol. iii, fol. pi', seq.

The primary demand made upon the monk is not: thou shalt live in this world and make this world a something which is worthy of life—but it is: thou shalt separate thyself from this world.

It is hardly necessary to say that any attempt to deduce from these enumerations of moral notions and sayings and narrations a connected code of morals, would be not less opposed to scientific truth than to scientific taste. Still, we find in the sacred texts expressions which point to a definite path of thought traversing the wide range of moral action and passion, a distribution of all that tends to happiness and deliverance under certain leading heads. Above all there recur continually three categories, to some extent like the headings of three chapters on ethic: uprightness, self-concentration, and wisdom.* In the narrative of Buddha's last addresses, the discourse in which he places before his followers the doctrine of the path of salvation, is time after time couched in the following words: "This is uprightness. This is self-concentration. This is wisdom. Pervaded by uprightness, self-concentration is fruitful and rich in blessing; pervaded by self-concentration, wisdom is fruitful and rich in blessing; pervaded by wisdom, the soul becomes wholly free from all infirmity, from the infirmity of desire, from the infirmity of becoming, from the infirmity of error, from the infirmity of ignorance." These three ranges of moral living are compared to the stages of a journey: the end of the journey is deliverance. The base of all is uprightness of walk, but inversely outward righteousness receives its finish only through wisdom. "As hand washes hand and foot washes foot, so uprightness is purified by wisdom, and wisdom is purified by uprightness. Where there is uprightness, there is wisdom: where there is wisdom, there is uprightness. And the wisdom of the upright

* The Pâli expressions are: sîla, samâdhi (or citta), paññâ.

and the uprightness of the wise, have of all uprightness and wisdom in the world the highest value."*

The will of a supreme lawgiver and ruler in the realm of the moral world, as the ground on which the fact and force of a moral command rest, is no more a factor of Buddhist thought than any bold claim, based on inherent necessity, of the universal, that the individual should be subordinate thereto. Nay more, the decided advantage of moral action over immoral arises wholly and solely from the consequence to the actor himself, which is naturally and necessarily attached to the one course of action or the other. In the one case reward—in the other punishment. "He who speaks or acts with impure thoughts, him sorrow follows, as the wheel follows the foot of the draught horse. He who speaks or acts with pure thought, him joy follows, like his shadow, which does not leave him."† "A peasant who saw a fruitful field and scattered no seed there, would not look for a crop. Even so I, who desire the reward of good works, if I saw a fine field for action and did not do good, should not expect the reward of works."‡ Thus morality has its sole weight in this, that it is the means to an end, in the lower degree the means to the humble end of happy life here on earth and in the forms of being yet to come, in the higher degree the means to the supreme and absolute end of happy deliverance.

We now pause in the next place to consider the requirement which Buddhism makes the precursor and preliminary of all higher moral perfection, the precept of "uprightness," and we find its purport expressed in a series of uniformly negative propositions. Upright is he, who keeps himself from all

* "Soṇadaṇḍa Sutta" ("Dîgha Nikâya").

† "Dhammapada," 1, 2.

‡ "Cariyâ Piṭaka," 1, 2.

impurity in word and deed. In the different series of prohibitions, into which this precept is analyzed in the sacred texts, a complex of five commandments takes a special place in the foreground, the regular observance of which constitutes the "five-fold uprightness." Their substance is:—

1. To kill no living thing;*
2. Not to lay hands on another's property;
3. Not to touch another's wife;
4. Not to speak what is untrue;
5. Not to drink intoxicating drinks.

For monks the injunction of absolute chastity was inserted instead of the third of these propositions, and there is added for them a long series of further prohibitions in which abstinence from worldly comforts and enjoyments, from all worldly intermeddling as well as self-indulgence, is laid down as their duty. In the detailed expositions, which we find appended to the several prohibitions, the limits of the pure negative are not unfrequently transgressed.† It could not but happen that, whether the fundamental principle of Buddhist ethic admitted of morality being conceived as a

* It is well known to what an extreme Buddhism, and Indian habits of thought generally, tends to push the regard for the life of even the smallest creature. This regard lies at the bottom of numerous regulations for the daily life of monks. A monk may not drink water in which animal life of any kind whatever is contained, and must not even as much as pour it out on grass or clay ("Pâcittiya," 20, 62). When monks wish to have silk cloths made for themselves, silkweavers murmur and say: "It is our misfortune, it is our ill-fate, that we are obliged to kill many little creatures for the sake of our living, for our wives' and children's sake." And Buddha forbids the monks on this account the use of silk cloths ("Vinaya Piṭaka," vol. iii, p. 224).

† Cf. the extensive section bearing on this subject in the "Sâmâññaphala Suttâ" (the Discourse on the Reward of Ascetism).

positively constituted power or not, the "thou shalt not" should gradually transform itself for the lively moral consciousness into "thou shalt." In this way we find the first of these prohibitions, that of killing, construed in a manner which scarcely falls short of the Christian version of that command, which "was said by them of old time: thou shalt not kill." "How does a monk become a partaker of uprightness?" asks Buddha, and then proceeds himself to furnish the answer in the following sentences: "A monk abstains from killing living creatures; he refrains from causing the death of living creatures. He lays down the stick; he lays down weapons. He is compassionate and tender-hearted: he seeks with friendly spirit the welfare of all living things. That is part of his uprightness." From the prohibition of backbiting a positive course is deduced in the same speech of Buddha's in the following way: "He abstains from calumnious conversation; he refrains from calumnious conversation. What he has heard here he does not repeat there, to separate this man from that; what he has heard there he does not repeat here, to separate that man from this. He is the uniter of the separated, and the confirmer of the united. He enjoys concord; he seeks to promote concord; he takes delight in concord; he is a speaker of concord-producing words. This also is a part of his uprightness."

In every case it is quite true that the prohibition is far more comprehensive than the command; the range of the command goes in but few cases beyond what is of itself implied in the gentle influence which good men exercise by their mere presence without action. As it is peculiarly characteristic of woman's nature to diffuse such an influence silently around her, we shall perhaps be justified in attributing a trace of the feminine to that type of morality to which Buddhism has given birth.

Some who have endeavoured to bring Buddhism up to Christianity, have given compassionate love of all creatures as the kernel of the Buddhist's pure morality. In this there is something of truth. But the inherent difference of the two moral powers is still apparent. The language of Buddhism has no word for the poesy of Christian love, of which that hymn of Paul's is full, the love which is greater than faith and hope, without which one, though he spake with the tongue of men or of angels, would be a sounding brass or a tinkling cymbal; nor have the realities, in which that poetry assumed flesh and blood within the Christian world, had their parallel in the history of Buddhism. We may say that love, such as it displays itself in Buddhist morality, oscillating between negative and positive, approaches Christian love without actually touching it, in a way similar to that in which the beatitude of the Nirvâna, though fundamently wholly different from the Christian idea of happiness, does to a certain extent, as we saw, swing towards it. Buddhism does not so much enjoin on one to love his enemy, as not to hate his enemy; it evokes and cherishes the emotion of friendly goodness and tender-heartedness towards all creatures, a feeling in which the motive power is not the groundless, enigmatic self-surrender of love, but rather intelligent reflection, the conviction that it is thus best for all, and not least the expectation, that the natural law of retribution will allot to such conduct the richest reward.

"He who keeps the angry passion," thus we read in the Dhammapada,* "within his control, like a rolling waggon, him

* Verses 222, 223, 3 seq. ("Mahâvagga," x, 3).

I call the real waggon-driver; any other is only a rein-holder." "Let a man overcome anger by not becoming angry: let a man overcome evil with good; let a man overcome the parsimonious by generosity, let a man overcome the liar with truth." "'He has abused me, he has struck me, he has oppressed me, he has robbed me'—they who do not entertain such thoughts, in such men enmity comes to an end. For enmity never comes to an end through enmity here below; it comes to an end by non-enmity; this has been the rule from all eternity."

The last of these verses is connected with a narrative, which is to be found in one of the canonical books,* and is worthy of the consideration of him who desires to know whether and how far the Christian thought, that "there is no fear in love, but perfect love casteth out fear," recurs in the ground of the Buddhist moral intelligence.

On one occasion when a dispute arises in the band of his disciples, Buddha narrates to the discontented the history of King Long-grief, whom his powerful neighbour Brahmadatta had driven from his kingdom and deprived of all his possessions. Disguised as a mendicant monk the vanquished king fled with his wife from his home and sought safety in concealment at Benares, the capital of his enemy. There the queen bore him a son, whom he named Long-life: who became a clever boy, proficient in all arts. One day Long-grief was recognized by one of his quondam courtiers and his place of concealment betrayed to the king, Brahmadatta: thereupon the king ordered him and his wife to be led bound through all the streets of the town, and then hewn into four pieces outside the town. But Long-life saw how his father and mother were being led in chains through the town. And he went up to his father, who said to him: "My son Long-life, look not too

* "Mahâvagga," x, 2.

far and not too near. For enmity comes not to an end by enmity, my son Long-life; by non-enmity, my son Long-life, enmity comes to an end."

Thereupon king Long-grief and his wife were put to death. But Long-life made the guards who were placed over the corpses drunk, and when they had fallen asleep, he burnt both the dead and walked with folded hands three times round the funeral pile. Then he went into the forest and wept and wailed to his heart's content, then washed away his tears, went into the town, and took service in the king's elephant-stalls. By his beautiful singing he won the favour of Brahmadatta, who made him his trusted friend. One day he accompanied the king out hunting. They two were alone: Long-life had so managed that the retinue took another road. The king became tired, laid his head in Long-life's lap, and soon fell asleep. Thereupon thought the youth Long-life: "this King Brahmadatta of Benares has done us much evil. He has taken away our army and baggage, and land, and treasure, and stores, and has killed my father and mother. Now is the time come for me to satisfy my enmity." And he drew his sword from the scabbard. But just then this thought occurred to the youth Long-life: "My father has said to me, when he was being led away to execution: 'My son Long-life, look not too far and not too near. For enmity comes not to an end by enmity, my son Long-life; by non-enmity, my son Long-life, enmity comes to an end.' It would not be right for me to transgress my father's words." So he put his sword back in the scabbard again. The desire for revenge comes over him three times: three times the recollection of his father's last words overcomes his hatred. Then the king starts up from sleep: an evil dream has awakened him; he has dreamed about Long-life, that he is taking his life with the sword. "Then the youth Long-life seized with his left hand the head of King Brahmadatta of

Benares, and with his right he drew his sword, and he said to Brahmadatta, the king of Benares: 'I am the boy Long-life, O king, the son of King Long-grief, of Kosala. Thou hast done us much evil; thou hast taken away our army and baggage, and land, and treasure, and stores, and hast killed my father and mother. Now is the time come for me to satisfy my enmity.' Then the King Brahmadatta of Benares, fell at the feet of the youth Long-life, and said to the youth Long-life: 'Grant me my life, my son Long-life: grant me my life, my son Long-life!' 'How can I grant thee thy life, O king? It is thou, O king, who must grant me life.' 'Then grant thou me life, my son Long-life, and I will also grant thee life.' Then the King Brahmadatta of Benares and the boy Long-life granted each other life, gave each other their hands, and swore to do each other no harm. And King Brahmadatta of Benares said to the youth Long-life: 'My son Long-life, what thy father said to thee before his death, "Look not too far and not too near. For enmity comes not to an end by enmity: by non-enmity enmity comes to an end" —what did thy father mean by that?' 'What my father O king, said to me before his death: "Look not too far," signifies: "Let not enmity long continue;" that was what my father meant when he said before his death: "Look not too far." And what my father, O king, said to me before his death: "Not too near," signifies: "Fall not out too readily with thy friends;" that was what my father meant when he said to me before his death: "Not too near." And what my father, O king, said to me before his death: "For enmity comes not to an end by enmity; by non-enmity enmity comes to an end," signifies this: Thou, O king, hast killed my father and my mother. Were I now, O king, to seek to take thy life, then those who are attached to thee, O king, would take my life, and those who are attached to me, would take their lives; thus our enmity would not come to an end by enmity. But now, O king, thou hast granted me life and I, O king, have granted thee life: thus by non-enmity has our enmity come to an end. This is what my father meant when he said to me before his death: "For enmity comes not to an end by enmity; by non-enmity enmity comes to an end."' Then King Brahmadatta of Benares reflected: 'Wonderful! Astonishing! What a clever youth is this Long-life, that he can expound in such detail the meaning of what his father has so briefly said.' And he gave him all that had belonged to his father, army and baggage, and land, and treasure, and store, and gave him his daughter to wife."

While Buddhism enjoins the forgiveness of the wrongs which others have done us, we ought not to overlook the thought which incidentally peeps out from this moral, that in the dealings of the world forgiveness and reconciliation are a more profitable policy than revenge. The proposition that enmity comes not to an end by enmity is verified in a very substantial way in the case of the clever lad Long-life: instead of losing his life, he obtains a kingdom and a king's daughter to wife.

The lesson of forgiveness and love of enemies finds a deeper and more beautiful expression in the pathetic narrative of prince Kunâla,* the son of the great Buddhist king Asoka (circ. 250 B.C.). Kunâla—this name was given to him on account of his wonderfully beautiful eyes, which are as beautiful as the eyes of the bird Kunâla—lives far from the bustle of the court, devoted to meditation on impermanence. One of the queens is burning with love for the beautiful

* The narrative is only known from northern Buddhist sources, which are scarcely of very ancient origin.—*Burnouf, Introduction*, p. 403, seq.

youth, but her solicitation and the menaces of disdained beauty are alike in vain. Thirsting for revenge, she contrives to have him sent to a distant province, and then issues an order to that quarter, sealed with the slyly stolen ivory seal of the king, for the prince's eyes to be torn out. When the order arrives, no one can be prevailed upon to lay hands on the noble eyes of the prince. The prince himself offers rewards to any one who should be prepared to execute the king's order. At last a man appears, repulsive to look on, who undertakes the performance. When, amid the cries of the weeping multitude, the first eye is torn out, Kunâla takes it in his hand and says: "Why seest thou no longer those forms on which thou wast just now looking, thou coarse ball of flesh? How they deceive themselves, how blamable are those fools, who cling to thee and say: "This is I." And when his second eye is torn out, he says: "The eye of flesh, which is hard to get, has been torn from me, but I have won the perfect, faultless eye of wisdom. The king has forsaken me, but I am the son of the highly exalted king of truth: whose child I am called." He is informed that it is the queen, by whom the command concerning him was issued. Then he says: "Long may she enjoy happiness, life, and power who has brought me so great welfare." And he goes forth a beggar with his wife; and when he comes to his father's city, he sings to the lute before the palace. The king hears Kunâla's voice; he has him called into him, but when he sees the blind man before him, he cannot recognize his son. At last the truth comes to light. The king in the excess of grief and rage is about to torture and kill the guilty queen. But Kunâla says: "It would not become thee to kill her. Do as honour demands and do not kill a woman. There is no higher reward than that for benevolence: patience, sire, has been commanded by the Perfect One." And he falls at the king's feet, saying: "O king, I feel no pain, and notwithstanding the inhumanity which has been practised on me, I do not feel the fire of anger. My heart has none but a kindly feeling for my mother, who has given the order to have my eyes torn out. As sure as these words are true, may my eyes again become as they were"—and his eyes shone in their old splendour as before.

Buddhist poetry has nowhere glorified in more beautiful fashion, forgiveness, and the love of enemies than in the narrative of Kunâla. But even here we feel that cool air which floats round all pictures of Buddhist morality. The wise man stands upon a height to which no act of man can approach. He resents no wrong which sinful passion may work him, but he even feels no pain under this wrong. The body, over which his enemies have power, is not himself. Ungrieved by the actions of other men, he permits his benevolence to flow over all, over the evil as well as the good. "Those who cause me pain and those who cause me joy, to all I am alike; affection and hatred I know not. In joy and sorrow I remain unmoved, in honour and in dishonour; throughout I am alike. That is the perfection of my equanimity."*

The Buddhists had a peculiar *penchant* for systematic and methodical devotion at fixed times to certain modes and meditations, for which they previously put themselves with due precision in appropriate postures. So we have rules which are highly characteristic of this almost extravagant, quaint peculiarity of Buddhist praxis, regarding the art and method by which a man is to foster within himself the disposition of kindly benevolence to all beings in the universe, following the course of the four-quarters of the heavens. Buddha says:

* "Cariyâ Piṭaka," iii, 15.

"After reflection, when I have returned from the begging excursion, I go into the forest. There I heap together the blades of grass or the leaves which are there to be found, and I sit down on them, with crossed legs, upright body, surrounding my countenance with vigilant thought (as with an aureola). Thus I remain, while I cause the power of benevolence, which fills my mind, to extend over one quarter of the world; in the same way over the second, the third, the fourth, above, below, across; on all sides, in all directions over the whole of the entire universe I send forth the power of benevolence, which fills my spirit, the wide, great, immeasurable (feeling) which knows naught of hate, which doeth no evil."*

Whoever bears benevolence within him, possesses therein as it were a magical power; men and beasts, when he lets fall on them a ray of this power, are thereby wondrously subdued and attracted. Devadatta, the Judas Iscariot among Buddha's disciples, lets loose on Buddha a wild elephant in a narrow street (p. 160). "But the Exalted One exercised on the elephant Nâlâgiri the power of his benevolence. Then the elephant Nâlâgiri, struck by the Exalted One with the power of his benevolence, lowered his trunk, went up to where the Exalted One was, and stopped before him."† On another occasion Ânanda entreats the Exalted One, to be pleased to convert to the faith Roja, one of the stranger noblemen of the

* There follow several repetitions of the same passage, in which instead of "power of benevolence," there occur: power of pity, power of cheerfulness, power of equanimity ("Anguttara Nikâya," vol. i, fol. caṃ.; cf. vol. ii, fol. chu, where the same spiritual exercises are attributed to Brahmanical ascetics also; "Saṃyutta Nikâya," vol. ii, fol. tho'; "Childer's Dictionary," p. 624).

† "Cullavagga," vii, 3, 12. The using of the power of benevolence over the different kinds of snakes as a protection against snake-bite is described previously in v, 6.

house of the Mallas, inimical to the doctrine of Buddha. "It is not difficult, O Ânanda, for the Perfect One to cause the Malla, Roja, to be won to this faith and this order." Thereupon the Exalted One extended to Roja, the Malla, the power of his benevolence, rose from his seat and went into the house. And Roja, the Malla, struck by the Exalted One through the power of his benevolence, went, like a cow that seeks her young calf, from one house to another, from one cell to another, and asked the monks: "Where, O venerable men, is he now dwelling, the Exalted One, the holy, supreme Buddha? I desire to see him, the Exalted One, the holy, supreme Buddha."*

Place may be given in this connection to one of those brief sketches, in which the fancy of the faithful loved to portray the conception of Buddha's previous existences. We possess a collection of such sketches and short stories, admitted into the sacred canon, which are arranged to illustrate the perfections or cardinal virtues of the later Buddha.† The following brief passage is devoted to the virtue of benevolence:—

"I lived under the name of Sâma,‡ in a forest on the mountain slope . . . , I drew to myself lions and tigers through the power of my benevolence. I lived in the forest surrounded by lions and tigers, by panthers, bears, and wild buffaloes, by gazelles and boars. No creature is in terror of me, and I have no fear of any being. The power of benevolence is my footing, therefore I dwell on the mountain slope."

It appeared important to follow up the idea of benevolence,

* "Mahâvagga," vi, 36, 4.

† The usual enumeration of these perfections, which are, however, not all represented in that text (the "Cariyâ Piṭaka") by illustrative narratives, comprises ten virtues; beneficence, uprightness, wishlessness, wisdom, power, patience, sincerity, steadfastness, benevolence, equanimity.

‡ The narrator is Buddha himself.

of forgiveness, of goodness even towards enemies, in the many various forms in which it meets us, now in the garment of sober reflections, again in the noble robe of pure and childlike poesy, and anon veiled in the surroundings of a quaint fantastic Methodism. It was not the emotion of a world-embracing love, but this peaceful feeling of friendly harmony, which gave its stamp to the common life of Buddha's disciples, and if the Buddhist faith permits even the animal world to participate in the blessing of this peace and this goodwill, this may serve to remind us of the charming tales which Christian legend has woven round a form like that of the saint Franciscus, the friend of all animals, and of all inanimate nature.

Among the remaining emotional virtues, which are wont to be named in conjunction with those of uprightness and benevolence, the virtue of beneficence occupied the most prominent place in the didactic poetry of the Buddhists. It is significant how completely, in the conception of this poetry, the picture of the highest ideal beneficence melts away into that of renunciation, of self-sacrificing endurance. Whoever sets perfection before him as his goal, must be prepared to unconditionally surrender everything, even what is dearest to him. The limits, which our conception would set to the inherent propriety of the gift, are not here applicable; without any regard to what is the measure of the real benefit thereby extended to the recipient of the gift, the legends set before us as a duty, the most unbounded generosity, pushed even to the extreme of self-destruction.* Though penances, as they

* On the question, as to what, apart from the moralistic poetic of legends, was the practical performance of beneficence in the actual life of the early order, we refer on the one hand o the remarks on the subject in the First Part (p. 143, 166, seq.), and on the other to the Part on the Life of the Order. We cannot refrain from thinking, that the

were then practised among the ascetics of India, were discarded by Buddha as "vexatious, unworthy, unprofitable," yet motives of the most closely kindred character maintained their place in Buddhist moral poetry: if Brahmanical poems tell of marvellous self-mortifications, by which the sages of the past obtained a power portentous to the gods themselves, it is not far to go from them to the Buddhist narratives of those displays of unlimited generosity, crowned with immeasurable heavenly reward, in which the proper element of beneficence vanishes into nothing behind that of ascetic self-sacrifice.

Thus, for instance, in the narrative of Prince Vessantara, *i.e.*, the later Buddha in the last but one of his earthly existences.* The king's son was unjustly driven from the kingdom by the people by a mistake. He gave his last treasures, even the waggon on which he rode, and the horses to beggars, and he went on with wife and children through the burning heat on foot. "When the children saw trees bearing fruit in the forest, they wept, longing for the fruit. When they saw the weeping children, the lofty, mighty trees bowed down of themselves and came down to the children." At last they came to the Vanka mountain; there they lived as hermits in a leaf-hut. "I and the princess Maddî, and the two children, Jâli and Kanhâjinâ, dwelt in the hermitage, each dissipating the sorrow of the others. I remained in the hermitage to guard the children; Maddî gathered wild fruits and brought them to us there for food. When I was there dwelling in the forest, there came a beggar, who asked me for my children, the two, Jâli and Kanhâjinâ. When I saw the beggar who

treatment of beneficence in Buddhist morals would have been more sound and less prolix, if it were not that here a virtue was being handled, in a position to practise which, the pauper monk could scarcely ever be.

* "Cariyâ Piṭaka," i, 9. Cf. Hardy, Manual, 118.

had come, I smiled, and I took my two children and gave them to the Brahman. When I made over my children to Jûjaka the Brahman, the earth quaked, the forest-crowned Meru shook. And again it came to pass, that the god Sakka came down from heaven in the form of a Brahman; he asked me for Maddî, the princess, the virtuous and true. Then I took Maddî by the hand, filled her hands with water,* and I gave Maddî to him with cheerful heart. When I gave him Maddî, the gods in heaven were glad, and again the earth quaked, and the forest-crowned Meru shook. Jâli and Kanhâjinâ, my daughter, and Maddî, the princess, the true wife, I gave away, and I counted it not loss so that I might win the Buddhahood."

Another of these narratives of Buddha's past existences is the following "Story of the wise hare."†

"And again in another life I was a hare, that lived in a mountain forest: I ate grass and vegetables, leaves and fruits, and did no being any harm. An ape, a jackal, a young otter, and I, we dwelt together and we were seen together early and late. But I instructed them in duties and taught them what is good and what evil: abstain from evil, incline to good. On holy days when I saw the moon full, I said to them: 'to-day is the holy day; have alms in readiness that ye may dispense them to the worthy. Give alms according to merit and spend the holy day in fasting.' Then said they: 'So be it,' and according to their power and ability they got their offerings ready and looked for one who might be worthy to receive them. But I sat down and sought in my mind for a gift, which I was to offer: 'If I find a worthy object, what is my

* For the solemn surrender of Maddî, with a libation of water as for the completion of a dedication.

† The narrator is Buddha himself.—*Cariyâ Piṭaka*, i, 10.

gift to be? I have not sesame, nor beans, nor rice, nor butter. I live on grass only; one cannot offer grass. If a worthy person comes to me and asks me to give him food, then I shall give him myself; he shall not go hence empty-handed.' Thereupon Sakka (the king of gods) discerned my thoughts, and came in the form of a Brahman to my cover to put me to the test and see what I would give him. When I saw him, I spake to him joyfully these words: ''Tis well that thou comest to me to seek food. A noble gift, such as hath not erst been given, shall I give thee this day. Thou observest the duties of uprightness; it is not thy character to inflict pain on any creature. But go gather wood and kindle a fire; I will roast myself; roasted thou mayest consume me.' He said: 'So be it,' and he gladly gathered wood and stacked it in a great heap. He put living coals in the middle and a fire was soon kindled; then he shook off the dust, which covered his powerful limbs, and sat down before the fire. When the great heap of wood began to send up flame and smoke, I leaped into the air and plunged into the midst of the burning fire. As fresh-water quenches the torment of heat for him who dives into it, as it gives vitality and comfort, so the flaming fire into which I leaped, like fresh-water, quelled all my torment. Cuticle and skin, flesh and sinews, bones, heart and ligaments, my whole body with all its members, I have given to the Brahman."

Buddha's last existence, the days of attained sanctity, of itinerancy and teaching, are not adorned in the narratives of the order with any such marvels of self-sacrifice. Good works are for him to do, who is pressing on to perfection. The Perfect One himself "hath overcome both shackles, good and evil."*

* "Dhammapada," 412. Buddhism here stands wholly on the ground of the Brahmanical philosophy which preceded it, *vide* supra, p. 48.

MORAL SELF-CULTURE.

The most important part of moral action does not lie according to Buddhist notions in duties which are owing externally, from man to man, or more correctly speaking, from each being to the being nearest him, but in the scope of his own inner life, in the exercise of incessant self-discipline: "Step by step, piece by piece, moment by moment, must he who is wise, cleanse his ego from all impurity, as the goldsmith refines silver."*

The ego, whose reality remained to metaphysics an unsolved enigma, here becomes for ethical speculation a determinate power, before which everything external to it vanishes into the background as something foreign. To find the ego is acknowledged to be the worthiest object of all search, to make a friend of the ego the truest and highest friendship. "By thine ego spur on thy ego; by thine ego explore thine ego; so shalt thou, O monk, well guarding thine ego and vigilant, live in happiness. For the protection of the ego is the ego; the refuge of the ego is the ego; therefore keep thy ego in subjection, as a horse-breaker a noble steed." "First of all let a man establish his own ego in the good; then only can he instruct others; thus shall the wise remain free from misery."†

We have already (p. 288) touched those three leading notions, constituting in a certain manner a succession of steps, into which Buddhist ethic has divided the different ranges of moral action: uprightness, self-concentration, and wisdom. To the duties of internal watchfulness, self-education, and self-purification, on the part of the ego, the scholastic system allots a

* "Dhammapada," 239.

† "Dhammapada," 379, seq., 158.

middle place, between the first and second of these ranges. External rectitude is the foundation, from which alone proceeding, can those internal and deeper tasks of morality be performed, and these tasks again occupy a preparatory position as the regards the last, finishing forces of spiritual effort, self-concentration and wisdom. The standard expressions, by which the language of the schools describes the class of moral duties in question and inserts them in the described manner in that threefold class, are the headings: government of the senses, vigilance and attention, to which is further added the idea of contentment (absence of the feeling of want).* We must keep the eye and all other senses in subjection, so that they may not, by dwelling on external objects, find pleasure in them and convey to the ego impressions which endanger its peace and purity. We are to direct all our movements with vigilant consciousness;† whether we walk or stand, whether we sit or lie down, whether we talk or

* In the Pâli: indriyasaṃvara, satisampâjañña, santuṭṭhi. The closer examination of these notions is to be found in the Sâmaññaphala Sutta and recurs elsewhere very frequently in the sacred texts.

† With this are connected several half-bodily, half-spiritual exercises, fostered by Buddhism with such great fondness, which, it seems probable, occupied a very prominent place in the monks' allotment of time. We here select only one of them, "vigilance in inhaling and exhaling." "A monk, O disciples, who dwells in the forest, or dwells at the foot of a tree, or dwells in an empty chamber, sits down with legs crossed, body bolt upright, surrounding his countenance with watchful thought. He inhales with consciousness, he exhales with consciousness. If he draws in a long breath, he knows: 'I am drawing in a long breath.' If he exhales a long breath, he knows: 'I am exhaling a long breath.' If he draws in a short breath he knows: 'I am drawing in a short breath,' and so on. Buddha calls this exercise profitable and enjoyable; it drives away the evil that rises in man ("Vinaya Piṭaka," vol. iii, p. 70, seq.). If the disciples are asked, how

be silent, we are to think of what we are doing, and take care that it be done becomingly. We should need nothing, but what we carry on our persons, like the bird in the air which has no treasure, and carries nothing with it but its wings, which bear it whithersoever it wishes.

In contact with people of worldly occupation the most scrupulous caution must be observed. "As one, who has no shoes, walks over thorny ground, watchfully picking his steps, so let the wise man walk in the village."* "As the bee damages not the colour or perfume of the flower, but sucks its juice and flies on, so let the wise man walk in the village."† When a man has completed his begging excursion through the village, he is to examine himself, whether he has remained free from all internal dangers. Buddha says to Sâriputta:‡ "A monk, Sâriputta, must thus reflect: 'On my way to the village, when I was going to collect alms, and in the places where I solicited alms, and on my way back from the village, have I in the forms which the eye perceives,§ experienced pleasure, or desire, or hatred, or distraction, or anger in my mind?' If the monk, Sâriputta, on thus examining himself, discovers: 'On my way to the village, etc., I have in the forms which the eye perceives, experienced pleasure, etc.,' then must this monk, O Sâriputta, endeavour to become free from these evil,

Buddha spends the rainy season, they are to answer, 'Buried in watchfulness of inhaling and exhaling, O friends, the Exalted One is wont to spend his time during the rainy season.' "—*Samyutta Nikâya*, vol. iii, fol. vi.

* "Theragâthâ," fol. gû.

† "Dhammapada," 49.

‡ Piṇḍapâtaparisuddhisutta (Majjhima Nikâya).

§ There follow after this repetitions of the same question in reference to "the sounds which the ear hears," and the other senses with their objects.

treacherous emotions. But if the monk Sâriputta, who submits himself to this test, finds: 'I havé not experienced pleasure, etc.,' then should this monk, O Sâriputta, be glad and rejoice: Happy the man who has long accustomed his mind to good!"

"As a woman or a man," it is said in another Sutta,* "who is young and takes a delight in being clean, looks at his face in a bright, clear mirror, or in a clear stream of water, and, if he discovers therein any smudge or spot, takes pain to remove this smudge or spot, but if he sees therein no smudge or spot, is glad: 'That's good! I am clean!' so also the monk, who sees that he is not yet free from all those evil, treacherous emotions, must endeavour to become free from all those evil, treacherous emotions. But if he sees that he is free from all those evil, treacherous emotions, this monk is to be glad and rejoice: Happy the man, who has long accustomed his mind to that which is good!"

Incessantly and ever in new forms, we find the admonition repeated, not to take the show of moral action for the reality, not to remain clinging to the external, when salvation can come alone from within. It is all very well to guard the eye and ear from evil, but mere not-seeing and not-hearing avail nothing; else were the blind and deaf the most perfect.† The purpose, with which we speak and act, is decisive of the value of word and action; the word alone is worthless, where acts are wanting: "Our whole existence depends on our thought; thought is its noblest factor; in thought its staté consists. He who speaks or acts with impure thoughts, him sorrow follows, as the wheel follows the foot of the draught animal. Our whole existence depends on our thought; thought is its noblest factor; in thought its state consists.

* Anumânasutta (Majjhima Nikâya).

† Indriyabhâvanâsutta (Majjh. N.).

He who speaks or acts with pure thoughts, him joy follows, like the shadow which never forsakes him." "He who speaks many wise words, but does not act up to them, the fool is like a herd who counts the cows of others; he has no share in the nobility of the monks. He who speaks only a few wise words, but walks in the law of truth, who gets rid of love and hate, and of infatuation, who has knowledge and whose mind has found deliverance, who hankers after nothing in heaven or on earth, he has part in the nobility of the monks."*

MÂRA, THE EVIL ONE.

The toil, by which the spirit seeks purity, rest, and deliverance, pictures itself to the religious consciousness of Buddhism as a struggle against a hostile power. This power of the evil, of the sorrow, which opposes a resistance to man's escape from its shackles,—whence comes it? Buddhist thought holds aloof from this problem. If the question of the "origin of sorrow"† be asked, this question merely directs itself to ascertaining how sorrow originates in us, by what sluice the world-deluging stream of sorrow-fraught impermanence finds its way into our existence. But if one were to seek to know, whence it comes that there is sorrow at all, Buddhism would add this to the too inquisitive questions, on which the Exalted One has revealed nothing, because they are not profitable to happiness. To be curious about the origin of evil and of sorrow would amount to nothing less than prying into the origin of the universe, for the innermost essence of the world

* "Dhammapada," 1, 2, 19, 20.

† Remember the second of the four sacred truths and the formula of causality.

according to Buddhism consists in this, that it is subject to evil, that it is a state of continual sorrow.

It is not, therefore, as the one by whom evil has come into the world, but rather as the supreme lord of all evil, as the chief seducer to evil thought, word and deed, that the creed of the Buddhas looks upon Mâra, the Evil One, the Prince of Death, for Mâra means death.* The kingdom of this world with its pleasures is the kingdom of death. In the highest of the spheres of the universe, which are given over to the dominion of pleasure, he rules with his hosts as a powerful god; thence he comes down to earth, when it is his object to attack the kingdom of Buddha and his saints.

To simple faith Mâra is a personal existence, a personality, limited by the confines of time and space, every whit as real as Buddha, as all men and all gods. But philosophic thought, which sees the enemy of peace and happiness in the impersonal power of a universal law swaying the external world, regulating origination and decease, has naturally a tendency either to push this conception of Mâra into the background or to amplify his personal existence into a universal. Without Mâra's actually ceasing to be looked upon as a person, the limits of his being become so wide as to have room to embrace the contents of the whole universe subjected to sorrow. Wherever there is an eye and form, wherever there is an ear and sound, wherever there is thinking and thought, there is Mâra, there is sorrow, there is world.† Râdha says to Buddha:‡ "Mâra, Mâra, thus people say, O sire. Wherein, O sire, consists the being of Mâra?" "Where there is cor-

* Concerning the mythological elements, which have supplied the materials for the conception of Mâra, we refer to p. 54 seq., note p. 89.

† "Saṃyutta Nikâya," vol. ii, fol. khu.

‡ Ibid, vol. i, fol. no.

poreal form*, O Râdha, there is Mâra (Death), or he who kills, or he who is dying. Therefore, O Râdha, look upon corporeal form as being Mâra, or that it is he who kills, or he who is dying, or sickness, or an abscess, or a wounding dart, or impurity, or impure existence. Whoever regards it thus, understands it correctly."

Mâra is not everlasting, as there is nowhere in the domain of origination and decease an everlasting permanent. But as long as worlds revolve in their orbits and beings die and are born again, new Mâras are evermore appearing with ever new hosts of gods, who are subject to them; and thus we may say that the existence of Mâra is actually eternal in that sense in which alone eternal existence can be conceived by Buddhist speculation.

In those discourses and legends which speak of Mâra, the tempter, we meet with none of that gloomy tragedy with which we are accustomed to fancy the diabolical, deadly foe of good surrounded. The colours and grand outlines for the dark form of a Lucifer were not at the command of the Buddhist monk-poets. They narrate petty, often poorly enough conceived, legends of the attacks of Mâra on Buddha and his pious followers, how he appears at one time as a Brahman, and at another as a husbandman, at another as an elephant-king, and in many other different forms comes to shake their sanctity by temptations, their faith and their knowledge by lies.†

If a holy man makes his excursion for alms in vain and

* Then similarly: where sensation is—where perception is—where formation is—where consciousness is.

† A few such narratives have already been touched upon, supra, p. 116, 258. The "Saṃyutta Nikâya" gives a whole collection of them in the Mârasaṃyutta.

nowhere obtains a gift, it is Mâra's work; if the people in a village ridicule pious monks with derisive gestures, Mâra has entered into them; when Ânanda in the critical moment before Buddha's death neglected to ask the Master to prolong his earthly existence to the end of this mundane period, it so happened because Mâra had bewildered his mind. "At one time," as we read,* "the Exalted One was living in the land of Kosala, in the Himalaya, in a log-hut. When the Exalted One was thus living retired in hermitage, this thought entered his mind: 'It is possible really to rule as a king in righteousness, without killing or causing to be killed, without practising oppression or permitting oppression to be practised, without suffering pain or inflicting pain on another.' Then Mâra, the Evil One, perceived in his mind the thought which had arisen in the mind of the Exalted One, and he approached the Exalted One and spake thus: 'May the Exalted One, O sire, be pleased to rule as a king, may the Perfect One be pleased to rule as a king in righteousness, without killing or causing to be killed, without practising oppression or permitting oppression to be practised, without suffering pain or inflicting pain on another.' Buddha challenges him: 'What dost thou see in me, thou Evil One, that thou speakest thus to me?' Mâra says: 'The Exalted One, O sire, has made the fourfold miraculous power his own—: if the Exalted One, O sire, desired, he could ordain that the Himalaya, the king of mountains, should become gold, and it would turn to gold.' Buddha motions him away: what would it profit the wise man, if he possessed even a mountain of silver or of gold? 'He who has comprehended sorrow, whence it springs, how can he bend himself to desire? He who knows that earthly existence is a fetter in

* "Saṃyuttakâ Nikâya," vol. i, fol. ghâ'.

this world, let him practise that which sets him free therefrom.' Then Mâra, the Evil One, said, 'The Exalted One knows me, the Perfect One knows me,' and disconcerted and disheartened he rose and went away"—the invariable obvious conclusion of these narratives: Buddha looks through the Evil One and turns his temptations to naught.

Of the precautions which the religious should adopt with constant vigilance against the machinations of Mâra, Buddha speaks in the fable of the tortoise and the jackal.* There was once a tortoise, that went in the evening to the bank of a river to seek her food. And there went also a jackal to the river to seek for prey. When the tortoise saw the jackal, she hid all her limbs in her shell and dived quietly and fearlessly into the water. The jackal ran and waited until she should put forth one of her limbs from her shell. But the tortoise did not move; so the jackal was obliged to give up his prey and go away. "Thus, O disciples, Mâra also is constantly and evermore lurking for you and cogitating: 'I shall gain access to them by the door of their eye—or, by the door of their ear, or of their nose, or of their tongue, or of their body, or of their thought, I shall gain access to them.' Therefore, O disciples, guard the doors of your senses . . . then will Mâra, the Evil One, give it up and forsake you, when he finds he cannot find any access to you, as the jackal was obliged to depart from the tortoise."

The Last Stages of the Path of Salvation—Abstractions—Saints and Buddhas.

Thus is the inimical purpose of Mâra in league with the inimical natural law of the sorrow-causing chain of causes and

* "Saṃyuttaka Nikâya," vol. ii, fol. ja.

effects. In the wilderness of the *sankhâras*, of restless, substanceless procession, in ever surging and undulating darkness, the solitary combatants stand, who struggle to find the exit from this labyrinth of sorrow. The struggle is neither slight nor brief. From that moment forward, when first the conviction dawns upon a soul, that this battle must be fought, that there is a deliverance which can be gained—from that first beginning of the struggle up to the final victory, countless ages of the world pass away. Earth worlds and heavenly worlds, and worlds of hells also, states of torment, arise and pass away, as they have arisen and passed away from all eternity. Gods and men, all animated beings, come and go, die and are born again, and amid this endless tide of all things, the beings who are seeking deliverance, now advancing and victorious, and anon driven back, press on to their goal. The path reaches beyond the range of the eye, but it has an end. After countless wanderings through worlds and ages the goal at last appears before the wanderer's gaze. And in his sense of victory there is mingled a feeling of pride for the victory won by his own power. The Buddhist has no god to thank, as he had previously no god to invoke during his struggle. The gods bow before him, not he before the gods. The only help, which can be imparted to the struggle, comes from those like himself, from those who have gone before, the Buddhas and their enlightened disciples, who have wrestled as he now wrestles, and who cannot, it is true, grant him the victory, but can show him the path to victory.

Buddhism, closely following a common feature of all Indian religious life which preceded it, regards as stages preparatory to the victory which is won, certain exercises of spiritual abstraction, in which the *religieux* withdraws his thoughts from the external world with its motley crowd of changing forms, to anticipate in the stillness of his own ego, afar from pain and pleasure, the cessation of the impermanent. The devotion of abstraction is to Buddhism what prayer is to other religions.

It cannot be doubted that protracted and methodically pursued efforts to superinduce states of abstraction have actually formed a very prominent element in the spiritual life of the monks. The prose as well as the poetry of the sacred texts bears ample testimony to this. Monks who by a noisy manner disturb their brothers at moments of abstraction are reprimanded; a careful housekeeper, when he assigns the brothers their resting places, does not omit to arrange for those of them who are endowed with the gift of abstraction, a separate lodging, so that they may not be disturbed by others.* And also through the poems of the monk-poets there runs a vein of delight in the solitude of the forest cheered by the blessing of holy abstraction. "If before me, if behind me, my eye sees no other, it is truly pleasant to dwell alone in the forest. Come, then! Into solitude will I go, into the forest, which Buddha praises: therein it is good for the solitary monk to dwell, who seeks perfection. In the *sîta* forest rich in blossoms, in the cool mountain cave, will I wash my body and walk alone. Alone without comrades in the lovely forest—when shall I have gained the goal? when shall I be free from sins?"† "When the thunderclouds in heaven beat the drum, when the floods of water choke the paths of the air, and the monk in a mountain cave surrenders himself to abstraction, he can have no greater joy. On banks of flower-bestrewn streams, which

* "Mahâvagga," v, 6; "Cullavagga," iv, 4, 4.

† "Theragâthâ," saying of the Ekavihâriya Thera (fol. khe).

are garlanded with motley forest-crowns, he sits joyfully wrapt in abstraction : he can have no higher joy."*

The descriptions in the prose Sûtras which deal with these conditions of the mind, although the scholastic accessories of doubtful or imaginary psychological categories materially impair the objectivity of the picture, leave no room to doubt that here circumstances of a pathological kind also, as well as qualities which a sound mind is in a position to induce, must have played a part. The predispositions to these were superabundantly at hand. In men who were by the power of a religious idea torn from existence in the regular relations of home-life, the physical consequences of a wandering mendicant life, combined with spiritual over-excitement, exhaustion of the nervous system, might easily produce a tendency to morbid phases of this kind. We hear of hallucinations of the sight as well as of the hearing, of "heavenly visions" and "heavenly sounds."† From the days when Buddha aspired to enlightenment, it is related how he sees "a ray of light and the vision of forms," or even a ray of light alone and again forms only.‡ The appearances of deities also, or of the tempter of whom the legends have so much to relate, betray the existence of hallucinations. Still, visions of this kind are, comparatively speaking, isolated occurrences. The normal type of "self-concentration" was that which appears in the "four stages of abstraction (jhâna)," mentioned and described times without number. In a quiet chamber, but oftener in the forest, a man sat down, "with crossed legs, body erect, surrounding his countenance with vigilant thought." Thus he persevered in

* "Theragâthâ," saying of the Thera Bhûta (fol. khû').

† *E.g.*, Mahâlisuttanta (Dîgha N.).

‡ Upakilesiya Suttanta (Majjhima N.).

long-continued motionlessness of body, and freed himself successively from the disturbing elements of "desire and evil emotions," of "deliberation and reflection," of joy and sorrow; at last even breathing stopped. Thus the spirit became "collected, purified, refined, free from impurity, free from sin, pliant, ready to be wrought, firm and unflinching." This was the condition in which the sense of clairvoyant knowledge of the rationale of the universe became active. As the secret of creation revealed itself to Christian enthusiasts in moments of ecstasy, so in this case men imagined they looked back over the past of their own ego through countless periods of transmigration, imagined they saw throughout the universe wandering beings, how they are dying and being born again, imagined they could penetrate the thoughts of others. Even the possession of miraculous powers, of the capability of vanishing and reappearing, of the capability of multiplying the individual ego, is alleged in connection with this state of abstraction. In addition to this there is talk of an otherwise acquired concentration of the mind, which, without pathological ingredients, rests solely on a progressive and methodical abstraction from the plurality of the phenomenal world.* "As this house of Migâramâtâ is empty of elephants and cattle, of stallions and mares, empty of silver and gold, empty of the crowds of men and women, and it is not empty only in one respect, viz., not empty of monks, so also Ânanda the monk gets rid of the notion 'man,' and thinks only on the notion 'forest,' . . . then he perceives that emptiness has entered his notions in respect of the notion 'village,' and emptiness has entered in respect of the notion 'man;' non-emptiness is alone present in respect to the notion 'forest.'" And next the notion "forest" also is got rid of, so that the notion

* Cûlasuññatasutta (Majjh. N.).

"earth" is attained with the omission of all the multitudinous variety of the earth's surface; thence the mind mounts in a similar way to the notion of "endlessness of space," of "endlessness of reason," of "nothing-whatever-ness," step by step approaching deliverance.*

As that which accomplishes deliverance is wisdom, *i.e.*, the knowledge of the Doctrine, the knowledge principally of the four sacred truths, wisdom and abstraction lend each other mutual support and aid: "There is no abstraction where there is not wisdom, no wisdom where there is not abstraction. Truly he is near the Nirvâna, in whom abstraction dwells and wisdom."†

Side by side with the doctrine of abstractions there was another doctrine matured, which, like it, had as its scope the last stages of the path of deliverance: the theory of the four graded classes in which believers who are approaching the goal are arranged, according to the greater or lesser perfection of their saintliness. In the older text this doctrine moved, comparatively speaking, in the background. Men were then

* It is not impossible that these imaginations, which are here attained in the normal path of progressive abstraction, appeared also in a pathological form, when it is said: "He raises himself to the stage of infinity of space, which is meant to convey: 'Endless is space'—he raises himself to the stage of nothing-whatever-ness, which means: 'There is nothing whatever.'" The pantheistic mysticism derived from Brahmanical speculation may here possibly join contact with the morbid conditions of spiritual void familiar to psychiatry. It sounds, in fact, like a translation from a Buddhist Sutra, where Schüle ("Geisterkrankheiten," p. 100) describes the "universal feeling of the nothing free from every effect:" "Nothing exists, and there is and will be nothing"—these being the words of a patient afflicted with this feeling. For Brahmanical doctrine parallel to the Buddhist doctrine of Abstractions, compare specially "Yogasutra," i, 42, seq.

† "Dhammapada," 372.

content with defining only a double event in the souls of those who hear and accept Buddha's teaching. At first the knowledge of the impermanence of all being dawns upon them, "then bursts upon them," as the standard expression of the texts runs, "the clear and spotless vision of the truth: everything whatever that is liable to origination, is also liable to decease." They discern painful impermanence necessarily inherent in the existence of all being. He who has attained this knowledge and perseveres as a monk in earnest endeavour, may hope to take even the last step and reach the stage where, "by the cessation of the hankering (after the earthly), his soul becomes free from sins:" the ultimate aim of spiritual aspiration, deliverance, and sanctity.*

We refrain from unfolding in this place the system of the four graded classes of believers, of later date, as it appears to be, and over weighted, as it is, with ever more increasingly cumbrous scholastic accessories.† To the belonging to one

* The narrative of Buddha's first discourses and conversions ("Mahâvagga," Book I) gives ample vouchers for both grades of this succession of steps.

† We reserve for the third excursus at the close of this work, a more detailed examination of the texts, which give the psychological attributes of the four stages. Here we content ourselves with stating the brief characteristics of those stages, which are not unfrequently met in the sacred writings (*e.g.*, *vide* "Mahâparinibbâna Sutta," p. 16, seq.). The lowest class is made up of the Sotâpanna, *i.e.* those who have attained the path (of sanctification). Of them it is said: "By the annihilation of the three ties, they have attained the path; they are not liable to re-birth in the lower worlds (hells, spirit worlds, and world of lower animals); they are sure (of deliverance); they shall attain the highest knowledge." The next higher class is that of the Sakadâgâmi ("those who return once"): "By the annihilation of the three ties, by the suppression of desire, hatred and frivolity, they have become 'once-returning:' when they have returned once only to this world, they shall attain the end of sorrow." Then follow the Anâgâmi ("the not-returning"): "By the

or other of these grades there were, moreover, attached no claims to a more or less prominent position in the Order; how far each individual had advanced in his approach to the goal of sanctity, was an affair, which wholly concerned his own heart only and of which the Order as such took no notice.* The highest of these stages, that of complete deliverance, was regarded as attainable by monks alone.† How could those who had renounced everything earthly for the sake of their salvation, concede that eternal freedom from the world and sorrows of the world is compatible with the continuance of the outer man in worldly life? Yet an exception was made in favour of pious lay-disciples, if not in the matter of their life, at least in their death: a believing, wise layman, who directs

annihilation of the five first ties they have come to be beings, who originate of themselves (*i.e.* who enter upon the state of being without being begotten or born; this is the case of the higher worlds of the gods); they attain the Nirvâna up there (in the world of gods); they are not liable to return from that world." It seems that in the construction of this class, special consideration for the laity, who have deserved well at the hands of the Order, had some share, to whom because of their lay standing perfect holiness could not be attributed, but to whom a condition very nearly approaching thereto could not be denied. The highest of the four stages and last is that of the Arhat, *i.e.*, the Saint. The view taken by Childers ("Dict.," p. 268, cf. 444), that any higher of the four stages could not be attained, without having passed the lower successively, is wholly inaccurate, at least as regards the older period of Buddhist dogmatic, on which alone I venture to give an opinion.

* Only in one place, as far as I know, does Buddhist Church-law attach any legal importance to a monk's belonging to one of the four stages: a man who had killed a saint could not receive monastic orders ("Mahâvagga," i, 66). Still, it is possible, that the word "saint" is here used, as a remnant of a very ancient mode of speech, in a non-technical signification, and that the injunction in its original sense prohibited generally the admission of a murderer of a monk to the Order.

† Strictly taken the word Arhat ("saint") signifies this, *i.e.*, "one who has a claim"—it is to be supplied: on pious charity and veneration.

his last thoughts, his last longings, to the cessation of earthly being, becomes participator in this prize. "I tell thee, O Mahânâma, that between a lay disciple, whose soul has reached this stage of deliverance, and a monk, whose soul is freed from all impurity, there exists no difference, as far as concerns the state of their deliverance."*

High above these four stages stand those perfect ones, "who have of themselves alone become partakers of the Buddhahood" (Paccekabuddha): they have won the knowledge that brings deliverance, not as disciples of one of the holy, universal Buddhas, but of their own power, yet their perfection does not extend so far that they could preach it to the world. The sacred texts seldom touch this notion of the Paccekabuddhas: it can only have played an entirely secondary part in the ancient Order's circle of conceptions. It appears that the Paccekabuddhas were thought to have lived chiefly in the earlier ages, when there were no universal Buddhas and no Orders founded by them; the notion of a Paccekabuddha seems to have been principally intended to imply that even in such periods the door of deliverance is not shut against earnest and powerful effort. But the doctrine later advanced, that the

* "Saṃyuttaka Nikâya," vol. iii, fol. lau.—The later doctrine, not yet advanced, as far as I know, in the sacred texts, construes this to mean, that even a layman can attain holiness, but that he is not able to sustain the weight thereof, just as a blade of grass is unable to support the weight of a heavy stone. He must, therefore, on the same day on which he attains holiness, either receive monastic orders, or, as the external requisites for this cannot always be complied with, he must enter into Nirvâna ("Milinda Pañha," p. 265).—In the same connection that wantonly formal conception, also, as far as I know, foreign as yet to the sacred texts, grows up, that the more highly endowed believers generally attain deliverance "in the barber's shop," *i.e.*, during the performance of tonsure, which marks the passage from the worldly to the religious life.

appearance of Paccekabuddhas is confined exclusively to those ages, is not, as far as it appears, in accordance with the dogmatic of the sacred Pâli texts. "In the whole universe," says Buddha,* "there is, except me only, no one who is equal to the Paccekabuddhas"—the existence of saints of this grade is consequently, to all appearance, admitted even in Buddha's own time.

Above the four grades of believers and saints, there stand last of all, embodying in themselves the essence of every supreme perfection, the "exalted, holy, universal Buddhas."

It may cause surprise, that it is only in this place that our sketch mentions the dogma of the Buddhas, somewhat as an appendix to other more essential groups of thought. Is the doctrine of Buddha's personality a secondary matter, must it not be a fundamental part of the Buddhist faith, quite as much as in our regard the doctrine of the personality of Christ is a fundamental, nay, *the* fundamental part of the Christian creed?

At hardly any other point does the general similarity of these two lines of evolution appear to diverge more determinately than at this point. It may sound paradoxical, but it is undoubtedly correct to say, that the Buddhist doctrine might be in all essentials what it actually is, and yet admit of the idea of the Buddha being conceived apart from it. That the ineffaceable memory of Buddha's earthly life, that the belief in Buddha's word as the word of truth, subjection to Buddha's law as the law of holiness—that all these considerations were

* "Apadâna," fol. kî of the Phayre MS. Also when it is said, that two holy universal Buddhas can never appear in the same world-system at the same time ("Anguttara Nik.," vol. i, fol. kaṃ), it seems thereby to be implied, that the contemporaneous appearing of a universal Buddha with Paccekabuddhas is not excluded.

of the utmost importance in the formation of religious life and experience in the Order of Buddha's disciples, scarcely needs to be said. But as far as the dogmatic treatment of that one great problem is concerned, with which alone the whole of Buddhist dogmatic deals, the question of pain and deliverance, the dogma of Buddha stands in the background. In the creed-formula of the four sacred truths the word Buddha does not occur.

The key to the explanation of this remarkable attitude of the idea of Buddha towards the central ideas of the Buddhist circle of thought, is to be found, I believe, in pre-Buddhist history.

Where a doctrinal system, like the Christian, grows up on the basis of a strong faith in a God, it is natural that in the consciousness of the community a reflection, aye, more than a reflection of the grandeur and fulness of the almighty and all-good God should fall on the person of him who, as master, teacher, example, is in every way of immeasurable significance to the life of his followers. The grace of God is said to bestow eternal life on man: the Master becomes the mediator by whom the grace of God extends to man. His nature is raised in supernatural dignity to unity with God's nature; his earthly doings and sufferings appear to be the world-delivering doings and sufferings of God.

The preconditions did not exist, under which an analagous evolution of notions regarding Buddha's person might have taken place. The faith in the ancient deities had been obliterated by the pantheism of the Âtman theory; and the Âtman, the eternal inactive universal One, was not a god, who could evince pity for man by a display of delivering activity. And even the belief in the Âtman itself had been effaced or lost, and as ruler over the world longing for deliverance there remained no more a god, but only the natural law of the necessary concatenation of causes and effects. There stood man alone as the sole operative agent in the struggle against sorrow and death; his task was, by a skilful knowledge of the law of nature, to aim at gaining a position against it, in which he was beyond the reach of its sorrow-bringing operations.

The data, which must determine the dogmatic treatment of Buddha's person, were hereby given. He could not be a god-sent deliverer, for man looked not for deliverance from a god. Knowledge is to deliver; my knowledge is to deliver me: so he must be the great knower and bringer of knowledge for all the world. He must be a being, who has no inherent supernatural nobility beyond other beings,* but by higher, more powerful effort first discovers that path, in which others after him, following his footsteps, walk. In a certain sense we may say, that every disciple, who is pressing on to holiness, is also a Buddha as well as his Master.† This idea of essential

* The fact that Buddha, before he is born to his last life on earth, lives as a god in the Tusita heavens and thence descends to earth, in no way implies that a superhuman, god-and-man nature is claimed for him. One who is a god in one existence, may in the next existence be born again as an animal or in a hell. As Buddha in his last life but one was a Tusita god, he had been in earlier existences also a lion, a peacock, a hare, and so on; but in his last appearance on earth he was a man and in every way only a man.

† The customary terminology does not indeed designate Buddha's saintly followers themselves as Buddhas, but still it is evident on several occasions, that such an expression was felt to be really allowable. Thus, when the Sotâpanna (note 2, p. 319) is defined as a person, who "will attain the highest knowledge (sambodhi)." Especially in poetical texts it is often doubtful, whether the word buddha is used in its narrower sense or with reference to every saint. *Vide* "Dhammapada," v. 398 (cf. v. 419).

resemblance between Buddha and all delivered men is very significantly set forth in the following words: "As when, O Brahman, a hen has laid eggs, eight or ten or twelve, and the hen has sat on them long enough, and kept them warm and hatched them: when then one of the chickens first breaks the egg-shell with the tip of its claw or with its beak, and creeps successfully out of the egg, how will men describe this chicken, as the oldest or the youngest?" "It will be called the oldest, venerable Gotama, for it is the oldest of them." "So also, O Brahman, of those beings, who live in ignorance and are shut up and confined as it were in an egg, I have first broken the egg-shell of ignorance and alone in the universe obtained the most exalted, universal Buddhahood. Thus am I, O Brahman, the eldest, the noblest, of beings."* Buddha does not deliver beings, but he teaches them to deliver themselves, as he has delivered himself. They accept his declaration of the truth, not because it comes from him, but because, verified by his words, personal knowledge of that whereof he speaks, dawns on their minds.†

This is not, however, to be understood, as if Buddha's form had not in the belief of the Order exceeded the limits of earthly-human reality, as if dogmatic had disdained to cast round Buddha's head the halo of a glory that illuminates the universe. The land of India was not like the Athens of Thukydides and Aristophanes, in which care was taken that Sammâsambuddhas

* "Suttavibhanga, Pârâjika," i, 1, 4.

† It is said in one of Buddha's addresses, after a prefatory exposition of the causality formula: "If ye now know thus, and see thus, O disciples will ye then say: We respect the Master, and out of reverence for the Master do we thus speak?"—"That we shall not, O sire."— . . . "What ye speak, O disciples, is it not even that which ye have yourselves known, yourselves seen, yourselves realized?"—"It is, sire."—*Mahâtaṇhâsakhaṃya Sutta, Majjhima Nikâya.*

and god-men should not appear on earth. The eye of the Indian was accustomed at every step to regard the natural course of events within their earthly limits as interwoven in fanciful continuity with infinite distance. The longer thought occupied itself with any speculation, the oftener it recurred to it, the more the human, the earthly in it vanished behind the dreamy, the typical, the universal. The age in which the doctrines of the sorrow of everything earthly and of deliverance first engaged young thought, could look upon a Yâjnavalkya and a Çândilya as merely wise and pure men; viewed as the Buddhist viewed them, the floating outlines of such forms were bound to fix themselves after the type of the exalted, holy universal Buddhas appearing at fixed times according to an eternal law of the universe.

It could scarcely be otherwise than that the historical form of the one actual Buddha multiplied itself under dogmatic treatment to a countless number of past and coming Buddhas. It might satisfy a faith, which measured the past of this world by thousands of years, its future by years, or perhaps by days, to see standing out above the span of time the form of one Saviour, to whom the past prophetically pointed, whose second coming puts an end to the brief future. For the Indian no horizon bounds the view of world-life; from immeasurable distance to immeasurable distance, through innumerable, immense ages of the world, extends the gigantic course of origination, decease, and re-origination. How could he regard what appeared to stand in the centre of his own world, of his own time, as the universal middle point of all worlds,* of all times?

* The allotment of time to the Buddhas in the different ages of the world is not an equal one. In one of the Pâli-Sûtras (Mahâpadânasutta) the statement is found, that the last Buddhas appeared at the following

As an effort to reach the light that gives deliverance extends throughout the whole coming and going of ages, throughout the whole of being, enveloped in dark sorrow, so must at certain times certain beings obtain a glimpse of this light; they must become Buddhas and fulfil the career ordained from everlasting, of a Buddha. They are all born in the Eastern half of central Hindostan;* they all come of Brahman or Kshatriya families; they all attain delivering knowledge, sitting at the foot of a tree. Their lives are of different duration according to the ages in which they appear, and the doctrine also which they teach, maintains its hold, sometimes for a longer, sometimes for a shorter period, but in each case for a definite length of time. "Five hundred years, Ânanda, will the doctrine of the truth abide," says Buddha to his beloved disciple.† Then the faith vanishes from the earth, until a new Buddha appears, and again "sets in motion the Wheel of the Law."

It follows that as the line of Buddhas extends throughout

times: one in the ninety-first age of the world, back from the present, two in the thirty-first age; our present age is a "blessed age" (bhaddakappa); it possesses five Buddhas, of whom Gotama is the fourth; the appearing of Metteyya is still looked for. It is hardly necessary to observe, that all these Buddhas, Gotama Buddha alone excepted, are purely imaginary forms. (In the corresponding teaching of the Jaina-sect regarding the Jinas of ancient times, Jacobi, "Indian Antiquary," 1880, p. 158, seq., believes he can find elements of actual fact. I cannot convince myself of it.)

* So already the canonical Pâli tradition, "Cullavagga," xii, 2, 3. The passage is instructive, inasmuch as it shows how ancient Buddhism, far from that cosmopolitan breadth of view, which people are wont to conceive as inherent in the Buddhist nature, regards its own narrow fatherland as the only chosen land.

† "Cullavagga," x, 1, 6. Later on, when this prophecy was contradicted by events, the numbers were naturally made greater. Cf. "Köppen," i, 327.

the immeasurable extent of time, so also the not less immeasurable expanses of space have their Buddhas. The sacred texts appear to touch very slightly this idea of Buddha appearing in distant systems of worlds, but the conception is quite in keeping with Indian fancy, that even in those worlds separated from us by infinities the same struggle of beings for deliverance repeats itself, which is going on on this earth. "It cannot happen, O disciples," says Buddha, "it is impossible for two holy, universal Buddhas to appear in one world-system at one time, not one before or after the other"*—in these words we may perhaps see a hint given, that in other systems, apart from what is occurring in our world, similar triumphs of light over darkness are won, to that which Buddha has secured under the tree at Uruvelâ.

We hope to be excused from expanding in detail the scholastic predicates, which dogmatic attributes to the exalted, holy, universal Buddhas, from speaking of the ten Buddha faculties, of the thirty-two external marks of a Buddha, and so on. Instead of this we shall try to exhibit the *tout ensemble*, which the union of all these perfections produced in the imagination of the believer, the picture of supreme power, supreme knowledge, supreme peace, supreme compassion.

We shall speak in the words of the texts.

Buddha says: "The all-subduing, the all-knowing, am I, in everything that I am, without a spot. I have given up everything; I am without desire, a delivered one. By my own power I possess knowledge; whom should I call my master? I have no teacher: no one is to be compared to me. In the world, including the heavens, there is no one like unto me. I am the Holy One in the world; I am the supreme

* "Anguttara Nikâya," *vide* supra, note, p. 322.

Master. I alone am the perfect Buddha; the flames are extinct in me; I have attained the Nirvâna."* "The Exalted One," Kaccâna names him,† "the bringer of joy, the dispenser of joy, whose organs of life are placid, whose spirit is at rest, the supreme self-subduer and peace-possessor, the hero, who has conquered self and watches himself, who holds his desires in check." "He appears in the world for salvation to many people, for joy to many people, out of compassion for the world, for the blessing, the salvation, the joy of gods and men."‡ Thus have the Buddhas of bygone ages appeared, thus shall the Buddhas of coming ages appear.

Will their succession ever have an end? Will the victory become complete, so that all beings shall have crossed over to deliverance?

The faithful of ancient days directed their thoughts but seldom to this last question as to the future. But they did not wholly pass it over. In the narrative of Buddha's death we read the exclamation to which the god Brahma gave utterance when the Holy One entered into the Nirvâna:

> "In the worlds beings all put off corporeity at some time,
> Just as at this present time Buddha, the prince of victory, the supreme master of all worlds,
> The mighty, Perfect One, hath entered into Nirvâna."

Thus beings shall all reach the Nirvâna. Then, when animated, sorrow-susceptible beings have vanished from the domain of being, will the procession of the Sankhâras, the origination and decadence of worlds, continue in eternity? Or, after the extinction of all consciousness in which this procession was reflected, will the world of the Sankhâras fall

* "Mahâvagga," i, 6, 8.

† *Vide* supra, p. 146.

‡ "Anguttara Nikâya," vol. 1, fol. ko. and elsewhere.

to pieces, sinking in its own ruins? Will the Nirvâna, in the depths of which the realms of the visible have disappeared, be the One and All?

We ask too much. "The Exalted One has not revealed this. As it does not conduce to salvation, as it does not conduce to holy life, to separation from the earthly, to the extinction of desire, to cessation, to peace, to knowledge, to illumination, to Nirvâna, therefore has the Exalted One not revealed it."

PART III.

THE ORDER OF BUDDHA'S DISCIPLES.

CHAPTER I.

The Constitution of the Order and its Codes of Laws.

We now turn from the examination of the faith which held together the band of Buddha's followers, to the consideration of the outward observances, which religious custom and religious discipline have prescribed for the life of this monastic fraternity. It appears from the very beginning to have been a society governed by law. The completion of a procedure prescribed by law was necessary to the reception of a postulant into the society. The law of the Order pointed out to him his course of action and of omission. The society itself as a court of discipline secured conformity to the ecclesiastical rules by keeping up a regular judicial procedure.

This early appearance of a form of associated life strictly governed by law can cause no astonishment. It is the counterpart of the equally early appearance of a matured and formulated dogmatic; the same characteristic features of the period in which Buddhism developed itself, the same forces of preceding history upon which it rests, explain the one phenomenon as well as the other. The monastic orders professing other faiths, preceding and coeval with Buddha's Order, and, in a not less degree, the common source of all these sects, Brahmanism, have furnished for the formation of a Church polity, as they did in the case of dogmatic speculation, a set of ready-made forms, which Buddhism had only to appropriate.

Quickly as the formation of canonical observances seems to have attained a complete state, still there is no need of proving that it cannot have been the work of a moment. In the texts, which contain the rules for the life of the members of the Order, traces are clearly enough discernible which enable us to distinguish earlier and later phases of development. We can trace how a complex of injunctions first grew up, which were regularly propounded about the time of full moon and new moon in the confessional meetings of the Order; constantly recurring technical expressions described in all these rules what degree of guilt the monk incurred who transgressed them. It is quite possible that this old collection of prohibitions, which has come down to us under the title of Pâtimokkha ("unburdening"), the basis of the whole body of Buddhist Church-law, goes back to Buddha's own time, to the confessional meetings held by him with his disciples.* A later layer of the sacred texts shows us how further on the necessity made itself felt in the next period, of supplementing by new regulations

* Not, indeed, in the Pâtimokkha itself, but in another portion of the Church ordinances, bearing likewise the stamp of high antiquity, there is a clue which appears to point directly to the origin of the rules in question within Buddha's own lifetime. In the description of the persons who are not permitted to receive ordination, "he who has shed blood" appears. It cannot be meant that every one is rejected who has inflicted on another a bloody wound, for not even all murderers are excluded, but only parricides, matricides, and murderers of a holy man. Therefore it can hardly be doubted that the traditional explanation is correct, which

the principles laid down in the Pâtimokkha. But no one ventured to add anything on his own authority to the old hallowed formulas. They therefore left the Pâtimokkha itself untouched, but undertook, in the form of commentaries and in new works, a revised and enlarged edition of the canonical rules. They did not hesitate, indeed, to prescribe punishments for transgressions which were not specified as such in the Pâtimokkha. Yet they did not presume in doing so to use the same expressions which had been adopted in the Pâtimokkha, but they employed new words and introduced new forms of disciplinary procedure for bringing to punishment any offences against the newly-constituted ordinances.* Thus the succession of earlier and later periods reveals itself to our research more certainly still and more clearly in the development of the system of connexional law than in that of dogmatic.

But, we must add, although the Order of Buddha's disciples, or members thereof specially called on and qualified to do so, have virtually acted as law-makers, yet in theory the community has distinctly disclaimed all legislative functions. The authority to frame a law for the community belongs to Buddha alone according to Buddhist theory. All commands and prohibitions received their character as binding rules from the fact that Buddha has enunciated, or is supposed to have enunciated them. With his death both the possibility and the necessity for creating new laws has become extinct. The Order has only to apply and expound Buddha's regulations, in the same way

here understands: "who has so wounded Buddha that his blood has flowed." That this definition originated in a time when it had a meaning will be regarded, if not as absolutely certain, at any rate as more than natural. For the elucidation of the passage in point ("Mahâvagga," i, 67), cf. "Cullav." vii, 3, 9.

* Cf. the Introduction to my edition of the "Vinaya Piṭaka," vol. i, p. xvii, seq.

that it has to carefully preserve the doctrine revealed by Buddha, but it is not called upon nor is it competent to improve or extend. "The Order does not lay down what has not been laid down (by Buddha), and it does not abolish what he has laid down; it accepts the ordinances as he has prescribed them, and abides by them"—so traditional legend represents a Church council to have resolved shortly after Buddha's death.* In the sacred texts, accordingly, all regulations, even those obviously belonging to later periods, appear as if they had been issued by Buddha himself. The inconsistency with which, from this very desire to be consistent, they came to act, is characteristic: they had no scruple in giving out as orders of the exalted, holy Buddha, those very rules made by themselves which they shrank from clothing in the time-hallowed form of the Pâtimokkha institutes. The liturgical conscience was stronger than the historical—if, indeed, that complete indifference with which men in India have at all times regarded or rather have not regarded, literary and historical authenticity will allow us in this case to speak of an historical conscience.

The ancient compilations of the laws of the Order share to the fullest extent in all those peculiarities which cause some sections of Buddhist dogmatics to appear to us to be a so very pathless waste. The same subtlety here as there, the same inexhaustible capability of enjoying long abstract series of notions purely for their own sake. Here we have, not rules drawn from life for life, but scholastic lucubrations, unpractical and, strictly speaking, not even clear. The form in which they

* "Cullavagga," xi, 1, 9, cf. "Suttavibhanga, Nissaggiya," xv, 1, 2. The narrative of the council at Vesâlî ("Cullavagga," xii), also clearly illustrates how the Church, according to the current theory, limited itself throughout to the authentic interpretation of the spiritual law ordained by Buddha.

are usually introduced is most simple. In every case the same outline: At this time, when the exalted Buddha was staying in such and such a place, this and that irregularity occurred. The people who came to know of this were irritated, murmured, and complained: How can monks, who follow the son of the Sakya house, commit such offences, like wanton worldlings—or: like unbelieving heretics, as the case in point has occurred. The spiritual brothers hear the whisperings of the people; they too are irritated, murmur and complain: How can the venerable N. N. be guilty of the like! They mention the matter to Buddha; he calls the disciples together, delivers to them an admonitory address, and then issues the order: I order, O disciples, that so and so shall or shall not be done. Whoso does this is liable to such and such a punishment. Stereotyped like this narrative itself, which recurs thousands of times, are also the figures of the culprits who appear in the narrative, and by their actions afford occasion in every instance for Buddha's interference. A specific brother turns out to be the culprit, if the matter be an inordinate exaction of pious beneficence. If offences of a lascivious description occur, the actor, as a rule, is the venerable Udâyi. But the longest catalogue of crimes attaches to the Chabbaggiyas, six monks associated together in all mischievous artifices. Whatever Buddha may prescribe, the Chabbaggiyas always find a way of circumventing the law, or, while they comply with it, of mixing up some evil with their performance. When Buddha declares that the twigs of certain plants are to be used for cleaning the teeth, the Chabbaggiyas take long and massive twigs, and beat the novices with them. If a transgressor is to be censured before the Order, the Chabbaggiyas raise objections and thereby defeat the enforcement of discipline. On one occasion when the nuns had dirty water poured over them, the Chabbaggiyas were the actors, and so on through the long texts of the Rules for the Order the Chabbaggiyas figure everywhere as the arch-criminals, whose new discoveries in all regions of mischief the spiritual legislation enacted by Buddha follows up step by step. There is in these narratives undoubtedly many an authentic memory of the evil deeds of this and that black sheep of the flock. But, taken as a whole, it needs scarcely to be said, a picture of what was wont to occur within the Order, based on these cases of spiritual discipline, would only be correct to the same extent as if, for example, one were to admit Stichus, the much renowned slave of the Digests, to pass for an illustration of Roman slaves in general.

We shall now endeavour to present in a connected form the regulations of the Order, as they are illustrated in the descriptions of countless occurrences scattered here and there in the canonical texts.

The Order and the Dioceses—Admission and Withdrawal.

The band of disciples gathered round Buddha, out of which grew the Order and the Church, rested, as without doubt did also the other monastic orders of India so numerous in that age, on the forms, which under the older Brahmanical system governed the relation between the religious teacher and his religious disciples. The use of the same words, which, in this case as as well as in that, constituted the solemn expression of this relationship, warrant our inferring the homogeneousness of the last-named system. The youth who desires to commit himself to the guidance of a Brahmanical teacher to learn the Veda, steps before him and says: "I am come for the Brahmacarya (spiritual discipleship). I desire to be a Brahmacâriu (spiritual disciple)." And the teacher "ties the girdle round him, gives him the staff into his hand and explains him the Brahmacarya, by saying: 'Thou art a Brahmacârin; drink water; perform service; sleep not by day; study the Veda obediently to thy teacher.'"* In the very same way, according to Buddhist tradition, the coming Buddha goes in the time of his quest of delivering knowledge to the spiritual teacher Uddaka and says: "I desire, O friend, according to thy teaching and thy direction, to walk in the Brahmacarya." Uddaka receives him, and the relation thus established is indicated with the very expressions, which are those regularly adopted in the Brahmanical mode of speech, as that subsisting between Âcârya (teacher) and Antevâsin (scholar).† And in the same way later on, when Buddha himself as a teacher receives the first students of his gospel, tradition represents him as doing so in these words: "Come hither, O monk, the doctrine is duly preached; walk in the Brahmacârya, to put an end to all sorrow."

The Order of Buddhists presents, as long as the Master is alive, a union of teacher and scholars after the Brahmanical model. The transition of such a community, so to speak, from a monarchical type to a republican, its passing somehow, when the teacher dies, into a confederacy of independent members existing side by side, is wholly unknown to the religious system of the Brahmans.‡ This very transition has completed itself in

* "Âçvalâyana G.," i, 22; cf. "Pâraskara," ii, 2, 3; "Çat. Br.," xi, 5, 4, seq.

† Thus also when the Buddhists say: "Uruvelakassapo mahâsamaṇe (*i.e.* bhagavati) brahmacariyaṃ carati," this amounts to the same as when it is said in the "Chândogya Upanishad": "Maghavân Prajâpatau brahmacaryam uvâsa;" when Indra resolves to enter into this relation of pupil, it is said of him "abhipravavrâja."

‡ Not even in that case in which we should be especially inclined to

Buddhism. Buddha died, and his disciples, already at that time scattered over the greater part of India, survived as a monastic community, which had no visible head and saw its invisible head only in the doctrine and ordinance declared by Buddha.* "Be your own light, be your own refuge," says Buddha, when approaching death, "have no other refuge. Let the truth be your light and your refuge; have no other refuge." Thus became fixed, what has been described as the trinity of Buddhism, the triad of those sacred powers, in which the newly-entering monk or lay-brother by solemn declaration "takes his refuge:" Buddha, the Doctrine, the Order. Not without hesitation I here venture to hazard a conjecture, which has no support and can have none in tradition: I think that the formula of this sacred triad does not go back to the time of Buddha's life, but that it had its origin in connection with those very changes which his death wrought for the community of his disciples. Must not Buddha alone, as long as he lived, and the Doctrine of deliverance preached by him have appeared to the believers their refuge? Could anyone call the disciples his refuge, as long as the Master was with them? His death changed everything. Now the Order stood as the sole visible exponent of the idea hitherto embodied in Buddha, as the sole possessor of delivering truth; now he

expect to find such a transition, that, namely, where the pupils of the deceased teachers had been life-long (naishṭhika) Brahmacârins. Cf. the statements as to the scholars, whose teacher dies, in "Gautama," iii, 7, seq., "Manu," ii, 247, seq.; Bühler on "Âpastamba," i, 1, 1, 12.

* Considering the great number and the scattered residences of the members of the Order, it is natural to think it is even probable, that already in Buddha's lifetime the fraternities of his disciples had an existence independent of Buddha's personality in essential features. Buddhist tradition also points to this. More intimate knowledge of the facts bearing on this matter is obviously not obtainable by us.

who desired to become a partaker of this truth, was obliged to take his refuge also with the Order.

The confession of this sacred triad has been couched in these articles, to which has been added in the fourth place the expression of the determination to abide by the precepts of holy living. The formula runs :—

"To Buddha will I look in faith: he, the Exalted, is the holy, supreme Buddha, the Knowing, the instructed, the blessed, who knows the worlds, the Supreme One, who yoketh men like an ox, the Teacher of gods and men, the Exalted Buddha.

"To the Doctrine will I look in faith: well-preached is the Doctrine by the Exalted One. It has become apparent; it needs no time; it says 'come and see;' it leads to welfare; it is realized by the wise in their own hearts.

"To the Order will I look in faith: in right behaviour lives the Order of disciples of the Exalted One; in proper behaviour lives the Order of the disciples of the Exalted One; in honest behaviour lives the Order of the disciples of the Exalted One; in just behaviour lives the Order of the disciples of the Exalted One, the four couples, the eight classes of believers;* that is the Order of the disciples of the Exalted One, worthy of offerings, worthy of gifts, worthy of alms, worthy to have men lift their hands before them in reverence, the highest place in the world, in which man may do good.

"In the precepts of rectitude will I walk, which the holy love, which are uninfringed, unviolated, unmixed, uncoloured, free, praised by the wise and not counterfeit, which lead on to concentration."†

* The different grades of the holy.

† So according to the "Saṃyuttaka Nikâya," vol. iii, fol. sâ; cf.

But if the Order be regarded as the ideal unit of believing monks over the whole face of the earth, as the bearer of a holiness which resembles the holiness of Buddha and his Doctrine, yet in actual life the Order never appears in this universal sense. There is really not one order, but only orders, communities of the monks sojourning in the same diocese. Devout persons might indeed present gifts and endowments to the "Church of the four quarters of the world, those present and those absent;" then the monks happening to be present, or the monks present of the diocese concerned, appear to have been regarded as the legitimate representatives of the "Church of the four quarters" for the receiving of such a gift and the administration of property so acquired: but regular standing organization for the superintendence of its concerns the collective Church had none; for the forming of any resolution, the completion of any act in its name, there was a total absence of legal form.

The difficulties, which were bound to arise from this, and which have as a fact arisen, are obvious. The band of disciples, which had gathered round Buddha, had grown with unparalleled rapidity into a great spiritual power. Throughout all India and soon beyond the confines of India, in the woods, through the villages, went the Buddhist monks preaching and begging. How then was the "Church of the four quarters, those present and those absent" to undertake in fact the administration of their common concerns? This object could only have been secured by creating a powerful centre, a spiritual regency in which the will of the whole Church would

"Mahâparin, S.," p. 17, seq.; "D'Alwis, Kachcháyana," p. 77. He who keeps the vows expressed in this confession, has reached the grade of the "Sotâpanna" (*vide* p. 310, note 2) on the path of holiness.

have concentrated itself.* But we find that not even the slightest attempt has been made in the whole Church-regulations for carrying out such arrangements.† The centre of gravity of all operations of Church-government, if we may speak of such a thing at all, lies within the circumference, within the small corps of brethren dwelling in the same circuit. But in the wandering life of these mendicant monks, in their constant coming and going, which only the three months of the rainy season bring to a certain standstill, the composition of these limited corps is naturally always changing. These monks to-day, to-morrow those have been thrown together, to-day these, to-morrow those exercise decisive

* We have already referred (p. 158, note 2) to the fact that after Buddha's death none of the disciples was regarded as called to what may be styled the succession. We here insert further the following passage: "At one time the venerable Ânanda was sojourning at Râjagaha . . . , shortly after the Exalted One had entered into Nirvâna. At that time the king of Magadha, Ajâtasattu, the son of the Vedehî princess, was fortifying Râjagaha against the King Pajjota." The minister, who is directing these fortifications, Vassakâra, asks Ânanda: "Venerable Ânanda, has any special monk been marked out by the venerated Gotama of whom he has said: 'This shall be your refuge after my death'—in whom you can now find your shelter?" Ânanda answers the question in the negative. The minister further asks: "Has then the Church named a specific monk, has a multitude of elders appointed him and given an order: 'He shall after the death of the Exalted One be our refuge'—?" This also Ânanda answers in the negative. "If you thus have no refuge, revered Ânanda, how does unity exist among you?" "There is no want to us of a refuge, O Brahman; we have a refuge, the Doctrine.', ("Gopakamoggallâna Suttanta" in the "Majjhima Nikâya." Cf. also supra, p. 198.)

† How far the official construction of Church history current in Ceylon has understood the post of the Vinayapâmokkhâ ("Heads of the Church Law") as that of a primate, I do no pretend to determine. But this very notion of the Vinayapâmokkhâ, wholly foreign to the ancient Church law, shows that here we meet a not happy fictitious construction of history.

authority among the brothers. Continuity and succession in the direction of matters of common interest could not, under these circumstances, possibly exist—and how could there be wanting in the life of this vast ecclesiastical corporation matters which demanded a continuous direction? If the synod of a particular district had come to any resolution for the decision of a doubtful point, or as to the right and wrong in a dispute between spiritual brothers, it was open to every other synod to resolve the contrary, and higher authority there was none, either to re-establish harmony in a synod divided within itself, or to reconcile the rival claims of different synods.* In the early times after Buddha's death the personal authority of the disciples, who had stood nearest to the Master, may possibly have operated to compensate this want and have checked the outbreak of serious discord: but a condition of things, which depends on the weight of individuals, not upon the sure structure of legal institutions, bears in itself the germ of dissolution. The sacred texts, which became fixed some time towards the end of the first century after Buddha's death, show clearly what disorder and confusion must have prevailed in the Church at that time; there is reflected in these texts the deep feeling of disaster, which dissensions among the brethren were bound to cause and were already causing, and at the same time the utter incapacity to prevent this disaster. The chapter on Schisms in the Church is constantly treated of, whenever the topic of spiritual life is discussed; the guilt of him who has given occasion for such dissensions is reckoned among the gravest sins; the most impressive admonitions to the brethren are put in Buddha's mouth, to live in harmony with each other

* Of the disorder, which hence arising prevailed in the Church law and subsequently undoubtedly also in the Church life, "Cullavagga," iv, 14, 25, for example, gives us a glimpse.

and to make concessions, even when in the right, rather than to allow divisions to arise in the Order. More effective still than these admonitions would have been institutions, possessing the power to watch over the relations between communities and members of communities, over the co-operation of all; such institutions were wholly wanting.

The defect, which lay here, shows itself in nothing more observably than in those very features which a cursory examination might be inclined to regard as its remedy: in the great councils to which such transcending importance is attached in old Buddhist tradition. The sacred texts mentions two such councils. The first is said to have been held at Râjagaha a few months after Buddha's death, for the purpose of compiling an authentic collection of Buddha's discourses and precepts. The second took place, as it is said, a hundred years later at Vesâlî, occasioned by a difference of opinion as to certain licenses, which had come to be practised by the monks of that town. This narrative of the council at Râjagaha is, we admit, to all appearance quite unhistorical, but the legal construction, on which it rests, is not on that account anything the less instructive for us. In the great gathering of disciples, who came together at Kusinârâ after Buddha's death, thought turns upon collecting and arranging Buddha's discourses, so as to possess in them a weapon against profane innovators. It is decided that five hundred chosen brethren of known holiness should perform this great task at Râjagaha, and the assembled monks give them a commission in this behalf by a formal resolution. This resolution decides that the five hundred are to pass the rainy season at Râjagaha and that no other monk is permitted to remain then in that town. Thus the council is held; the arrangement and the wording of the canonical texts is fixed by the five hundred fathers. Now then, if we ask what is the legal nature of this assembly, it is evident, that it is nothing more and nothing less than the assembly of the brethren sojourning in the diocese of Râjagaha. There have come together, because of the resolution passed at Kusinârâ, specially numerous and specially qualified persons, and, in pursuance of that resolution, unqualified persons have kept themselves aloof from that diocese,* but that in no way alters the case, that the deliberations of this so-called council are in fact only the proceedings of one specially prominent diocese, brought about by the resolution of another similar diocesan meeting, but not a Church-proceeding, resting on the authority of the "Church of the four quarters of the world." It seems that tradition itself was clearly sensible of this, and that it desired to give expression to this, when it represented the venerable Purâna, a monk who had not been a sharer in the deliberations, coming to Râjagaha at their close, and being told: "The fathers, my dear Purâna, have fixed the canon of the Doctrine and Law; accept this canon." But he answers: "The canon of the Doctrine and Law, my friends, has been admirably fixed by the fathers, but I will adhere to that which I have myself heard and received from the Exalted One." The fathers make no reply, and cannot, indeed, say anything in reply; the right of the individual to take as much or as little notice as he pleased of the resolution of an assembly such as that at Râjagaha was, could not be disputed with propriety on the basis of this form of Church.†

* A cogent necessity to do so can scarcely have been brought about by such a decree; the right of every brother to live where he pleases, could hardly be set aside by a resolution like that here spoken of.

† It is the same as to the Council at Vesâlî. To remedy the abuses which had arisen in Vesâlî, a number of elders come together in that

The force of existing circumstances and the authority of influential personages might perhaps for a time help to make up for, or conceal the utter want of organization; finally, however, the inherent impossibility of a Church without Church-government, with ordinances which were only applicable to the narrow circle of a *coterie*, was certain to lead to ever increasingly momentous consequences. Those deeply incisive schisms, which early arose and never disappeared, the weakening of the resistance opposed to the Brahmanism at first so successfully attacked, are phenomena certainly not unconnected with that fundamental defectiveness of Buddhist Church-organization. If at last, after a long death-struggle, Buddhism has vanished from its Indian home, leaving not a trace behind, we venture to think, that in the old rules of the community, in what they say and not less in what they leave unsaid, no small part of the preparatory history leading to that distant future is clearly enough depicted.

Entry into the Order* was, as a rule, open to everyone. As earthly suffering affects all, as all are bound as it were by bands to the paths of metempsychosis, so too must the liberation from these bands, which Buddha's teaching promises, embrace all who choose to accept it. Buddha utters at the commencement of his career these words:—

> "Open thou, O Wise One, the door of eternity;
> Let be heard what thou, O Sinless One, hast discovered."

Nevertheless it could not but be that practical necessity

place; the resolutions of the "Council" are in reality only resolutions of the diocese of Vesâlî, to which every monk, who comes to Vesâlî, *eo ipso*, belonged, and the composition of which was modified appropriately to the importance of this special cause.

* We confine our observations for the present to the Order of Monks. We shall speak of the nuns farther on.

should cause the imposition of certain restrictions on admission into the Order. The reception of those afflicted with serious bodily deformities and sicknesses was, as a matter of course, forbidden; it was the same with confirmed criminals. Then there were above all several categories of persons excluded, whose entry into the spiritual status would have involved an interference with the rights of third parties: persons who were in the royal service, especially soldiers, could not be admitted, as that would have interfered with the rights of the king as commander of the forces; debtors and slaves could not, for this would have been an infringement of the rights of their creditors and owners; sons, whose parents had not given their consent were similarly excluded. Children, too, were considered unfit for admission into the Order: a person might be received as a novice at the earliest at the age of twelve years,* and as a fully-accredited member at twenty.†

The ceremony of initiation is completed in two grades: there

* These twenty years are reckoned not from birth but from conception, by a method of computation occurring also in the spiritual law of the Brahmans. ("Mahâvagga," i, 75; cf. "Çânkhâyana G.," ii, 1, seq.)

† The statements having reference to invalidity of reception ("Mahâvagga," i, 49, seq.; 61, seq.) prohibit, partly the completion of the lower, and partly that of the higher grade of initiation (*vide* infra). In cases of the latter kind the initiation granted contrary to rule must be cancelled; the old codex of the "Pâtimokkha" goes even farther, and, in the only case of the kind which it touches, declares the initiation granted to be *ipso jure* invalid ("Pâcitt.," 65). For cases of the first kind on the contrary there is no such clause; it appears, that in this case the initiation remained in force, even though it had been conceded contrary to rule. Thus we might here have a distinction which may be compared to that of *impedimenta dirimentia* and *impedientia* in the legal system of our own times. In detail the separation of cases falling under the two classes mentioned gives rise to manifold doubts; the *redaction* of the "Mahâvagga" is in this point not without embarrassment.

is a lower, to a certain extent preparatory ordination, Pabbajjâ, *i.e.*, the outgoing, and a higher Upasampadâ, *i.e.*, the arrival. The Pabbajjâ is the going out from a prior state, from the lay-life or from a monastic sect holding another faith; the Upasampadâ is the entry into the circle of the Bhikkhus, the fully-accredited members of the Buddhist Order: just as in Buddha's own life, the departure from home is distinct from the Upasampadâ, the attainment of delivering knowledge, which coincides with the founding of the Order.* Between the two steps of initiation, if the postulant has not yet attained the age of twenty years, lies the noviciate, or if he has previously belonged to another monastic order, a probationary period extending over four months.† To outsiders, who look upon the Order as a whole, without considering the difference based on its internal relationship, he is during this term, as well as all his brethren, an "ascetic who follows the son of the Sakya house;"‡ but in the Order he is first treated as a Bhikkhu, a real member, when he has received the higher initiation. Where the grounds mentioned for separating the two steps of initiation did not exist, they appear to have been gone through, as a rule, at the same time.

We directed attention above (p. 336) to the analogy which prevails between the reception of a Buddhist believer into the Order and the reception of the young Brahman by his teacher. This is the place to institute a comparison between the first of the two steps in Buddhist initiation and another stage in the Brahmanical system, the entry of the Brahman

* "Milinda Pañha," p. 76; "Mahâvastu," vol. i, p. 3.

† So according to "Mahâvagga," i, 38. I give this view the preference to that stated in the "Mahâparinibbâna Sutta," p. 59, according to which the probationary period precedes the Pabbajjâ.

‡ *Vide e.g.*, "Mahâvagga," i, 46.

into the state of a hermit or wandering beggar. "When the Brahman," we read in Manu's Institutes, "who is living in the state of a householder, sees his skin becoming wrinkled and his hair becoming grey, if he sees his son's son, then let him go forth into the forest. Let him leave all food, such as one enjoys in the village, and all household furniture behind him; to his sons let him commit his wife, and let him go to the forest, or let him go forth with his wife. Let the Brahman make the Prajâpati-offering and give all his possessions as remuneration of sacrifice; his holy fire let him take up in his own body, and thus *let him go forth* from his house.* For the Brahman, who leaves his home and becomes a homeless ascetic, his own act of *outgoing* only is necessary; and Pabbajjâ, *i.e.*, "the outgoing" is therefore used by the Buddhists of the first step of initiation, by which the change of a layman into an ascetic takes place, "outgoing from home into homelessness" (agârasmâ anagâriyaṃ pabbajjâ).

Pabbajjâ, as is implied by its very essence, is a one-sided act on the part of the "outgoer." He alone speaks, and of what he says the Order as such takes no notice; every older, fully-accredited monk can receive his declaration. The candidate puts on the yellow garment of the *religieux*, has his hair and beard shaved off, and says three times in reverential attitude to the monk or monks present: "I take my refuge in the Buddha. I take my refuge in the Doctrine. I take my refuge in the Order."

To full membership of the Order, to be a Bhikkhu, the novice was raised by the ordination of Upasampadâ, which, differing from the lower form, consisted of a ceremony com-

* The word "going forth" (pra-vraj) can be used equally well, whether the entry upon the condition of a hermit or upon that of a mendicant monk be spoken of. "Âpastamba," ii, 9, 8. 19.

pleted before the Order and by their participation. The outer forms were most simple; the old Order was wont when it undertook ceremonial operations, to express what had to be expressed, with bare business-like precision, and nothing more. We find in the ceremony of ordination nothing of the ceremonies which we are accustomed to look for in Church observances, no sound, in which we might hear ringing the depths and the poetry of the religious idea. Instead, we here meet, in truly Indian fashion, the careful concise expression of all the precautions, which the Order takes before admitting a new member into their midst. The postulant speaks before the assembled chapter of the monks, cowering reverently on the ground, raising his joined hands to his forehead, saying: "I entreat the Order, reverend sirs, for initation. May the Order, reverend sirs, raise me up to itself; may it have pity on me. And for the second—and for the third time I entreat the Order, reverend sirs, for initiation. May the Order, reverend sirs, raise me up to itself; may it have pity on me." Now follows a formal examination of the postulant. "Hearest thou me, N. N.? Now is the time come for thee to speak truly and to speak honestly. I ask thee, how things are. What is, thou must say thereof: It is. What is not, thou must say thereof: It is not. Art thou afflicted with any of the following diseases: leprosy, *goître*, white leprosy, consumption, epilepsy? Art thou a human being?* Art thou a man? Art thou thine own master? Hast thou no debts? Art thou not in the royal service? Has thou the permission of thy father and mother? Art thou full twenty years of age? Hast thou the almsbowl and the garments? What is thy name? What is thy teacher's name?" If the answer to all these

* That is, not a serpent-demon in human form, and the like.

questions be satisfactory, the motion for the conceding of initiation is put to the Order and repeated thrice: "Reverend sirs, let the Order hear me. N. N. here present desires as pupil of the venerable N. N. to receive ordination. He is free from the obstacles to ordination. He has the almsbowl and garments. N. N. entreats the Order for ordination with the said N. N. as his teacher. The Order grants N. N. ordination with the said N. N. as his teacher. Whoever of the venerable is for granting the said N. N. ordination with the said N. N. as his teacher, let him be silent. Whoever is against it, let him speak." If, after thrice repeating this motion, no dissentient voice is heard, it is declared passed. "N. N. has from the Order received ordination with the said N. N. as his teacher. The Order is in favour of this; therefore it is silent; thus I understand." Next, when they have measured the shadow, *i.e.*, determined the time of day, in order to fix the *ancienneté* of the newly-ordained member, and have announced the particulars therefore, they communicate to the young member of the Order the four rules of monastic austerity in external life: The food of him, who has gone from home into homelessness, shall be the morsels which he receives by begging. His clothing shall be made out of the rags which he collects. His resting-place shall be under the trees of the forest. His medicine shall be the stinking urine of cattle. If pious laymen prepare him a meal, if they give him clothing, shelter, medicine, it is not forbidden him to take them, but he is to look upon this harsh form of mendicancy as the proper and appointed mode of life for a monk.

Finally the four great prohibitions are communicated to the member, the fundamental duties of monastic life, by an infringement of which the guilty person brings about his inevitable expulsion from the Order :—

"An ordained monk may not have sexual intercourse, not even with an animal. The monk who has sexual intercourse, is no longer a monk; he is no disciple of the son of the Sakya house. As a man whose head is cut off, cannot live with the trunk, so also a monk who practises sexual intercourse is no longer a monk: he is no disciple of the son of the Sakya house. Thou must abstain therefrom all thy life.

"An ordained monk may not take what has not been given to him, what is called a theft—not even a blade of grass. The monk, who takes ungiven a pâda* or a pâda's worth or more than a pâda, (commits) what is called a theft, is no longer a monk; he is no disciple of the son of the Sakya house. As a dry leaf which has separated itself from the stalk cannot again become green, so also a monk, who takes ungiven a pâda or a pâda's worth or more than a pâda, what is called a theft, is no longer a monk; he is no disciple of the son of the Sakya house. Thou must abstain therefrom all thy life.

"An ordained monk may not knowingly deprive any creature of life, not even a worm or an ant. The monk, who knowingly deprives a human being of life, even by the destruction of a fœtus, is no longer a monk: he is no disciple of the son of the Sakya house. As a great stone, which has been split into two parts, cannot again be made into one, so also a monk —and so on.

"An ordained monk may not boast of any superhuman perfection, as much as to say: 'I like to dwell in an empty house.' The monk, who with evil intent and from covetousness falsely and untruly boasts of a superhuman perfection,†

* A coin or a trivial metallic weight.

† When we here, next to the offences of unchastity, theft and murder, find the false and fraudulent assumption of spiritual perfections mentioned

be it a condition of abstraction, or of rapture, or of concentration, or of elevation, or of the path of deliverance, or of the fruit of deliverance, he is no longer a monk; he is no disciple of the son of the Sakya house. As a palm-tree, the top of which has been destroyed, cannot again grow, so also a monk —and so on."

The communication of these four great prohibitions concludes the ceremony of ordination. We see, that in it no liturgical elements come to the front which might to a certain extent serve to express by solemn symbolism the putting off of the natural man and the putting on of a new man, or the cohesion of the old believers and the young member into a spiritual unity.* We have before us merely a process of spiritual law, not

as the fourth of the major sins, this entitles us to infer, with what offensive preference this branch of religious swindling must have been cultivated already even in that age in Indian monastic circles. The sacred texts ("Vinaya Piṭaka," vol. iii, p. 87, seq.) narrate as an illustration to Buddha's ruling on this point, that a community of monks in the Vajji territory once endured great distress by famine. It was proposed that they should take service with the laity to obtain the means of living; a more quick-witted monk, however, advised that every brother should attribute the highest spiritual perfections to the other brethren in the hearing of the laity: "This monk has attained such and such a degree of abstraction"—"this monk is a saint"—"this monk possesses the threefold knowledge"—and more of the like. The suggestion is accepted, and the laity say in astonishment: "It is lucky, very lucky for us that such monks are spending the rainy season in our midst. Never in days gone by have monks come to us for the rainy season such as these monks are, rich in virtue and noble." Naturally then the liberality of the laity corresponds in full to the high opinion which they entertain of the spiritual merit of their guests, so that the latter survive the period of famine, "blooming, well-fed, with healthy complexion and healthy skin."

* The assertion often made, that the person entering the Order changes his family-name for a cloister-name, is erroneous or at any rate supported

a mystic transformation which comes over and permeates the person of the ordained. The consequence of this conception, as rational as it is bare, is that there is nothing to prevent the breaking off of the relation thus established, either on the part of the Order* or on the part of the ordained. If the latter be guilty of any serious transgression, especially if he infringe the four great prohibitions, imposed on him at ordination, it becomes the right and the duty of the Order to renounce him. On the other side, to the monk, who has a lingering fondness for a worldly life, the exit from the Order is always open: the Order makes no effort to detain him. It is better for him "to renounce monastic practice and to admit his weakness," than, remaining in the spiritual state, to commit sin. Whoever says: "My father is in my thoughts," or "my mother is in my thoughts," or "my wife is in my thoughts," or "the laughter and the jest, the pleasantry of old days is in my thoughts," may return to the world. He can do so silently —the Order permits him to depart—; but the proper way for him is to declare before a witness, who hears and understands him,† his resolution, that he renounces Buddha, the Doctrine, and the Order. He departs without enmity; if he desires again to re-establish his connection as a lay-brother or as a novice with the comrades of his quondam spiritual life,

only by solitary cases. Ânanda, as member of the brotherhood, is called "the venerable Ânanda," Kassapa of Uruvelâ is called "the venerable Kassapa of Uruvelâ."

* The technical expression for this is: the Order "destroys him" (nâseti). A list of the cases in which this occurred—these are by no means confined only to offences against the four great prohibitions—may be found compiled in the Index to the "Vinaya Piṭaka," vol. ii, p. 346 (s. v. nâseti).

† It does not appear to have been required that this declaration should be made before a monk. Cf. "Vinaya Piṭaka," vol. iii, p. 27.

they do not repel him. Though this unlimited possibility of recession may have brought evils in its train—it is admitted, that it has led to gross abuses in the present day*—yet its influence on the moral health of monastic life may be regarded as more beneficial than otherwise. Apart from the fact that the Order would have been wholly deficient in the external power to bind its members by forcible means of any kind whatever, nothing could have been more decidedly opposed to the nature of Buddhism than such constraint. Every man might go the way which the strength or the weakness of his nature, the merit or demerit of past existences led him: the doors of the Order stood open, but no impatient or pertinacious zeal pressed the reluctant to enter or impeded the return of the wayward to the world.

PROPERTY—CLOTHING—DWELLING—MAINTENANCE.

"Community of mendicants" (Bhikkhusangha) was the name given to themselves by this fraternity of fully-accredited, ordained monks. This name indicates that among their duties that of poverty ranked next in order to chastity. This had always been so, ever since there was a monastic system in India. A Vedic text belonging to the age of the first rudiments of this monasticism says of the Brahmans

* "It happens every day that monks who have entered the cloister under the compulsion of parents, or to avoid the service of the king, or from poverty, from laziness, from a love of solitude or of study, or from any other worldly motive, again quit the cloister, to succeed to an inheritance, to marry, &c. In further India it is even the custom for young men, even princes, to assume the monk's cowl for a term only, at least for three months."—*Köppen*, i, 338.

who renounce the world: "They cease from seeking for children, and seeking for possessions, and seeking the worldly, and they itinerate as beggars. For what seeking for children is, that is also seeking for possessions; what seeking for possessions is, that is also seeking for the worldly; the one is seeking as much as the other."* So the Buddhist monk also renounces all property. No express vow imposes on him the duty of poverty; both the marriage tie and the rights of property of him who renounces the world, are regarded as *ipso facto* cancelled by the "going forth from home into homelessness."† Property was felt to be a fetter, which holds in bondage the spirit struggling for freedom: "Very straitened," it is said, "is life in the home, a state of impurity: freedom is in leaving the home"—"Leaving all property behind must one go thence"—"In supreme felicity live we,

* "Çatapatha Br.," xiv, 7, 2, 26.

† More accurately expressed: the monk, who is resolved to remain true to the spiritual life, looks upon his marriage as dissolved, his property as given away. The wife whom he has forsaken, is strictly termed in the texts "his quondam partner" (purâṇadutiyikâ, "Mahâvagga," i, 8, 78; "Suttavibhanga," Pâr. i, 5); he addresses her, like every other woman, as "sister" (Pâr. l.c. § 7). It is in no way inconsistent with this, if the family of a monk, which desires his return to a worldly status, looks upon his marriage and his rights of property as continuing, and if he himself, longing for a worldly life, says to himself: "I have a wife, for whom I must provide"—"I have a village, on the income of which I desire to live"—"I have gold, on it I shall live" ("Suttavibhanga," Pâr. i, 8, 2).—In one direction the spiritual law permitted a noteworthy operation of the old rights of property surrendered by the monk to take effect: in certain cases where the receiving of any new article whatever for monastic house-keeping was forbidden, *e.g.*, a new almsbowl, he was permitted to take the object in question, if it had been made for him "from his own means." ("Suttav. Nissaggiya," xxii, 2, 2; xxvi, 2, seq.) Cf. Mayr, "Indisches Erbrecht," p. 145.

who possess nothing; cheerfulness is our diet, as of the gods of the regions of light"—"As the bird, wherever he flies, carries nothing with him but his wings, so also a monk is content with the garment, which he is wearing, with the food, which he has in his body. Wherever he goes, he everywhere carries his property with him."

The simple needs, which in the climate of India belong to the life of a monk, and the common life of a monastic order, are easily satisfied. "Clothing, food, lodging, medicine for the sick"—this is the standing enumeration of what the Order looked for from the pious beneficence of the laity, and seldom looked for in vain. What did not come within the narrow circle of these immediate necessaries of life, could as little constitute part of the property of the Order as that of the individual monk.* Lands, slaves, horses and live stock, the Order did not possess, and was not allowed to accept. It did not engage in agricultural pursuits, nor did it permit them to be carried on on its account. "A monk," as the old confessional formula says, "who digs the earth or causes it to be

* That the Order was allowed to have any kind of possession whatever, which was forbidden to the individual brethren, has been often asserted, but, as far I can see, quite groundlessly. The more important items of property which belonged to the Order, could not indeed by gift or division pass into the possession of individual monks ("Cullavagga," vi, 15, 16), but it was not unallowable for a monk to possess things of this description ("Mahâvagga," viii, 27, 5). Then after his death they fell into the property of the "Church of the four quarters of the world, the present and the absent," while smaller articles of a deceased monk were divided among the brethren with a special regard for those who had attended to him during his sickness. Mention, however, is made of death-bed bequests: "A nun said when dying: after my death my property is to go to the Order" ("Cull.," x, ii). Whether any other heirs but the Order of the monks or of the nuns could be nominated, is not known.

dug, is liable to punishment."* But most strictly was the receiving of gold and silver forbidden to Buddha's disciples, individually as well as collectively. The benefactor, who desires to give a monk not the things themselves which he requires, but their money value, delivers the money to operatives, and the monk then receives from them what is intended for him. The provisions of the rules of the Order to meet the case, where a brother permits gold or silver to be tendered to him in spite of the prohibition, show how lively was the feeling of what was here at stake for the spirit of their common life, and how care was taken with an anxiety which has something touching about it, to guard against the dangerous consequences of such sinful greed. When the guilty monk has penitently confessed his transgression before the assembled monks, if one of the laity attached to the Order be in the neighbourhood, the gold is given to him, with these words: "Friend, take this into thy keeping." If he wishes, he can then purchase for the monks what they are permitted to receive, butter, oil, or honey. This they may all enjoy; only he who has received the gold, is not allowed to have any share of it. Or the layman may cast the gold away. If it is not possible for the Order to get rid of the dangerous possession in this way, one of the brethren is to be chosen to be the "thrower away of the gold," who has five qualities: who is

* Of Buddha's Order the same may be said which the Brahmajâla Sutta represents people saying to each other regarding Buddha himself: "From receiving bondsmen and bondswomen, the ascetic Gotama refrains —from receiving elephants, cattle, horses and mares, the ascetic Gotama refrains—from receiving arable land the ascetic Gotama refrains." In the Vinaya texts, accordingly, nothing is found which points to the pursuit of agriculture, except only one, quite solitary passage, "Mahâvagga," vi, 39, which hardly refers to anything more than the occasional sowing of seed in the land belonging to the Ârâmas.

free from desire, free from hate, free from infatuation, free from fear, and who knows what casting away and what not casting away means. He is to throw the gold or the silver away, and is to take care that the place where it lies is not to be recognized by any sign. If he makes any signs, he is liable to punishment. Already at an early date severe struggles arose in the Order regarding this prohibition of the receipt of gold and silver,* but it was successfully maintained in its integrity for centuries. By nothing so clearly as by this prohibition and by the obedience which it has obtained, is it guaranteed that the ancient Buddhist Order did really remain free and pure from all hankering after worldly power as well as worldly enjoyment. Never could it have so completely surrendered the possession of gold and therewith all possibility of outer action, had it not been in truth precisely that alone which it professed to be, a community of those who sought for peace and deliverance in separation from everything earthly.

The dwelling, food, and clothing of the monks are laid down in detailed regulations. The character of these rules is very decided: the abstaining from everything which implies comfortable enjoyment, being at one's ease in worldly possessions, is just as urgently demanded, as on the other side excesses of ascetic praxis are wholly eschewed. Here we find none of those strange features, with which a fanciful inquirer has recently made up the picture of what he calls original Buddhism: a society of ascetics, who were allowed to live under no roof, but to pass their whole life under the open heavens, sitting in cremation-grounds or under trees, whose whole appearance bears upon it the stamp of deformity and

* Apparently in the Council of Vesâli (circ. one century after Buddha's death) the dispute touching the receipt of gold and silver was the particularly essential among a series of secondary and subtle differences.

impurity.* In truth all negligence in outer appearance, especially in clothing, is most strictly tabooed. In the case of younger monks, who are placed under the superintendence of an elder brother, the latter has to pay attention to the appearance of those committed to his care; he is required to see, that they make their clothes right, dye them, and wash them properly. The sanitation and ventilation of the quarters occupied by the monks, the cleaning of furniture, the sunning of all articles that require it, are prescribed with the greatest minuteness in the works on the rules of the Order. Touching the greater or less degree of abstinence from the necessities and comforts of regular life, a certain freedom is allowed to the individual, to allow scope for his individual likes and dislikes. Whoever wished might take a vow to live only on the food which he might obtain on his begging expedition from house to house, but no one was forbidden to accept the invitations of pious laymen to dine, and we read that Buddha himself accepted such invitations on numberless occasions. Whoever wished might patch together rags, which he had collected, to make himself a monk's yellow garment; wandering monks, who happened to come to a cremation-ground, used perhaps to gather there the shreds from which they made their clothes.

* "Wassiljew, der Buddhismus," p. 16, seq. (of the German translation). *Inter alia*, it is there said: "In fact we see the Buddha in the legends, notwithstanding the specious splendour with which they invest him, every day in his own person going out of the grove of Anâthapindika and walking to the nearest town to collect alms. In the face of this, what meaning have the cloister rules, the directions for associated life, and whatever else of the kind meets us in the Vinaya? Is it consistent with this, that a host of scholars surround the Buddha and have satiated themselves with his doctrine and have taught others?" Of course, how could scholars indeed satiate themselves with the teaching of a man, who daily goes out of a wood in person!

But no one was forbidden to dress himself in the garments, which laymen presented to the monks. "I grant you, O monks, that he who wears clothes given by the laity, may also wear clothes made up from gathered rags. If you have a fancy for both, O monks, I have no objection to it."* Whoever wished, might dwell in the forest or in the caves of the mountains, but no one was forbidden to take up his abode near a village or a town. With sticks gathered in the forests, and grass, every monk could easily construct a hut for himself, and laymen not unfrequently even lent their assistance or caused building operations to be carried on at their expense for the Order, so that monks' houses (vihâras), detached buildings or a complex whole, with assembly-rooms, council-chambers, dining-halls,

* The following passage of the "Theragâthâ" (fol. khe) describes briefly and graphically the life of a monk, who adheres to the stricter ordinances in dress, food, and so on: "In solitude and quiet where the wild beasts have their dwelling and the gazelles, there let the abode of the monk be, that he may be able to dwell in retirement and seclusion. On dunghills, on cremation-grounds, and on the streets, let him seek wherewith he may prepare himself clothing; rough let the garment be which he wears. With submissive air let the monk move, watching the doors of his senses and keeping himself in check, from house to house in order to beg for food. Let him be content also with poor food; let him not desire anything else, many savoury things. He who is fond of savoury things, his spirit is not fond of abstraction. Needing nothing, content, apart from the world, let the wise man live; layman and anchorite, both let him avoid. Like a dumb or a deaf man let him show himself; let him not speak, who is wise, at an unseasonable moment in the Order." The dangers, which forest life must daily and hourly cause to spiritual personages, were obviously not fewer in those days than now, when year after year hermits are killed in hundreds by snakes and wild beasts in Indian forests. A particular section of the sacred texts, entitled "the imminent dangers of forest life," contains admonitions to zealous acceleration of spiritual effort, when every moment may bring violent death.

structures for warm baths and ablutions, as well for the Order in its entirety as for the members individually, were at their disposal.* On the whole we have undoubtedly to picture to ourselves monks, those even who had chosen a life in the forests,† dwelling rather in huts or houses than under the open sky, perchance under the shade of a tree. Even wanderers had as a rule a shelter at their disposal. Novices and scholars used generally to go on ahead and see that quarters were prepared for their teachers among the communities, whose places of residence they passed through. The younger brethren went out to meet the older monks, who came on their wanderings; they took their overalls and almsbowls from them, got water ready for them to wash their feet and showed them to their quarters for the night. During the three months of the rainy season in which itinerating ceased, the monks were expressly forbidden to resort to a place of rest in the open, at the foot of a tree. Thus the tradition of the Singhalese represents Mahinda, the converter of the island, and his spiritual companions, before the rainy season sets in, dwelling

* We are not to think of the vihâras of ancient times as cloisters, which had been erected for the reception of a great number of residents. On the whole it seems to have been the rule, that one vihâra accommodated only one monk; such vihâras usually lay near one another in greater or smaller numbers. The vihâra is described as especially great which is mentioned in the "Cullavagga" (vi, 11), in which seventeen monks arranged themselves for a rainy season. Six other monks come thither, and still there is room for them also. Possibly we have to look upon both parties as accompanied by scholars, novices, and so forth. Stone, brick, and wood are named as the usual materials for the buildings of the Order.

† Compare the rules for the house and the day for monks living in the forest, which we read in the "Cullavagga," viii, 6. The stately vihâra, which the venerable Udâyi had built for himself in the forest, is described in the "Suttavibhanga," Sangh. ii, 1, 1.

near the capital in a park, which the king had placed at their disposal, "with a good view and rich in shade, adorned with flowers and fruit, truly lovely . . . there is a beautiful lotus pool, covered with lotuses, white and blue; there is fresh water in beautiful springs, scented by sweet flowers." But when the rainy season comes round, when in India damp weather sets in—in Ceylon itself these are the finest months of the whole year—Mahinda leaves the park and goes with the other monks to the mountain of Missaka, there to provide himself accommodation in the holes of the rocks. The king hears of this and hastens out: "Why hast thou left me and mine and come to this mountain?" And Mahinda replies: "Here we wish to pass the rainy reason, three months long. Near a village or in the forest, or in a dwelling-place, the door of which can be shut, has Buddha commanded the monks to dwell, when the rainy season comes."* Then the king gives an order for eight and sixty cells to be hollowed out in the rock for the monks—cells such as throughout the whole of India and Ceylon, lying often several stories one over the other, still mark indelibly to-day the old rallying points and centres of monastic life.

In the village itself, or in a town, the monk is not permitted to reside except in cases of urgent necessity, nor even as much as to set foot in them between noon and the appearance of dawn on the following day.† But he is tied to the neighbour-

* With this passage of the "Dîpavaṃsa" (14, 64) compare the rules of the Order on this subject, "Mahâvagga," iii, 12.

† "Pâcittiya," 85. On one occasion when Buddha in his wanderings approaches his native town, Kapilavatthu, he sends on one of the faithful, saying: "Go, Mahânâma, and seek in Kapilavatthu a lodging, in which I can find shelter to-day for one night" ("Anguttara Nik.," vol. i, fol. jhau). Instances of this kind occur only quite isolated.

hood of village and town by the necessity of supporting life. Even he, who has taken a vow to live in the forest, lives just near enough to the village to be able to reach it on his begging excursion.* Carrying in his hands the bowl, in which he places the food handed to him, he is to go from house to house, whether believers dwell in them or unbelievers; only he is to pass by the houses of poor people, of whom the Order know that they would give the begging monks food beyond what they could afford, and would then themselves to suffer hunger. Enveloped in his overall, with downcast look, without bustle, and in neither hasty nor careless fashion, the monk is to enter the houses. He is not to stand too near nor too far off, he is not to stay too long nor to go away too quickly. He is to wait in silence, until something is given to him; then he is to hold out his bowl, and, without looking at the face of the giver, receive what she gives him. Then he spreads his overall over the almsbowl, and goes slowly on. "When they leave the

* "Cullavagga," viii, 6. For illustration take the narrative in the "Commentary on the Dhammapada," p. 81, seq. The saintly monk Pâlita comes with sixty accompanying brethren in his wanderings, when the rainy season is near, to a great village, and makes his begging-excursion through it. "The people saw these monks, who were adorned with right demeanour, and they prepared seats for them with believing heart, invited them to sit down, entertained them with the best food, and asked them: 'Reverend sirs, whither does your way lie?' They replied: 'Where we may find a place good to dwell in, O believer.' The clever people saw: 'The venerable men are looking for a dwelling and an abode,' and they said: 'If you, venerable sirs, be willing to dwell here for these three months, we shall take our refuge in the faith, and observe the requirements of upright life.' Pâlita accepts the invitation, whereon the villagers erect a vihâra in the forest (l.c. p. 85, line 13). Thence the monks go every morning into the village to collect alms. When one of the monks becomes blind, and can go no longer to the village, the residents of the village send him food daily into the forest."

village," says an old poem,* "they look back on nothing. Without looking round they walk about; therefore dear to me are the monks." When the monk has returned from the begging excursion, there follows about midday the hour for eating, the one meal in the whole day. "The monk," it is said in the confessional formula, "who at an improper time† takes or enjoys hard or soft food, is liable to punishment." The meal consists chiefly, as Indian custom requires, of bread and rice, with which water is drunk. The enjoyment of flesh and fish is limited; spirituous liquors are most strictly forbidden.

For a monk to dwell alone, without having other brethren in his neighbourhood, is quite the exception, even in the case of those who have chosen a forest-life. The provisions of the laws of the Order are wholly based on the supposition that small knots of brethren living near each other come together, who depend on each other to unite for confession, to instruct one another, to strengthen one another in doubt and temptation, to care for one another in sickness, and to keep up spiritual discipline among themselves. "For," says the old confessional formula, "the band of the disciples of the Exalted One is so bound together that one exhorts the other and one stablishes the other." Especially on the young monk is it enjoined as a duty to seek the company of the older and more experienced brethren, to be instructed in the doctrines of the faith as well as in the external rules of conduct, even down to the directions for the wearing of clothes and carrying of the almsbowl. During the first five years, which every monk passes in the Order, he is required to place himself under the guidance and

* "Therîgâthâ," fol. ṅi.

† *I.e.*, between the hour of midday and the dawn of the following day.

instruction of two able monks,* who shall have belonged for at least ten years to the Order. These he accompanies in their wanderings and begging excursions; he looks after the cleaning of their cells, and serves them at their meals. "The teacher is to look upon the scholar as a son; the scholar is to look upon the teacher as a father. Thus both are to permit respect, attachment and unanimity of life to prevail between them, that they may be able to grow, progress, and stablish themselves in this Doctrine and this Law."† "He who has left his home for the faith, he who has come hither in early years and is young, let him attach himself to noble friends, to unwearying persons of pure walk. He who has left his home for the faith, who has come hither in early years and is young, a monk who is intelligent, let him abide in the Order and practise the rules."‡

There was nothing in the way of differences of rank in the circles of brethren, but the natural privileges and claims to respect, which belong to greater seniority—*i.e.* to the greater length of spiritual standing, which was reckoned from the date of ordination. In the proceedings, which had to be conducted before the Order, any "experienced and able monk" could take the initiative. The numerous office-bearers whom we find mentioned bear by no means a hierarchical character; they have to do chiefly with the care of external necessities and the discharge of domestic duties; thus there was a caretaker of the sleeping places, a caretaker of the council chambers, a rice distributor, a fruit distributor, the overseer of the novices, and

* One of them is denominated Upajjhâya, the other Âcariya (both are synonymous for "teacher"). As to the relation of these two appointments, see Davids's and my note to "Mahâvagga," i, 32.

† "Mahâvagga," i, 25, 6; 32, 1.

‡ "Theragâthâ," fol. kau'.

other similar officers. As unanimity was necessary as a general rule in most of the resolutions of the Order, these appointments also depended as a whole on the unanimous choice of the brethren present in the diocese.

Ordinary labour of any kind whatever was always foreign to this monastic life; it was deeply embedded in the Buddhist conception of the moral that the educative value of labour could not be acknowledged here. The whole life and all the energies were claimed for spiritual exercises. Already at early morn, before the hour for begging excursions had arrived, in the chambers of the vihâras, in the halls and under the trees of the cloister-gardens, might be heard the monotonous, half-singing recitation of the sacred sayings and discourses of Buddha. The oldest of the brethren present himself recited or directed one of the others to recite. Or there came forward, as questioner and answerer, two of the brethren who were versed in the rules of the Order, and discoursed before the assembly on important and difficult points of monastic law and of rules of the Order.* Then after the begging excursion, after dinner and the hours of rest which followed, when evening brought the brethren again together, they sat on far into the night—the time allotted to the monks for sleeping was very scant†—silently or in converse with one another. There were also times when friends made compacts with each other, like that of Anuruddha and his two comrades, who kept awake one night every five days, propounding the Doctrine and discussing it together.‡ "He who abides in the Order," we

* In this form of discussion, which is treated of at "Mahâvagga," ii, 15, 6-11, the proceedings, for instance, of the Council at Vesâli regarding the ten disputed points of the rules of the Order were carried on (p. 343).

† The regular time for rising was about dawn.

‡ "Mahâvagga," x, 4, 5.

read,* "talks not of many topics and talks not of vulgar things. He expounds the word himself, or stirs another up to its exposition, or he esteems even sacred silence not lightly."

Of the very profane interruptions to which sacred silence was liable, especially at the greater centres of monastic life, at places where hundreds, probably sometimes, indeed, thousands of monks flocked together from all parts of India, the texts do not speak very much with relish. An old verse† says with special reference to the spiritual brothers: "Like Brahma men live alone; like gods they live in twos; like a village they live in threes; where there are more there is bustle and turmoil." Particularly in the last clause of this saying will he fully concur who has seen and especially who has heard the commotion of a crowd of people, or better still of a crowd of wrangling and scolding faqirs in India. Thus many among Buddha's disciples withdrew from the bustle of the masses, from the great *âramas* in the neighbourhood of the towns into the solitude of the forest.‡ There they lived in the huts they built for themselves, in small communities, in twos or threes, or even quite alone and only just near enough

* "Anguttara Nikâya," vol. iii, fol. ki.

† "Theragâthâ," fol. kau'.

‡ The comparative estimation of solitude and of life with others could naturally be only a purely personal matter, and so it appears in the sacred texts. Sometimes we read expressions like these: "Let him seek out remote places, therein to dwell; there let him walk, that he may become free from all bands. If he does not find peace there, let him live in the Order, guarding his soul from sins with watchful spirit" ("Saṃy. N.," quoted in the "Milinda Pañha," p. 402). And then it is said again: "If he finds a wise associate, a noble comrade of upright walk, then let him live with him, overcoming all temptation, cheerful and with a watchful spirit. If he does not find a wise associate, a noble comrade of upright walk, then let him go forth alone, as a king who abandons his conquered kingdom, like the elephant into the forest" ("Dhammap.," 328, seq.).

to others to be in reach of one another for holding the meetings of the chapter prescribed for confessional and other purposes. Perhaps nowhere have the sayings of Buddha, the earnest thoughts of the suffering of everything earthly, and the great, pure expectations of the happy cessation of impermanence, so fully satisfied human hearts, as among these anchorites in their small and quiet forest bands. "When shall I," says one of the spiritual poets,* "dwell alone in mountain grotto without companions, viewing instability in every form of being? When will such be my lot? When shall I, as a sage clad in garments made of rags, in yellow garb, calling nothing my own and without occupation, desisting from love and hate, ceasing from infatuation, dwell cheerfully in the forest? When shall I, seeing the instability of my body, which is a nest of murder and disease, oppressed by old age and death, dwell free from fear, alone in the forest? When will such be my lot?" "The broad, heart-cheering expanses, crowned by *kareri* forests, those lovely regions, where elephants raise their voices, the rocks make me glad. Where the rain rushes, those lovely abodes, the mountains, where sages walk, where the peacock's cry resounds, the rocks make me glad. There is it good for me to be, the friend of abstraction, who is struggling for salvation. There is it good for me to be, the monk, who pursues the true good, who is struggling for salvation."† Not in many places on earth will the charms of contemplative solitude have been enjoyed so fully as there, in the forests on the Ganges and at the foot of the Himalaya, among the yellow-robed monks of Buddha's Order.

* "Theragâthâ," fol. gau.

† "Theragâthâ," fol. go.

The Cultus.

Twice in the month, at full moon and at new moon, the monks of each district, wherever they may happen to be sojourning, come together to celebrate the fast-day.*

The observance of the fast-day is the most prominent and almost the only observance of the ancient Buddhist cultus, if the word "cultus" can be at all applied to these most simple and plain external forms of mutual religious life. For a faith, which looks upon man's own heart as the sole place in which decisions between happiness and ruin can be carried into effect, what the lip utters and what the hand does, can have a value only in so far as it is a concomitant of, a symbol corresponding to, that internal process. And above all in the first age of the young Buddhist community must that very opposition to the old faith with its ceremoniousness, with its animal sacrifices and soma-offerings, with its hosts of singing and mumbling priests, have been especially keenly felt and led to the result, that so much the more earnest heed was taken to preserve the internal character of the individual faith free from every non-essential. We must keep before us the fact, that anything in the way of a mysterium, such as that from which the early Christian cultus drew its vitality, was foreign to Buddhism; the conception that the divine Head of the Church is not absent from his people, but that he dwells powerfully in their midst as their lord and king, so that all cultus is nothing else but the expression of this continuing living fellowship. Buddha, however, has entered into Nirvâna; if his believers desired to invoke him, he could not hear them. Therefore Buddhism is a

* The designation of this day as a fast-day rests on the ancient usages of the Vedic cultus. With an actual fast the Buddhist Order had nothing to do.

religion without prayer. The preaching of Buddha's doctrine, the practice of spiritual abstractions, in which they thought they possessed so powerful an aid to religious effort, permeated the whole life of the brethren, but they found no expression in the forms of a regularly organized cultus; for this last there was little room left in that universal sway, conceivable only in a monastic Order, of religious thought over every word which the believer utters, and over every step he takes.

Among the operations of this quasi-cultus stands, as already mentioned, in precedence of everything else, the confessional celebration observed on the "fast-day," the check, so to speak, employed to determine whether the duties of spiritual life have been truly and fully performed by all the brethren. These confessional meetings give above all a lively expression to the cohesion of the members of the Order.

The eldest among the monks in every district calls the meeting, and at evening on the fast-day all the brethren, who are sojurning within the limits of the diocese, come together in the vihâra chosen for the purpose or whatever other place is selected by the Order, be it a building or a cave in the mountain. No one is permitted to absent himself. Only in the case of insanity can a dispensation be granted, and sick brethren can be allowed to remain away, if they can cause an assurance of their purity from the transgressions mentioned in the confessional formula to reach the assembled brethren through a comrade. If there be no one to convey this assurance, the invalid must be brought on his chair or on his bed to the assembly, or if this cannot be done without danger to him, the Order must go in a body to his bedside for the celebration. But under no circumstances is it permitted to go through the sacred office in an assembly short of the full number.

By the light of a torch the monks take their places in the

place of assembly on the low seats prepared for them. No layman, no novice, no nun may be present, for the law of the Order, which is now to be recited in the form of a confessional formula, is regarded as a reserved possession of the monks alone.* This confessional formula, the liturgy Pâtimokkha ("unburdening"), the oldest of the brethren, or he who otherwise able and qualified, now recites with a loud voice:—

"Reverend sirs," he says, "let the Order hear me. To-day is fast-day, the fifteenth of the half month. If the Order is ready, let the Order keep fast-day and have the formula of confession recited. What must the Order do first? Report the declaration of purity, reverend sirs.† I shall recite the formula of confession."

* "The monk, who makes an unordained person a partaker verbatim of the Dhamma, is liable to punishment" ("Pâcittiya," 4). I believe, not altogether in harmony with the ancient commentator in this passage, that by the term Dhamma the maxims of the confessional formula of the Pâtimokkha are to be understood. It can hardly be assumed that a monk, who, like Mahinda, for example, before the Ceylonese king, retailed the sayings or preachings of Buddha, thereby incurred the penalty of an offence. There were, moreover, among the laity themselves "preachers of the Dhamma" (dhammakathika), as the first of whom Citta is mentioned by name in one of the sacred texts ("Anguttara Nikâya," vol. i, near the beginning); and similarly the case is mentioned in the "Vinaya," where a layman summons the monks to deliver to them a discourse of Buddha's, with which he is acquainted, and of which the knowledge is in danger of being lost ("Mahâvagga," iii, 5, 9). As regards the character of the Pâtimokkha as a secret lore, cf. "Milinda Pañha," p. 190, seq. From this it also follows, when tradition represents a person like the young Moggaliputta, who is put forward as the model of a quickly progressing scholar, as still learning during the four years of his noviciate only the collections of the Suttas and the Abhidhamma, that the Vinaya was an Arcanum, which became accessible to him after his ordination, and not till then.—*Vinaya Piṭaka*, vol. iii, p. 299.

† *I.e.*, the declaration in the name of the brethren absent on account of

The Order present replies: "We all, who are here present, hear and consider it well."

"Whoever has committed a transgression," the leader goes on, "let him confess it. Where there is no transgression, let him be silent. From your silence I shall infer that you are clear, reverend sirs. As an individual man, to whom a question is put, is supposed to answer, so is it in the case of an assembly like the present, when the question has been put three times. A monk, who on the question being put three times does not confess a fault, which he has committed and which he remembers, is guilty of an intentional lie. But intentional lying, reverend sirs, brings destruction;* thus has the Exalted One said. Therefore a monk, who has committed a fault, remembers it, and seeks to be pure therefrom, is to confess his fault. For what he confesses, will lie lightly on him."

Now the enumeration of the transgressions which are to be confessed begins. The most serious stand first, those four sins, of which every newly entering brother is already warned at ordination, that whoever commits them, can no longer belong to the Order (p. 351). "If a monk," the leader begins, "who has chosen the exercises and the fellowship of the monks, has carnal intercourse with any creature whatever, down even to a beast, without renouncing these exercises† and without admitting his weakness, then this involves a defeat (by evil) and expulsion from the Order." Similar terms deal with the three other gravest sins, theft, murder, and the false assumption of spiritual perfections. At the close of this

sickness, that they have committed no transgression enumerated in the confessional formula.

* *I.e.*, it prevents the attainment of sanctification.

† *I.e.*, leaving the Order.

enumeration of transgressions, which bring with them "defeat and expulsion from the Order," the leader turns himself to the brethren present with the thrice repeated question: "Here now I ask the venerable: Are you free from these transgressions? And for the second time I ask: Are you free? For the third time I ask: Are you free?" And if all are silent*—"Free are the venerable from these, therefore they are silent; so I take it."

The enumeration is now directed to the less serious transgressions, to those, which the Order visits with a temporary degradation, and to those, which are atoned for without any action of the Order by the mere admission of the guilty party. For example, it is said:—

"The monk who lowers himself to touch a woman's person with corrupt thoughts, while he clasps her hand or clasps her

* The wording of the formula shows beyond doubt, that according to the original intention anyone who felt himself guilty of a transgression, had at this point to confess it before the Order. The later texts ("Khandhaka") give directions which are at variance with this construction. No one could carry unatoned guilt with him into the confessional meeting. He had previously to confess and, where any penance is attached, perform it. Also when he calls to mind an offence first only during the celebration, he has not to answer the question of the leader, but he has to absolve himself, by anticipation as it were, for the period of the celebration, by saying to his neighbour: "Friend, I have committed this and that offence; when I shall have risen from this place, I shall purify myself therefrom." Whoever was cognizant of the transgression of another, had to hold the guilty party to penance before the celebration of the confession, or "to forbid the confession" in his case by veto, until he had complied with his duty. We see in this maxim: "No man, on whom a transgression lies, is allowed to keep the ceremony of the fast-day" ("Mahâvagga," ii, 27; cf. "Cullavagga," ix, 2) clearly the more scrupulous conception of a late period, as compared with the old institution, which had created the observance of the fast-day quite particularly for those who were burdened by a sense of guilt.

hair or touches one part or another of her body, the Order inflicts on him degradation."

"The monk who in any house belonging to the Order knowingly so arranges his quarters that he thereby incommodes a monk who has come before him, and says within himself: 'Who finds it too narrow, may go out,' having just this and nothing else in view; he is guilty of sin."

"The monk who in anger or enmity extrudes a monk from a house belonging to the Order, or causes him to be extruded, he is guilty of sin."

In this manner, in more than two hundred paragraphs thrown together somewhat unsystematically, are specified those injunctions, which govern the daily life of the monks, their residence, eating and drinking, clothing, and their intercourse with each other and with nuns and laity. Even the most external and the most trivial matter finds a place; to the painful fondness for rule, which is here traceable in every word, nothing is unessential. In the fact that the Buddhist Order has not been able to invest its most prominent liturgical creation with any other form than that of a paragraphic collection of monastic rules we may perhaps detect an element of illiberality; but insipidity and paltriness he alone will call it, to whom serious and scrupulous obedience to rule even in the most trivial matters appears insipid and paltry.

Next to the half-monthly confessional days the yearly recurring simple and beautiful celebration must be borne in mind, which bears the name of *invitation* (Pavâraṇâ). When the three months of the rainy season have gone by, before the wandering begins, the brethren in each diocese, who have passed this time in common retirement—they are for the most part friends closely attached to each other—unite in a solemn conference, in which every one, from the oldest to the youngest, sitting in a reverential attitude on the ground, raising his clasped hands, asks his spiritual comrades, if he has been guilty of any sin during this period, to name it to him. "Reverend sirs," it is then said, "I invite the Order, if ye have seen anything on my part, or have heard anything, or have any suspicion about me, have pity on me, reverend sirs, and speak. If I see it, I shall atone for it."*

In these few ceremonious observances has been described the narrow range of that, which, with the disciples of Buddha, takes the place of regular acts of public worship. It will be seen that this cultus, if we wish to call it so, goes only into the outer court of the religious life; it has only to do with maintaining among the monks external correctness in decent behaviour and dealing. Whatever goes beyond this, the keeping up of instructive meditation and religious concentration, is left wholly to the unfettered action of the individual brother, of the individual group of brethren.

It may be here observed that at least the first rudiments of a cultus of another stamp, separated in broad distinction from that which we have discussed, go back into the times with which our sketch has to deal: the rudiments of the veneration attaching to holy places and to Buddha's relics. Four places, it is said,† are deserving that believing, noble youths should

* According to the original custom every one then, as a matter of course, said what he had to say in reply to this appeal, and when doubts existed, these were explained before the Order. The "Khandhaka Texts" here adopted apparently, exactly as we have already (note p. 373) seen they did in the confessional celebration, the standpoint of a later age. No one, it is said in this connection, who is under the burden of guilt, can take part in the solemnization of the "Invitation;" what every one has to cast up to the other, must be previously brought to an issue.—*Mah.* iv, 6; 16,

† "Mahâparinibbâna Sutta," p. 51.

see them and that their hearts should be moved by them: the place where the holy Buddha was born; the place where he has obtained the highest illumination;* the place where he has "set in motion the Wheel of the Law," the place where he, delivered from everything earthly, has entered into the perfect Nirvâna. To these places monks and nuns, lay-brothers and lay-sisters have a desire to travel. "For he, O Ânanda, who dies in the faith on the pilgrimage to such holy places, will, when his body dissolves, beyond death, walk the good road and be born again in the heavenly world."

The care of Buddha's relics and the institution of festivals in their honour are committed exclusively to the piety of believing laity. "What are we to do," Ânanda asks of the Master, when his end is drawing near,† "with the body of the Perfect One?" "Let not the honours due to the body of the Perfect One trouble you, O Ânanda. Seek ye rather holiness, O Ânanda; be intent on holiness: live in holiness without blemish, in holy haste, seeking after perfection. There are, Ânanda, wise men among the nobles, the Brahmans, and the

* Already one of the texts belonging to the sacred canon points to festivals, which are kept at the "Tree of Knowledge." "At the great Tree of Knowledge of the Buddha Padumuttara there was a festival celebrated. Then I took vessels of many kinds and offered sweet-smelling water. When the Tree of Knowledge was to be bathed, a great rainfall began," and so on. "At the supremely holy foot of the Knowledge-tree of the Buddha Padumuttara, I planted cheerfully, with cheerful heart a banner."—*Apadâna*, fol. ghi', ghî, of the Phayre MS.

† "Mahâp." p. 51, seq. Cf. "Milinda Pañha," p. 177, seq. It is noteworthy, that, as at this place the care for Buddha's remains is not represented as belonging to the disciples, so the Vinaya texts are nearly altogether silent as to the last honours of deceased monks. To arrange for their cremation was perhaps committed to the laity.—*Vide e.g. Hardy, Manual*, second edn. p. 226; cf. however, *Bhikkhunîvibhanga Pâcittya*, 52.

citizens, who believe in the Perfect One; they will do the honours to the body of the Perfect One." So then after Buddha's death his relics are divided out to a number of princes and nobles, each of whom "builds a stûpa (monument for relics) and institutes a festival"—festivals at which offerings of flowers, ablutions and illuminations on a grand scale usually play the chief part. The Order of monks as such has nothing to do with this pompous show of veneration; the old rules of the Order have not a word to say about it.

The Order of Nuns.

We have already undertaken in a previous passage (p. 164, seq.) to show the position of women in Buddha's teaching. We saw with what decided antipathy Buddha's disciples stood aloof from the female sex, and how admission to the Order was conceded to women only with reluctance and under conditions which involved their absolute subjection to the monks. The social law of the Indians also kept woman all her life long in complete dependence. "In childhood," says an oft-quoted sentence in the Institutes of Manu, "let her be subjected to the will of her father; in adult life to the will of the man who has led her home; to her son's will, when her husband has died; a woman is not permitted to enjoy independence." The rules which Buddhist Church-law lays down for the spiritual life of nuns might pass for an amplification of this position of Manu; as the wife is placed under the guardianship of her husband, the mother under the guardianship of her sons, so the Order of nuns* is placed under the guardianship of the Order of monks.

* The nuns constitute by themselves an Order of their own (Bhikkhunî-sangha), which is co-ordinate with, or rather subordinate to, the Order of

To a certain extent the fundamental law for the Order of the nuns is contained in the "eight high ordinances," which Buddha is said to have enjoined on the first nuns at their ordination.*

"A nun," so run these propositions, "if she have been ordained even a hundred years ago, must bow most reverentially before every monk, even though he be ordained only on this day, rise in his presence, raise her clasped hands, duly honour him. This rule shall she observe, esteem sacred, keep, respect, and through her whole life not transgress."

"A nun is not permitted to pass the rainy season in any district in which monks are not residing. This rule also shall she observe, esteem sacred, &c.

"The nuns are to go once in the half-month to the monks for two things: they are to ask for the confessional ceremony,† and to apply to the monks for the preaching (of the sacred word). This rule also, &c.

"At the end of the rainy season the nuns are to give the

the monks (Bhikkhusangha). The two Orders are together denominated "the two-sided Order" (ubhatosangha). The two-sided Order represents, however, no particular unifying organism: the term is only a collective expression, which amounts merely to "the Order of monks and the Order of nuns." The two-sided Order nowhere appears acting on a common platform. If a layman gives garments to the two-sided Order, all members, monks and nuns, do not obtain equal shares, but one-half belongs to the Order of monks, the other half to the Order of nuns. "Even if there be many monks there and only one nun, she obtains the half."—*Mahâvagga*, viii, 32.

* "Cullavagga," x, 1, 4.

† The nuns have to observe the half-monthly confessional ceremony, with an extended liturgy of confession corresponding to the special circumstances of the Order of the nuns. It is incumbent on the monks to impart instruction to them regarding this ceremony, as well as regarding the atonement of any transgressions committed.—*Cullavagga*, x, 6.

threefold invitation to both sides of the Order:* (to accuse them of the crime) if anyone has seen, or has heard of anything, or has any suspicion against them. This rule also, &c.

"A nun who has been guilty of a grave offence must submit herself to a half-monthly discipline of penance before both sides of the Order. This rule also, &c.

"Ordination is to be applied for from both sides of the Order only when the *postulante* has lived for a probationary period of two years in the six rules.† This rule also, &c.

"Under no circumstances is a nun to revile or scold a monk. This rule also, &c.

"From this day forward is the path of speech against the monks closed to the nuns. Yet is not the path of speech against the nuns closed to the monks.‡ This rule also," &c.

The eight "high ordinances" show clearly enough the subordination in which the Order of nuns is kept to the monks. None of the more important transactions required by the rules of the Order could be completed by the nuns, which did not require to be submitted for confirmation by the chapter of the monks. If a maiden or a woman, who desires to obtain the initiations, has kept the vow of the "six rules"§

* When the nuns have finished the celebration of the invitation among themselves (*vide* supra, p. 364), they send a messenger to the monks on the following day, who conveys to them in the name of the nuns the invitation, to state to the nuns any offence of theirs, seen, heard, or suspected. A corresponding invitation of the monks to the nuns does not follow (loc. cit. x, 19).

† *Vide* infra, n. §.

‡ The meaning of this expression cannot be that the nun is not allowed to speak to the monk at all. It is probably meant that the nun is not allowed to charge a monk with an offence, to hold him to penance therefor, eventually to veto his participation in the ceremonies of the confession and invitation (cf. "Cull." x, 20).

§ She has to promise expressly: "I undertake, as an inviolable vow, to through a probationary period of two years, and has obtained ordination from the Order of nuns, she is still regarded as only "ordained on one side," and not fully accredited, as long as she has not appeared before the chapter of monks and in its presence gone through the whole ceremony of ordination anew. In the same way the confessional observances and invitation ceremonies of the nuns' Order, the atonement for transgressions, and the settlement of differences of all kinds, are subject to control and partly to confirmation by the monks' Order. Every half-month the nuns betake themselves to the monk, who has been named to them by a resolution of the brotherhood, to receive his spiritual instruction and admonition. In the presence of another monk, that monk sits waiting the nuns, and when they have made their appearance, bowed themselves to the ground, and sat down before him, he speaks to them of the eight high ordinances, and expounds to them, either by way of sermon or by question and answer, what he deems profitable of the teaching and maxims of Buddha.*

That, as for the rest, strict separation prevailed between monks and nuns, is self-apparent. Even the monk, who had to preach to the nuns, was not allowed to set foot in the nunnery, except when one of the sisters lay ill and required his consolation. To make a journey with a nun, to go aboard

abstain from killing any living creature during two years"—in the same way she then vows not to steal, to commit no unchastity, not to lie, to drink no intoxicating beverages, and not to eat at the forbidden hours (*i.e.*, between noon and the break of dawn next day).

* That these discourses do not represent the particular scholastic traditions of the sacred texts within the Order of nuns and that the latter was formed chiefly through nun-teachers, follows from the circumstances of the case, and is confirmed, *e.g.*, by the statements in 18th cap. of the Dîpavaṃsa. "Cullavagga," x, 8, when properly understood is not contradictory of this.

the same boat with her, to sit with her alone and without witness, was strictly forbidden to the monks. The daily life, the religious exercises of the nuns were not essentially different from those of the monks, except that solitude, in which the latter found so rich a source of spiritual joys, if not absolutely forbidden to the nuns, was at least restricted and was necessarily so: to live in forest hermitages was forbidden them; they took up their abode rather within the walls of the village or town, in huts or nunneries, by twos or in greater numbers, for a sister was not allowed to live alone. From such places they made their begging excursions and set out also on those greater pilgrimages which were deemed for them as well as for the monks a necessary element of ascetic life. In number they were apparently far behind the monks,* and therefore it is to be doubted also, whether at any time there was inherent in the spiritual sisterhood a degree of influence which could be felt, bearing on the Buddhist community as a whole. The thoughts and forms of life of Buddhism had been thought out and moulded solely by men and for men.

The Spiritual Order and the Lay World.

Buddha's Church is a Church of monks and nuns. "Very straitened," it is said, "is life in the home, a state of impurity; freedom is in leaving the home." He who cannot or will not gain this freedom, is not a member of the Church. But the

* An illustration of this is given, for example, in the statements of the "Dīpavaṃsa" (7, i.) regarding the number of the monks and nuns, who have assisted at a great festival instituted by Asoka. Though the numbers themselves are inordinately exaggerated, yet they throw a certain light on the relation of the two sides. The chronicle speaks of 800 millions of monks and of only 96,000 nuns.

nature of the case was such, and the external existence of the the Church even demanded, that regular relations should be maintained between it and the worldly circles, which were favourably disposed to the interests of the Order. Without a laity, which professed a faith in Buddha and Buddha's teaching, and evinced this faith in pious offices, above all in works of helpful beneficence, an order of mendicants could not be thought of, and the religious movement of Buddhism would have been shut out from contact with the broad surface of popular life. Tradition, therefore, as we have pointed out, represents, assuredly with propriety, not merely monks and nuns, but also "male votaries" (upâsaka) and "female votaries" (upâsikâ) as gathering round Buddha from the very beginning, persons who while remaining in the worldly state, "take their refuge" in Buddha, in the Doctrine, and in the Order, and show by word and deed their adherence to this holy triad.*

But while there was framed from the beginning for the monastic Church an organization, clothed with strict forms of spiritual procedure, there was no attempt made at creations of a similar kind for the quasi-Church of lay-brothers and lay-sisters. Certain customs of spiritual life and practical beneficence must obviously have arisen even here; definite institutions have not followed. There was not so much as any sharply drawn line between the laity, who were to be regarded as adherents of the Order of Buddha, and those who stood aloof therefrom; entry into the circle of "votaries" was dependent on no qualification and followed regularly upon a form fixed by custom, but not determind by rule,† namely upon

* *Vide* supra, p. 161, seq.

† Any one who is conversant with the method of description prevailing in the Vinaya Texts, will admit the conclusion, that, if the form for

the person taking the step declaring in the presence of a monk, either on his own behalf alone, or jointly with wife, children, and servants, that he takes his refuge in Buddha, the Doctrine, and the Order of Disciples. Then there was also, it is true, inculcated on the lay-disciples on the part of the Order, the observance of certain duties of temperance and rectitude,* but neither was the profession of a formal vow by them insisted upon, nor did the Church keep watch in any way whatever over the actual fulfilment of these duties. A formal excommunication of unbelieving, unworthy, or scandalously-living lay-brothers there was not, and, as a result of circumstances, there could not be. The only procedure prescribed in the regulations of the Church against laity, who had given cause of complaint, shows clearly how little the ideas of admission and expulsion had been applied to this relation: namely, the Order might resolve "to withdraw the almsbowl" from such a layman (*i.e.*, take no gifts from him) "and refuse

the admission of an Upâsaka had been looked upon as one determined by rule, some narrative of the introduction of this form by an injunction of Buddha must also exist. In truth he is an Upâsaka, who shows himself to be so by his acts. It cannot therefore cause astonishment, if occasionally people, who show honour to monks and entertain them, are addressed by them as Upâsakas, although they do not make a declaration of their taking refuge until afterwards ("Dhp. Atth.," p. 81). Cf. also supra, note p. 162.

* Certain business pursuits were regarded as unallowable for a lay-disciple, for instance, dealing in arms, in intoxicating liquors, in poison ("Anguttara Nikâya," vol. ii, fol. caṃ.).—As a counterpart to the confessional celebration observed by the monk on the first day, there is also enjoined on the laity the observance of an "eightfold abstinence;" the refraining from killing living creatures, from the appropriation of another's property, from lying, from the enjoyment of intoxicating liquors, from unchastity, from eating after midday, from perfumes and garlands; and the sleeping on low, hard couches or on the ground (*idem*, vol. iii, fol. ghau').

their company to him at table"*); if after this he reformed and conciliated the Order, then by a new resolution "the almsbowl would be again presented to him, and the company (of the Order) at table be granted to him." It is evident, that what is here dealt with, is not the deprivation or the re-conferring of a legal qualification of a kind such as we are in these days accustomed to associate with membership of a Church community, but merely the interruption or revival of a purely factitious relation of daily intercourse, the giving and receiving of material gifts and spiritual instruction.

It is entirely in keeping with the manner and method in which the position of the lay believers has been treated, that regular spiritual gatherings were not instituted for them, and much less were they admitted to be present at the ceremonious proceedings of the Order, or even to a share of any kind whatsoever in the administration of the business affairs of the Order. The daily begging excursion of the monks maintained the usual contact between them and the believing laity, and gave a natural opening for attentions of a pastoral kind. The laity also on their part came to the parks of the community near the gates of the town with gifts of every kind, with food and medicine, with garlands and perfumes; there they paid their respects to the monks, and listened to the exposition of the sacred discourses and sayings. Or they erected buildings

* This separation was not desired in the case of a scandalous mode of living—of this the Order as such took no notice—but only as a punishment for an affront or injury done to the Order. There are eight cases noted, in which this resolution was to be passed against a layman: "He endeavours to prevent the monks obtaining gifts; he endeavours to cause the monks to suffer injury; he endeavours to cause the monks not to obtain lodgings; he abuses or scolds the monks; he causes dissensions among the monks; he speaks evil of Buddha; he speaks evil of the Doctrine; he speaks evil of the Order."—*Cullavagga*, v, 20, 3.

for the uses of the Order, and invited the monks to the dedicatory and opening celebrations. "May it please the venerable ones to come to me," the message ran somewhat thus, which they sent to the Order, "I wish to present a gift and to hear the preaching of the Doctrine and to see the monks." Such invitations the Order is to receive, and even during the rainy season, when otherwise it is forbidden the monks to travel, they are allowed in a case of this kind to be absent from their place of residence for a period of seven days. Or the believers of a township requested the monks to pass the rainy season in their neighbourhood; then they provided lodgings for their guests, and gave them daily food when they made their begging excursions; and before the monks proceeded on their wanderings on the expiration of the rainy season, the lay believers were in the habit of giving them a farewell meal, with which was connected a distribution of clothing, or of stuff for clothing, to the parting spiritual pilgrims. Not unfrequently, too, a circle of laymen clubbed together to establish among themselves a "roster of dinners" for the Order, each taking his turn, and in dear times, when the entertaining of all the brethren would have exceeded the ability of one layman, there were instituted "dinners by arrangement," "dinners by invitation," "dinners on subscriptions," "fortnightly dinners." They promised the brethren to furnish, be it constantly or only for a limited period, the medicines of which they might be in need, or benefactresses of the Order went through the gardens of the monasteries and asked from house to house: "Who is sick among you, reverend sirs? To whom are we to bring anything, and what?" That the monks then, on their part, were not sparing in promising to the givers every heavenly reward, was a matter of course. "To give houses to the

Order," it is said,* "a place of refuge and joy, so that we may there exercise concentration and holy intuition, has been commanded by Buddha as the most noble gift. Therefore let a wise man, who understands what is best for himself, build beautiful houses, and receive into them knowers of the Doctrine. He may give food and drink, clothes and lodging to such, the upright with cheerful heart. These preach to him the Doctrine which drives away all suffering; if he apprehends the Doctrine here below, he goes sinless into Nirvâna." In another place it is said:† "Well is it for a man always to dispense boiled-rice if he have a desire for joy, whether he seek heavenly joy or long for earthly happiness." That occasionally the givers, for whom the drafts on a heavenly reward-fund in return for earthly benefaction had so much attraction, must have allowed themselves to be laid very wantonly under contribution by pretentious comrades among the begging stewards of heavenly treasures, is only natural. Certainly those narratives are drawn from life, as they are not unfrequently told of such occurrences in the Vinaya: of the man who had incautiously offered to give to the venerable Upananda whatever he required, and from whom he immediately demanded the clothes he was wearing, or of the pious potter, of whom the monks demanded almsbowls in such numbers that his business was thereby ruined. A long series of statements in the confessional liturgy was directed against this unauthorized exaction of pious charity, and confined within narrow limits the little, which monks receive, and the still less, for which they were allowed to ask. Apparently the criticism was by no means regarded with indifference, which might be practised in lay

* "Cullavagga," vi, 1, 5.
† "Mahâvagga," vi, 24, 6.

circles, and which the rival religious orders certainly did not neglect to maintain vigilantly and keenly. Monks who exercised in any way whatever an evil influence upon the laity, or caused them mortification, were most severely discountenanced, and in every way the laity were regarded as an ally on whose friendship they knew how to put a proper value.

As an ally, but at the same time as nothing more. The feeling of having a share as a citizen in the kingdom of Buddha's children, was denied to the laity, much more so even than was such a feeling denied in the old Brahmanical sacrificial-faith to the non-Brahman who, albeit only through the medium of the priest, could draw near to the god equally with the priest himself. The Buddhist believer, who did not feel in himself the power to renounce the world, could console himself with coming ages; he could hope for this, that it might then be vouchsafed to him, as a disciple of Metteyya, or of one of the countless Buddhas, who shall come after him, to don the garb of a monk and to taste the bliss of deliverance.

For to but a few chosen ones, thus the Doctrine says, was it given, already in this age to attain the goal as disciples of the Son of the Sakya house, and short term was allotted to the existence of the Church on earth. When in the cloister-gardens at Râjagaha and Sâvatthi the discourses of Buddha were recited among the assembled brethren, they bethought themselves also of the prophecy: "Not a long time, Ânanda, will holy living remain preserved; five hundred years, Ânanda, will the Doctrine of the truth abide." Who then foresaw, that after five hundred years the Church of the Buddhists would overspread India, and that its missionaries far beyond India, traversing the ocean, crossing the snowy ranges of the Himalaya, wandering through the deserts of Central Asia, would bring the faith of Buddha to nations, whose name even was not then named in India—to nations among whom this faith survived and still survives to this day, while in its parent-land the spirit of the Indian people, which in endless play dashed into ever new spheres of thought and fancy, which relegated to nothingness the wreck of ruined worlds and rebuilt lost beauty, not always in greater stateliness,* has long since permitted the Doctrine of Buddha to decay.

* The reader of the original will observe the happy use which Dr. Oldenberg has made of the Chorus of Spirits in Göthe's "Faust," Pt. I.

Weh! Weh!
Du hast sie zerstört
Die schöne Welt
Mit mächtiger Faust;
Sie stürzt, sie zerfällt!
Ein Halbgott hat sie zerschlagen!
Wir tragen
Die Trümmern ins Nichts hinüber
Und klagen
Ueber die verlorne Schöne.
Mächtiger
Der Erdensöhne,
Prächtiger,
Baue sie wieder,
In deinem Busen baue sie auf!

EXCURSUS.

FIRST EXCURSUS.

On the relative Geographical Location of Vedic and Buddhist Culture.

Those of the Indian peoples, among whom Buddhism has its home,* especially the people of Magadha, dwell far to the east of the territories, to which the poetry of the *Ri*gveda introduces us. Were they then already residing in the east, or were they at least in the act of penetrating to the east, when the hymns of the Veda were being sung in the west, in the Panjâb and on the Sarasvati? Or were they then within the circle of the Vedic world, and have they not moved eastward until a later period? The question may also be expressed thus: If in the epic-Buddhist age there was an Aryan culture in India, as partakers in which we find the Kurus and Pañcâlas, the people of Magadha and Kosala and so on, did all these peoples at one time participate in the ancient Vedic culture, or did the Vedic culture in the Vedic age within the Indian Aryandom cover a narrower field, which, for example, included the Kurus and Pañcâlas, and on the other hand did not comprise the people of Videha and Magadha?

We have (p. 9) declared our adherence to the latter of these two views, and we here intend to more accurately define and support our view, according to which the culture of the Vedas was indigenous to but one portion of the Aryan peoples of Hindostan, and from them reached the other afterwards only at second hand.

* What the approximate geographical extent of the most ancient Buddhism was, is stated *inter alia* in the "Mahâparinibbâna Sutta," p. 55. The chie towns, in which many and respected nobles, Brahmans, and Vaiçyas, who confess adherence to the faith of Buddha, dwell, are there named: Campâ, Râjagaha, Sâvatthi, Sâketa, Kosambî, Bârâ*n*asî.

Even, *à priori*, considering the wide spread of the Aryan territory and Aryan peoples in India, it must be considered probable, that already in the Vedic age a community of culture had no longer continued to prevail throughout this vast tract. The analogies of kindred nations which force themselves on our attention indicate this. As, though we do not shut our eyes to the reciprocal influences, we are entitled to say that the Dorians of the Peloponnesus created for themselves a culture apart from the Æolians or Ionians, and that to a late period Umbrians, Latins, and Oscans, pursued their own path of religious, political, and literary development, so the historical treatment of India will in a similar way have to separate between western stocks with their Vedic culture, which went ahead in spiritual development, and the eastern peoples, which developed themselves more slowly, between Kurus and Pañcâlas on one side and the peoples of Kosala, Videha, and Magadha on the other. It will have to make this distinction here, even though it is true that the races of India by on means in themselves, and still less for us, presented so sharply imprinted, distinguishing individualities, as did the Grecian stocks; we cannot expect, it is self-apparent, to realize for ourselves the national life of the Kurupañcâlas on the one hand and of the Videha or Kosala peoples on the other hand, in the same way that we know Dorians and Athenians as clearly different types.

It is necessary for us in our inquiry, at first to leave the *Ri*k-Sa*m*hitâ out of sight, and first to ask the question, what stocks have had a share in the spiritual movements, which are indicated by the Brâhma*n*a texts and kindred literature. On the basis of the results hereby gained we shall then attempt to determine how the group of peoples appearing in the *Ri*k-Sa*m*hitâ are related to the great Indian cultured peoples of later times.

The ethnological table in the "Aitareya Brâhma*n*a" (8, 14) shows how the Indian stocks group themselves from the standpoint of this text, where the incisions are, which separate the differently constituted divisions. In the middle "asyâ*m** dhruvâyâm madh-

* In treating of the other territories, instead of asyâm the word etasyâm is used: asyâm contains a significant hint that the compiler of the text belongs to this very territory. *Vide* Weber, "Ind. Lit. Gesch.,"[2] p. 49.

yamâyâm pratishṭhâyâm diçi" lie the realms of the Kurupañcâlas together with Vaças* and Uçinaras. To the south of this Land of the Middle there dwell the Satvats, eastward the Prâcyas (we shall necessarily think chiefly of the Kâçi, Kosala,† Videha, and Magadha peoples), westward the Nîcyas, Apâcyas. In the north the Middle Land is bounded by the Himalaya, for as peoples north of the Middle those are named, who dwell pareṇa Himavantam, the Uttarakurus and Uttaramadras.

With the sketch of the distribution of Indian peoples, which is thus given, now admirably fit in the data, which are supplied by Manu—probably following older Sûtra texts. The land of the Brahmarshis, whose customs and rights are taken as a model, whose

* This is the accepted and, as I believe, the correct translation of savaçoçînarâṇâm. The Vaças will be identical with the Vaṃsas in the Buddhist enumeration of peoples (*vid. infra*, p. 407, n. 2,), but can hardly have anything to do with the Vaças introduced by the Petersburgh Lexicon from the "Mahâbhârata," i, 6684 (if the reading of the Calc. Edition be correct), who are classed together with the Yavanas, Barbaras, Cînas, and other Mlecchas. The Lexicon finds, apparently correctly, a mention of the Vaças also in the "Gop. Br.," 2, 9: imeshu Kurupañcâleshu Añgamagadheshu Kâçikauçalyeshu Çâlvamatsyeshu Çavasa (lege: savaça) uçînareshûdîcyeshu. Now, from a comparison of "Ait. Br.," 8, 14, and "Gop. Br.," 2, 9, the relevancy also of a third passage seems to me to be established, "Kaush. Upan.," iv, 1: so 'vasad Uçînareshu savasan Matsyeshu Kurupâñcâleshu Kâçivideheshv iti. The "savasan," which here occurs between the names of the Uçînaras and the Matsyas, cannot be disassociated from the "çavasa," which stands between the same names in the "Gop. Br.," and the "savaça," which occurs in the "Ait Br." in conjunction with the name of the Uçînaras. Thus, I think, that in this passage the conjecture "savaçamatsyeshu" should be preferred to the emendation "Satvan-Matsyeshu," recommended by the Pet. Lex. and by Professor Max Müller ("Upanishads," Introd., p. lxxvii).

† The Kosala people are by the Buddhists also counted among the Prâcyas. As the Sakyas belonged to the Kosalas, Buddha himself was considered a Kosala; but as to the Buddhas the rule held good: puratthimesu janapadesu buddhâ bhagavanto uppajjanti ("Cullav." xii, 2, 3). In the same way it follows that Benares belonged to the eastern land, for the Buddha Kassapa was born in the kingdom of the king Kiki of Bârâṇasî (Mahâpadâna Sutta). Moreover the Buddhist texts make the king of Kosala rule over Benares also (Lohiccasutta in the "Dîgha Nikâya": râjâ Pasenadi Kosalo Kâsikosalaṃ ajjhâvasati); in the territory of Kâsi Pasenadi fights his battles against Ajâtasutta (Kosala Saṃyutta).—Cf. further "Mahâvagga," viii, 2. The distinction of a northern and southern Kosala kingdom ("Burnouf," Intr., p. 22, vol. i) is not in accordance with the Pâli Piṭakas.

warriors are the bravest, is Kurukshetra and the territory of the Matsyas, the Pañcâlas and Çûrasenas (2, 19; 7, 193). Thus the land of the Brahmarshis embraces what is set down in the Aitareya as madhyamâ diç and as south;* but what is regarded in the Aitareya as west and east, above all the eastern peoples of Kâçi, Kosala, Videha, and Magadha, is in Manu excluded from the land of the Brahmarshis.

Thus we have here a distinction between those stocks, who felt themselves to be the qualified champions of Aryan culture, and those who were Aryans, it is true, but were not regarded as equally accredited partakers in this culture. Momenta of many kinds may have co-operated to bring about and enhance this difference. Association with non-Aryan elements, to which the stocks that had migrated to the greatest distances were especially exposed, may have been at the same time in play.† But it hardly lay in this only, that the Kurus claimed to be something other and better than the Magadhas. Rather here appears to be the place where the ancient lines of distinction become apparent, which had come down from an immemorial past, drawn between the different leading groups and leading types of the Indian Aryan stocks, and the existence of which we might be entitled to assume almost with *à priori* certainty. We must, for the testing of this supposition,

* Of the peoples of the madhyamâ diç the Kurus and Pañcâlas occur again in Manu; that the small stocks of the Vaças and Uçînaras are not expressly named, is no cause of astonishment. In the south new tribal names have arisen: the Çûrasenas, who are not named at all in the old texts, are now the chief people of the south. As to the connection between the Satvats, Bhojas, Yâdavas, Çûrasenas, *see* Lassen, "Ind. Alt.," i, 757; cf. Weber, "Ind. St.," i, 211.

† So it is said in the "Baudhâyanadharmaçâstra," i, 1 (according to MSS. Burnell 39 and 40 in the India Office Library):

Avantayo 'ñga-Magadhâs Surâsh*t*râ-Dakshi*n*âpathâ*h*
Upâv*r*it-Sindhusauvîrâ ete sa*m*kîr*n*ayona*h*.

Âra*tt*ân Kâraskarân Pu*n*d*r*ân Sauvîrân Vañga-Kaliñgân prâna*r*inâniti cadagatvâ (? *sic*, the last word being corrected to codag gatvâ, one MS.; the other reads: prâna*r*inân iti ca gatvâ) punastomena yajeta sarvap*r*ish*t*h*a*yâ vâ. 'thâpy udâharanti:

padbhyâ*m* sa kurute pâpa*m* ya*h* Kaliñgân prapadyate,
*r*ishayo nishk*r*iti*m* tasya prâhur vaiçvânara*m* havi*h*.

next submit the Brâhmana texts and finally the *Rik*-Samhita to an examination as to their bearing on the peoples of the different groups indicated by us.

If, as we hold, in the Brâhmana period the home of Brahmanic civilization has been with the Kuru-Pañcâlas and the stocks of the west standing in closer union with them, we cannot, nevertheless, and we do not, expect to find this disclosed in the exclusive mention of peoples of the western groups in the Brâhmana texts. But the cases of their being mentioned, specially of the Kurus and Pañcâlas, and in a second degree of the Bharatas,* surpass at once beyond all comparison in frequency the mentioning of the eastern peoples, and then the texts frequently attribute to the western peoples unmistakably the weight of an older and higher sacral authority, than to the eastern groups, which latter are plainly named in a hostile or contemptuous tone, or at least appear as peoples who have received from the west instruction in the spiritual knowledge, which has its home there.

A selection of the very amply existing materials bearing on this matter will suffice for the illustration of what has been said.

The Kurukshetra is the place of sacrifice of the gods ("Çat." iv, 1, 5, 13; xiv, 1, 1, 2). From the Camasa, which the gods used in the sacrifice, was produced the sacred tree Nyagrodha; the first-born of the Nyagrodha trees grow on the Kurukshetra ("Ait." 7, 30). In the tale of the Purûravas and Urvaçis the Kurukshetra plays a part ("Çat." xi, 5, 1, 4; "Ind. Studien," i, 197). The offerings which must be performed at the Sarasvatî, D*ri*shadvatî and Yamunâ, are known (v. "Çâñkh. çr." 13, 29; "Kâty." 24, 6; "Pañcav. Br." 25, 10 seq). In the north, among the Kurupañcâlas, is the country, where the Vâc has her peculiar home; the Vâc, as she there is, is truly (nidânena) to be called a Vâc ("Çat." iii, 2, 3, 15).† Some prefer the Pañcâvattam to the Caturavattam, but the Caturavattam follows the custom of the Kurupañcâlas, therefore let it be given the preference ("Çat." i, 7, 2, 8). A saying of the Kurupañcâlas with reference to the kings of the

* Concerning these and their relation to the Kurus, see farther on.

† Cf. the Çâñkh. Brâhm., "Ind. Stud.," ii, p. 309.

Kurupañcâlas, who have performed the Râjasûya-sacrifice, v. "Çat." v, 5, 2, 5. A form of the Vâjapeya-offering, which bears the name Kuru-vâjapeya, is explained at "Çâñkh. çr." xv, 3, 15. To a disaster which the Kurus sustained by a shower of stones, reference is made in "Chând. Up." i, 10, 1. An old verse, in which it is said, "The mare saves the Kurus," is quoted at id. iv, 17, 9. "The Kurus shall be obliged to fly from Kurukshetra," a Brahman threatens and his threat is fulfilled; "Çâñkh. çr." xv, 15, 10."—Cf. also "Taitt. Br." i, 8, 4, 1, 2.

The brilliant part is well known, which Janamejaya, the king of the Kurus, plays in a series of the Brâhma*n*a texts, as well as that noble ode in praise of his father, the Kuru king Parikshit, which we have preserved in "Av." xx, 127, 7 seq.

As Parikshit and Janamejaya among kings, so Âru*n*i among those versed in sacrifice stands on a high, perhaps on the highest platform.* To Âru*n*i is attributed the formula with which the morning and evening sacrifice is celebrated: agnir jyotir agni*h* svâhâ; sûryo jyotir jyoti*h* sûrya*h* svâhâ ("Çat." ii, 3, 1, 34), and in others also of the Yajus formulæ are found traces of Âru*n*i's hand ("Çat." iii, 3, 4, 19, vgl. "Taitt. Âr." i, 12, 4). But Aru*n*i is mentioned as a Kaurupañcâla brahman ("Çat." xi, 4, 1, 2); the

* When the time shall have come for the inquiries, which will have to be made to create order out of the chaotic mass of names of teachers and other celebrities of the Brâhma*n*a period, it may turn out that the most important centre for the formation and diffusion of the Brâhma*n*a doctrine will have to be looked for in Âru*n*i and in the circles which surrounded him. The most divergent lines of tradition meet in the person of Uddâlaka Âru*n*i. He is named as the teacher of Yâjnavalkya ("Çat. Br." xiv, 9, 3, 15; 9, 4, 33; cf. of the other books of this text V. 5, 5, 14). But also in the texts belonging to the *Ri*gveda he plays a prominent part. As the Va*m*ça at the end of the "Çat. Br." makes the teacher, who in this text enjoys leading authority, namely, Yâjnavalkya, a pupil of Âru*n*i's, so the Kaushîtaki Âra*n*yaka (XV) represents Kaushîtaki and through him also his pupil Çâñkhâyana derive his wisdom from Âru*n*i ("Gu*n*âkhyâc Châñkhâyanâd asmâbhir adhîta*m*, Gu*n*âkhya*h* Çâñkhâyanâ*h* Kaholât Kaushîtake*h*, Kahola*h* Kaushîtakir Uddâlakâd Âru*n*e*h*," etc.). And also the teacher, whose name we find at the head of another branch of *Ri*gveda school tradition, Madhuka Paiñgya (cf. regarding him "Kaush. Brâhm." xvi, 9; "Çat. Br." xi, 7, 2, 8), is through the medium of Yâjnavalkya brought into connection with Âru*n*i ("Çat. Br." xiv, 9, 3, 16). Cf. also "Chând. Up." iii, p. 178 ed. Roer.

Mahâbhârata (i, 682, ed. Calc.) defines him more closely as a Pañcâlya, with which the fact is in keeping, that we find his son Çvetaketu* appear in an assembly of the Pañcâlas ("Çat." xiv, 9, 1, 1; "Chând. Up." v, 3, 1), and that a man from Kauçâmbî is mentioned as Âru*n*i's pupil ("Çat." xii, 2, 2, 13).

Certain peculiarities of recitation are laid claim to as belonging to the Pañcâlas, others to the Prâcyas ("Çâñkh. çr." xii, 13, 6; "*Ri*k-Prâtiç. Sûtra" 137 and 186); we shall perhaps be permitted to conclude, that on the whole the method of Vedic recitation has arisen among the Kurus.

The passages bearing on the Bharatas, standing to all appearance in closest union with the Kurus, will be set forth and explained farther on. Here we merely mention the saying in "Taitt. Âr." ii, 20: namo Gañgâyamunayor madhye ye vasanti . . . namo Gañgâyamunayor munibhyaç ca.

To the evidence here collected† of the prominent importance of the Kurupañcâlas in the Vedic world—evidence, a part of which is drawn from the "Çatapatha Brâhma*n*a"—will be opposed the important part, which the people of Videha, living far in the east, and their king Janaka play in this very text. The attitude of the "Çatapatha Brâhma*n*a" to the eastern parts of Hindostan is so instructive on the matters which now engage our attention, that we shall go into greater detail on this point.

In the last books of the "Çatapatha Brâhma*n*a," the debates, which are carried on between the Brahmans at the Court of the Videha king Janaka, bear leading prominence. The hero of these contests, and at the same time the teacher, whose authority on spiritual questions is regarded as decisive,‡ is Yâjnavalkya. Some passages of the Brâhma*n*a make it, if not absolutely certain, at any rate highly probable, that he belonged by descent, not to the Kurupañcâlas but

* The same, who in a noteworthy passage of the Âpastamba (i, 2, 5, 6) is cited as an example of the appearance of Çrutarshayas still in later ages.

† Compare with these also the very rich collections of Weber, "Ind. St." i, 189 seq.; the relevant passages from the "Kâ*th*aka" are quoted at iii, 469, 471.

‡ For brevity's sake we may here be permitted to omit notice of Books vi-x, xiii, the bearing of which is avowedly peculiar (Weber, "Ind. Stud." xiii, 265-269; Delbrück, "Die Altindische Wortfolge," p. 45).

—we may venture to add conjecturally—to the Videhas.* Thus we have here a proof, from which it is clear that Brahman-Vedic culture was held in honour at a court far east from the land of the Kurupañcâlas, and also that, in all probability, the most respected teacher of this court was himself a native of that eastern kingdom.

This fact cannot be thrown into relief by itself alone, without setting it in its true light by means of other facts drawn from that same Brâhma*n*a. The "Çatapatha Br." shows itself in the clearest way, that Brahmanic culture among the Videhas is only an offshoot from the Kurupañcâlas. Yâjnavalkya himself is a pupil of Âru*n*i (note p. 396), who, as we saw, was a Pañcâla. The groups of Brahmans, who flock to Janaka, are—except Yâjnavalkya—Kurupañcâlânâm brâhma*n*â*h* (xiv, 6, 1, 1, etc.); the king of the east, who has a leaning to the culture of the west, collects the celebrities of the west at his court—much as the intellects of Athens gathered at the court of Macedonian princes. How fully throughout the whole text, which actually appears to have been compiled in the east, the authority of the west, of the Kurupañcâlas, is felt and acknowledged, the passages collected above amply show.† And most clearly in the well-known narration of the "Çatapatha Br." i, 4, 1, 10 seq.‡ has the memory been preserved, that there was a time, when the sacrificial system, as it flourished on the Sarasvatî, was still a stranger to the land of the Videhas§: Videgha Mâthava,

* XIV, 6, 1, 1-3 and especially 6, 9, 20.

† Holding as we do with Weber that the "Çat. Br." was compiled in the east, it is very readily explained how this text not only knows those peoples, kings and teachers, as do the other texts, but in addition also knows Yâjnavalkya and Janaka, of whom the other texts are almost wholly ignorant (Weber, "Lit. Gesch."[2] p. 146, note 2). The other texts originated at the very centre, the "Çat. Br." at the periphery of Vedic culture; in the provinces people know the great folks of the capital, but not *vice versâ*.

‡ Cf. Weber, "Ind. Stud." i, 170 seq.

§ What river that Sâdanîrâ here, named as a boundary, is, cannot, as far as I see, be determined with certainty. Weber (*loc. cit.* 172, 181) identifies it with the Ga*n*d*akî, which in later times formed the boundary between the territories of Kosala and Videha. Against this the fact seems to speak, that the Mahâbhârata on one occasion makes its heroes cross "Ga*n*d*akîñ ca Mahâço*n*am Sadânîrân tathaiva ca" (ii, 794 ed. Calc.; also vi, 325, 332 the two rivers stand beside each other in a long list); this passage is, of course, not decisive, for the

the national hero of the Videhas, goes eastward across the Sadânîrâ and there establishes the rule of the Videhas. But Agni Vaiçvânara, who comes from the Sarasvatî, does not accompany him across; he cannot burn beyond the Sadânîrâ. Therefore in earlier ages no Brahmans went across the Sadânîrâ to the east, for it was bad land, whereof Agni Vaiçvânara had not tasted. "Now, however, eastward of that dwell many Brahmans; . . . now is it indeed good land, for now have Brahmans made it enjoyable through offerings." The difference between the ancient Vedic land of culture in the west and the east, where there was Aryan land, but not yet for a long time a home of Vaiçvânara, can scarcely be more significantly expressed. Certainly the limits between the two tracts here appear to have been already pushed forward a stage farther toward the east; the Kosalas have entered earlier than the Videhas into the community of Vedo-Brahmanic culture.*

Still farther off from the old centres of Vedic culture than the races already named stand the Magadhas. In a well-known passage of the Atharva-Veda (5, 22, 14) the fever is washed away to the Gandhâris† and Mûjavants, and to the Añgas and Magadhas; and

knowledge of the true Sadânîrâ, which has been lost to later lexicographers in every instance—for the Karatoyâ cannot possibly be identified with the S.—may have been already wanting to the poets who composed these passages of the Mahâbhârata.

* It is quite in accordance with this that among the names of the stocks not held in full esteem as though being non-Aryan, which are at the same time applied as the designations of mixed castes, Vaideha occurs as well as Magadha (Manu x, 11; cf. Gautama iv, 17), but not Kausalya. We also find the names of the Nicchivis (Licchavis) and the Mallas (Manu x, 22), the rulers of Kusinârâ and Pâvâ and the near neighbours of the Sakyas. Probably, then, the latter also belonged to the stocks little affected by Brahmanic influences.

† The Gandhâras in the north-west will have to be regarded by us as standing outside the pale of Vedic culture, in the same way as the Magadha people did in the south-east (cf. Roth, "zur Literatur," see 42). Of course they are known to the Vedic texts. But their mention in "Chândogya Upan." vi, 14 does not imply that the compiler of that text was specially near to the Gandhâras, so that we cannot conclude with Prof. Max Müller (p. 105 of his Translation) regarding the high antiquity of the text or the northern origin of its compiler. The passage seems to me rather to favour the opposite (cf. also Weber, "Ind. St." i, 219 note). The matter dealt with is a comparison of a man, who is led (ânîya) away by the Gandhâras with closed eyes, and who then inquires his way back from village to village. The

a host of other passages in the Vedic literature combine to show that the Magadhas were looked upon as strangers, and were regarded by no means with favour.*

If our inquiry up to this point, which has been based essentially on the Brâhma*n*a Text, has yielded the probability, that, for the history of the spread of Vedic culture, a sharp distinction must be drawn between Kurus, Pañcâlas, and the peoples connected with them on the one hand, and the Eastern stocks, especially the Videhas and Magadhas on the other, now is the time to examine this hypothesis by the data which the *R*ik-Sa*m*hitâ supplies. We ask: Can we discern among the stocks, which are mentioned in the *R*ik-Sa*m*hitâ, a prominence or even an exclusive appearance of the circle which groups itself round the Kuru-Pañcâlas? We believe we shall have to answer this question in the affirmative.

passage means the more, the farther the Gandhâras are made to reside from the land where this may have been said. With the Buddhists the capital of the Gandhâras, Takkasilâ, figures constantly as the place to which anyone travels, when he desires to learn something good, *e.g.* "Tat. A*tth*." ii, 2; 39 etc. and already in the Vinaya Pi*t*aka: "Mahâvagga," viii, 1, 5, seq.

* Vide the quotations in Professor Weber's "Lit. Gesch.," second edition, p. 86, 123 seq. 156. I cannot agree with Weber in tracing the light esteem of the Brahmans (or quasi-Brahmans, for they do not apparently pass as pure) of Magadha expressed in the passages in point, to the success of Buddhism in that country. If the Brahmans of Magadha as such are spoken of in a sneering tone, it is, I think, more natural to think of the light esteem in which their fatherland was held, than of a circumstance—the Buddhist faith—which affected only single individuals among them, but affected, instead, Kosala Brahmans, etc., quite as much. If this faith and not the origin of the Magadha Brahmans were the real point, why then was not, for example, the well-known prescript regarding Vrâtyastoma based on the faith and not on the descent? Data of any kind whatever, which might stand in any connection whatever with Buddhism, I have not been able to discover in the whole range of the statements regarding the Vrâtyas. The *rôle* which the Magadha people here play, is amply explained by the feeling of national antipathy, or of contempt, which was harboured towards them. Prof. Weber seems to me to hit the mark, when he, "Lit. G.,"[2] p. 305, surmises that the land of Magadha was not wholly Brahmanized. But we need not suppose that here "the aborigines always preserved a kind of influence." The Aryan immigrants themselves were not wholly Brahmanized, *i.e.*, not wholly permeated by the culture of the Kuru-Pañcâlas.—We may here also refer to "Kaush Âr." 7, 14: atha ha smâsya (*i.e.*, of the Hrasva Mâ*nd*ukeya) putra âha Madhyama*h* Prâtibodhîputro Magadhavâsî. Thus, dwelling in the Magadha territory is mentioned as something unusual.

It is admitted that the status of Indian family-stocks, as it is given in the *Ri*k-Sa*m*hitâ, corresponds at first sight only partially with that which is set forth in the Brâhma*n*a. A series of the most important race-names given in the *Ri*k-Sa*m*hitâ have vanished wholly, or as good as wholly, in the Brâhma*n*a: *e.g.*, the Pûrus, Turvaças, Yadus, T*r*itsus, and so on. *Vice versâ*, of the names of Kurus and Pañcâlas, which stand in the front in the Brâhma*n*a, not one is named, directly at least, in the Sa*m*hitâ. There arose apparently on the one side new names instead of the old (note the well-known change of Krivi and Pañcâla), on the other, in the many migrations and struggles in numerous places, the countless small stocks of the older days cohered into few greater peoples;* naturally such events might easily necessitate a change in the names. Finally the possibility also must not be overlooked, that one and another among the stocks, which had participated in the culture of the *Ri*k-Sa*m*hitâ, withdrew later from the circle, in which the Vedic culture has further developed itself, and new stocks entered this circle.

The investigation will now naturally take this course: first those stocks of the *Ri*k-Sa*m*hitâ will be enumerated, which reappear under the same names in the Brâhma*n*a. Then will be mentioned the unfortunately only few cases, in which the identity of the name is indeed wanting, but where from further considerations of some kind or other a connection between the one case and the other is rendered probable.

Of instances of the first kind I may cite the following:—

Kurus, in the *Ri*k-Sa*m*hitâ at least indirectly named, Zimmer, "Altind. Leben," p. 130 seq.; Ludwig, "Mantraliteratur," p. 205.

Krivis (=Pañcâlas), s. Zimmer, p. 102 seq. The small importance of the Krivis in ancient times as compared with the later great prominence of the Pañcâlas suggests the supposition, that the change of names is connected with further changes, some such

* Compare the analogous occurrences in ancient Germany, where, for example, the Chamavi, Sigamberi, Ampsivarii of ancient times combined to form the composite race of the Franks.

as a cohesion of the Krivis with other elements to form the Pañcâla stock; we shall return to this matter later on, p. 404 seq.

Matsyas, Zimmer, p. 127. The passage quoted from Manu (supra, p. 393) and numerous other evidences establish their connection with the great western groups of peoples.

Uçînaras, Zimmer, p. 130. Their belonging to the group of the Kurus and Pañcâlas is clear from the genealogical table of the Aitareya.

S*ri*ñjayas, Zimmer, p. 132; Ludwig, "Mantra Lit." p. 153 seq.; Weber, "Ind. Stud." i, 208; iii, 472. Their close connection with the Kurus has been rightly inferred by Zimmer from "Çat." ii, 4, 4, 5; cf. also "Çat." xii, 9, 3, 1 seq.

Ruçamas, Zimmer, p. 129. In the Brâhma*n*a we meet with at least one Ruçamâ ("Pañc. Br." xxv, 13); this one runs round Kurukshetra for a bet made with Indra.

Cedis, Zimmer, p. 129. I here insert this stock, although, as far as I know, it does not meet us again in the Brâhma*n*a, but only in the great Epic: Pañcâlâç Cedi-Matsyâç ca Çûrasenâ*h*, etc. (iv. 11). The Cedis are set up as the model of upright living (i, 2342 seq.). They lie, judging by their later settlements, of all these peoples farthest to the south-east, s. Lassen, I², 688 A. 3; Cunningham "Archæol. Survey," ix, 54 seq.

Of the Bharatas we shall treat farther on.

Already this of itself confessedly scanty list of names indicates unmistakably that the *Ri*k-Sa*m*hitâ has its home among those groups of peoples, who are found later on gathered round the centre of the Kurupañcâlas. The instances to the contrary are unimportant. They are the following:—

The Gandhâris, Zimmer, p. 30. *Vide* supra, p. 399.

The Kîka*t*as, Zimmer, p. 31. These, according to the lexicographers, would have to be taken as identical with the Magadha people. But, on the one hand, they are mentioned in a way which appears to point to their distance from, rather than to their nearness to, the compiler of the poem, and on the other it is more than uncertain that they are to be really identified with the Magadha stock. Yâska (Nir. 6, 32) was only able to say of the Kîka*t*as that they were non-Aryans. If he was justified in this, then they were not the Magadhas, if these were Aryans. But if Yâska knew nothing really of the Kîka*t*as and drew what he said of them only from the passage of the *Ri*gveda, it is then difficult to believe that the lexicographers knew more.

A connection of the Añga Aurava, who according to the Anukrama*n*î is represented to be compiler of *R*v. 10, 138, with the people of the Añgas, we have no reason to suppose.

Ikshvâkus, Zimmer, p. 133, cf. p. 104 note. The later ages trace back the royal race of Eastern Hindostan to Ikshvâku; the race also, to which Buddha belonged, regarded itself as a race of Ikshvâkuidæ. If Ikshvâku stands outside the circle with which, according to our investigation, the *Ri*k-Sa*m*hitâ otherwise deals, the mention of a mighty prince in this way would of itself scarcely be used against us as an instance opposed to our result. But the case itself is questionable: the "Çatapatha Brâhma*n*a" (xiii, 5, 4, 5) knows Purukutsa as an Ikshvâkuid;* but Purukutsa was prince of the Pûrus (Zimmer, p. 123), whom no one will seek to identify with those eastern peoples (regarding the Pûrus see our remarks presently). Are we to suppose that the eastern stocks, when they came into closer contact with the Vedic culture, have appropriated to their most venerated kingly races ancestors of Vedic nobility, and that for that purpose the name of Ikshvâkuidæ, belonging correctly to the Pûrus, has been selected?

We now pass on to consider the cases, in which the identity or connection of stocks which we mentioned in the Sa*m*hitâ, and such as are mentioned in the Brâhma*n*a, is to be rendered probable, not directly by resemblance of name but in some other way.

The Pûrus are, as is known, brought in the genealogical system of the great epic into the closest connection with the Kurus. In the Brâhma*n*a there are unfortunately wanting evidences, but internal probability really speaks for our inferring a connection between the people, which stands in the age of the *Ri*k-Sa*m*hitâ in

* Probably it serves to confirm this statement, that according to the "Pañcav. Br." xiii, 3, 12 Tryaru*n*a Traidhâtva was an Aikshvâka; but a Tryaru*n*a we know from *Ri*gv. v. 27 to be a descendant of Trasadasyu.

the centre of Vedic civilization, and that which occupies the same position in the case of the Brâhmana.* It also deserves to be noted that the Kuruçravana, cf. Rv. x, 33, 4, is denominated Trâsadasyava; but Trasadasyu was a prince of the Pûrus. I believe that the Pûrus were only one among other elements, which combined to form the people of the Kurus; another I shall attempt to point out as we proceed (p. 408 seq.).

The Turvaças, standing in closest connection with the Yadus, belong of course to the stocks most frequently mentioned in the Rik-Samhitâ; they are sometimes mentioned in a friendly and sometimes in an unfriendly tone. From the Brâhmana their name has almost completely vanished;† nevertheless we have one passage which gives us a key to the place in which we have to search for the ancient Turvaças among the people of the later age. In the lists of kings who have offered the Açvamedha, we find the Pañcâla king Çona Sâtrâsâha ("Çat." xiii, 5, 4, 16), regarding whose horse-sacrifice a Gâthâ is quoted: "When Sâtrâsâha makes the Açvamedha offering, the Taurvaças arise, six thousand and six and thirty clad in mail (varminâm)." The commentary explains: Taurvaçâh açvâh; the construction (cf. also the following Gâthâ, § 17) clearly shows that the Taurvaças are rather the "varmin," *i.e.*, the mail-clad escort of noble races, who have to follow the offered horse (or the horses offered), so that it be not lost ("Çat." xiii, 1, 6, 3; 4, 2, 16; "Kâty. çr." xx, 2, 11).

We expressed above our doubt that the Krivis of ancient time alone, without admixture of other elements, are to be set down as being the same with the Pañcâla: now we have found bands of the Turvaça youth actively engaged in the offering of a Pañcâla king. Thus the conjecture is justified that we are to look to find in the people of the Pañcâlas, of the stock of the Rik Samhitâ, the Turvaças also as well as the Krivis. The union of the Turvaças, frequently

* Cf. the remarks of Ludwig, "Mantralit." p. 205.

† That they are identical with the *Vrićivants* also named in the Brâhmana, as Zimmer (p. 124) would have them, Rv. vi, 27, does not justify us to assume. This passage is satisfactorily explained also if the *Vrićivants* are treated only as confederates of the Turvaças (cf. Ludwig, "Mantra L.," p. 153).

with the Yadus, and occasionally with the Matsyas (*Rv.* vii, 18, 6), falls in completely with this conjecture.

In order to define the position which the Tr*i*tsus, whose brilliant victories are so highly celebrated in the Vasish*th*a Hymns, occupy among the stocks of the Vedic age, we point next to the connection in which they stand with the Sr*i*ñjaya (*vide* supra, p. 402), a connection which is undoubtedly to be regarded as an alliance. Both have the same enemies: that the Tr*i*tsus stand opposed to the Turvaças in battle we know from vii, 18, 6; 19, 8, and so on; of the Sr*i*ñjayas we gather the same from vi, 27, 7. In the hymns of the Bharadvâja book (Ma*nd*. vi) an equal friendship for the Sr*i*ñjayas and the Tr*i*tsu prince Divodâsa appears; the praises of the gifts and honours which the bard has received from Divodâsa, and of those which he has received from the Sârñjaya (*i.e.*, Daivavâta), are united in the same poem (vi, 47).* Now we have already mentioned the union of the Sr*i*ñjayas and Kurus appearing in the Brâhma*n*a; as the bard of vi, 47 posed as the Purohita of the Tr*i*tsu and Sr*i*ñjaya princes, so Devabhâga Çrautarsha ("Çat. Br." ii, 4, 4, 5) united the purohital dignity of the Kurus and Sr*i*ñjayas. Thus we shall be led by probabilities to allot to the Tr*i*tsus their place within the circle of stocks, among which later on the name of the Kurus played the most prominent part.

Much clearer results are obtained if we accept the important and acute supposition of Ludwig,† who declares the Tr*i*tsus to be identical with the Bharatas. I think that there is, in fact, more than one consideration in support of this conjecture. The Tr*i*tsus are mentioned under this name exclusively in the seventh Ma*nd*ala; but it is *à priori* in the highest degree improbable that the race which thus plays so brilliant a part should be wholly unknown to

* Among the vouchers for the connection of the Tr*i*tsus and Sr*i*ñjayas I also reckon *Rv.* vii, 19, 3, although of course the weight of this passage is diminished by the mention of Trasadasyu and the Pûrus being made therein at the same time. As Vîtahavya and Sudâs there stand beside each other, it appears to me to be clear that Vîtahavya is to be understood as a proper name of the Sr*i*ñjaya prince, cf. "Ath. V.," v, 19, 1; "Taitt. Sa*m*h." v, 6, 5, 3; "Pañc. Br." xxv, 16, 3. A Vîtahavya is also lauded in the Bharadvâja book, which is, as is well known, friendly to the Sr*i*ñjayas (*Rv.* vi, 15, 2, 3). Aliter Zimmer, p. 132.

† "Mantraliteratur," p. 175.

the remaining parts of the *Ri*gveda; there is in them no deficiency of passages where mention is made of the T*ri*tsu king Sudâs and his father, Divodâsa Atithigva, the conqueror of Çambara. If we are thus authorized to presuppose that the T*ri*tsus are identical with one of the elsewhere-mentioned stocks—and certainly in all probability with one of those frequently mentioned—there thus remain, in fact, as the Five Peoples are excluded on account of their enmity against the T*ri*tsus, apparently only the Bharatas of whom we can entertain a thought. That vii, 33, 6, can be used as well to support as to controvert this view is evident. Direct support of this identification of the T*ri*tsus with the Bharatas is found* in the following considerations:—

T*ri*tsus, like Bharatas, are enemies of the Purus, mentioned elsewhere in the *Ri*k-Sa*m*hitâ as a rule in a friendly tone, and certainly the poet belonging to the Vasish*th*idæ sides with the T*ri*tsus as with Bharatas; cf. vii, 8, 4; 18, 13, etc.

The king of the T*ri*tsus is Sudâs; the praise of Sudâs and of the Bharatas is found coupled in iii, 53, 9. 12. 24.

In vi, 16, 4. 5, cf. v, 19, the prayer for Divodâsa and for the Bharatas is united in such a fashion that one can scarcely help taking Divodâsa for a Bharata. But Divodâsa is, according to viii, 18, 25, the father of Sudâs, the king of the T*ri*tsus.

The question of the historical position of the T*ri*tsus thus merges in that of the position of the Bharatas, and to this latter question we have now to address ourselves.

The Brâhma*n*a texts tell us of Bharata heroes in a distant antiquity as well as of such as must be regarded as belonging to a not very remote past. In the list of Açvamedha offerers ("Çat." xiii, 5, 4) two Bharata princes appear: Bharata himself, the son of Dushyanta, and Çatânîka Sâtrâjita; the accompanying verses on both occasions point to the incomparable nobility of the Bharata or Bharatas, whose greatness is as far beyond that of other mortals as the heavens are above the earth. The family, as belonging to which those two princes were regarded by the compilers of the Brâhma*n*a text, proceeds from the person of the priests, who are

* To a great extent already cited by Ludwig, p. 175.

named in connection with them: Bharata Daushyanti has received the kingly installation from Dîrghatamas Mâmateya, therefore from a *Ri*shi of the *Ri*k-Sa*m*hitâ ("Ait." viii, 23), Çatanîka Sâtrâjita on the contrary from Somaçushman Vâjaratnâyana ("Ait." viii, 21), therefore from a man, whom his name already stamps as belonging to a later epoch.

That the existence and prominent importance of the Bharatas continued down to the age of the compiler of the Brâhma*n*a is also evident from a series of other passages,* in which reference is made to customs of the Bharatas usually in such a way that the Bharatas appear in what they say and do as the rule for correct procedure, once ("Ait." iii, 18) also in such a manner that the knowledge of the Bharata custom is freely designated as something which not every one has.

In the lists of tribes in "Ait. Br." 8, 14, and in Manu the Bharatas are wanting; as little do we meet them in the Buddhists' enumeration of peoples,† or in the numerous references made by the Buddhist texts to the peoples through whose country Buddha wanders or who figure in any other place in Buddhist sacred history.‡ And anyone who goes through the mentionings made of the Bharatas in the Brâhma*n*a texts will find that there, in a certain way, the course is being prepared already for the vanishing of the

* "Ait." ii, 25; iii, 18 (twice); "Çat." v, 4, 4, 1. Whoever considers these passages by themselves and in comparison with the evidence to be explained further on, will scarcely adhere to the signification "mercenary soldier" for Bharata (*vide* Pet. Lex.), but see in it solely the name of the tribe. I emend Satvanâm in "Ait." ii, 25, to Satvatâm (according to "Çat." xiii, 5, 4, 21, which reading—as opposed to the Lex.—is supported by "Ait." viii, 14), and translate: "therefore even now go the Bharatas forth for plunder against the Satvats, and their charioteers say: For a fourth part," etc.

† One Sutta of the "Añguttara Nikâya" (A*tth*anipâta); so*l*asanna*m* mahâjanapadâna*m* . . . seyyath' îda*m*: Añgâna*m* Magadhâna*m* Kâsîna*m* Kosalâna*m* Vajjîna*m* Mallâna*m* Cetiyâna*m* Va*m*sâna*m* (so agreeing two MSS. consulted by me. In the Janavasabhasutta I find Kâsikosalesu Vajjimallesu Cetiva*m*sesu Kurupañcâlesu Macchasûrasenesu). Kurûna*m* Pañcâlâna*m* Macchâna*m* Surasenâna*m* Assakâna*m* Avantîna*m* Gandhârâna*m* Kambojâna*m*.

‡ The only mention known to me of the Bharatas in the sacred Pâli texts occurs in the Govindasutta ("Dîgha-Nikâya"). It is there narrated how in old times, after the death of the king Disampati (cf. "Dîpav." 3, 40), the Brahman

Bharata name out of the circle of Indian tribal names which are wont to be mentioned. The Bharatas are referred to with great deference, but in quite another tone than that adopted with regard to the peoples influencing the life of the Kurus, Videhas, etc.; in the incidental way in which, for example, Brahmans of the Kurupañcâla stock are spoken of, or in which it is said that some one wanders in the country of the Matsyas or Uçînaras, the Bharatas do not appear. The peculiar importance and at the same time the isolation of the Bharatas shows itself, perhaps, in the most decisive manner when Agni is spoken of as brâhma*n*a Bhârata ("Çat. Br." i, 4, 2, 2), and is invited to dispose of the offering Manushvad Bharatavat (*ibid.* i, 5, 1, 7).

We may, perhaps, be allowed to surmise that in the Bharatas we have to do with a stock which in the time of the Brâhama*n*a had politically merged in, or was about to merge in, one of the great peoples of India in that age, but which had attaching to its name the splendour of great memories and sacral precedence. If we ask after the people, which may have absorbed the Bharatas, it is most natural to seek them in those tracts to which in the Brâhma*n*a period especially the highest sacral authority appertains in the domains of the Kurupañcâla. It fits in with this that, according to "Çat. Br." xiii, 5, 4, 11. 21, one Bharata king has obtained a victory over the Kâçis, another has made offerings to Gaṅgâ and Yamunâ. It further tallies with the fact that the formula of the king's proclamation (esha vo, N. N., râjâ) for the people that is addressed, the following variants occur: Kurava*h*, Pañcalâ*h*, Kuru-

Govinda divided the kingdom between Re*n*u, the son of the king, and the "aññe cha khattiyâ." It is said of this :—

"Tatra suda*m* majjhe Re*n*ussa rañño janapado hoti.
Dantapura*m* Kaliṅgâna*m* Assakâna*m* ca Potama*m*
Mahîyata Avantîna*m* Sovîrânañ ca Roruka*m*
Mithilâ ca Videhâna*m* Campâ Aṅgesu mâpitâ
Bârâ*n*sî ca Kâsîna*m* ete Govindamâpitâ 'ti.
Sattabhû Brahmadatto ca Vessabhû Bharato saha
Re*n*u dve ca Dhatara*tth*â tadâsu*m* satta Bhâratâ 'ti.

It is seen how here the name of the Bharatas is used in a wider sense, embracing the whole of India (cf. Bhâratavarsha), or at any rate its princes.

pañcâlâ*h*, and Bharatâ*h* (*vide* Weber, "Ind. Lit. G."[2] p. 126, note). With this, above all, fits in the conception running through the epics. Also those who, like us, do not rate highly the confused representations of the Mahâbhârata regarding the stocks of antiquity in general, will not be able to avoid giving a certain weight to the evidences which the great epic at every step, and, indeed, even by its name, furnishes to prove that the royal family of the Kurus was a Bhârata family.*

Our discussions hitherto regarding the Bhâratas have not as yet dealt with the evidence furnished by the *R*ik-Sa*m*hitâ. We now inquire, how does its testimony stand to the view of the Bharatas hitherto conjecturally evolved.

In the hymns of the *R*ik we meet the Bharatas as one stock among many others†; the Viçvâmitra odes are well known in praise of the deeds of the Bharatas, the Vasish*th*a ode referring to their (quondam) defeat.

Also we find in the *R*ik-Sa*m*hitâ trace of a peculiar position occupied by the Bharatas, a special connection of theirs with important points of sacred significance, which are recognized throughout the whole circle of ancient Vedic culture. Agni is Bhârata, *i.e.*, propitious or belonging to the Bharata or Bharatas; among the protecting deities, who are invoked in the Âprî-odes, we find Bhâratî, the personified divine protective power of the Bharatas.

We find the Sarasvatî constantly named in connection with her; must not the sacred river Sarasvatî be the river of the holy people, the Bharatas? In one ode of the Ma*nd*ala, which specially extols the Bharatas (iii, 23), the two Bhâratas, Devaçravas and Devavâta,

* In this connection we may also point to the fact that the list of the Açvamedhayâjinas, "Çat. Br." xiii, 5, 4, generally states with reference to each king the people over which he ruled (Purukutsa is designated as Aikshvâko râjâ, Marutta as Âyogavo râjâ, Kraivya as Pañcâlo râjâ, and so on), but in three cases this detail is omitted apparently as superfluous: these cases are those of Janamejaya and his brothers, as well as Bharata and Çatânika. The first-named was, as is well-known, a Kuru prince; the two last were Bharata kings.

† See the passages in Grassmann's Lexicon, and Ludwig, p. 175, Zimmer p. 127 seq. Cf. also "Taitt. Âr." i, 27, 2.

are spoken of, who have generated Agni by friction: on the D*ri*shadvatî, on the Âpayâ, on the Sarasvatî may Agni beam. We find thus Bharata princes sacrificing in the land on the D*ri*shadvatî and on the Sarasvatî. Now the land on the D*ri*shadvatî and on the Sarasvatî is that which is later on so highly celebrated as Kurukshetra. Thus the testimonies of the Sa*m*hitâ and the Brâhma*n*a combine to establish the close connection of the ideas Bharata, Kuru, Sarasvatî.*

Out of the struggles in which the migratory period of the Vedic stocks was passed, the Bharatas issued, as we believe we are entitled to suppose the course of events to have been, as the possessors of the regions round the Sarasvatî and D*ri*shadvatî. The weapons of the Bharata princes and the poetical fame of their *Ri*shis may have co-operated to acquire for the cult of the Bharatas the character of universally acknowledged rule, and for the Bharatas a kind of sacral hegemony: hence Agni as friend of the Bharatas, the goddess Bhâratî, the sacredness of the Sarasvatî and D*ri*shadvatî.

Then came the period, when the countless small stocks of the Sa*m*hitâ age were fused together to form the greater peoples of the Brâhma*n*a period. The Bharatas found their place, probably together with their old enemies, the Pûrus,† within the great complex of peoples now in process of formation, the Kurus; their sacred land now became Kurukshetra.

We return from this digression bearing on the Bharatas, to state the result of our main investigation.

We found that the literature of the Brâhma*n*as points to a certain definitely circumscribed circle of peoples as its home, as the

* On the fact, that in the epic Ilâ and Sarasvatî are named among the divine ancestors of the Bharatas ("M. Bh." i, 3760, 3779, etc.) I will lay no stress. More worthy of note, considering the close connection of the Bharatas and Kuçikas (Zimmer, p. 128), is the fact that a tributary of the D*ri*shadvatî bears the name Kauçikî ("M. Bh." iii, 6065).—Regarding the relation of the son of Ilâ, Purûravas, to Kurukshetra, see "Çat. Br." xi, 5, 1, 4.

† Is it to be taken as connected with the vanishing of this enmity, that already in the *Rik*-Sa*m*hitâ on some occasions Sudâs, or Divodâsa on the one side and Purukutsa, or Trasadasyu on the other, are named together in a friendly tone? i, 112, 14; vii, 19, 3.

home of genuine Brahmanism. We found that this circle of peoples corresponds with those whom Manu celebrates as upright in life. We found finally, that the names of the stocks named in the *Ri*gveda, especially the most prominent of them, the Pûrus, Turvaças, Bharata-T*ri*tsus, go back to the same circle of peoples.

In this way we shall be permitted to consider established the statement premised to this inquiry, that this circle of stocks has formed from of old a community in itself closely inter-connected, separated from the Videhas, Magadhas, and also probably, though less clearly, from the Kosalas. Inasmuch as at the time when those stocks were pressing forward through the Panjâb towards their later habitations, we find this association and that separation already existing, we are entitle to assume that the Kosalas, the Magadhas, the Videhas had at that time already pressed forward farther to the east, down the Ganges. Vedic culture has not had its home, originally at least, among these stocks of the east, but among the peoples of the western group.

It will be an interesting task to follow out the distinction here indicated also on the lines of the dialects;* but the time for its performance will not have come until Indian epigraphic has been based on wider and surer foundations than the first volume of the Corpus Inscriptionum presents.

SECOND EXCURSUS.

Annotations and Authorities for the History of Buddha's Youth.

The several points noted in the account given in the text of the family from which Buddha sprang, are derived from "Cullavagga," vii, 1 seq. (cf. "Dhp. Atth." p. 351), as well as the following passages: So*n*ada*n*dasutta ("Dîgha N."): sama*n*o khalu bho Gotamo pahûta*m* hirañña*m* suva*nna*m ohâya pabbajito bhûmigata*m* ca

* Also the little which we can gather from Buddhist sources regarding the mythology of eastern lands and their religious terminology, so far as this is not overgrown by the Veda, coincides by no means with what the western literature yields.

vehâsa*tth*a*m* ca —, sama*n*o khalu bho Gotamo a*ddh*akulâ pabbajito mahaddhanâ mahâbhogâ. — "Apadâna," fol. khâ*h*: a*ddh*e kule mahâbhoge nibbattissatti tâvade.

"Apadâna," fol. ko':

aparimeyye ito kappe Ukkâkakulasambhavo (sic)
Gotamo nâmagottena satthâ loke bhavissati.

Idem. fol. ga*m*' seq.:

aparimeyye ito kappe bhûmipâlo mahiddhiko
Okkâko nâma nâmena râjâ râ*tth*e bhavissati.
so*l*asitthisahassâna*m* sabbâsa*m* pavarâ ca yâ
abhijâtâ khattiyânî nava putte janissati.
nava putte janitvâna khattiyânî marissati,
taru*n*avâ (sic) piyâ kaññâ mahesitta*m* karissati.
Okkâka*m* tosayitvâna vara*m* kaññâ labhissati,
vara*m* laddhâ ca sâ kaññâ putte pabbâjayissati.
pabbâjitâ ca te sabbe gamissanti naguttama*m*
jâtibhedabhayâ sabbe bhaginihi sa*m*vasissare.
ekâ 'va kaññâ byâdhihi bhavissati purakkhatâ,
mâ no jâti pabhijja (sic) ti nikha*n*iyanti khattiyâ.
khattiyo niharitvâna tâya saddhi*m* vasissati:
bhavissati tadâ bhedo Okkâkakulasambhavo.
tesa*m* pajâ bhavissanti Koliyâ nâma jâtiyâ,
tattha mânusaka*m* bhoga*m* anubhossanti nappaka*m*.

Here we must also compare the data given in the Amba*tth*asutta ("Dîgha Nikâya") for the descent of Buddha from Okkâka, as well as Sutta Nipâta, "Pârây. Vatthug." v, 16 ("Fausböll," p. 186). The Rohi*n*î as a boundary stream between the Sakyas and the Koliyas: passantu ta*m* Sâkiyâ Ko*l*iyâ ca pacchâmukha*m* Rohiniya*m* taranta*m* ("Theragâthâ," fol. khû').

Amba*tth*asutta ("Dîgha N."): The young Brahman Amba*tth*a says to Buddha: eka*m* idâha*m* bho Gotama samaya*m* âcariyassa brâhma*n*assa Pokkharasâtissa kenacid eva kara*n*îyena Kapilavatthu*m* agamâsi*m* yena Sakyâna*m* santhâgâra*m* ter' upasa*m*kami*m*. tena kho pana samayena sambahulâ Sakyâ c'eva Sakyakumârâ ca santhâgâre uccesu âsanesu nisinnâ honti aññamañña*m* aṅgulipatodakena sa*m*jagghantâ sa*m*kî*l*antâ aññadatthu maññeva mamañ ñeva anojagghantâ na na*m* koci âsanena pi nimantesi. tayida*m* bho

Gotama na cchanam tayidam na ppatirûpam yad ime Sakyâ ibbhâ samânâ na brâhmane sakkaronti, etc. In the "Añg. Nik." (vol. i, fol. kau) Bhaddiya Kâligodhâya putta is mentioned as uccâkulikânam agga among the Bhikkhus, apparently the same of whom "Cull." vii, 1 speaks. Dhammacetiyasuttanta ("Majjh. N.;" King Pasenadi is speaking): bhagavâ pi Kosalako aham pi Kosalako. The supremacy of Pasenadi over the Sakyas appears from the following passage: Sakyâ kho pana Vâsettha rañño Pasenadikosalâssa anantarâ anuyuttâ bhavanti; karonti kho Vâsettha Sakyâ rañño Pasenadimhi Kosale nipaccakâram abhivâdanam paccutthânam añjalikammam sâmîcikammam (Aggaññasutta, "Dîgha N.").

Buddha's claim to the "gotta" of Gotama I cannot satisfactorily explain. The question must here be put in general terms: how is the appearance of a gotta-name among members of the Khattiya caste to be explained?

I give first of all the essential facts bearing on this point, so far as they are known to me.

Each of those oft-mentioned noble families, in whose hands lies the government of separate towns and their adjacent territory, seems to have borne a gotta-name. Thus the Mallas of Kusinârâ are denoted as Vâsetthâs ("Mahâparinibb. Sutta," p. 55, etc.), the Mallas of Pâvâ bear the same gotta (Samgîtipariyâyasutta in the "Dîgha-Nikâya"), the Koliyas are styled Byagghapajja (often in the "Añguttara Nikâya"). Is the name of their town Vyâghrapura connected herewith? (Sp. Hardy, "Manual," p. 139.) In the Mahâpadhânasuttta is explained the descent, gotta and so on, of the six Buddhas, who have preceded the Buddhas of the present age in the holy dignity. Three of these six Buddhas are Khattiyas, but of these, as well as of the other three, who are Brâhmanas, the gotta is mentioned as something existing as a matter of course; the three Khattiyas are Kondaññas, the three Brâhmanas are Kassapas. The last Buddha himself is a Gotama, apparently because his whole family are (*v.* Burnouf, "Introd." p. 155); at least his father is addressed as Gotama ("Mahâvagga" i, 54, 4); likewise his cousin Ânanda ("Vañgîsathera Samyutta," fol. câ, of the Phayre MS.); Mahâpajâpatî, who at the same time belongs to the Sakya race

("Lal. Vist." p. 28 ed. Calc.; "Mahâva*m*sa," p. 9), bears the name Gotamî; so also her sister Mâyâ ("Theragâthâ," fol. khû'); finally we have in "Jât A*tth*." i, 60 and elsewhere Kisâ Gotamî, who is to be regarded apparently as a young Sakya woman.—Numerous other instances of the application of a gotta-designation to persons of the Khattiya class are to be found in the Jinacaritra of the Jainas and in inscriptions (it is enough to refer at present to Cunningham, the "Stûpa of Bharhut," p. 128 seq., and Bühler's notice therewith given).

From these data it appears to me to follow with great probability, that according to that view of custom which is disclosed by the Buddhist and Jainist texts, every family of the Khattiya as well as of the Brâhma*n*a caste bears the gentile name of one of the Vedic Brahman-gottas. If in the case of kings like Bimbisâra or Pasenadi such a gotta cannot be pointed to, the reason of this seems not to be that they had no gotta name, but rather that the appellation mahârâja or deva was looked on as more respectful and consequently more correct than Vâse*tth*a or Gotama.

That in the appropriation of these Brahmanical names we have to do with a universal usage, not with a special right of individual families, dependent for instance on relationships of affinity, is also rendered probable by the verse often quoted in Buddhist suttas:

khattiyo se*tth*o jane tasmi*m* yo gottapa*t*isârino.

An extension of the mode of distinction here referred to, to persons of the third class, does not appear to have taken place; otherwise traces of it could scarcely have been omitted in the numberless cases, where they must have been expected to occur in our texts.

The designation of Buddha as Gotamides is usually traced to this, that the dignity of purohita may have lain in the case of the Sakyas in the hands of the Gautama-race.* As is well known, according to the Brahmanical custom of offering at the Pravara ceremony, instead of the naming of the ancestors of the person making the

* An express statement that this was the case, of course is not found in our translation.

offering, in case the latter is not a Brahman, the naming of the ancestors of his purohita must or can take place (Weber, "Indische Studien," x, 73, 79; Hillebrandt, "Das Altindische Neu- und Vollmondsopfer," S. 81, A. 1). But from the usage of calling upon the Agni as the Agni who has served the Gotama, in the case of the offering of a man who has a Gautama as purohit, to the designation of the man himself and his whole house as "descendants of the Gotama," seems to me far too wide a step for us to be able to accept that mode of explanation without hesitation. Here there may be fictions and expressions of caste-rivalry at play, which to lay bare even by conjecture the materials at present at our disposal do not suffice.

To the question of the position of the Sakya kingdom and of the town of Kapilavatthu we need not return in detail after what has been said above, p. 92, 25 seq. That Kapilavatthu itself lay immediately on or in the Himalaya cannot be admitted in face of the silence which Fa Hian and Hiouen Thsang observed as to the mountain in their descriptions of the town. True, it is said in the Pabbajjâsutta regarding the Sakyas ("Sutta Nipâta," cf. Fausböll's Trans., p. 68): uju*m* janapado . . . Himavantassa passato; but this warrants a conclusion as to the situation at the Himalaya of the territory only of the Sakyas, not of their capital. That Kapilavatthu, if it did not lie in the mountain, may not even have lain in the girdle of damp hollows (the so-called Tarai) which surrounds the southern margin of the mountain, that it must thus have lain south of the Tarai, cannot be alleged with certainty. The condition of the land and air has not been here at all times the same; in tracts of the Nepalese tarai, where now malaria prevails and only tiger and wild boar live, are to be found the splendid ruins of great ancient cities (Hodgson in the "Journ. As. Soc.," Bengal, 1835, p. 121 seq.).

The death of Mâyâ is often narrated in the texts of the Sutta Pi*t*aka.

To the circle of testimony collected on this point, the following passages also belong: "Sa*m*yutta Nikâya," vol. iii, fol. hâ: ida*m* bhante Kapilavatthu iddhañ c'eva phîtañ ca bâhujaññam âki*nn*amanussa*m* sambâdhabyûha*m*, se khv âha*m* . . . sâya*n*hasamaya*m* Kapilavatthu*m* pavisanto bhante na pi hatthinâ samâgacchâmi bhante na pi assena . . . rathena . . . saka*t*ena . . . na pi purisena samâgacchâmi. — Mahâsaccakasutta ("Majjh. N."): abhijânâmi kho panâha*m* pitu Sakkassa kammante sîtâya jambucchâyâya nisinno vivicc' e[va kâme]hi vivicca akusalehi dhammehi . . . pa*th*amajjhâna*m* upasampajja viharattâ (sic). To this later on was added the known legend of the Vappamañgala, "Jât. A*tth*." i, p. 57 seq.

The following leads me to deny the antiquity of the tradition, which makes Buddha's father a king. When (as in the So*n*ada*n*-*d*asutta of the "Dîghâ N.") the external claims of Buddha to respectful consideration are discussed, it is always admitted merely that he has come of an "uccakula, khattiyakula, a*ddh*akula;" it is emphasized that he, when he entered on a spiritual career, forsook relatives and friends, gold and silver; the kingly dignity of the family is not alluded to. If anywhere, it is with reference to a circumstance of this kind, which assuredly could not have been suppressed, that the *argumentum ex silentio* is applicable. To this another consideration must be added. Anyone who knows the uniform care with which the titulary appellation of persons appearing in the Pi*t*akas is observed, will also find this difference decisive, that Buddha's father is there named merely Suddhodhana Sakka ("Mahâvagga," i, 54, and cf. the passage cited above from the "Mâhasaccakasutta"), just as mention is made of Anuruddha Sakka, Upananda Sakyaputta, &c., while Bhaddiya, who was really king of the Sakyas—if we may call this petty râjâ a king—is regularly introduced as Bhaddiya Sakyarâjâ ("Cullav." vii, 1, 3 seq.). Moreover, Suddhodana is addressed "Gotama" ("Mahav." l. c.), as the Mallas are called Vâse*tth*â, the Koliyas Byagghapajjâ, but no one says to him "Mahârâja" as to Bimbisâra or Pasenadi.—The oldest evidence which attributes to Suddhodana the kingly dignity, as far as I know the only passage of the kind in the Tipi*t*aka, occurs in the Mahâpadhânasutta ("Dîgha N."), where a series of notices of the lives of the last seven Buddhas is thrown together. In a systematic manner, exactly as in the passage apparently modelled on this Sutta, "Dîp." xvii, 3 seq., there is recorded the length of life, the parentage, home, tree of knowledge, Sâvakayuga, &c., of these Buddhas. The three first were kings' sons, the following three Brahmans' sons, the last is again a king's son, the son of Suddhodhana râjâ. Possibly similar is the statement also in the concluding portion of the Buddhava*m*sa—it would be quite in keeping with the character of this text; I regret not to be able to make any statement on this part of the said texts as it is not accessible to me at present. There is no need of enlarging to show that in any case evidence of this description must retire before the momenta previously brought to bear on this question. From the Buddhava*m*sa (Phayre MS., fol. ju') I have noted the verse :—

mayha*m* janettikâ mâtâ Mâyâdevîti vuccati.

Cf. Râhulamâtâ devî, "Mahâvagga," i, 54.

As the birthplace of the Bodhisatta later tradition names the Lumbinî grove: from the Tipi*t*aka itself tho only passage bearing on this question known to me, is the following from the Nâlakasutta of the Sutta Nîpâta :—

—jâto
Sakyâna*m* gâme janapade Lampuneyye.*

The wonders connected with the conception and birth of the Bodhisatta are detailed in the Acchariyabahutasutta of the "Majjh. Nikâya" (cf. "Mahâparinibbâna Sutta," p. 27); there the law is laid down as universally valid, that the mother dies seven days after the birth of the child, and is born again in the heaven of the Tusita deities; also the so-called Sîhanâda ("aggo 'ham asmi lokassa," &c., cf. "Jât. A*tth*." i, p. 53) is there mentioned. The presentation of the child to the *R*ishi Asita (or as he is named in the "Jât. A*tth*." i, p. 54, Kâ*l*adevala) is narrated in the just-mentioned Nâlakasutta of the Sutta Nipâta† (v. Fausböll's translation).

* So the Phayre MS.; cf. Fausböll's translation, p. 125. The compiler of the passage seems to have been hampered by metrical necessity he wished undoubtedly to say: Sakyâna*m* janapade gâme L°.

† Also this Sutta belongs to the texts, in which we could not but assuredly

Touching the youth of the Bodhisatta the most important passage is found in the "Añguttara Nikâya" (I give it exactly according to the MS., vol. i, fol. ñu'): sukhumâlo aham bhikkhave paramasukhumâlo accantasukhumâlo. mama sukham bhikkhave pitu nivesane pokkharaniyo hâriyâkâ honti, ekattha sukham bhikkhave uppalam vappati ekattha padumam ekattha punnarikam yâvad evam atthâya. na kho pana es' âham bhikkhave kâsikam candanam dhâremi, kâsikam bhikkhave su me tam vethanam hoti kâsikâ kañcukâ kâsikam nivâsanam kâsiko uttarâsañgo. rattidivam kho pana me su tam bhikkhave setachattam dhâreyya mâ nam phussi sîtam vâ unham vâ tinam vâ rajo vâ ussâvo vâ 'ti. tassa mayham bhikkhave tayo pâsâdâ ahesum (this is shown to be a universal custom by comparing "Mahâvagga," i, 7, 1; "Cullavagga," vii, 1, 1) eko hemantiko eko gimhantiko eko vassiko 'ti. so kho aham bhikkhave vassikapâsâde vassike cattâro mâse nipppurisehi turiyehi paricâriyamâno na heṭṭhâ pâsâdâ orohâmi. yathâ kho pana bhikkhave aññesam nivesane dâsakammakarâporisassa kanâjakam bhojanam diyyati bilañgadutiyam evam eva su me bhikkhave pitu nivesane dâsakammakaraporisassa sâlimamsodano diyyati. Now follows the narrative translated at p. 102 seq., how the thought of old age, disease, and death is awakened in him: therewith ends the part of that text bearing on this matter. Let it be observed that the origin of these thoughts is not here attributed to an external occurrence like the well-known four excursions. The history of these excursions has been transferred to the later legends, as is almost expressly stated in the "Jât. Atth." i, p. 59, from the Mahâpadhânasutta ("Dîgha Nikâya"), where it is introduced as referring to the Buddha Vipassi* (there and in the Mahâpurisa-

expect a reference to the birth of the Bodhisatta in a royal house, unless this feature first belonged to the later tradition. In Professor Fausböll's translation of this Sutta Suddhodana's house is designated a "palace," and the child frequently a "prince;" the Pâli text has *bhavana* and *kumâra* respectively.

* When the compiler of this commentary there says for brevity's sake, that the dialogue between the Bodhisatta and the charioteer may be supplied after that Sutta, it follows apparently that a Sutta which narrated the corresponding occurrence regarding Gotama, was quite as unknown to the commentator as it is to me. Also, the appeal made in "Jât.," i, 59, line 39, to the commentary-tradition shows that there was no text to which an appeal could have been made.

lakkhaṇasutta of the "Dîgha N.," the 32 Lakkhaṇas of the Mahâpurisa are also discussed). Of Gotama Buddha the excursions are, as far as I know, never narrated in the Tipiṭaka.*

Regarding the wife and child of Buddha the chief passage is "Mahâvagga," i, 54;† Râhula is frequently mentioned in the Sutta texts as Buddha's son, without any prominent *rôle* being ascribed to him among the circles of disciples by the ancient tradition.

Touching the Pabbajjâ, first of all we must quote the Pabbajjâsutta in the "Jât. *Atth.*," i, p. 66, which stands in the Sutta Nipâta (Fausböll's translation, p. 67, seq.). It begins:

> Pabbajjaṁ kittayissâmi yathâ pabbaji cakkhumâ
> yathâ vimaṁsamâno so pabbajjaṁ samarocayi.
> sambâdh' âyaṁ gharâvâso rajassâyatanaṁ iti
> abbhokâso ca pabbajjâ iti disvâna pabbaji.
> pabbajitvâna kâyena pâpakammaṁ vivajjayi,
> vacîduccaritaṁ hitvâ âjîvaṁ parisodhayi.
> agamâ Râjagahaṁ buddho, and so on.

Then follows a narrative of the meeting of the coming Buddha and king Bimbisâra, presented in the "Jât. *Atth.*" i, p. 66. After this Sutta there comes next the following fragment of the

* Here also the verses of the Mâṇava Thera ("Therag." fol. ku) may be inserted:

> jiṇṇaṁ ca disvâ dukhitañ ca byâdhitaṁ
> matañ ca disvâ gataṁ âyusaṁkhayaṁ
> tato ahaṁ nikkhamituṁna pabbajiṁ
> pahâya kâmâni manoramâñiti.

(To all appearance we here have the Form nikkhamitûna, after which what has been said by me in Kuhn's "Zeitschr. N. F." v, 323 seq., is to be supplied.)

So of the Buddha Dîpaṁkara ("Buddhavaṁsa," fol. cai of the Phayre MS.):

nimitte caturo disvâ hatthiyânena nikkhami.

Similarly of the Buddha Koṇḍañña (ibid. fol. co.):

nimitte caturo disvâ rathayânena nikkhami.

Similarly of the following Buddhas. Whether at the close of the Buddhavaṁsa the same is directly said of Gotama Buddha, I cannot state at this moment. Improbable it is not; here, as also elsewhere, the traces of later legend-building may already be discernible in the most recent parts of the Piṭakas themselves; a fact which naturally would not be able to shake the elsewhere acquired inference regarding the earlier and later form of representations of Buddha's life.

† Cf. Dr. Davids's and my note to our translation of this passage.

So*n*ada*nd*asutta ("Dîgha N.") recurring at many other places, translated at p. 105: sama*n*o khalu bho Gotamo daharo samâno susukâ*l*ake sobhadrena yobbanena samannâgato pa*th*amena vayasâ agârasmâ anagâriya*m* pabbajito; sama*n*o khalu bho Gotamo akâmakâna*m* mâtâpitunna*m* assumukhâna*m* rudantâna*m* kesamassu*m* ohâretvâ kâsâyâni vatthâni acchâdetvâ agârasmâ anagâriya*m* pabbajito. Cf. also the passages quoted later on (p. 421). The narrative given in later legends (*e.g.* "Jât. A*tth*." i, p. 61) of the night scene in Buddha's bedroom, which precedes his flight, is to be found, if nothing have escaped me, in the Tipi*t*aka, told not of Buddha himself, but of one of his earliest converts, Yasa ("Mahâvagga," i, 7, 1. 2) and seems to have been thence transferred at a later time to the legends of Buddha. The age of the Bodhisatta at the time of his Pabbajjâ is stated in the "Mahâparinibbânasutta," p. 59, to have been twenty-nine years.

Regarding the time from the Pabbajjâ to the Sambodhi the tradition of the Tipi*t*aka is to be found in the following passages.

The duration of this period is frequently set down at seven years, *i.e.*, it is said that Mâra pursued the Bodhisatta for seven years up to the last vain attack he made on him; Padhânasutta of the Sutta-Nipâta:

> satta vassâni bhagavanta*m* anubandhi*m* padâpada*m*
> otâra*m* nâdhigacchissa*m* sambuddhassa satimato.

Similarly in the Mârasa*m*yutta of the "Sa*m*y. Nikâya" (vol. i, fol. ghî'): tena kho pana samayena (namely, when Buddha shortly after attaining deliverance sat under the tree) Mâro pâpimâ satta vassâni bhagavanta*m* anubaddho hoti otârâpekho otâra*m* alabhamâno.

The consecutive narrations touching this period represent the Bodhisatta after his Pabbajjâ confiding himself to the guidance of Â*l*âra Kâlâma,* and Uddaka Râmaputta (the place where these

* We find two versions side by side in the sacred Pâli-Kanon; on the one side it is related that Buddha left his home and went to Râjagaha, where the meeting with Bimbisâra took place; on the other it is said that he left his home and went to Â*l*âra Kâlâma. The later texts naturally arrange the different occurrences in one series. It is worthy of remark that the southern tradition and the northern

persons lived is not given); then he goes on to Uruvelâ; then follow the three comparisons (cf. "Lal. Vist." p. 309), his labours to obtain the goal by penances, at last the attainment of the Buddhahood and the first incidents thereon following.

This recital is to be found in different passages of the "Majjhima Nikâya," namely, in the Ariyapariyosânasutta (here are omitted the three comparisons and the Dukkarakârikâ); in the Mahâsaccasutta, the Bodhirâjakumârasuttanta, and the Sañgaravasuttanta.

I furnish from the sources indicated a selection of what appears to me most essential.

From the Mahâsaccakasutta:

Idha me Aggivessana pubbeva sambodhâ anabhisambuddhassa bodhisattass' eva sato etad ahosi: sambâdho gharâvâso rajapatho abbhokâso pabbajjâ. na yida*m* sukara*m* . . . (cf. "Mahavagga," v, 13, 1) . . . pabbajeyyan ti. so kho aha*m* Aggivessana aparena samayena daharo 'va samâno susukâlako sobhadrena yobbanena samannâgato pa*th*amena vayasâ akâmakâna*m* mâtâpitunna*m* assumukhâna*m* rudantâna*m* kesamassu*m* ohâretvâ kâsâyâni vatthâni acchâdetvâ agârasmâ anagâriya*m* pabbajito samâno ki*m*kusalagavesî anuttara*m* santivarapada*m* pariyesamâno yena Âlâro Kâlâmo ten' upasa*m*kami*m*, etc.

From the Ariyapariyosânasutta (cf. "Lal. Vist." p. 295, seq.):

Atha khv âha*m* bhikkhave yena Âlâro Kâlâmo ten' upasa*m*kami*m* upasa*m*kamitvâ Âlâra*m* Kâlâma*m* etad avoca*m*: kittâvatâ no âvuso Kâlâma dhamma*m* saya*m* abhiññâya sacchikatvâ upasampajja viharâmîti pavedesîti. eva*m* vutte bhikkhave Âlâro K. âkiñcaññayatana*m* pavedesi. tassa mayha*m* bhikkhave etad ahosi: na kho Âlârass' eva Kâlâmassa atthi saddhâ mayham p' atthi saddhâ. na kho Âlârass' eva Kâlâmassa atthi viriya*m* . . . sati . . . samâdhi . . . paññâ mayham pi atthi paññâ. yan nûnâha*m* ya*m* dhamma*m* Âlâro K. saya*m* abhiññâya sacchikatvâ upasampajja

have done so in different ways. The former represent Buddha as first going to Râjagaha and then to Â*l*âra ("Jât.," i, 66), the latter has the opposite course ("Lal. Vist.," p. 296 seq.): it is seen significantly how here the two branches of later tradition have, independently of each other, gone on building for themselves on a common basis, which is to us represented by the Pâli-Pi*t*akas.

viharâmîti pavediti tassa dhammassa sacchikiriyâya padaheyyan ti. so kho aham bhikkhave na cirass' eva khippam eva tam dhammam sayam abhiññâ sacchikatvâ upasampajja vihâsim. atha khv âham bhikkhave yena Âlâro K. ten' upasamkamim, upasamkamitvâ Âlâram K. etad avocam: ettâvatâ no âvuso Kâlâma imam dhammam sayam abhiññâ sacchikatvâ upasampajja pavedesîti. ettâvatâ kho âvuso imam dhammam sayam abhiññâ sacchikatvâ upasampajja pavadesîti (pavedemîti ?). aham pi kho âvuso ettâvatâ imam dhammam sayam abhiññâ sacchikatvâ upasampajja viharâmîti. lâbhâ no âvuso suladdham no âvuso ye mayam âyasmantam tâdisam sabrahmacârim passâma, iti yâham dhammam sayam abh. s. upasampajja pavedemi tam tvam dhammam sayam abh. s. upasampajja viharasi, yam tvam dhammam sayam abh. s. upasampajja viharasi tam aham dhammam sayam abh. s. upas. pavedemi, iti yâham dhammam jânâmi tam tvam dhammam jânâsi, yam tvam dhammam jânâsi tam aham dhammam jânâmi, iti yâdiso aham tâdiso tvam, yâdiso tvam tâdiso aham. ehi dâni âvuso ubho 'va santâ imam ganam pariharâmâ 'ti. iti kho bhikkhave Âlâro Kâlâmo âcariyo me samâno antevâsim samânam attano samasamam *th*apesi ulârâya ca mam pûjâya pûjesi. tassa mayham bhikkhave etad ahosi: nâyam dhammo nibbidâya na virâgâya na nirodhâya na upasamâya na abhiññâya na sambodhâya na nibbânâya samvattati yâvad eva âkiñcaññâyatanûpapattiyâ 'ti. so kho aham bhikkhave tam dhammam analamkaritvâ tasmâ dhammâ nibbijja pakkamim. so kho aham bhikkhave kimkusalagavesî anuttaram santivarapadam pariyesamâna yena Uddako Râmaputto ten' upasamkamim, upasamkamitvâ Uddakam Râmaputtam etad avocam: icchâm aham âvuso imasmim dhammavinaye brahmacariyam caritun ti. evam vutte bhikkhave Uddako Râmaputto mam etad avoca: viharâyasma, tâdiso ayam dhammo yattha viññû puriso na cirass' eva sakam âcariyakam sayam abhiññâ sacchikatvâ upasampajja vihareyyâ 'ti. so kho aham bhikkhave na cirass' eva khippam eva tam dhammam pariyâpunim. so kho aham bhikkhave tâvataken' eva o*tth*apahatamattena lapitalâpanamattena ñâ*n*â (sic) vadâmi theravâdañ ca jânâmi passâmîti pa*t*ijânâmi ahañ c'eva aññesam ca (sic). tassa mayham bhikkhave etad ahosi: na kho Râmo imam dhammam kevalam sabbâmantakena (sic) sayam abhiññâ sacchikatvâ upasampajja viharâmîti pavedesi, addhâ Râmo imam dhammam jânam passam vihâsîti. atha khv âham bhikkhave yena Uddako Râmaputto ten' upasamkamim, upasamkamitvâ Uddakam Râmaputtam etad avocam: kittâvatâ no âvuso Râmo (sic) imam dhammam sayam abhiññâ sacchikatvâ upasampajja pavedesîti. evam vutte bhikkhave Uddako Râmaputto nevasaññânâsaññâyatanam pavedesi. tassa mayham bhikkhave etad ahosi: na kho Râmass' eva ahosi saddhâ mayham p'atthi saddhâ (etc., the following, as above, is the story of Âlâra Kâlâma. Râmaputta finally says): ehi dâni âvuso tvam imam ganam pariharâ 'ti. iti kho bhikkhave Uddako Râmaputto sabrahmacârî samâno âcariyatthâne mamam thapesi ulârâya ca mam pûjâya pûjesi. tassa mayham bhikkhave etad ahosi: nâyam dhammo nibbidâya . . . samvattati yâvad eva nevasaññânâsaññâyatanûpapattiyâ 'ti. so kho aham bhikkhave tam dhammam analamkaritvâ tasmâ dhammâ nibbijja pakkamim. so kho aham bhikkhave kimkusalagavesî anuttaram santivarapadam pariyesamâno Magadhesu anupubbena cârikam caramâno yena Uruvelâ senânigamo tad avasarim. tatth' addasam ramaniyam bhûmibhâgam pâsâdikam ca vanasandam nadim ca sandantim setakam supatittham ramanîyam samantâ ca gocaragâmam. tassa mayham bhikkhave etad ahosi: ramanîyo vata bho bhûmibhâgo pâsâdiko ca vanasando nadî ca sandati setakâ supatitthâ ramanîyâ samantâ gocaragâmo alam ca tidam (sic) kulaputtassa padhânatthikassa padhânâyâ 'ti. so kho aham bhikkhave attanâ jâtidhammo (. . . jarâdhammo, vyâdhidhammo, maranadhammo, sokadhammo, samkilesadhammo . . .) samâno jâtidhamme (. . . jarâdhamme, etc.) âdînavam viditvâ ajâtam (. . . ajaram etc.) yogakkhemam nibbânam pariyesamâno ajâtam anuttaram yogakkhemam ajjhagamam . . . asamkilittham anuttaram yogakkhemam nibbânam ajjhagamam; ñânañ ca pana me dassanam udapâdi: akuppâ me cetovimutti, ayam antimâ jâti, n' atthi dâni punabbhavo 'ti. tassa mayham bhikkhave etad ahosi: adhigato kho me, etc. (*vide* "Mahavagga," i, 5, 2).

As a rule we find between the period of instruction by Âlâra and Uddaka and the attainment of Sambodhi, a description of the

Dukkarakârikâ inserted, which on the whole corresponds to what is narrated in "Lal. Vist.," p. 314 seq. (excepting naturally the episode referring to Mâyâ devî). Also the three Upamâs of "Lal. Vist.," p. 309 seq., are found already in the Pali-Tipi*t*aka (in the Mahâsaccakasutta).

I quote from the last named Sutta the close of this section which ends in the narration of the Sambodhi :—

So kho aha*m* Aggivessana o*l*ârika*m* âhâram âhâresi*m* odanakummâsa*m*. tena kho pana ma*m* Aggivessana samayena pañca bhikkhû paccupa*tth*itâ honti* yan no sama*n*o Gotamo dhamma*m* adhigamissati ta*m* no âcarissâma 'ti. yato kho aha*m* Aggivessana o*l*ârika*m* âhâra*m* âhâresi*m* odanakummâsa*m* atha kho te pañca bhikkhû nibbijja pakkami*m*su bâhuliko sama*n*o Gotamo padhânavibbhanto âvatto bâhullâyâ 'ti. so kho aha*m* Aggivessana o*l*ârika*m* âhâra*m* âharito (sic) bala*m* gahetvâ vivicc' eva kâmehi . . . (then follows the well known description of the attainment of the four Jhânas, then the attainment of the three Vijjâs—pubbenivâsaññâ*n*a*m*, dibba*m* cakkhu, dic ariyasacca—in the three Yâmas of the night; next:) tassa me eva*m* jânato eva*m* passato kâmâsavâpi citta*m* vimuccittha, bhavâsavâpi citta*m* vimuccittha, di*tth*âsavâpi c. v., avijjâsavâpi c. v., vimuttasmi*m* vimutt' amhîti ñâ*n*a*m* ahosi, khî*n*â me jâti, vusita*m* bramacariya*m*, kata*m* kara*n*îya*m*, nâpara*m* itthattâyâ 'ti abbhaññâsi*m*.

This is the usual description of the Sambodhi, as it is found also, *e.g.*, in the introduction to the Vibhaṅga ("Vinaya Pi*t*aka," iii, p. 4 seq.), in the Bhayabheravasutta ("Majjh. Nikaya"), and in the Dvedhâvitakkasutta (ibid). To the ancient Order the kernel and the sole essential to the event of Sambodhi (*i.e.*, the attainment of Buddhahood) appeared to be the springing forth of such and such a knowledge, and of such and such qualities in the mind of the Buddha, and nothing else.

This shows itself also in the somewhat abbreviated narratives of

* Cf. also "Mahâvagga," i, 6, 5, and specially with reference to Ko*nd*añña Apadana, fol. khe' :—

nikkhantenânupabbajji (sic), padhâna*m* sukata*m* mayâ,
kilese jhâpanatthâya pabbajji*m* (sic) anagâriya*m*.

a similar kind, in which the attainment of delivering knowledge by certain disciples, male and female, is described. Thus in the history of the Pupphacha*dd*aka (see above, p. 159, n. 1, "Thera-gâthâ," fol. kho—kho'):

so 'ha*m* eko araññasmi*m* viharanto atandito
akâsi[*m*] satthu vacana*m* yathâ ma*m* ovadi jino.
rattiyâ pa*th*ama*m* yâma*m* pubbajâti*m* anussari[*m*],
rattiyâ majjhima*m* yama*m* dibbacakkhu*m* visodhayi*m*,
rattiyâ pacchime yâme tamokhandha*m* padâlayi*m*.
tato ratyâ vivasâne* suriyuggamana*m* pati
Indo Brahmâ ca âgantvâ ma*m* namassi*m*su añjali:
namo te purisâjañña, namo te purisuttama,
yassa te âsavâ khî*n*â, dakkhi*n*eyy' asi mârisa.

Similarly in the verses of the Vijayâ, "Therîgâthâ," fol. gha*m*:

bhikkhunî† upasa*m*kamma sakkacca*m* paripucch' aha*m*,
sâ me dhamma*m* adesesi dhâtuâyatanâni ca.
cattâri ariyasaccâni indriyâni balâni ca
bojjhaṅga*tth*aṅgika*m* magga*m* uttamatthassa pattiyâ.
tassâha*m* vacana*m* sutvâ karontî anusâsani*m*
rattiyâ purime yâme pubbajâti*m* anussari*m*,
rittiyâ majjhime yâme dibbacakkhu*m* visodhayi*m*,
rattiyâ pacchime yâme tamokkhandha*m* padâlayi*m*,
pîtisukhena ca kâya*m* pharitvâ vihari*m* tadâ;
sattamiyâ pâde pasâremi, tamokkhandha*m* padâlayi [*m*].

Compare also the narrative of the Jainas couched throughout in similar style, of how Mahâvîra obtained the delivering knowledge, "Jinacaritra," p. 64, ed. Jacobi.

I here insert the prophecy of the Buddha Dîpa*m*kara regarding Gotama's Buddhahood, contained in the Buddhava*m*sa (fol. ci' of the Phayre MS.):

padhâna*m* padahitvâna katvâ dukkarakârika*m*
Ajapâlarukkhamûlasmi*m* nisîditvâ tathâgato

* So the MS.; originally it may have been vivasâno.
† Lege: bhikkhuni*m*.

tattha pâyâsa*m* paggayha (comp. "Jat.," i, p. 69) Nerañjaram upehiti.
Nerañjarâya tîramhi pâyâsam adaso jino
pa*t*iyattavaramaggena bodhimûlam upehiti,
tato padakkhi*nam* katvâ bodhima*nd*am anuttaro
assattharukkhamûlamhi bujjhissati mahâyaso.

The narratives of Mara's attacks do not stand in the sacred texts in immediate connection with the history of the attainment of Sambodhi. *Before* the Sambodhi is placed that conversation recited in the Padhânasutta ("Sutta Nipata," p. 69 of Fausböll's translation), of which a northern Buddhist version, pretty closely corresponding with the Pâli text, occurs in the metrical portion of the "Lalita Vistara," pp. 327–329. *After* the Sambodhi, within the period which Buddha passed under the tree Ajapâla, falls the similar narrative of the Mâra Sa*m*yutta ("Sa*m*y. Nikâya," vol. i, fol. ghî–ghû; here after the temptation by Mâra comes that by his daughters).

As regards the historical trustworthiness of the traditions, which relate to the period intervening between Buddha's flight from his home and the commencement of his public career, I am inclined to recognize in the leading points therein mentioned real facts. The names of Â*l*âra Kâlâma and Uddaka Râmaputta are as trustworthy as possible; if there had here been an intention to invent, more famous names would have been preferably furnished, names of teachers, who have adopted later on a pronounced attitude, whether friendly or hostile, to Buddha's own public operations. Â*l*âra, as far as I know, besides being named in this connection, is elsewhere mentioned only in the "Mahâparinibb. Sutta," p. 44; of Uddaka also we hear but little.*

* "Sa*m*y. Nik.," vol. ii, fol. ghî': Uddako suda*m* bikkhave Râmaputto eva*m* vâca*m* bhâsati: ida*m* jâtu vedagû ida*m* jâtu sabbaji ida*m* jâtu apalikhita*m* ga*nd*a-mûla*m* palikha*n*iti.—"Pâsâdikasutta" ("Dîgha-N."): Uddako suda*m* Cunda Râmaputto eva*m* vâca*m* bhâsati: passa*m* na passatîti. ki*m* ca passa*m* na passatîti? khurassa sâdhunissitassa talam assa passati dhârañ ca khv assa na passati, ida*m* vuccati Cunda passa*m* na passatîti.—The relations of the râjâ Eleyya to the sama*n*a Râmaputta are mentioned at "Añg. Nik.," vol. i, fol. ti.

THIRD EXCURSUS.

APPENDICES AND AUTHORITIES TOUCHING SOME MATTERS OF THE BUDDHIST DOGMATIC.

1. The Nirvâ*n*a.

In order to clearly set forth the dogmatic terminology of the Nirvâ*n*a doctrine, we must first of all go into the categories of the Anupâdisesanibbâna and of the Saupâdisesanibbâna (Nirvâ*n*a respectively without and with a residuum of "Upâdi"). Childers has, as is known ("Dict.," pp. 267, 526), propounded the theory that by Saupâdisesanibbâna is meant the condition of the perfect saint, in whom the five Khandas are still to the fore, but the desire which chains to being is extinct; Anupâdisesanibbâna, on the other hand, is said to designate the cessation of all being, the condition or non-condition ensuing on the death of the saint.

To the criticism, adverse to this view, which I propose to advance, I premise a collection of relevant passages from the texts.

In connection with the notion of Nirvâ*n*a the following outwardly similarly sounding expressions occur:—Upadhi; upâdâna connected with upâda, upâdâya, and anupâdâna con. with anupâdâ, anupâdâya; lastly upâdisesa, saupâdisesa and anupâdisesa. I give a few of the most important passages for each of these termini in order.

First for Upadhi.

Sunakkhattasuttanta (in the "Majjh. N."):—

So vata Sunakkhatta bhikkhu chasu phassâyatanesu sa*m*vutakârî upadhi dukkhassa mûlan ti iti viditvâ nirupadhi upadhisa*m*khaye vimutto upadhismi*m* vâ kâya*m* upasa*m*harissati citta*m* vâ anuppadassanti (mel. °dassati): n' eta*m* *th*âna*m* vijjati.

"Sa*m*yuttaka Nikâya," vol. i, fol. ñau' of the Phayre MS.:—

ya*m* kho ida*m* anekavidha*m* nânappakâraka*m* dukkha*m* loke uppajjati jarâmara*n*a*m* ida*m* kho dukkha*m* upadhinidâna*m* upadhisamudaya*m* upadhijâtika*m* upadhipabhava*m*; upadhismi*m* sati jarâmara*n*a*m* hoti; . . . upadhi panâya*m* ki*m*nidânâ etc.? upadhi ta*n*hânidâno ta*n*hâsamudayo etc.

"Itivuttaka," fol. kâh of the Phayre MS.:—

tisso imâ bhikkhave dhâtuyo. katamâ tisso? rûpadhâtu arupadhâtu nirodhadhâtu. ime (lege: imâ) kho bhikkhave tisso dhâtuyo 'ti.

rûpadhâtupariññâya arûpesu asa*n*th*i*tâ
nirodhe ye vimuñcanti (°ccanti?) te janâ paccuhâyino 'ti (maccuhâyino?)
kâyena amata*m* dhâtu*m* phusayitvâ nirûpadhi
upadhipa*t*inissagga*m* sacchikatvâna anâsavo
desesi sammâsambuddho asoka*m* virâja*m* padan ti.

"Sa*m*yuttaka N.," vol. i, fol. ki (=Suttanipâta, Dhaniyasutta.
The first distich is put in the mouth of Mâra):—

nandati puttehi puttimâ gomâ gobhi tath' eva nandati;
upadhîhi narassa nandanû na hi so nandati yo nirûpadhîti.
socati puttehi puttimâ gomâ gohi tath' eva socati;
upadhîhi narassa socanâ na hi so socati yo nirûpadhîti.

"Sa*m*yuttaka N.," vol. i, fol. ghâ':—

yo dukkha*m* addakkhi yatonidâna*m* kâmesu so jantu katha*m* nameyya?
upadhi*m* viditvâ sa*m*go 'ti loke tass' eva jantu vinayâya sikkhe 'ti.

Ibid. fol. ghu' (Buddha is speaking to Mârâ):

amaccudheyya*m* pucchanti ye janâ pâragâmino
tes' âha*m* pu*tth*o akkhâmi ya*m* taccha*m* ta*m* nirûpadhin ti.

Ibid. fol. ghu' (Mâra's daughters approach, tempting the Buddha):

atha kho bhagavâ na manas' âkâsi yathâ ta*m* anuttare upadhisa*m*khaye vimutto.

"Mahâniddesa," Phayre MS., fol. ko:—

katamo upadhiviveko? upadhî vuccanti kilesâ ca khandhâ ca abhisa*m*khârâ ca. upadhiviveko vuccati amata*m* nibbâna*m*.

Cf. also "Mahâvagga," i, 5, 2; 22, 4. 5; 24, 3; v, 13, 10; "Cullavagga," vi, 4, 4; "Dhammap. A*tth*ak.," p. 270; Burnouf, "Introd.," p. 591 seq.; M. Müller on the "Dhammapada," 418; Davids's and my note to the translation of the "Mahâvagga," i, 5, 2.

For Upâdâna and the termini connected therewith the following passage will suffice:—

"Majjhima Nikâya," fol. khai' (Turnour's MS.):—cattâr' imâni bhikkhave upâdânâni. katamâni cattâri. kamupâdânam di*tth*upâdânam silabbatupâdânam attavâdupâdânam.—Cf. "Mahânidâna Sutta," p. 248, ed. Grimblot.

"Sa*m*yuttaka Nikâya," vol. ii, fol. to seq.:—It is related that "sambahulâna*m* aññatitthiyasama*n*abrâhma*n*aparibbâjakâna*m* kutûhalasâlâna*m* sannisinnâna*m*" the conversation turned on this, that each of the six other teachers (Pûra*n*a Kassapa, etc.) "sâvaka*m* abbhatita*m* kâla*m*kata*m* upapattîsu byâkaroti asu amutra upapanno asu amutra upapanno 'ti, yo pi 'ssa sâvako uttamapuriso paramapuriso paramapattipatto tam pi sâvaka*m* abbhatita*m* kâla*m*kata*m* upapattîsu byâkaroti asu amutra upapanno asu amutra upapanno 'ti." Buddha, on the contrary, does the same only with regard to the other Sâvakas, "yo ca khv assa sâvako uttamapuriso—pa—asu amutra upapanno 'ti (sic!) api ca kho na*m* eva*m* byâkaroti acchejji ta*n*ha*m* vivattayi saññojana*m* sammâmânâbhisamayâ (sic) antam akâsi dukkhassâ 'ti." The Paribbâjaka Vacchagotta addresses to Buddha a request for the clearing up of this point. Buddha answers: "alañ hi Vaccha kaṅkhitu*m* ala*m* vicikicchitu*m*. kaṅkhânîyo ca pana te *th*âno vicikicchâ uppannâ. saupâdânassa khv âha*m* Vaccha upapatti*m* paññâpemi no anupâdânassa. seyyathâpi Vaccha aggi saupâdâno jalati no anupâdâno evam eva khv âha*m* Vaccha saupâdânassa upapatti*m* paññâpemi no anupâdânassâ 'ti. yasmi*m* bho Gotama samaye acchi vâtena khittâ dûram pi gacchati imissâ pana bhava*m* Gotamo ki*m* upâdânasmi*m* paññâpetîti. yasmi*m* kho Vaccha samaye acchi vâtena khittâ dûra*m* pi gacchati tam aha*m* vâtupâdâna*m* paññâpemi, vâto hi 'ssâ Vaccha tassi*m* samaye upâdâna*m* hotîti. yasmi*m* bho Gotama samaye imañ ca kâya*m* nikkhipati satto ca aññatara*m* kâya*m* anupapanno hoti, imassa pana bhava*m* Gotamo ki*m* upâdânasmi*m* paññâpetîti. yasmi*m* kho Vaccha samaye imassa (sic) kâya*m* nikkhipati satto ca aññatara*m* kâya*m* anupapanno hoti, tam aha*m* ta*n*hupâdâna*m* vadâmi, ta*n*hâ hi 'ssa Vaccha tasmi*m* samaye apâdâna*m* hotîti."

"Mahâpu*nn*amâya Suttanta" ("Majjhima Nikâya"):—

ime pana bhante pañcupâdânakkhandhâ kimmûlakâ 'ti. ime kho bhikkhu pañcupâdânakkhandhâ chandamûlakâ 'ti. tam yeva nu kho bhante upâdânam te pañcupâdânakkhandhâ udâhu aññatra pañcupâdânakkhandhehi upâdânam ti. na kho bhikkhu tam yeva upâdânam pañcupâdânam pañcupâdânakkhandhassa* na pi aññatra pañcupâdânakkhandhei [upâdânam]. upâdânam kho bhikkhu pañcupâdânakkhandhesu chandarâgo, tamtattha upâdânan ti.

We may mention in this connection also the place which the category of Upâdâna occupies in the causality formula: tanhâpaccayâ upâdânam.

"Samy. N." vol. ii, fol. ghe: samyojaniye ca bhikkhave dhamme desissâmi samyojanañ ca, tam sunâtha. katame ca bhikkhave samyojaniyâ dhammâ katamañ ca samyojanam. cakkhum bhikkhave samyojaniyo dhammo; yo tattha chandarâgo tam tattha samyojanam.—So on the other organs of sense to the mano. Then the Text goes on: upâdâniye ca bhikkhave dhamme desissâmi upâdânañ ca, tam sunâtha. There follows exactly the same detail.†

"Samy. N." vol. ii, fol. ña. It is related that Sakka Devânaminda puts the question: ko nu kho khante hetu ko paccayo yenam idh' ekacce sattâ ditth eva dhamme no parinibbâyanti, ko pana bhante hetu ko paccayo yenam idhekacce sattâ dittheva dhamme parinibbâyantîti.—The answer runs: santi kho Devânaminda cakkhuviññeyyâ rûpâ itthâ kantâ manâpâ piyarûpâ kâmopasamhitâ rajaniyâ. tañ ce bhikkhu abhinandati abhivadati ajjhosâya titthati tassa tam abhinandato abhivadato ajjhosâya titthato tamnissitam viññânam hoti tadupâdânam: saupâdâno Devânaminda bhikkhu no

* So the Turnour MS.

† Consequently the two words Upâdâna and Samyojana are synonymous. With this it is consistent, when on the one hand beings whirled along in the cycle of existence are designated as tanhâsamyojana, on the other hand tanhâ is termed an Upâdâna (in the quoted dialogue with Vaccha). Also the four Upâdânas, so named κατ' ἐξοχήν (kâma, ditthi, sîlabbata, attavâda), recur with tolerable exactness in the series of the ten Samyojana, where we meet the ideas, kâmarâga, avijjâ, sîlabbataparâmâsa, and sakkâyaditthi. The last is considered to be identical with attavâda (Childers s. v. sakkâya) and as a fact virtually comes to the same thing.

parinibbâyati — la — santi kho Devânaminda jivhâviññeyyâ rasâ (etc., down to manoviññeyyâ dha*m*mâ). aya*m* kho Devânaminda hetu aya*m* paccayo yenam idh' ekacce sattâ di*tth*eva dhamme no parinibbâyanti. santi kho Devânaminda cakkhuviññeyyâ rûpâ etc.; tañ ce bhikkhu nâbhinandati nâbhivadati na ajjhosâya ti*tth*ati tassa ta*m* anabhinandato anabhivadato no ajjhosâya ti*tth*ato na ta*m*nissita*m* viññâ*n*a*m* hoti na tadupâdâna*m*; anupâdâno Devânaminda bhikkhu parinibbâyati.

"Â*n*añjasappâya Suttanta" ("Majjh. Nikâya"):

. . . eva*m* vutte âyasmâ Ânando bhagavantam etad avoca: idha bhante bhikkhu eva*m* pa*t*ipanno hoti: no c' assa no ca me siyo na bhavissati na me bhavissati yad atthi, ya*m* bhûta*m* ta*m* pajahâmîti upekha*m* pa*t*iabhati. parinibbâyi)* nu kho so bhante bhikkhû 'ti? app etth' ekacco Ânanda bhikkhu parinibbâyeyya app etth' ekacco bhikkhu na parinibbâyeyya 'ti. ko nu kho khante hetu ko paccayo yena app etth' ekacco bhikkhu parinibbâyeyya app etth' ekacco bhikkhu na parinibbâyeyyâ 'ti. idhânanda bhikkhu eva*m* pa*t*ipanno hoti: no c' assa . . . ta*m* pajahâmîti upekha*m* pa*t*ilabhati. so ta*m* upekha*m* abhinandati abhivadati ajjhosâya ti*tth*ati, tassa ta*m* upekha*m* abhinandato . . .†) na parinibbâyatîti. kaha*m* pana so bhante bhikkhu upâdiyatîti. nevasaññânâsaññâyatana*m* Ânandâ 'ti. upâdânase*tth*a*m* kira so bhante bhikkhu upâdiyamâno upâdiyatîti. upâdânase*tth*a*m* so Ânanda bhikkhu upâdiyamâno upâdiyati; upâdânase*tth*a*m* h'eta*m* Ânandâ yad ida*m* nevasaññânâsaññâyatana*m*.‡

"Pañcattaya Suttanta" ("Majjh. N."). Of a "ekacco sama*n*o vâ brâhma*n*o vâ" it is said: "santo 'ham asmi nibbuto 'ham asmi anupâdâno 'ham asmîti samanupassati." Of this the Tathâgata says: addhâ ayam âyasmâ nibbâna*m* sappâyañ ñeva pa*t*ipada*m* abhivadati, atha ca paññya*m* bhava*m* samaño vâ brâhma*n*o vâ pubbantânudi*tth*im vâ upâdiyamâno upâdiyati aparantânudi*tth*im vâ up.

* Probably the Adj. parinibbâyî should be placed here, which we have in antarâparinibbâyî, etc.

† As above, p. 430.

‡ Now follows in exactly corresponding fashion the opposite case, where a Bhikkhu "ta*m* upekha*m* nâbhinandati;" anupâdâno Ânanda bhikkhu parinibbâyati.

up. kâmasaññojanam* vâ up. up. pavivekam vâ pîtim up. up. nirâmisam vâ sukham up. up. adukkhamasukham vâ vedanam up. up.; yañ ca kho ayam âyasmâ santo 'ham asmi nibbâno (sic) 'ham asmi anupâdâno 'ham asmîti samanupassati tad ap' imassa bhoto samanabrâhmanassa upâdânam akkhâyati.

From the "Rathavinîta Sutta" ("Majjh. Nik."): kimatthañ carah' âvuso bhagavati brahmacariyam vussatîti. anupâdâparinibbânattham kho bhagavati brahmacariyam vussatîti. kim nu kho âvuso sîlavisuddhi anupâdâparinibbânan ti. no h' idam âvuso. kim panâvuso cittavisuddhi — ditthivisuddhi — kaṅkhâvitaranavisuddhi — maggâmaggañânadassanavisuddhi—patipadâñânadassanavisuddhi anupâdâparinibbânan ti. no h' idam âvuso. kin nu kho âvuso ñânadassanavisuddhi anupâdâparinibbânan ti. no h' idam âvuso. kim panâvuso aññatra imehi dhammehi anupâdâparinibbânan ti. no h' idam âvuso. . . . yathâkatham panâvuso imassa bhâsitassa attho datthabbo 'ti. sîlavisuddhim ce âvuso bhagavâ anupâdâparinibbânam paññâpessa saupâdânam yeva samânam anupâdâparinibbânam paññâpessa. ditthivisuddhim . . . ñânadassanavisuddhim ce âvuso bhagavâ anupâdâparinibbânam paññâpessa saupâdânam yeva samânam anupâdâparinibbânam paññâpessa. aññatrañ ca† âvuso imehi dhammehi anupâdâparinibbânam abhavissa, puthujjano parinibbâyeyya, puthujjano âvuso aññatra imehi dhammehi.—Then follows the comparison of the journey of the king Pasenadi from Sâvatthi to Sâketa; he has relays (rathavinîta) lying between the two towns and arrives "sattamena rathavinîtena" at this palace in Sâketa. Evam eva kho âvuso sîlavisuddhi yâvad eva cittavisuddhattham . . . ñânadassanavisuddhi yâvad eva anupâdâparinibbânattham. anupâdâparinibbânattham kho âvuso bhagavati brahmacariyam vussatîti.

Buddhavamsa: nibbâyi anupâdâno yath' agg' upâdânasamkhayâ.

Cf. also "Dhammap." v. 89; "Mahâvagga," v, 1, 24 seq. Burnouf, "Intr." p. 495 seq., and so on.

Before we proceed to give evidences bearing on the expressions

* Kâmasaññojanânam the Turnour MS., which I follow in quoting this passage.

† So the Turnour MS.

Saupâdisesa and Anupâdisesa, we shall attempt to briefly point out the dogmatic signification of Upâdâna and Upadhi. These ideas are almost synonymous. The attainment or non-attainment of Nirvâ*n*a, victory or defeat in the struggle against suffering is made dependent upon the presence or non-presence of Upâdâna and quite as much so of Upadhi. In one of the above cited passages of the Sa*m*yuttaka Nikâya there is given a series of members which are joined together by causal nexus: From Ta*n*hâ comes Upadhi, from Upadhi comes old age, death, suffering. In exactly the same way the well-known formula of the twelve Nidânas makes Upâdâna come from Ta*n*hâ, and from Upâdâna (through a few middle links) old age, death, suffering. The difference between Upadhi and Upâdâna is further diminished, when we remember that beside the Upadhi of the Buddhist texts there occurs in the philosophic Sanscrit texts an Upadhi ("Colebroke Misc. Ess." I[2], 308 etc.) and also the participle Upahita.* Upa-dhâ signifies "to lay one thing on another, to give it a support," thus, of anything which would so to speak float in the air or fly about, to chain it to reality by a substratum, which is given to it to localize it. This substratum is exactly Upadhi. Upa-dâ or Upâ-dâ (middle), on the other hand, is "to lay hold of anything, to cling to anything," as the flame catches the fuel; this fuel, or that laid hold of by a being, to which it clings, as well as the act of this catching, is Upâdâna. It is clear, that in this way Upadhi and Upâdâna, although the ideas underlying them differ, must still acquire significations for Buddhist terminology, which cover each other or at least very nearly touch.

We shall now treat of the third of these closely connected ideas, that of Upâdi, which is known only in the compounds Sopâdisesa and Anupâdisesa.

"Itivuttaka," fol. kau of the Phayre MS.: vutta*m* h' eta*m* bhagavatâ vutta*m* arahatâ 'ti me suta*m*. dve 'mâ bhikkhave nibbânadhâtuyo. katamâ dve. saupâdisesâ ca nibbânadhâtu anupâdisesâ ca nibbânadhâtu. katamâ ca bhikkhave saupâdisesâ nibbânadhâtu? idha bhikkhave bhikkhu araha*m* hoti khî*n*âsavo

* It is characteristic in this connection, that in Sanscrit upadhi and upâdhi are exactly equivalent in the sense of "deceit."

vusitavâ katakaraṇîyo ohitabhâro anuppattasadttho* parikkhîṇabhavasaṃyojano sammadaññâvimutto. tassa tiṭṭhant' exa pañc' indriyâni yesaṃ avighâtattâ manâpaṃ paccanubhoti sukhadukkhaṃ paṭisaṃvediyati. tassa kho râgakkhayo dosakkhayo mohakkhayo. ayaṃ vuccati bhikkhave saupâdisesâ nibbânadhâtu. katamâ ca bhikkhave anupâdisesâ nibbânadhâtu? idha bhikkhave bhikkhu arahaṃ hoti . . . . sammadaññâvimutto. tassa idh' eva bhikkhave vedayitâni† anabhinanditâni sîtibhavissanti. ayaṃ vuccati bhikkhave anupâdisesâ nibbânadhâtu. imâ kho bhikkhave dve nibbânadhâtuyo 'ti. etam atthaṃ bhagavâ avoca. tatth' etaṃ itivuccati:—

> dve imâ cakkhumatâ pakâsitâ nibbânâdhâtu‡ anissitena tâdinâ:
> ekâ hi dhâtu idha diṭṭhadhammikâ saupâdisesâ bhavanettisaṃkhayâ,
> anupâdisesâ pana samparâyikâ yamhi nirujjhanti bhavâni sabbaso. |
> ye etad aññaya paraṃ§ asaṃkhataṃ vimutticittâ|| bhavanettisaṃkhayâ
> te dhammâ sârâdhikammakkhare¶ yathâ pahaṃsu te sabbabhavânitâdino 'ti. |

ayaṃ pi attho vutto bhagavatâ iti me sutan ti.

It is clear, that the chapter of the Itivuttaka here given supports throughout the already referred to theory of Childers. He who attains holiness, attains the Nirvâṇa; this is, as long as his earthly life still continues, saupâdisesa; the body, the sense-perceptions, and so on, are still present. When these also vanish, in the death of the saint, that is, his being thereby enters on the anupâdisesâ nibbânadhâtu.*

* anuppattapadatto the MS. † devayitâni the MS.

‡ So the MS. § saraṃ the MS.

|| Perhaps vimuttacittâ as an emendation.

¶ I cannot venture an emendation without further MS. materials. Apparently, considering the interchange of r and y so frequent in Burmese MSS., we should read kammakkhaye.

* So also the commentary on the "Dhammapada," p. 278 (cf. p. 196).

It must be in the highest degree astonishing that the limit between saupâdisesa and anupâdisesa is here removed to a wholly different place from the limit between saupâdâna and anupâdâna, or between the state of the nirupadhi and the burdened with upadhi. In the two last named cases we had to do with the ethical opposition of the internally bound and the internally free; in the case now before us, on the other hand, we could only have, according to the view of Childers and the passage quoted from the Itivuttaka, to do with the physical opposition of the internally free, whose external life still continues, and the internally free, whose external life has ceased. It is really very hard to believe that, of the three pairs of ideas which all belong to the Nirvâ*n*a doctrine, and which at first sight present an appearance of so close a parallelism, the third should actually have in view a point so thoroughly different from the first two, that the "anupâdisesâ nibbânadhâtu" should imply something wholly different from "anupâdâya citta*m* vimucci" or "anupadhisa*m*-khaye vimutto."

Notwithstanding, I should not venture to build only on considerations of this kind the supposition, that the meaning clearly and expressly given in the Itivuttaka to sa- and anupâdisesa does not express the true or the original doctrine of Buddhism: yet the canonical texts themselves give us further points, which strengthen the scruples we entertain against the testimony of the Itivuttaka.

In the "Satipa*tth*ânasutta" ("Majjh. N.") we read: yo hi koci bhikkhave bhikkhu ime cattâro satipa*tth*âne eva*m* bhâveyya satta vassâni* tassa dvinna*m* phalâna*m* aññatara*m* phala*m* pâ*t*ikaṅkhâ: di*tth*eva dhamme aññâ sati vâ upâdisese anâgâmitâ.

As is known, he who is born again as Anâgâmî, has still a small residue of sinful nature in him, from which to purify himself in the celestial existence, upon which he enters, is allotted to him. In the passage we have quoted, then, the Saupâdisesa is not, as in the Itivuttaka, he who is pure from sins, who remains still in the earthly state, but he who is burdened with a residuum of sin,

* It is afterwards stated that a still shorter time suffices.

who is re-born into a deified state. And the fully pure, still lingering on earth "ditthe va dhamme" is in one passage exactly the person in whom an Upâdisesa is no longer present. Thus Upâdisesa here has not the physical meaning of a residuum of earthly existence, but the ethical meaning of a residuum of impurity, the same signification which we have found in Upâdâna and Upadhi.

To the passage already quoted we add a proof, which we take from the "Vañgîsa Sutta" (Nigrodhakappa Sutta), a text* included in the "Sutta Nipâta." This Sutta begins: Evam me sutam. ekam samayam bhagavâ Âlaviyam viharati Aggâlave cetiye. tena kho pana samayena âyasmato Vañgîsassa upajjhâyo Nigrodhakappo nâma thero Aggâlave cetiye aciraparinibbuto hoti. atha kho âyasmato Vañgîsassa rahogatassa patisallînassa evam cetaso parivitakko udapâdi: parinibbuto nu kho me upajjhâyo udâhu no parinibbuto 'ti.†—Buddha is asked: Has the Brahmacariyam, in which he has lived, brought him any advantage? "Nibbâyi so âdu saupâdiseso; yathâ vimutto ahu tam sunoma." And Buddha replies:

Acchecchi tanham idha nâmarûpe 'ti bhagavâ, tanhâya‡ sotam dîgharattânusayitam
atâri jâtimaranam asesam icc abravî bhagavâ pañcasettho.

Here also the alternative is put in a way which does not harmonize with Childers's conception. "Has he entered into Nirvâna or is he Saupâdisesa?" Buddha is asked concerning a monk whose death had been announced. Saupâdisesa must consequently be he, who, on account of a not yet complete freedom from sinful nature, cannot yet become partaker of the Nirvâna.

Finally decisive are the data, which the Sunakkhatta Suttanta ("Majjhima Nikâya") supplies. It uses the expression, in the eluci-

* See Fausböll's Translation of the "Sutta Nipâta," p. 57 seq. Cf. also the "Kalahavivâdasutta," v, 15 (ibidem, p. 167).

† *I.e.*, as also the further detail clearly shows: the fact that Nigrodhakappa died, is known to him, but he does not know whether he is still liable to re-birth or not.

‡ So clearly the MS. of the Phayre collection consulted by me. Fausböll "Kanha's (*i.e.*, Mâra's) stream."

dation of which we are engaged, in reference to conditions of material life. A man, it is said in a parable, is wounded with a poisoned arrow. A physician treats his wound, "apaneyya visadosa*m* saupâdisesa*m** anupâdiseso ti maññamâno." He therefore treats the poison as having been overcome, while really a remnant of the poisonous stuff is still present in the patient. In opposition to this is placed a second case, where the danger has been fully overcome: "apaneyya visadosa*m* anupâdisesa*m* anupâdiseso ti jânamâno." The first patient thinks himself cured, lives carelessly, and so falls a victim to his wound. The second patient lives carefully and makes a complete recovery. While then the spiritual meaning of this parable is being unfolded, the expression nirupadhi occurs in place of the expression anupâdiseso. Of the monk who perseveres successfully, to whom the second of the two patients is compared, it is said: so vata Sunakkhatta bhikkhu chasu phassâyatanesu sa*m*vutakârî upadhi dukkhassa mûlan ti iti viditvâ nirupadhi upadhisa*m*khaye vimutto upadhismi*m* vâ kâya*m* upasa*m*harissati citta*m* vâ anuppadassati†: n'eta*m* *thâna*m vijjati. — Thus it is apparent that here also saupâdisesa and anupâdisesa point to the presence or absence of a last remnant of deadly peril in a spiritual sense, and the passage establishes at the same time the identity of the upâdi contained in this word with the word upadhi. Now, as is well known, the anupâdisesa of the Pâli in the northern Buddhist texts corresponds with anupadhiçesha or nirupadhiçesha (Burnouf, "Intr." 590). In the same way reads a Sanscritified Singhalese inscription of the twelfth cent. A.D. ("Ind. Antiquary," 1877, p. 326): nirupadhiçeshanirvvâ*n*adhâtuwen. We shall from these considerations have no scruple in declaring the problematic upâdi to be only a spelling of the word upadhi peculiar to the Pâli—probably we should rather say, peculiar to our modern Pâli manuscripts. The origin of this orthography, if we consider the significant fact that this upâdi occurs only in connection with sesa, is not hard to account for. As the Pâli manuscripts write the name of the god Skanda Khandha obviously under the influence of Khandha = Sansk. skandha, or as the Sansk. sm*ri*ti is written

* Visadosa upâdisese the MS.

† Anuppadassanti the MS.

sammuti in the Pâli, under the influence of the word sammuti "nomination," so, it appears to me, the manuscript tradition of the Pâli has caused the word anupadhisesa to resemble the word sa*m*ghâdisesa so very familiar to all copyists of sacred texts, probably by the co-operation of the influence of anupâdâya, and thus has arisen the orthography anupâdisesa.

That, if this supposition be correct, then also the signification of sa- and anupâdisesa, corresponding to that of upadhi, must be: "one with whom there is, or is not, respectively, still present a remnant of earthly, sinful nature," is self-apparent. How it has come to pass that a so thoroughly different meaning has been given to both terms in the Itivuttaka, can naturally not be explained otherwise than by conjecture. It appears to me, that the expression anupâdisesâ nibbânadhâtu, which contains in fact a tautology —for the nibbânadhâtu implies the absence of upadhi— might by its form easily suggest to a misinformed mind the opposition of a saupâdisesâ nibbânadhâtu, while the word saupâdisesa, rightly comprehended, as we have pointed out from the Satipa*tth*âna Sutta and the Vañgîsa Sutta, excludes the idea of Nirvâ*n*a. But if once this adjective had been employed regarding the nibbânadhâtu by an error like that we have supposed, if once the opposition of an anupâdisesâ and a saupâdisesâ nibbânadhâtu had been set up, then it was scarcely possible to attach a more passable meaning to these words, than that given to them in the Itivuttaka.

The preceding explanation regarding the expressions, in which the main difficulty of the Nirvâ*n*a terminology lies, has already given us occasion to quote a series of the passages of the canonical texts relevant to this doctrine. We shall now proceed to set forth in the Pâli text the more essential of the materials upon which our previously expounded (antea, pp. 267 seq.) view of the Nirvâ*n*a doctrine rests, and therewith also some passages which we have given above in translation.*

In the "Sa*m*yuttaka Nikâya" there comes after the above quoted (p. 429) passage on the conversation of Buddha with Vacchagotta

* Reference may here also be made to the communication of Dr. O. Frankfurter, in the "Journ. R. Asiatic Soc.," Oct. 1880.

paribbâjaka, the following (cf. antea, p. 272 seq.): Atha kho Vacchagotto paribbâjako yena bhagavâ ten' upasa*m*kami, upasa*m*kamitvâ bhagavatâ saddhi*m* sammodi, sammodanîyam katha*m* sâra*n*îya*m* vîtisâretvâ ekamanta*m* nisîdi, ekamanta*m* nisinno Vacchagotto paribbâjako bhagavanta*m* etad avoca: ki*m* nu kho bho Gotama atth' attâ 'ti. eva*m* vutte bhagavâ tu*n*hî ahosi. ki*m* pana bho Gotama n' atth' attâ 'ti. dutiyam pi kho bhagavâ tu*n*hî ahosi. atha kho Vacchagotto paribbâjako u*tth*âyâsanâ pakkâmi. atha kho âyasmâ Ânando acirapakkante Vacchagotte paribbâjake bhagavanta*m* etad avoca: ki*m* nu kho bhante bhagavâ Vacchagottassa paribbâjakassa pañha*m* pu*tth*o na byâkâsîti. aha*ñ* c' Ânanda Vacchagottassa paribbâjakassa atth' attâ 'ti pu*tth*o samâno atth' attâ 'ti byâkareyya*m*, ye te Ânanda sama*n*abrâhma*n*â sassatavâdâ tesa*m* eta*m* saddha*m* abhavissati*. aha*ñ* c' Ânanda Vacchagottassa parribbâjakassa n' atth' attâ 'ti pu*tth*o samâno n' atth' attâ 'ti byâkareyya*m*, ye te Ânanda sama*n*abrâhma*n*â ucchedavâdâ tesa*m* eta*m*† abhavissa. aha*ñ* c' Ânanda Vacchagottassa . . . atth' attâ 'ti byâkareyya*m*, api nu me ta*m* Ânanda anuloma*m* abhavissa ñâ*n*assa upâdâya‡ sabbe dhammmâ anattâ 'ti. no h' eta*m* bhante. aha*ñ* c' Ânanda . . . n'atth' attâ 'ti byâkareyya*m*, sa*m*mû*lh*assa Ananda Vacchagottassa paribbâjakassa bhiyyosammohâya abhavissa ahuvâ me nanu pubbe attâ so etarahi n'atthîti.

"Sa*m*yuttaka Nikâya," vol. ii, fol. *no*. seq. (cf. antea, p. 278 seq.):

Eka*m* samaya*m* bhagavâ Sâvatthiya*m* viharati Jetavane Anâtha pi*n*dikassa ârâme. tena kho pana samayena Khemâ bhikkhunî Kosalesu cârika*m* caramânâ antarâ ca Sâvatthim antarâ ca Sâketa*m* Tora*n*avatthusmi*m* vâsa*m* upagatâ hoti. atha kho râjâ Pasenadi Kosalo Sâketâ Sâvatthi*m* gacchanto antarâ ca Sâketa*m* antarâ ca Sâvatthi*m* Tora*n*avatthusmi*m* ekarattivâsa*m* upagacchi. atha kho râjâ Pasenadi Kosalo aññatara*m* purisa*m* âmantesi: ehi tva*m* ambho purisa Tora*n*avatthusmi*m* tathârûpa*m* sama*n*a*m* vâ brâhma*n*a*m* vâ jâna yam aha*m* ajja payirupâseyyan ti. eva*m* devâ 'ti kho so puriso

* So the MS.; lege abhavissa. On saddha*m* cf. Abhidhân. 1147.

† Here undoubtedly saddha*m* is to be inserted. ‡ Lege uppâdâya.

rañño Pasenadissa Kosalassa pa*t*isutvâ kevalakappa*m* Tora*n*avatthu*m* ahi*nd*anto nâddasa tathârûpa*m* sama*n*a*m* vâ brâhma*n*a*m* vâ ya*m* râjâ Pasenadi Kosalo payirupâseyya. addasa kho [so] puriso Khema*m* bhikkhuni*m* Tora*n*avatthusmi*m* vâsa*m* upagata*m*, disvâna yena râjâ Pasenadi Kosalo ten' upasa*m*kami, upasa*m*kamitvâ râjâna*m* Pasenadikosala*m* etad avoca: n' atthi kho deva Tora*n*avatthusmi*m* tathârûpo sama*n*o vâ brâhma*n*o vâ ya*m* devo pairupâseyya, atthi ca kho deva Khemâ nâma bhikkhunî tassa bhagavato sâvikâ arahato sammâsambuddhassa, tassâ kho pana ayyâya eva*m* kalyâ*n*o kittisaddo abbhuggato pa*nd*itâ viyattâ medhâvî bahusuttâ cittakathî kalyâ*n*apa*t*ibhânâ 'ti, ta*m* devo payirupâsatû 'ti. atha kho râjâ Pasenadi Kosalo yena Khemâ bhikkhunî ten' upasa*m*kami, upasamkamitvâ Khema*m* bhikkuni*m* abhivâdetvâ ekamanta*m* nisîdi. ekamanta*m* nisinno kho râjâ Pasenadi Kosalo Khema*m* bhikkhuni*m* etad avoca: ki*m* nu kho ayye hoti tathâgato para*m* mara*n*â 'ti. abyâkata*m* kho eta*m* mahârâja bhagavatâ hoti tathâgato para*m* mara*n*â 'ti. ki*m* pan' ayye na hoti tathâgato para*m* mara*n*â 'ti. eta*m* pi kho mahârâja abyâkata*m* bhagavatâ na hoti tathâgato para*m* mara*n*â ti. ki*m* nu kho ayye hoti ca na ca hoti tathâgato para*m* mara*n*â 'ti. abyâkata*m* kho eta*m* mahârâja bhagavatâ . . . ki*m* pan' ayye n' eva hoti na na hoti tathâgato para*m* mara*n*â 'ti. eta*m* pi kho mahârâja abyâkata*m* bhagavatâ . . . The king now asks why she has given no other answer to all his questions, and goes on: ko nu kho ayye hetu ko paccayo yena ta*m* abyâkata*m* bhagavatâ 'ti. tena hi mahârâja tañ ñev' ettha pa*t*ipucchissâmi, yathâ te khameyya tathâ na*m* byâkareyyâsi. ta*m* ki*m* maññasi mahârâja, atthi te koci ga*n*ako vâ muddiko vâ sa*m*khâyako vâ yo pahoti Gaṅgâya vâluka*m* ga*n*etu*m* ettakâ vâlukâ iti vâ ettakâni vâlukasatâni ita vâ ettakâni vâlukasahassâni iti vâ ettakâni valukasatasahassâni iti vâ 'ti. no h' eta*m* ayye. atthi pana te koci ga*n*ako vâ muddiko vâ sa*m*khâyako vâ yo pahoti mahâsamudde udaka*m* ga*n*etu*m* ettakâni udaka*l*hakâni iti vâ . . . ettakâni udaka*l*hakasatasahassâni iti vâ 'ti. no h' eta*m* ayye. ta*m* kissa hetu. mahâsamuddo gambhîro appameyyo duppariyogâho 'ti. evam eva kho mahârâja yena rûpena tathâgata*m* paññâpayamâno paññâpeyya ta*m* rûpa*m* tathâgatassa pahîna*m* ucchinnamûla*m* tâlavatthukata*m* anabhâva*m* kata*m** âyati*m* anuppâdadhamma*m*. rûpasa*m*khâya vimutto kho mahârâja tathâgato gambhîro appameyyo duppariyogâho seyyathâpi mahâsamuddo. hoti tathâgato para*m* mara*n*â 'ti pi na upeti, na hoti t. p. m. 'ti pi na upeti, hoti ca na ca hoti t. p. m. 'ti pi na upeti, n'eva hoti na na hoti t. p. m. 'ti pi na upeti. yâya vedanâya . . . yâya saññâya . . . yehi sa*m*khârehi . . . yena viññâ*n*ena tathâgata*m* paññâpayamâno paññâpeyya . . . ti pi na upetîti. atho kho râjâ Pasenadi Kosalo Khemâya bhikkhuniyâ bhâsita*m* abhinanditvâ anumoditvâ u*tth*âyâsanâ Khema*m* bhikkhuni*m* abhivâdetvâ padakkhi*n*a*m* katvâ pakkâmi. The text then further relates how the king later on put the same questions to Buddha himself, and obtained from him the same answers word for word as the nun Khemâ had given him.

"Sa*m*yuttaka Nikâya," vol. i, fol. de (cf. antea, p. 281 seq.): tena kho pana samayena Yamakassa nâma bhikkhuno evarûpa*m* pâpaka*m* di*tth*igata*m* uppanna*m* hoti : tathâha*m* bhagavatâ dhamma*m* desita*m* âjânâmi yathâ khî*n*âsavo bhikkhu kâyassa bhedâ ucchijjati vinassati na hoti para*m* mara*n*â 'ti. (Sâriputta resolves to put the misbeliever on the right track and says to him :) ta*m* ki*m* maññasi âvuso Yamaka rûpa*m* nicca*m* vâ anicca*m* vâ 'ti. anicca*m* âvuso† . . . ta*m* ki*m* maññasi âvuso Yamaka rûpa*m* tathâgato 'ti samanupassasîti. no h'eta*m* âvuso. vedana*m* tathâgato 'ti samanupassasîti . . . ta*m* ki*m* maññasi âvuso Yamaka rûpasmi*m* tathâgato 'ti samanupassasîti. no h' eta*m* âvuso. aññatra rûpâ tathâgato 'ti samanupassasîti. no h' eta*m* âvuso.‡ ta*m* ki*m* maññasi âvuso Yamaka rûpa*m* vedana*m* sañña*m* sa*m*khâre viññâ*n*a*m* tathâgato 'ti samanupassasîti. no h' eta*m* âvuso. ta*m* ki*m* maññasi âvuso Yamaku aya*m* so arûpî avedano asaññî asa*m*khâro aviññâ*n*o tathâgato 'ti samanupassasîti. no h' eta*m* âvuso. ettha ca te âvuso Yamaka di*tth*eva dhamme saccato te tato tathâgato anupalabbhiyamâno. kalla*m* nu te ta*m* veyyâkara*n*a*m* tathâha*m* bhagavatâ dhamma*m* desita*m* âjânâmi . . . na hoti

* Lege gata*m*.

† The same then regarding the other Khandas, and the usual conclusions drawn therefrom as in the "Mahâvagga," i, 6, 42-46.

‡ Then similarly: vedanâya, aññatra vedanâya, &c.

param maranâ 'ti. ahu kho me tam âvuso Sâriputta pubbe aviddasuno pâpakam ditthigatam, idam ca panâyasmato Sâriputtassa dhammadesanam sutvâ tam c' eva pâpakam ditthigatam pahînam dhammo ca me abhisamito. sace tam âvuso Yamaka enam puccheyyum, yo so âvuso Yamaka bhikkhu araham khînâsavo so kâyassa bhedâ param maranâ kim hotîti: evam puttho tvam âvuso Yamaka kinti byâkareyyâsîti. sace mam âvuso evam puccheyyum, yo so . . . kim hotîti, evam puttho aham âvuso evam byâkareyyam: rûpam kho âvuso aniccam, yad annicam tam dukkham, yam dukkham tam niruddham tad atthamga tam. vedanâ, saññâ, samkhârâ, viññânam aniccam . . . atthamgatan ti. evam puttho aham âvuso evam byâkareyyan ti sâdhu sâdhu âvuso Yamaka.

"Udâna," fol. ghau (Phayre MS., cf. antea, p. 283): . . . imam udânam udânesi: atthi bhikkhave tad âyatanam yattha n'eva pathavî na âpo na tejo na vâyo na âkâsânañcâyatanam na viññânânâñcâyatanam na âkiñcaññâyatanam na nevasaññânâsaññâyatanam nâyam loko no paraloko ubdo candimasuriyâ, tam aham bhikkhave n'eva âyatim vadâmi na gatim na thitim na upapattim: appatittham apavattam anârammanam eva tam, es' ev' anto dukkhassâ 'ti.*

Ibid. fol. ghau' (="Itivuttaka," fol. kau; antea, p. 283): atthi bhikkhavo ajâtam abhûtam akatam asamk hatam. no ce tam bhikkhave abhavissa ajâtam . . . asamkhatam na yidha jâtassa bhûtassa katassa samkhatassa nissaranam paññâyetha. yasmâ ca kho bhikkhave atthi ajâtam . . . tasmâ jâtassa . . . nissaranam paññâyatîti.

Ibid. fol. ghau'—gham: nissitassa ca calitam, anissitassa calitam n' atthi, calite asati passadhi, passaddhiyâ sati rati na hoti, ratiyâ asati âgatigati na hoti, âgatigatiyâ asati cutûpapâto na hoti, cutûpapâte asati n' ev' idha na huram na ubhayamantare. es' ev' anto dukkhassâ 'ti.

"Añguttara Nikâya" (Phayre MS.), vol. i, fol. *nu*: cattâro 'me

* It is well here to bear in mind the quite similar mode of expression of the Jainas. "Jinacaritra," 16: sivam ayalam aruyam anamtam akkhayam avvâbâham apunarâvatti-siddhi-gai-nâmadheyam *thânam*.

bhikkhave puggalâ santo sa*m*vijjamânâ lokasmi*m*. katame cattâro? idha bhikkhave ekacco puggalo di*tth*eva dhamme sasa*m*khâraparinibbâyî hoti, idha pana bhikkhave ekacco puggalo kâyassa bhedâ sasa*m*khâraparinibbâyî hoti, idha pana bhikkhave ekacco puggalo di*tth*eva dhamme asa*m*khâraparinibbâyî hoti, idha pana bhikkhave ekacco puggalo kâyassa bhedâ asa*m*khâraparinibbâyi hoti. kathañ ca bhikkhave ekacco puggalo di*tth*eva dhamme sasa*m*khâraparinibbâyî hotî? idha bhikkhave bhikkhu asubhânupassî kâye viharati âhâre pa*t*ikûlassaññî sabbaloke anabhiratisaññî sabbasa*m* khâresu aniccânupassî, mara*n*asaññâ kho pan' assa ajjhatta*m* supati*tth*itâ hoti. so imâni pañca sekhabalâni upanissâya viharati saddhâbala*m* hiribala*m* ottappabala*m* viriyabala*m*, paññâbala*m*, tass' imâni pañc' indriyâni adhimattâni pâtubhavanti saddhindriya*m* viriyin driya*m* satindriya*m* samâdhindriya*m* paññindriya*m*. so imesa*m* pañcanna*m* indriyâna*m* adhimattattâ sasa*m*khâraparinibbâyî hoti. eva*m* kho khikkhave puggalo di*tth*eva dhamme sasa*m*khâraparinibbâyî hoti. kathañ ca bhikkhave ekacco puggalo kâyassa bhedâ sasa*m*khâraparinibbâyî hoti? idha bhikkhave bhikkhu asubhânupassì (&c. as above, for adhimattâni, adhimattattâ read mudûni, muduttâ). kathañ ca bhikkhave ekacco puggalo di*tth*eva dhamme asa*m*khâraparinibbâyî hoti? idha bhikkhave bhikkhu vivicc' eva kâmehi -pa- pa*th*amajjhâna*m* . . . . cattutha*m* jhâna*m* upasampajja viharati. so imâni pañca sekhabalâni (&c. as above, then corresponding to the fourth case, but instead of adhimattâni read mudûni). ime kho bhikkhave cattâro puggalâ santo sa*m*vijjamânâ lokasmin ti.

"Añguttara Nikâya," Navanipâta, vol. iii, fol. ñû: eka*m* samayam âyasmâ Sâriputto Râjagahe viharati Ve*l*uvane Kalandakanivâpe. tatra kho âyasmâ Sâriputto bhikkhû âmantesi: sukha*m* ida*m* âvuso nibbânan ti. evam vutte âyasmâ Udâyi âyasmanta*m* Sâriputta*m* etad avoca: kim pan' ettha âvuso Sâriputta sukha*m* yad ettha n' atthi vedayitan ti? etad eva khv etthâvuso sukha*m* yad ettha n' atthi vedayita*m*. pañc' ime âvuso kâmagu*n*â. katame pañca? cakkhuviññeyâ rûpâ i*tth*â kantâ manâpâ piyrûpâ sâtarûpâ kâmupasañhitâ rajaniyâ, sotavineyyâ saddâ, . . . ime kho âvuso pañca kâmagu*n*â. ya*m* kho âvuso ime pañca kâmagu*n*e pa*t*icca uppajjati sukham somanassam idam vuccat' âvuso kâmasukham. idhâvuso bhikkhu vivicc' eva kâmehi -pa- paṭhamam jhânam upasampajja viharati, tass ce âvuso bhikkhuno iminâ vihârena viharato kâmasahagatâ saññâ manasikârâ samudâcaranti sv âssa hoti âbâdho. seyyathâpi âvuso sukhino dukkham uppajjeyya yâvad eva âbâdhâya, evam ev' assa te kâmasahagatâ saññâ manasikârâ samudâcaranti, sv âssa hoti âbâdho. yo kho panâvuso âbâdho dukkham idam vuttam bhagavatâ. iminâpi kho etam âvuso pariyâyena veditabbam yathâ sukham nibbânam. puna ca param âvuso bhikkhu vitakkavicârânam . . . dutiyam jhânam upasampajja viharati. tassa ce âvuso bhikkhuno iminâ vihârena viharato vitakkasahagatâ saññâ manasikârâ samudâcaranti (see as above). In the third Jhâna, the disturbing element is described as pîtisahagatâ saññâ, in the fourth upekhâsukhasahagatâ saññâ. The exposition then proceeds in the analogous way also through the highest stages of abstraction.

As in the two last quoted passages the term nibbâna is used of the happy condition of him who has attained the Jhâna, so also this occurs in the following passage:

"Añg. Nikâya," *loc. cit.* fol. *ṭha*:

sandiṭṭhikam nibbânam sandiṭṭhikam nibbânan ti âvuso vuccati. kittâvatâ nu kho âvuso sandiṭṭhikam nibbânam vuttam bhagavatâ 'ti? idhâvuso bhikkhu vivicc' eva kâmehi -pa- paṭhamam jhânam upasampajja viharati. etthâpi kho âvuso sandiṭṭhikam nibbânam vuttam bhagavatâ pariyâyena. (Similarly of the following Jhânas and the stages of higher ecstasy. Finally:) puna ca param âvuse bhikkhu sabbaso nevasaññânâsaññâyatanam samatikkamma saññâvedayitanirodham upasampajja viharati paññâya c'assa disvâ âsavâ parikkhînâ honti. ettâvatâ kho âvuso sandiṭṭhikam nibbânam vuttam bhagavatâ nippariyâyenâ 'ti.* Then follows a series of exactly similar passages: nibbânam nibbânan ti âvuso vuccati -pa- parinibbânam parinibbânan ti, tadañganibbânam tadañganibbânan ti, diṭṭhadhammanibbânan diṭṭhadhammanibânan ti âvuso vuccati . . . vuttam bhagavatâ nippariyâyenâ 'ti.

The fact that here the Parinibbâna is treated as exactly equal

* Here pariyâyena (cf. "Dîpavamsa," 5, 34) means "in metaphorical sense,' nippariyayena, "without metaphor, in the exact sense."

with the nibbâna and the di*tth*adhammanibbâna, as well as the fact that in one of the earlier quoted passages the "di*tth*eva dhamme sasa*m*khâraparinibbâyâ" is spoken of, gives me occasion to here refer to the theory advanced by Dr. Rhys Davids, according to which nibbâna and parinibbâna are as a rule so used differently, that the former denotes arhatship, the latter the end of the saint, his disappearance from the world of the transitory. As a fact the usage of the canonical texts follows, on the whole, the rule laid down by Davids. Yet it seems to me, that here we have to do only with a tendency of the usage of speech, which is liable to exceptions, in the same way as usage fluctuates between Buddha and Sambuddha, Paccekabuddha and Paccekasambuddha. Thus, the word parinibbuta is used of the saint already during his earthly life, "Dhp." v, 89, and "Sa*m*yutta Nikâya," vol. ii, fol. ja:

kummo va añgâni sake kapâle samodaha*m* bhikkhu manovitakko anissito aññamaññam apothamâno parinibbuto na upavadeyya kiñci

and *vice versâ* nibbuta is also occasionally used of the saint entering into the hereafter. Anuruddha says ("Theragâthâ," fol. gu):

Vajjina*m* Ve*l*uvagâme aha*m* jîvitasa*m*khayâ
he*tth*ato Ve*l*ugumbasmi*m* nibbâyissam anâsavo.

Bakkulattherassa-Acchariyabahutasutta ("Majjh. Nikâya"): atha kho âyasmâ Bakkulo aparena samayena apâpura*n*a*m* âdâya vihârena vihâra*m* upasa*m*kamitvâ evam âha: abhikkamathâyasmanto abhikkamathâyasmanto, ajja me nibbâna*m* bhavissatîti . . . atha kho âyasmâ Bakkulo majjhe bhikkhusa*m*ghassa nisinnako parinibbâyi.

Compare also the strophe of the Vimânavatthu, which is found quoted at "Dhp. *Atth.*" p. 350.

2. Nâmarûpa.

To the observations made in note 2, p. 23, regarding the terminus Nâmarûpa, *i.e.* "Name and form," or "Name and corporeal form," I desire to here add a few of the more important passages of the texts.

The expression Nâmarûpa is known to have had its origin in the

Brâhma*n*a and Âra*n*yaka period of Indian literature. In the name of beings the wisdom of those ages finds, as is natural, specially deep mysteries. Jâratkârava Ârtabhâga says:* "Yâjnavalkya! what is that which does not forsake a man when he dies?" And Yâjnavalkya answers: "The name! An infinite thing in truth is the name, infinite (innumerable) are all the Gods; infinite fulness he attains thereby." Thus the name of beings or of things is represented as a self-existing power beside their external form. Name and form are the two "monster powers" of the Brahma, by which it has got at the worlds or into the worlds. When the universe lay in chaotic confusion, by "name and form" clearness was created; therefore they say, when they wish to make a man knowable: "he is called so-and-so; he looks so-and-so." "In this this universe consists, in form and in name"—or, as it is said on another occasion: "A triad is this world: name, form, act."†

The cessation of the individual being, the attainment of the everlasting goal presents itself as well to the Brahman as to the Buddhist method of thought and speech as the cessation of "name and form." He who has attained the highest wisdom, unites with the universal spirit, "delivered from name and form, as the streams, the flowing streams, enter into rest in the sea, leaving name‡ and form behind;" thus we read in the "Mu*nd*akopanishad."§ And in the "Suttanipâta"|| it is said: "What thou hast asked after, Ajita, that will I tell thee; where name and form cease without a residuum: by the cessation of consciousness,** there that ceases."

As regards the idea of "name" in this connection, it is to be understood in its literal meaning, when in the Mahânidâna sutta††

* "Çat. Br." xiv, 6, 2, 11.

† "Çat. Br." xi, 2, 3, 3 fg.; xiv, 4, 2, 15; 4, 4, 1 fg. Cf. the N*ri*si*m*hatâpanîya Upanishad, "Ind. Studien," ix, 134.

‡ It is clear, that here "name" is to be taken quite in the literal sense, cf. "Cullavagga," ix, 1, 4.

§ P. 322 of the edition in the "Bibl. India."

|| Fol. ghau' of the Phayre MS.; Fausböll, p. 191.

** *I.e.*, the Nirvâ*n*a, cf. *supra*, p. 266 seq.

†† P. 253, 255, ed. "Grimblot."

the attainability of the form-world through the "contact by means of naming" is traced back to the existence of the "name-world," and when it is there said, "that the domain of naming, the domain of expression, the domain of manifestation," extends as far as "name and form together with consciousness." As a rule, however, another meaning of "name" meets us in the Buddhist texts, so far as this idea appears in connection with that of form. Thus already in the "Sutta Pi*t*aka" ("Sammâdi*tth*i Suttanta" in the "Majjhima Nikâya," fol. khu of the Turnour MSS.), where a reply is given to the question regarding the definition of Nâmarûpa: vedanâ saññâ cetenâ phasso manasikâro ida*m* vuccat' âvuso nâmarûpa*m*,* cattâri ca mahâbhûtâni catunna*m* ca mahâbhûtânam upâdâya rûpa*m* ida*m* vuccat' âvuso rûpa*m*.—Similarly in the Abhidhamma texts. "Vibhañga," fol. ci' (Phayre MS.): tattha katama*m* viññâ*n*a-paccayâ nâmarûpa*m*? atthi nâma*m* atthi rûpa*m*. tattha katama*m* nâma*m*? vedanakkhandho saññâkhandho sa*m*khârakkhandho ida*m* vuccati nâma*m*. tattha katama*m* rûpa*m*? cattâro ca mahâbhûtâ catunna*m* ca mahâbhûtâna*m* upâdâya rûpa*m* ida*m* vuccati rûpa*m* iti' idañ ca nâma*m* ida*m* vuccati viññâ*n*apaccayâ nâmarûpa*m*.—"Nettippakara*n*a," fol. kû' (Phayre MS.): tattha ye pañc' upâdânakkhandâ ida*m* nâmarûpa*m*. tattha ye phassapañcamakâ dhammâ† ida*m* nâma*m*, yâni pañcindriyâni rûpâni ida*m* rûpa*m*. tadubhaya*m* nâmarûpa*m* viññâ*n*asampayutta*m*.

How this explanation of Nâma has arisen, is evident. The category of "form" or "corporeity" (rûpa), like that of consciousness, is to be met as well in the combination "name and form together with consciousness," as in the system of the five khandhas "form, sensations, perceptions, conformations, consciousness." Now the very natural conceit suggested itself to identify the two series of notions, which had actually arisen wholly independently of each other, having the members "form" and "consciousness" in common, and thus the three khandhas "sensations, perceptions,

* It appears to me we should read nâma*m*.

† *I.e.*, the five categories mentioned in the passage quoted from the Sammâdi*tth*i Sutta, among which phassa is named, not indeed in the last, but in the fourth place?

conformations (Sa*m*khârâ = Cetanâ)" of the one series remained over for the category of "name" in the other series.

Cf. further "Milinda Pañha," p. 49; Burnouf, "Intr." 501 seq.

3. The Four Stages of Holiness.

It is not my intention here to expound in all its bearings the doctrine of the Cattâro Maggâ, on the whole rather unprofitable to the comprehension of Buddhist religious thought. I shall here only attempt to show how, in the statement of the psychological attributes which were attributed to the saints of the four stages, the earlier and later texts of the sacred Kanon differ from each other, in a manner which is characteristic of the history of the development of dogmatic literature.

As far as I know, we possess, regarding the psychological attributes of saints of the four grades, no older expressions than those which occur in the "Mahâparinibbâna Sutta," p. 16 seq., and conformably very often afterwards in the "Sutta Pi*t*aka." The four stages are there defined in the following way:

1. ti*nn*a*m* sa*m*yojanâna*m* parikkhayâ sotâpanno avinipâtadhammo niyato sambodhiparâyano.

2. ti*nn*a*m* sa*m*yojanânam parikkhayâ râgadosamohâna*m* tanuttâ sakadâgami sakid eva ima*m* loka*m* âgantvâ dukkhass' anta*m* karissati.

3. pañcanna*m* orambhâgiyâna*m* sa*m*yojanâna*m* parikkhaya opapâtiko tatthaparinibbâyî anâvattidhammo tasmâ lokâ.

4. âsavâna*m* khayâ anâsava*m* cetovimutti*m* paññâvimuttim di*tth*eva dhamme saya*m* abhiññâ sacchikatvâ upasamyajja vihâsi.

These definitions show evidently that there was a conventionally arranged series of Sa*m*yojanas and this lay at the bottom of the speculations upon progressive sanctification. We can scarcely doubt that this series is the same which is uniformly given by commentators, and already occurs in the "Sutta Pi*t*aka":* the five Orambhâgiva Sa*m*yojana are Sakkâyadi*tth*i, Nicikicchâ,

* "Sa*m*yutta Nikâya," vol. iii, fol. dhe.

Sîlabbataparâmâsa, Kâmarâga, Paṭigha; the five Uddhambhâgiva Saṁyojana: Rûparâga, Arûparâga, Mâna, Uddhacca, Avijjâ.

It will be seen how quite unsymmetrically couched the definitions given of the four stages are, with reference to this series. Sometimes three, sometimes five of the Saṁyojanas are overcome; the categories of Râga, Dosa, Moha, are introduced, of which only the first figures in the list of the Saṁyojanas; in the second stage, it is said, these three vices are almost overcome; how it fares with them in the third stage is not stated; but for the definition of the third grade recourse is again had exclusively to the Saṁyojana categories. Thus these formulas give a veritable picture of the confusion which usually prevails in the long and abstruse series of ideas in ancient Buddhist dogmatic.

It is interesting to observe how the later generation of dogmatists, whose systematizing and harmonizing labours lie before us in the Abhidhamma Piṭaka, endeavoured to introduce some order and arrangement into this confusion. One of the Abhidhamma texts, the Puggalapaññatti,* deals exclusively with the different grades of beings in relation to the goal of holiness. Thus the four classes (by the side of which stand the corresponding subdivisions of the "phalasacchikiriyâya paṭipannâ," already, by-the-bye, frequently mentioned in the older Piṭakas, *e.g.*, "Cullavagga," ix, 1, 4) are defined as follows:

1. yassa puggalassa tîṇi saṁyojanâni pahînâni ayaṁ vuccati puggalo sotâpanno.

2. yassa puggalassa kâmarâgabyâpâdâ tanubhûtâ ayaṁ vuccati puggalo sakadâgâmî.

* Puggala (Sansk. pudgala), the subject bound in transmigration, or correspondingly the subject delivered therefrom, is synonymous with Satta, and Puggala-Satta stands against the pair of synonyms, Dhamma-Saṁkhâra (*vide* supra, p. 250). According to the old strict teaching there are only Dhammas, and Sattas are spoken of only in accordance with ordinary modes of expression. Regarding the juxtaposition of Satta-puggala and Dhamma-Saṁkhâra compare "Milinda Pañha," p. 317, where in characteristic style the topic is "atthisatta" and "atthidhamma;" the Jinâlaṁkâra in Burnouf, "Intr." 505 ("Buddho 'ti ko satto vâ saṁkhâro vâ"), and the northern Buddhist text, which is there quoted, p. 508 ("Sa pudgalo na dharmaḥ").

3. yassa puggalassa kâmarâgabyâpâdâ anavasesâ pahînâ ayam vuccati puggalo anâgâmî.

4. yassa puggalassa rûparâgo arûparâgo mâno uddhaccam avijjâ anavasesâ pahînâ ayam vuccati puggalo arahâ.

The system rests here exclusively on the series of the ten Samyojanas.* Whatever in the older form of the doctrine referred to the Samyojanas, is here adopted; the other categories which were there dealt with, Râga, Dosa, Moha, and the Âsavas, have vanished from the new wording, or have been replaced by notions from the Samyojana series. Thus, when we regard the Samyojanas numbered according to the order given above, the graded course of their conquest is the following: the Sotâpanna has got rid of 1—3; in the case of the Sakadâgâmî and Anâgâmi, 4 and 5 also vanished, and that in such a way that in the Sak. they were reduced to a small measure, in the Anâg. wholly annihilated; the Arahâ finally has extirpated the last vices also, 6—10.

Thus the doctrine of the four grades gives a picture of the way in which the confused series of notions contained in the suttas have been pondered by the theologians of the Abhidhamma, and their inconsistencies eliminated by them.

* That the notion which was designated in the above-quoted form of the Samyojana list as Patigha is identical with that here named Byâpâda, admits of no doubt.

2. INDEX TO SUBJECTS.

INDICES.

1. INDEX TO PROPER NAMES.

BOOKS IN PALI.

BUDDHIST SCRIPTURES IN PALI.

In 5 vols. 8vo. 21*s* each Volume.

THE VINAYA PIṬAKAM, one of the principal Buddhist Holy Scriptures in the Pâli Language. Edited by Dr. H. OLDENBERG. Vol. I. The Mahâvagga, with an Introduction. Vol. II. The Cullavagga. Vol. III. The Suttavibhaṅga, I. (Pârâjika, Saṃghâdisesa, Anyata, Nissaggiya). Vol. IV. The Suttavibhaṅga II. (end of Mahâvibhaṅga, Bhikkhunîvibhaṅga). Published with the assistance of the Royal Academy of Berlin, and of the Secretary of State for India in Council. Vol. V. in the press.

8vo. cloth, 21*s*.

THE DÎPAVAṂSA, an Ancient Buddhist Historical Record in the Pâli Language. Edited, with an English Translation, by Dr. H. OLDENBERG.

THE DÎPAVAṂSA is the most ancient Historical Work of the Ceylonese; it contains an account of the Ecclesiastical History of the Buddhist Church, of the conversion of the Ceylonese to the Buddhist faith, and of the Ancient History of Ceylon.

The study of Pâli is in India raised to the level of that of Sanskrit, and is made the subject of examination in the University of Calcutta. In the absence of Text-Books, the "Dîpavaṃsa" is specially adapted for the purpose, on account of the accompanying translation.

8vo. 21*s*.

THE MILINDA PAÑHA. Being Dialogues between King Milinda and the Buddhist Sage Nāgasena. The Pâli Text edited by V. TRENCKNER, of Copenhagen.

"A very interesting dialogue between Milinda and Nāgasena."—*Max Müller in Chips I.*

"Next in order of interest should undoubtedly be named the 'Milinda Panha; or, Questions of Menander.' Whatever be the origin of this remarkable work, there can be no doubt of its great antiquity, for it exhibits a familiarity with Greek names and places, and records a religious discussion between the Buddhist divine Nāgasena and a 'Yona' king Milinda, who can be identified with certainty with the Bactrian king Menander."—*Childers in Pâli Dictionary.*

Also, 8vo. 4*s*.

PÂLI MISCELLANY, by V. TRENCKNER. Part I. The Introductory Part of the Milinda Pañho, an English Translation and Notes.